Cells at Work!
はたらく細胞

02

AKANE SHIMIZU

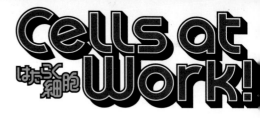

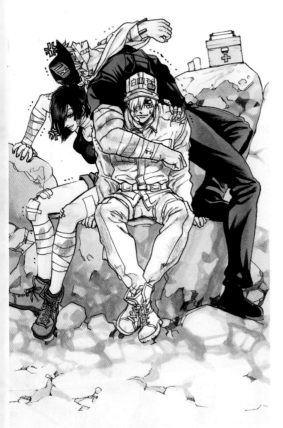

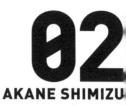

CONTENTS

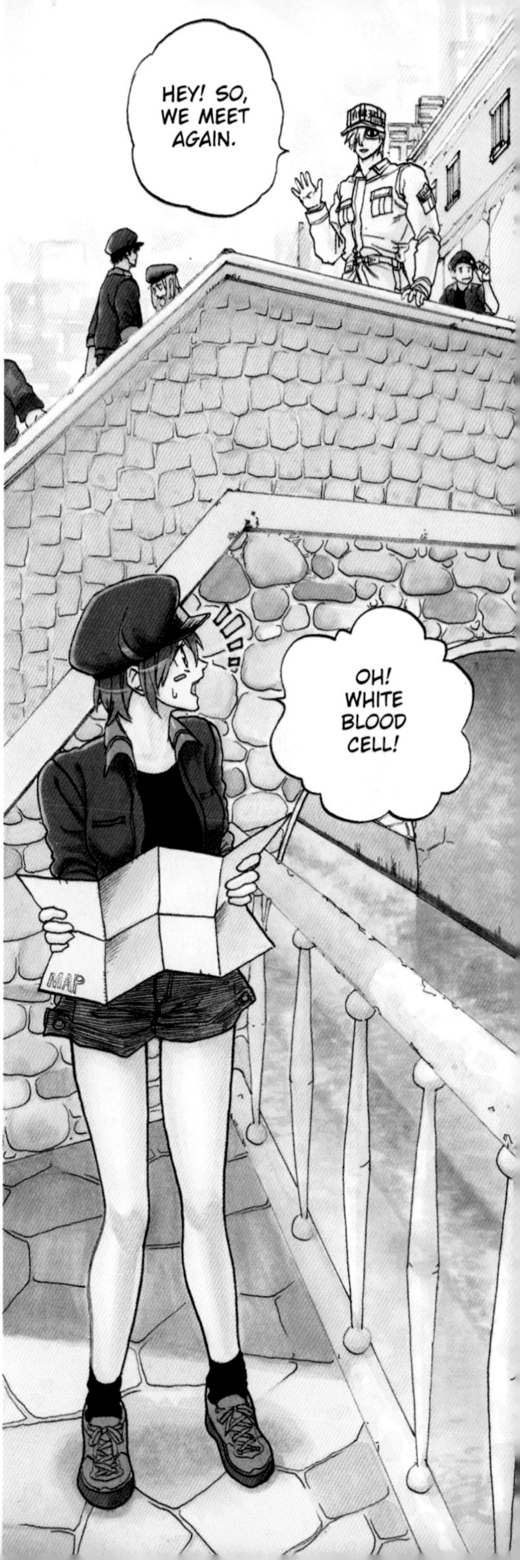

HEY! SO, WE MEET AGAIN.
OH! WHITE BLOOD CELL!
MAP

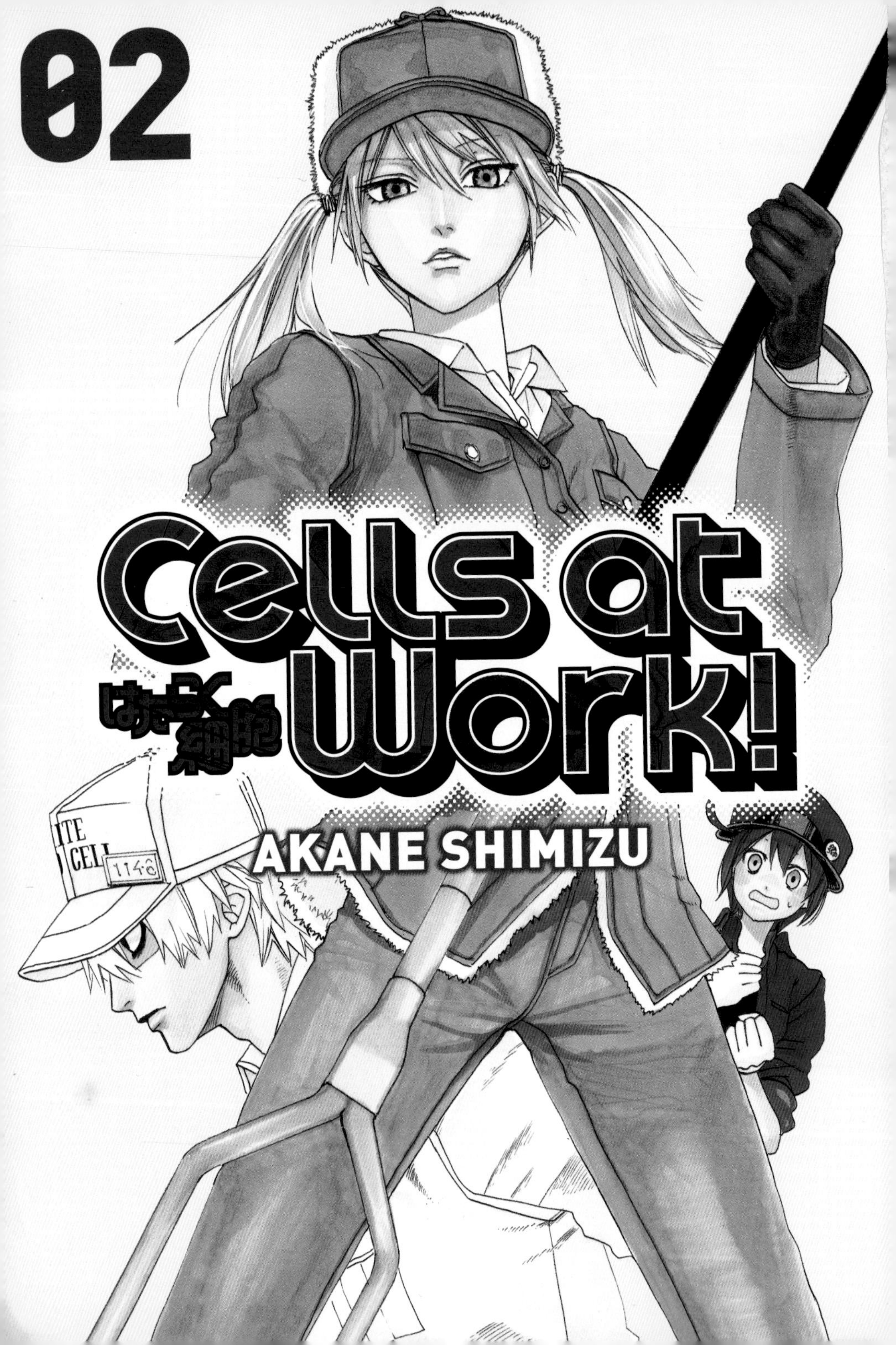
02
Cells at Work!
はたらく細胞
AKANE SHIMIZU
1146

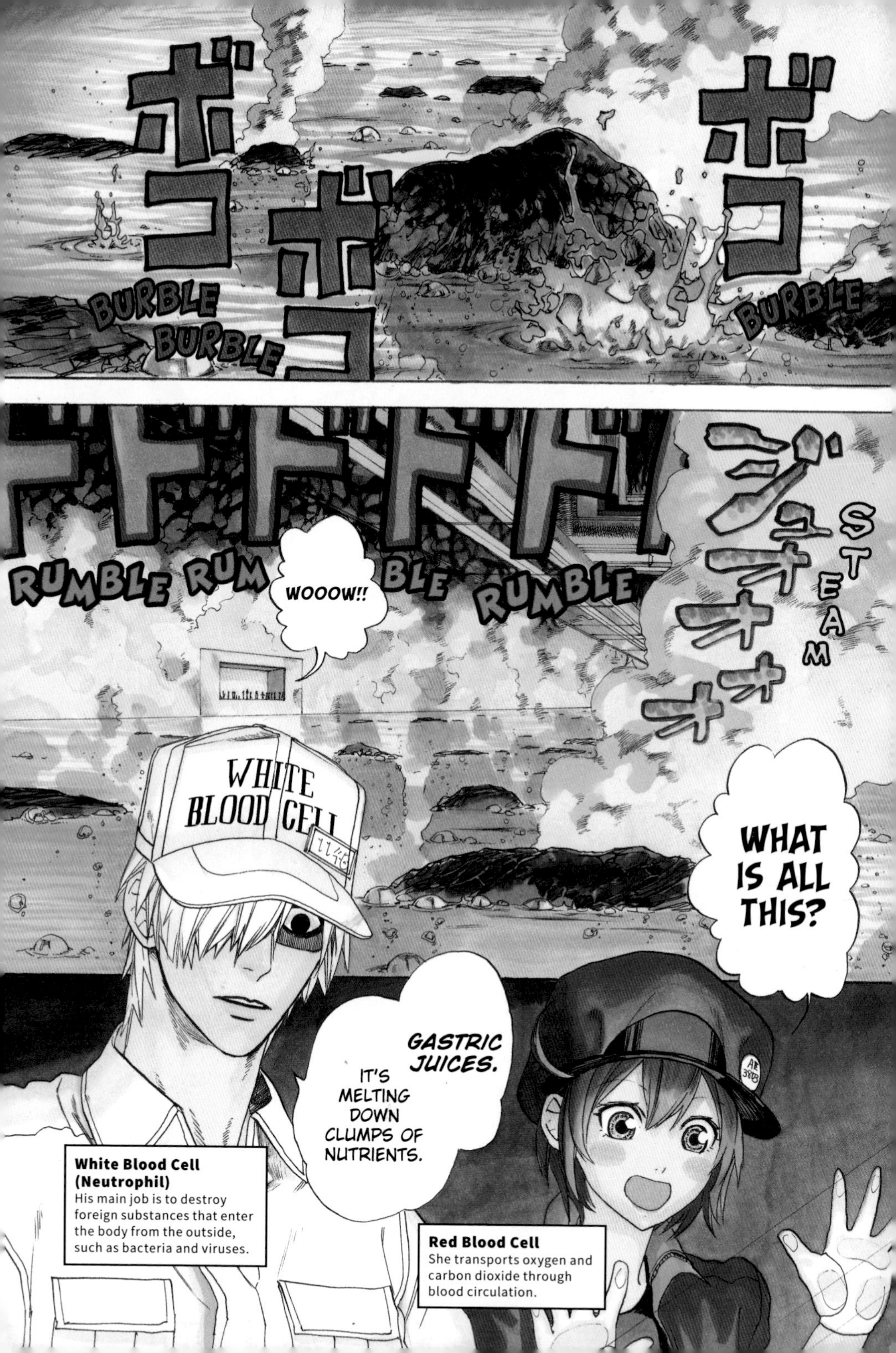

ボコ
BURBLE
ボコ
ボコ
BURBLE
BURBLE
ジュオオオ
STEAM
RUMBLE RUMBLE RUMBLE
WOOOW!!
WHAT IS ALL THIS?
GASTRIC JUICES.
IT'S MELTING DOWN CLUMPS OF NUTRIENTS.
WHITE BLOOD CELL
Red Blood Cell
She transports oxygen and carbon dioxide through blood circulation.
White Blood Cell (Neutrophil)
His main job is to destroy foreign substances that enter the body from the outside, such as bacteria and viruses.

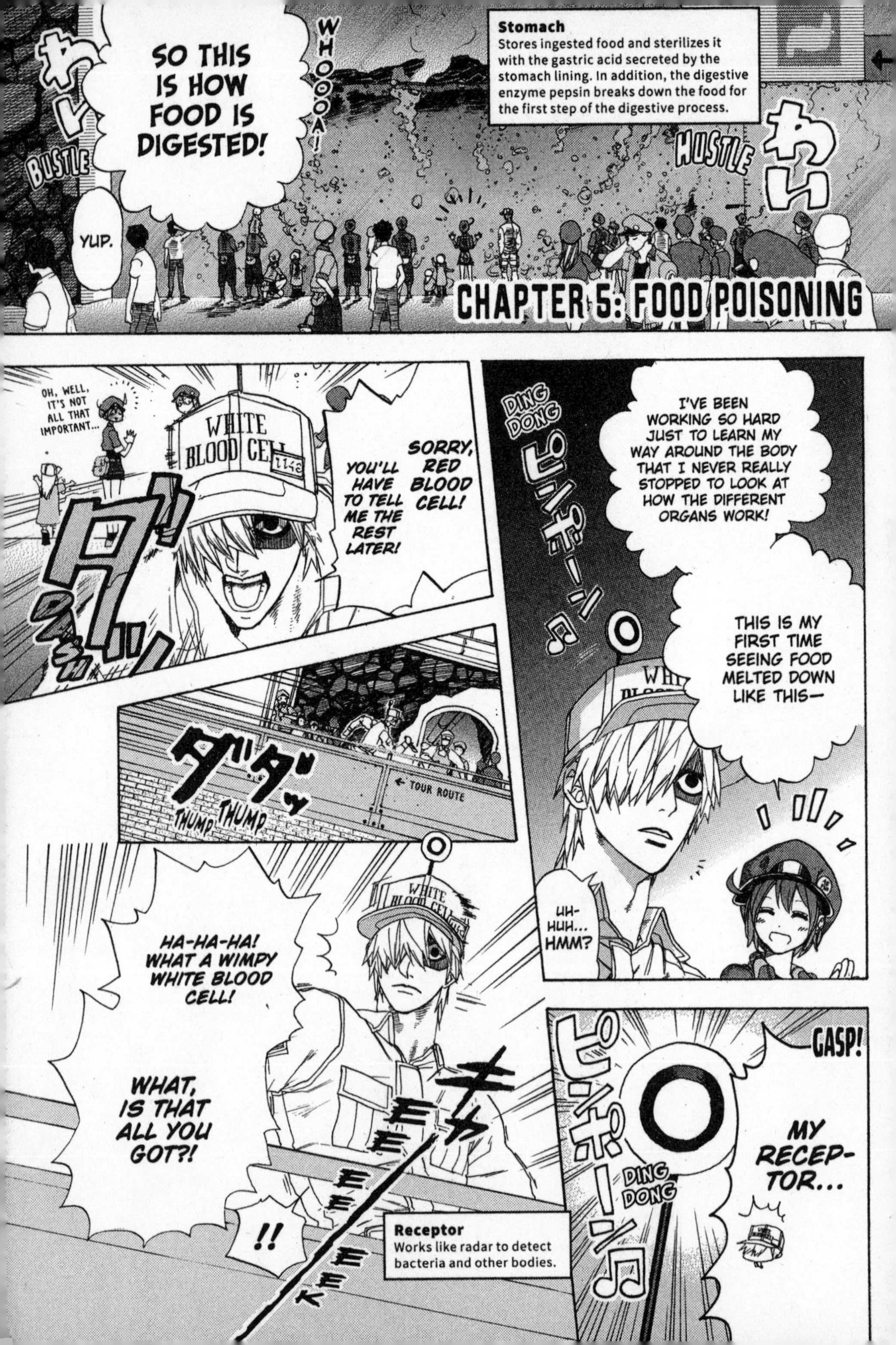

わい
HUSTLE
Stomach
Stores ingested food and sterilizes it with the gastric acid secreted by the stomach lining. In addition, the digestive enzyme pepsin breaks down the food for the first step of the digestive process.
WHOOOOA!
SO THIS IS HOW FOOD IS DIGESTED!
YUP.
わい
BUSTLE
CHAPTER 5: FOOD POISONING
I'VE BEEN WORKING SO HARD JUST TO LEARN MY WAY AROUND THE BODY THAT I NEVER REALLY STOPPED TO LOOK AT HOW THE DIFFERENT ORGANS WORK!
DING DONG
ピンポーン♪
THIS IS MY FIRST TIME SEEING FOOD MELTED DOWN LIKE THIS—
UH-HUH... HMM?
SORRY, RED BLOOD CELL!
YOU'LL HAVE TO TELL ME THE REST LATER!
OH, WELL, IT'S NOT ALL THAT IMPORTANT...
ダダッ
THUMP THUMP
← TOUR ROUTE
GASP!
ピンポーン♪
DING DONG
MY RECEPTOR...
HA-HA-HA! WHAT A WIMPY WHITE BLOOD CELL!
WHAT, IS THAT ALL YOU GOT?!
EEEEEEEEK
!!
Receptor
Works like radar to detect bacteria and other bodies.

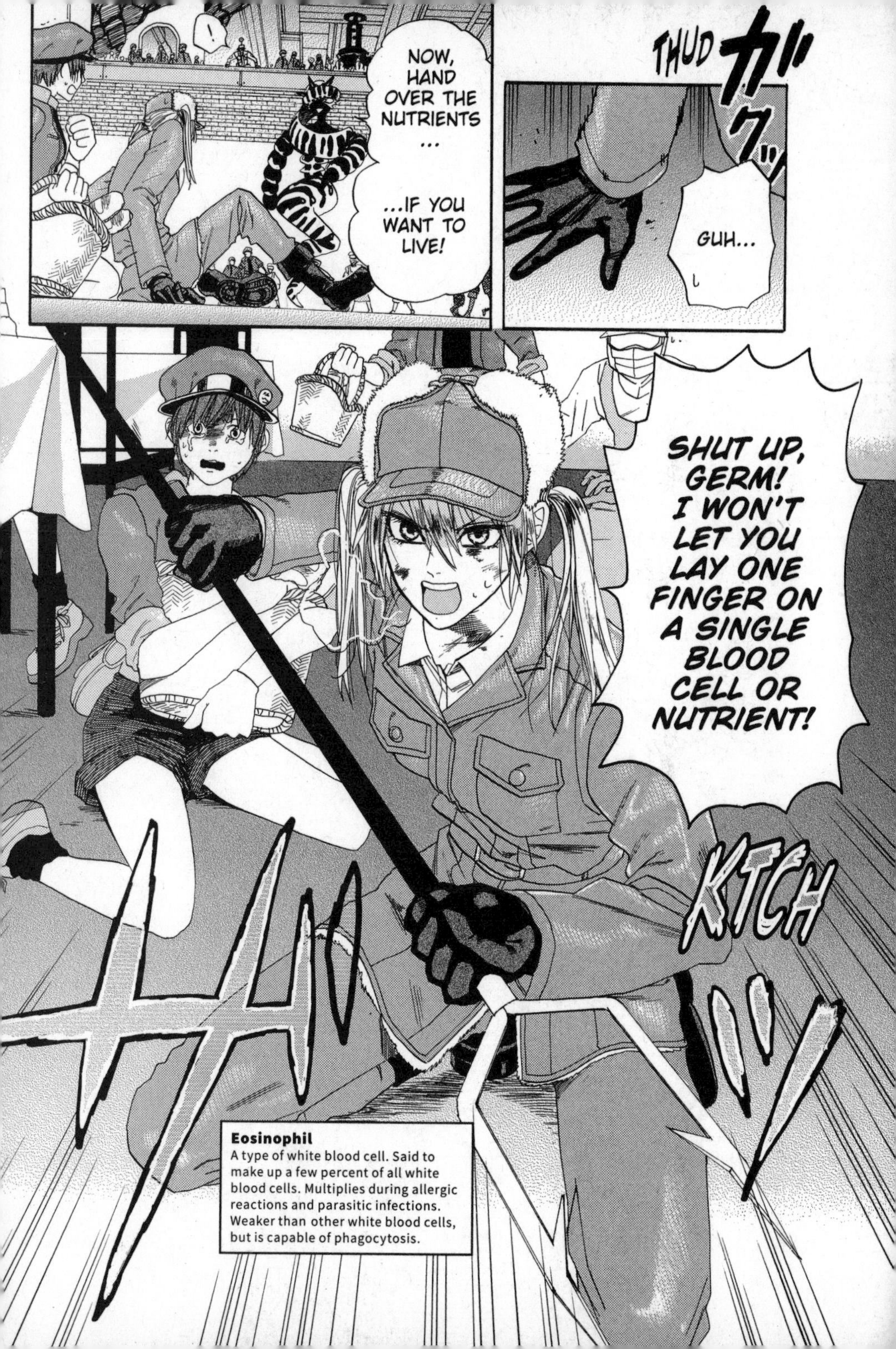
THUD
ガグッ
GUH...
!
NOW, HAND OVER THE NUTRIENTS ...
...IF YOU WANT TO LIVE!
SHUT UP, GERM! I WON'T LET YOU LAY ONE FINGER ON A SINGLE BLOOD CELL OR NUTRIENT!
KTCH
Eosinophil
A type of white blood cell. Said to make up a few percent of all white blood cells. Multiplies during allergic reactions and parasitic infections. Weaker than other white blood cells, but is capable of phagocytosis.

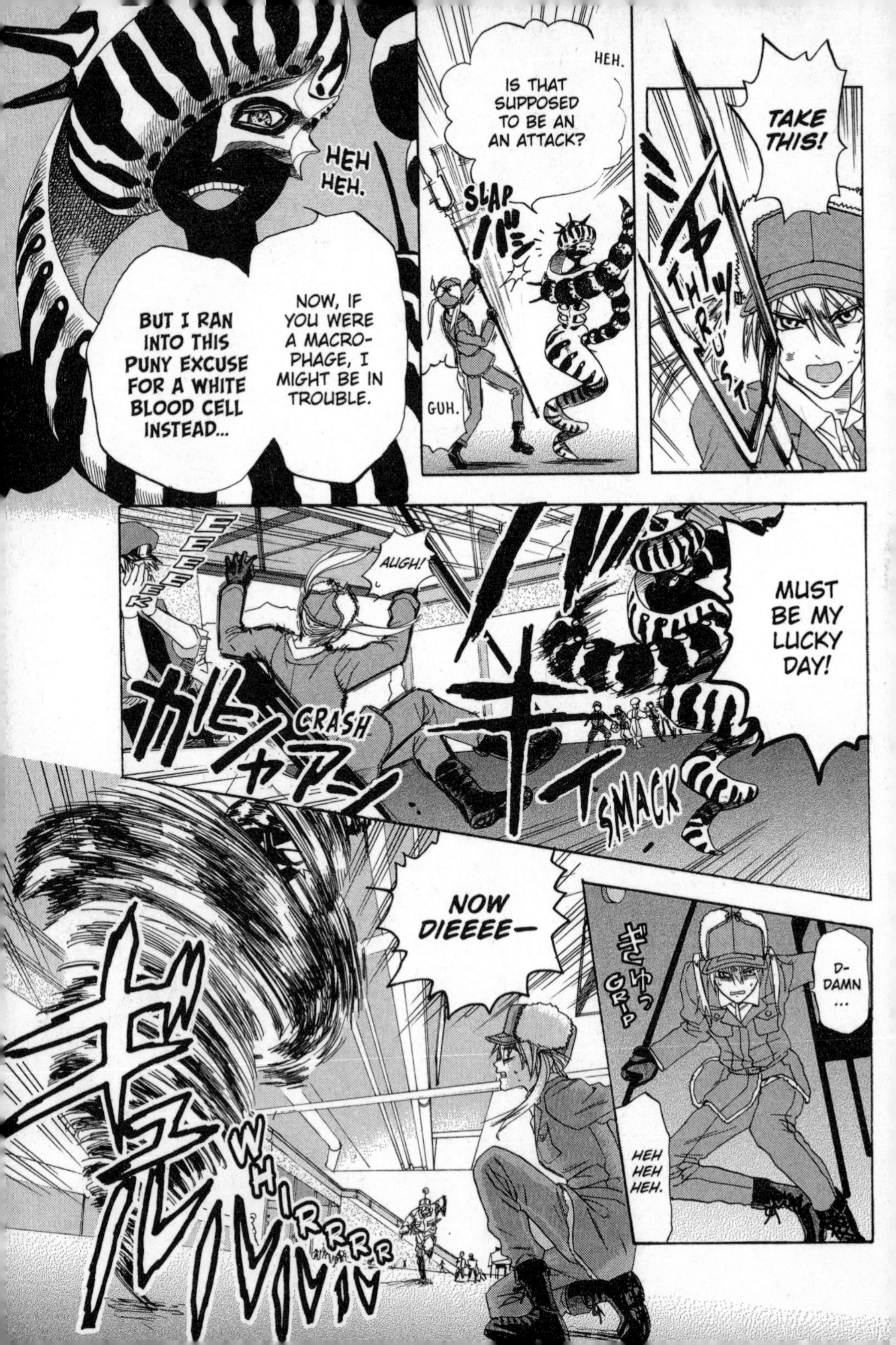
TAKE THIS!
THRUST
HEH.
IS THAT SUPPOSED TO BE AN AN ATTACK?
SLAP
GUH.
HEH HEH.
NOW, IF YOU WERE A MACROPHAGE, I MIGHT BE IN TROUBLE.
BUT I RAN INTO THIS PUNY EXCUSE FOR A WHITE BLOOD CELL INSTEAD...
MUST BE MY LUCKY DAY!
SMACK
AUGH!
CRASH
EEEEEEK
D-DAMN...
GRIP
HEH HEH HEH.
NOW DIEEEE—
WHIRRRRR

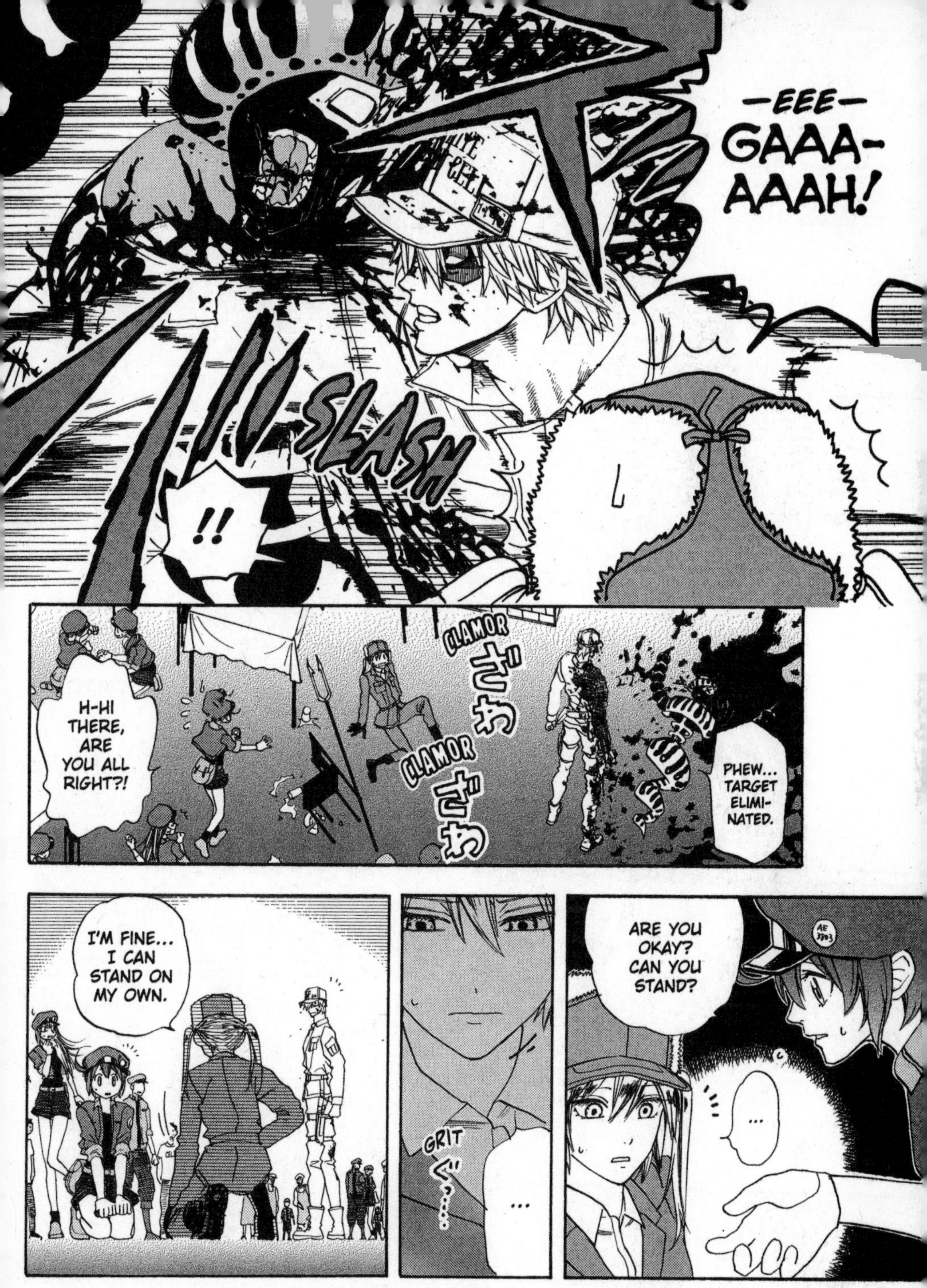
—EEE—
GAAA-AAAH!
SLASH
!!
PHEW... TARGET ELIMINATED.
CLAMOR ざわ
CLAMOR ざわ
H-HI THERE, ARE YOU ALL RIGHT?!
ARE YOU OKAY? CAN YOU STAND?
...
GRIT ぐっ……
...
I'M FINE... I CAN STAND ON MY OWN.

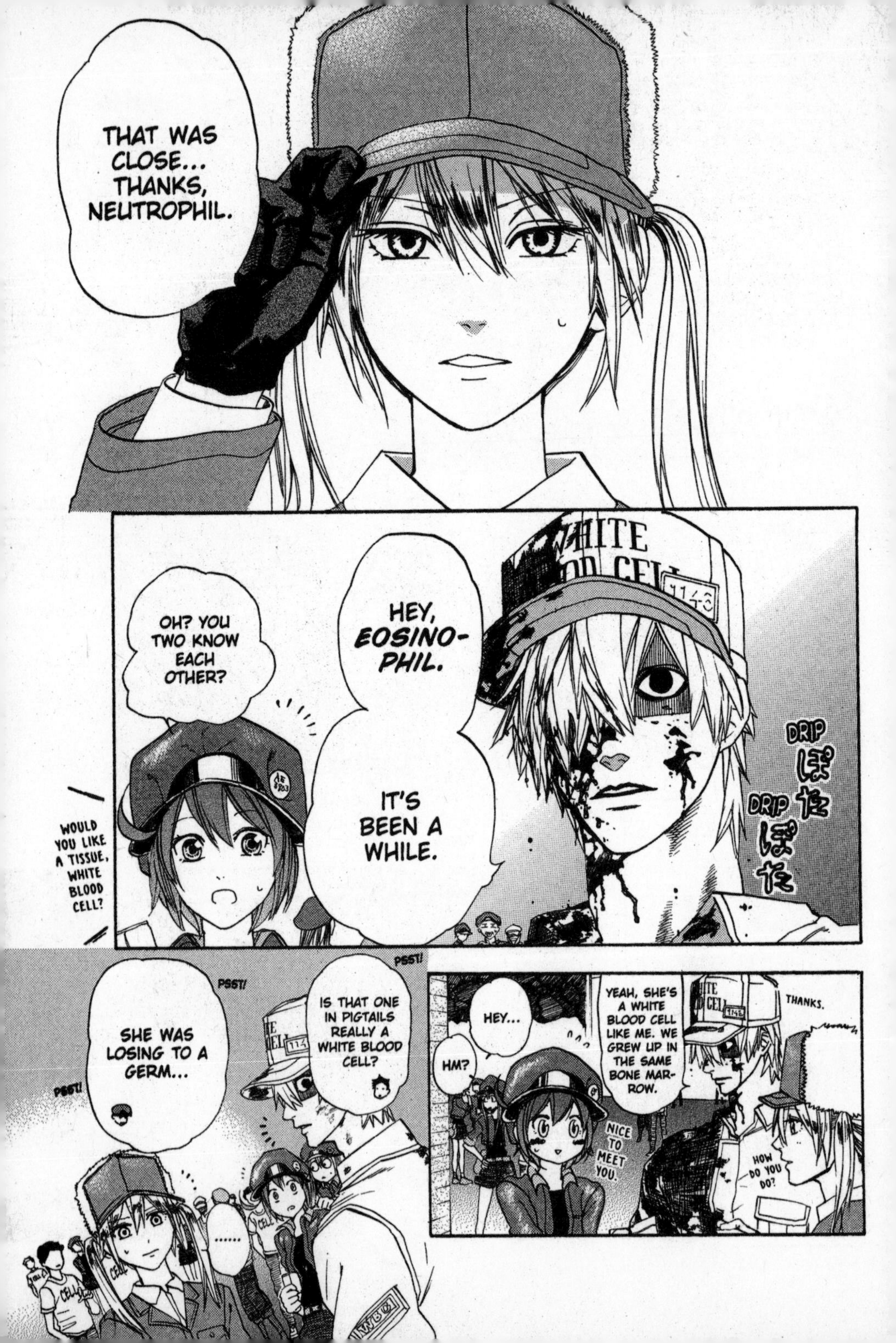
THAT WAS CLOSE... THANKS, NEUTROPHIL.
DRIP
ぽた
DRIP
ぽた
HEY, EOSINOPHIL.
IT'S BEEN A WHILE.
OH? YOU TWO KNOW EACH OTHER?
WOULD YOU LIKE A TISSUE, WHITE BLOOD CELL?
THANKS.
YEAH, SHE'S A WHITE BLOOD CELL LIKE ME. WE GREW UP IN THE SAME BONE MARROW.
HEY...
HM?
HOW DO YOU DO?
NICE TO MEET YOU.
PSST!
IS THAT ONE IN PIGTAILS REALLY A WHITE BLOOD CELL?
PSST!
SHE WAS LOSING TO A GERM...
PSST!
......

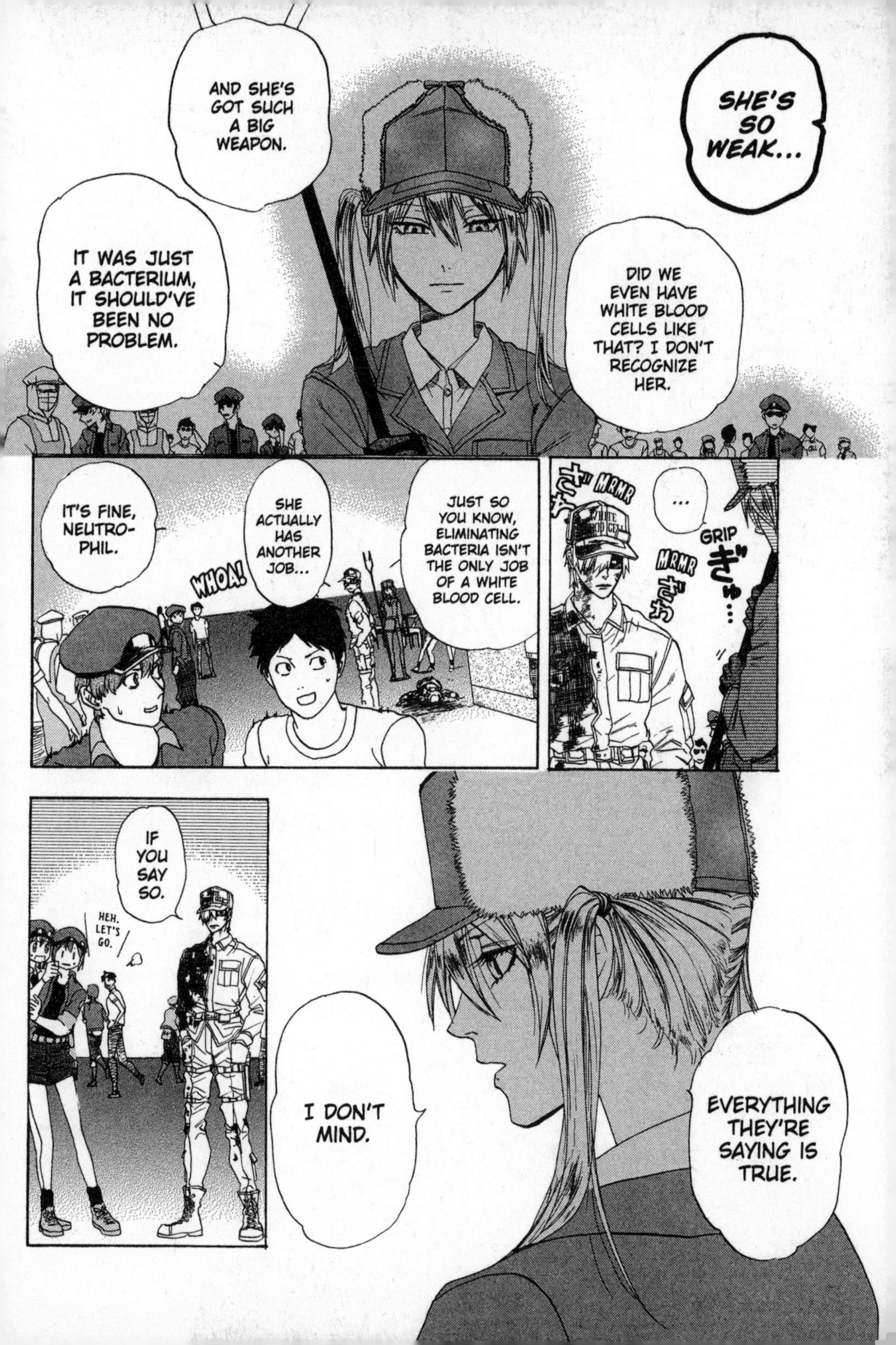
SHE'S SO WEAK...
AND SHE'S GOT SUCH A BIG WEAPON.
DID WE EVEN HAVE WHITE BLOOD CELLS LIKE THAT? I DON'T RECOGNIZE HER.
IT WAS JUST A BACTERIUM, IT SHOULD'VE BEEN NO PROBLEM.
MRMR
ざわ
...
GRIP
ぎゅ…
MRMR
ざわ
JUST SO YOU KNOW, ELIMINATING BACTERIA ISN'T THE ONLY JOB OF A WHITE BLOOD CELL.
SHE ACTUALLY HAS ANOTHER JOB...
WHOA!
IT'S FINE, NEUTROPHIL.
EVERYTHING THEY'RE SAYING IS TRUE.
I DON'T MIND.
IF YOU SAY SO.
HEH. LET'S GO.

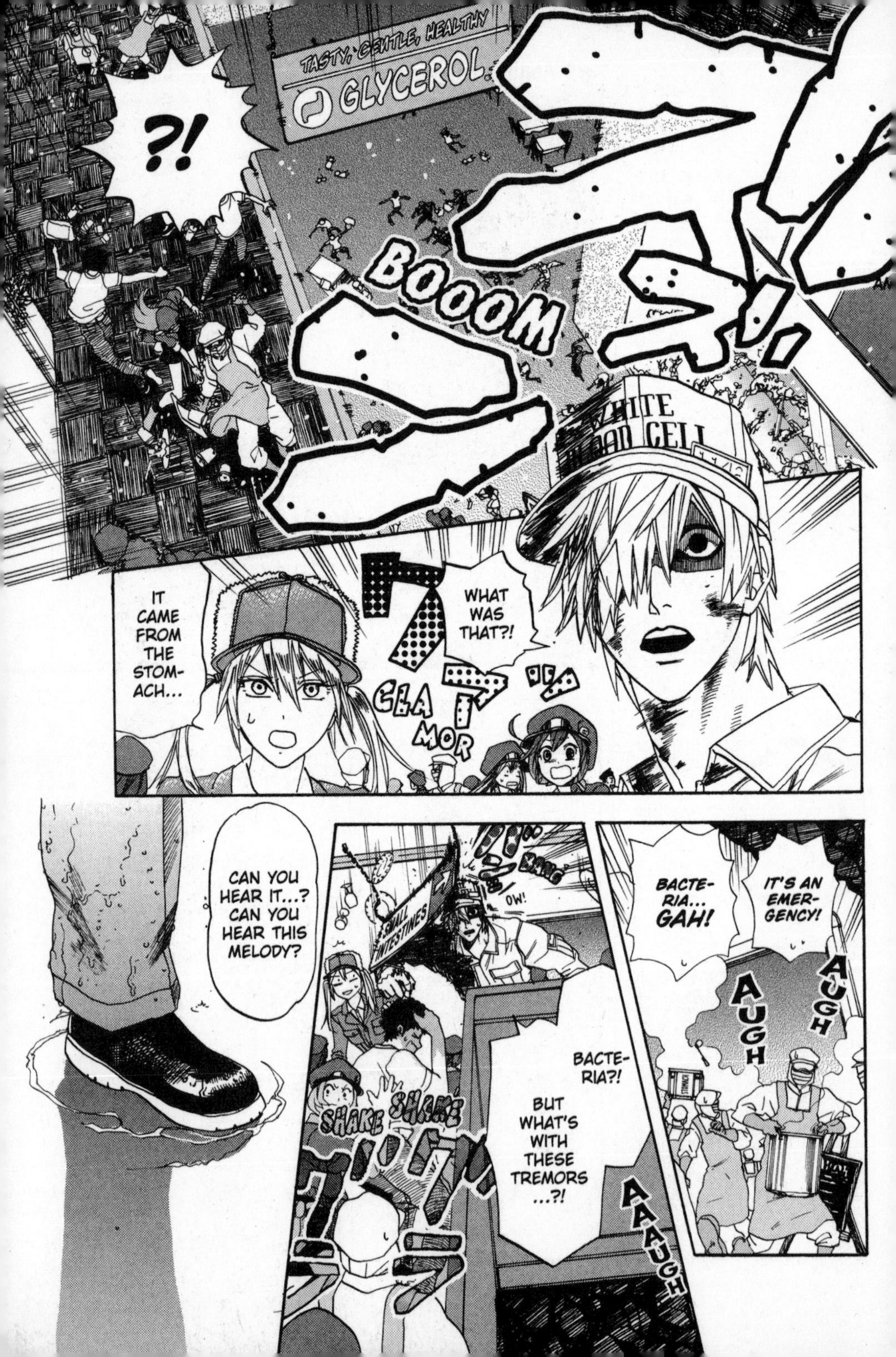
TASTY, GENTLE, HEALTHY
GLYCEROL
BOOOM
?!
WHAT WAS THAT?!
CLAMOR
IT CAME FROM THE STOMACH...
IT'S AN EMERGENCY!
BACTERIA... GAH!
AUGH
AUGH
OW!
SMALL INTESTINES
BACTERIA?!
BUT WHAT'S WITH THESE TREMORS...?!
SHAKE SHAKE
AAAUGH
CAN YOU HEAR IT...? CAN YOU HEAR THIS MELODY?

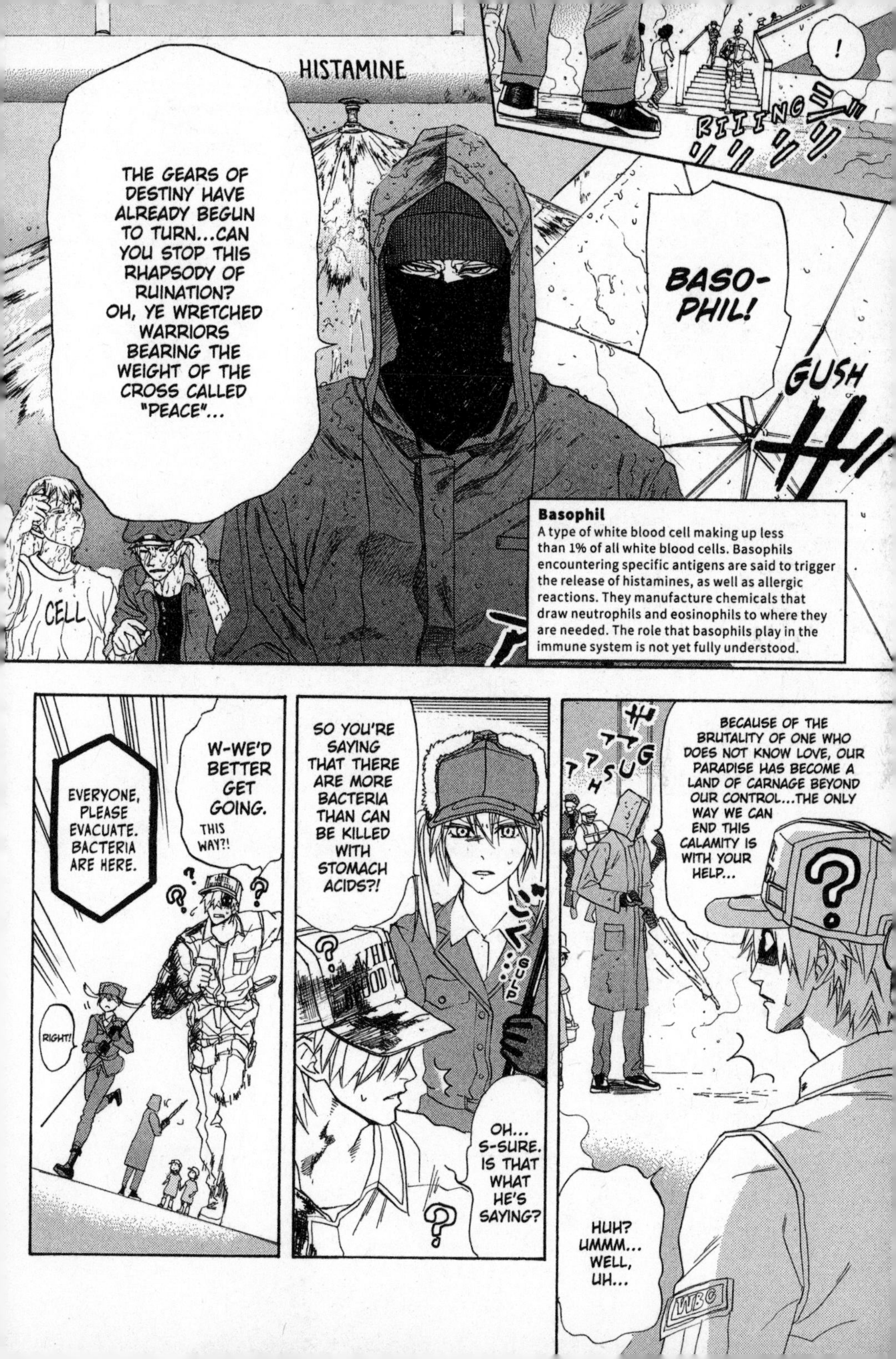

!
RIIING
BASO-PHIL!
GUSH
HISTAMINE
THE GEARS OF DESTINY HAVE ALREADY BEGUN TO TURN...CAN YOU STOP THIS RHAPSODY OF RUINATION? OH, YE WRETCHED WARRIORS BEARING THE WEIGHT OF THE CROSS CALLED "PEACE"...
CELL
Basophil
A type of white blood cell making up less than 1% of all white blood cells. Basophils encountering specific antigens are said to trigger the release of histamines, as well as allergic reactions. They manufacture chemicals that draw neutrophils and eosinophils to where they are needed. The role that basophils play in the immune system is not yet fully understood.
BECAUSE OF THE BRUTALITY OF ONE WHO DOES NOT KNOW LOVE, OUR PARADISE HAS BECOME A LAND OF CARNAGE BEYOND OUR CONTROL...THE ONLY WAY WE CAN END THIS CALAMITY IS WITH YOUR HELP...
THHSUG
HUH? UMMM... WELL, UH...
WBC
SO YOU'RE SAYING THAT THERE ARE MORE BACTERIA THAN CAN BE KILLED WITH STOMACH ACIDS?!
GULP
OH... S-SURE. IS THAT WHAT HE'S SAYING?
W-WE'D BETTER GET GOING.
THIS WAY?!
EVERYONE, PLEASE EVACUATE. BACTERIA ARE HERE.
RIGHT!

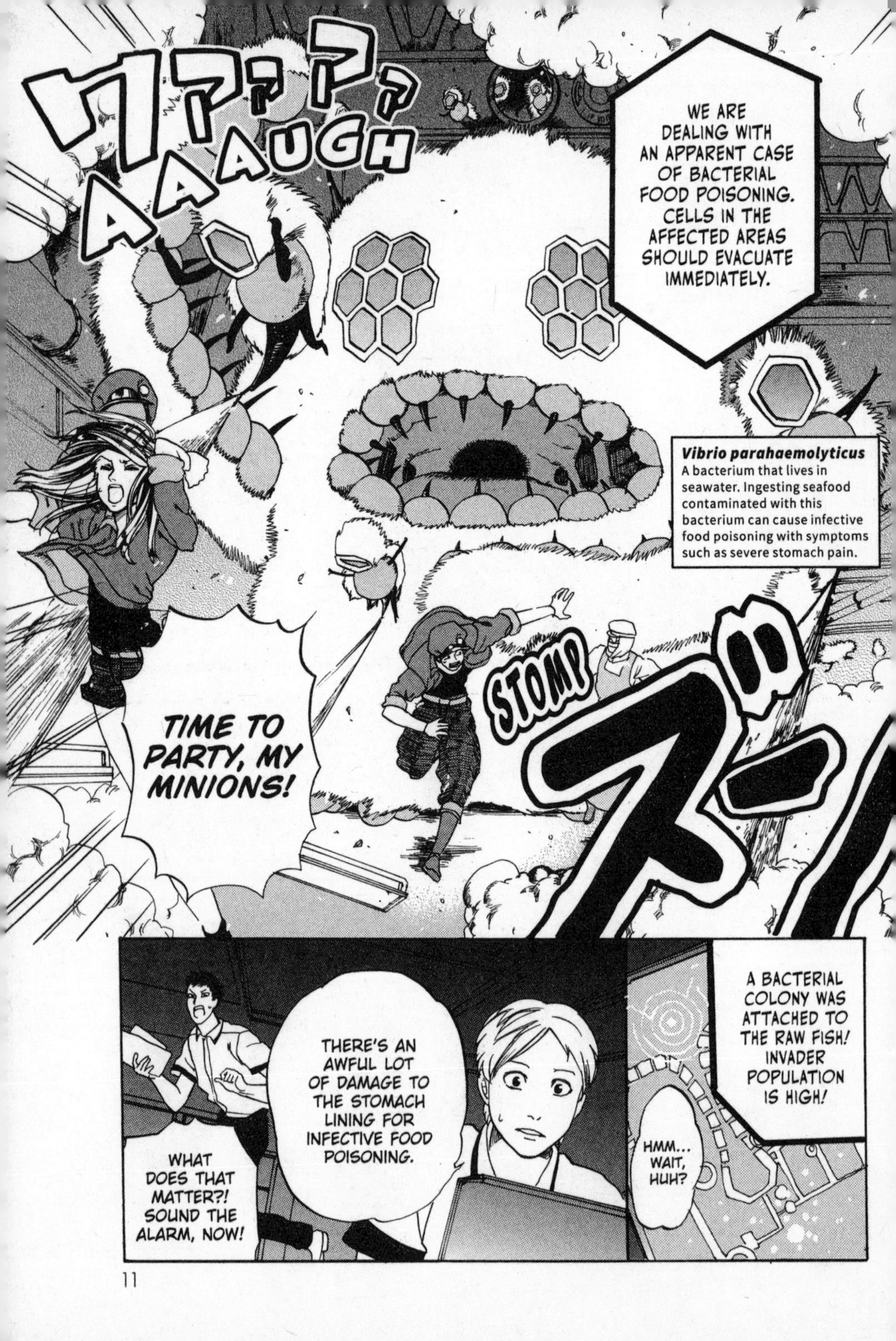
WE ARE DEALING WITH AN APPARENT CASE OF BACTERIAL FOOD POISONING. CELLS IN THE AFFECTED AREAS SHOULD EVACUATE IMMEDIATELY.
AAAUGH
Vibrio parahaemolyticus
A bacterium that lives in seawater. Ingesting seafood contaminated with this bacterium can cause infective food poisoning with symptoms such as severe stomach pain.
STOMP
TIME TO PARTY, MY MINIONS!
A BACTERIAL COLONY WAS ATTACHED TO THE RAW FISH! INVADER POPULATION IS HIGH!
HMM... WAIT, HUH?
THERE'S AN AWFUL LOT OF DAMAGE TO THE STOMACH LINING FOR INFECTIVE FOOD POISONING.
WHAT DOES THAT MATTER?! SOUND THE ALARM, NOW!

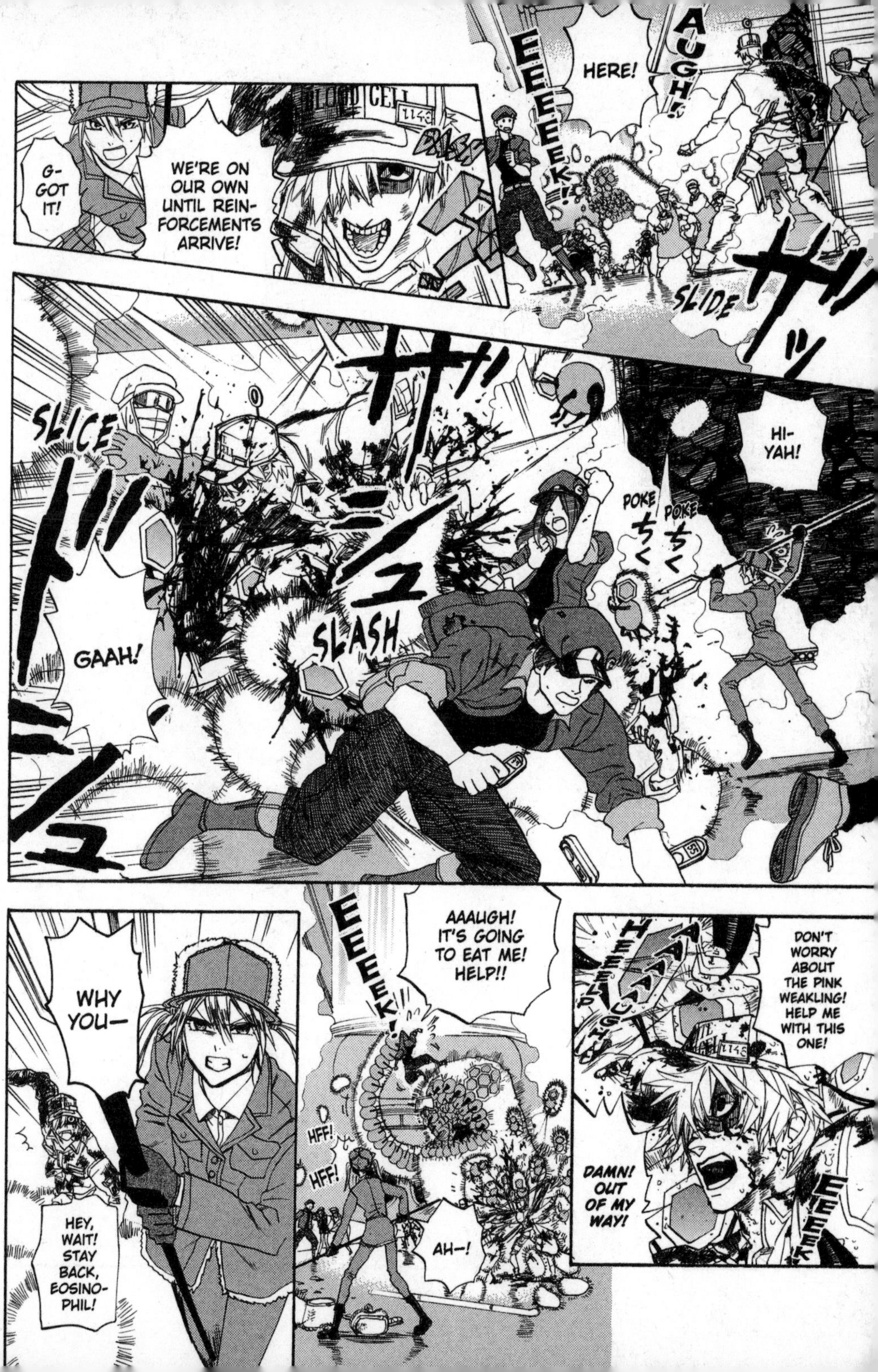
AUGH!
HERE!
EEEEEEK!!
WE'RE ON OUR OWN UNTIL REIN-FORCEMENTS ARRIVE!
G-GOT IT!
SLIDE
ザッ
HI-YAH!
POKE ちく
POKE ちく
SLASH
SLICE
GAAH!
DON'T WORRY ABOUT THE PINK WEAKLING! HELP ME WITH THIS ONE!
AAAAUGH
HEEELP
DAMN! OUT OF MY WAY!
EEEEK
AAAUGH! IT'S GOING TO EAT ME! HELP!!
EEEEK!
HFF!
HFF!
AH—!
WHY YOU—
HEY, WAIT! STAY BACK, EOSINO-PHIL!

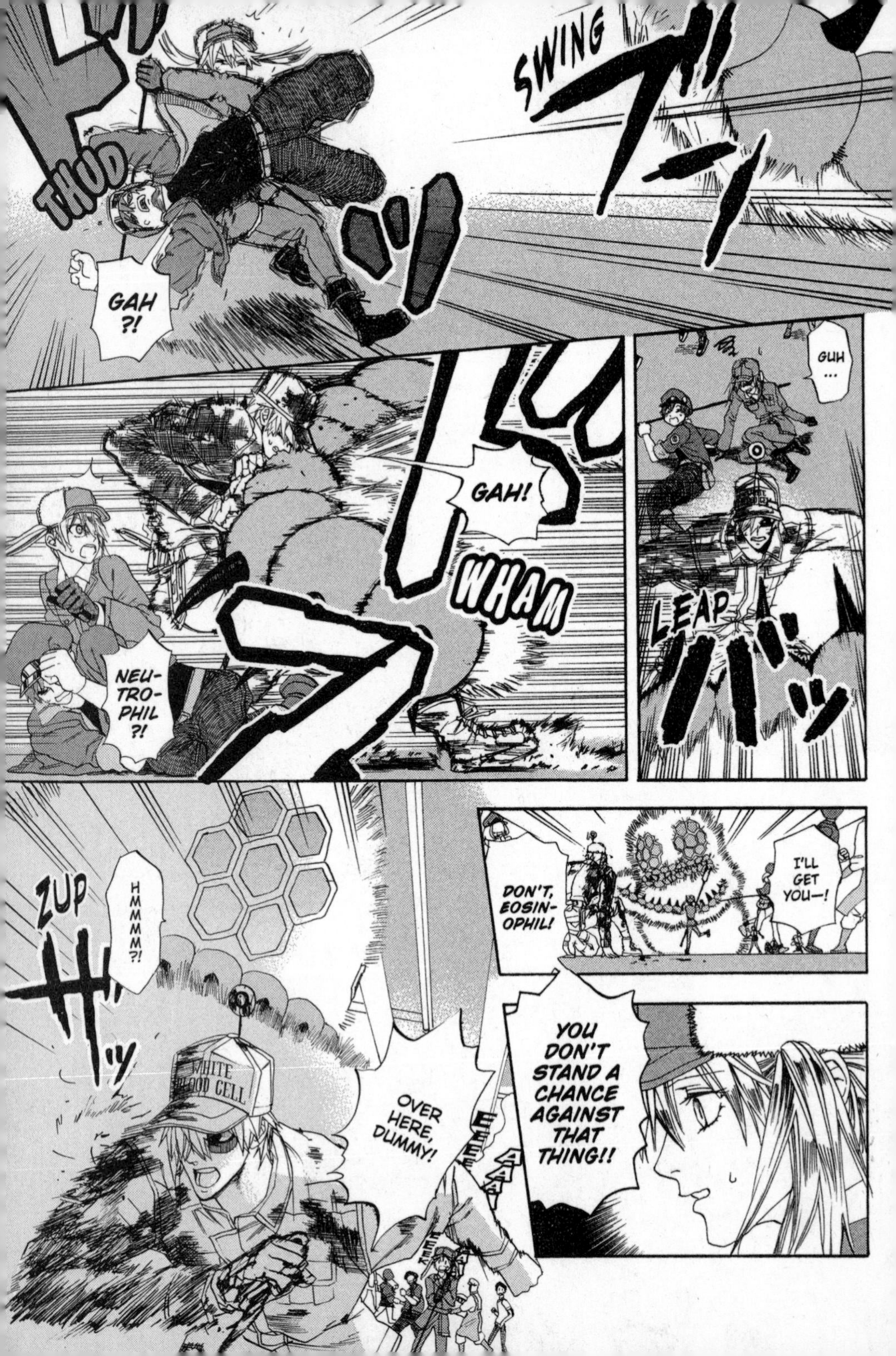
SWING
THUD
GAH ?!
GUH ...
LEAP
GAH!
WHAM
NEU-TROPHIL ?!
I'LL GET YOU—!
DON'T, EOSINOPHIL!
YOU DON'T STAND A CHANCE AGAINST THAT THING!!
HMMMMM?!
ZUP
WHITE BLOOD CELL
OVER HERE, DUMMY!

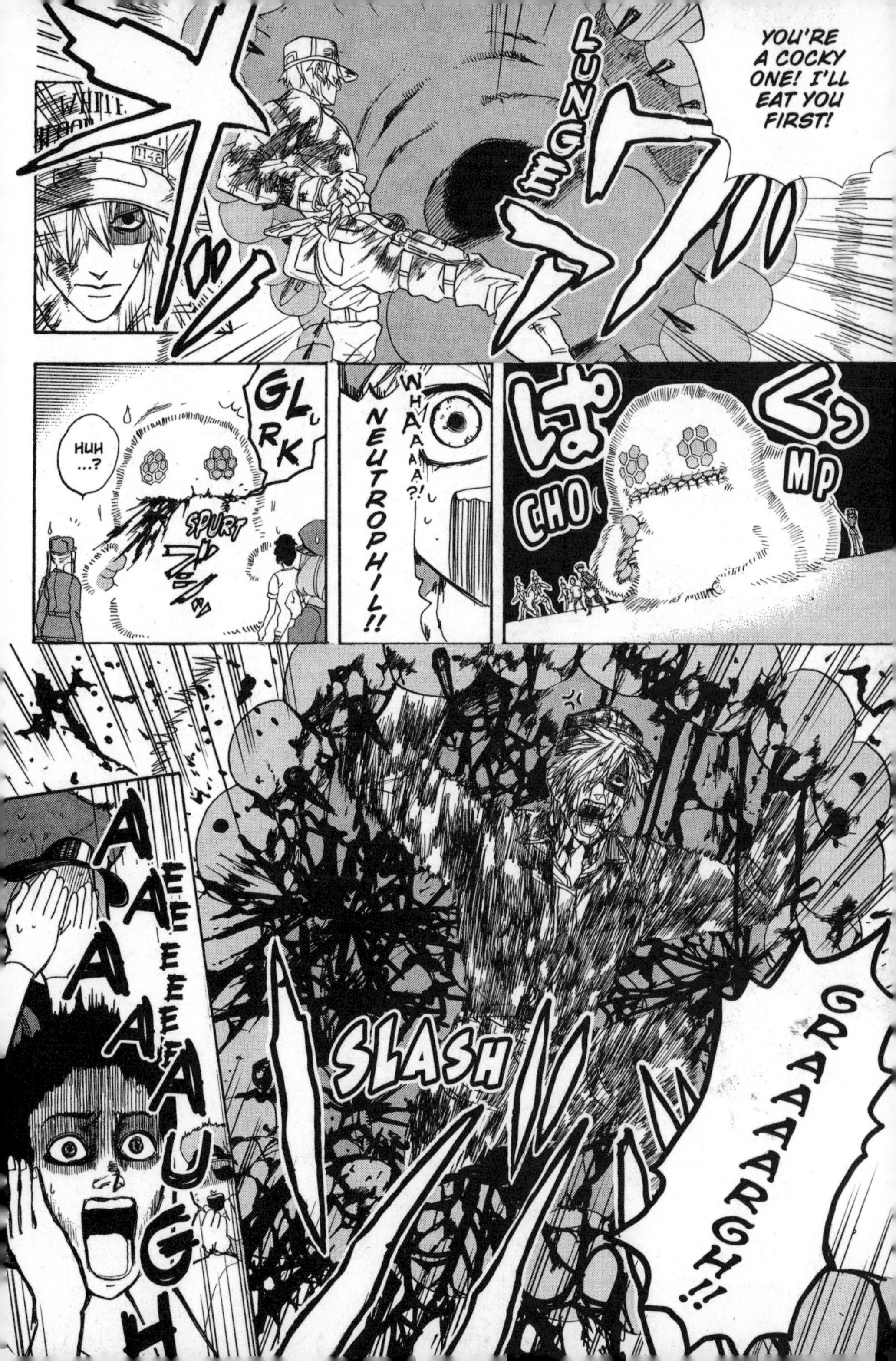
YOU'RE A COCKY ONE! I'LL EAT YOU FIRST!
LUNGE
ぱ
くっ
CHOMP
WHAAAAA?!
NEUTROPHIL!!
GLRK
HUH ...?
SPURT
GRAAAAARGH!!
SLASH
AAAAAUGH
EEEEEE

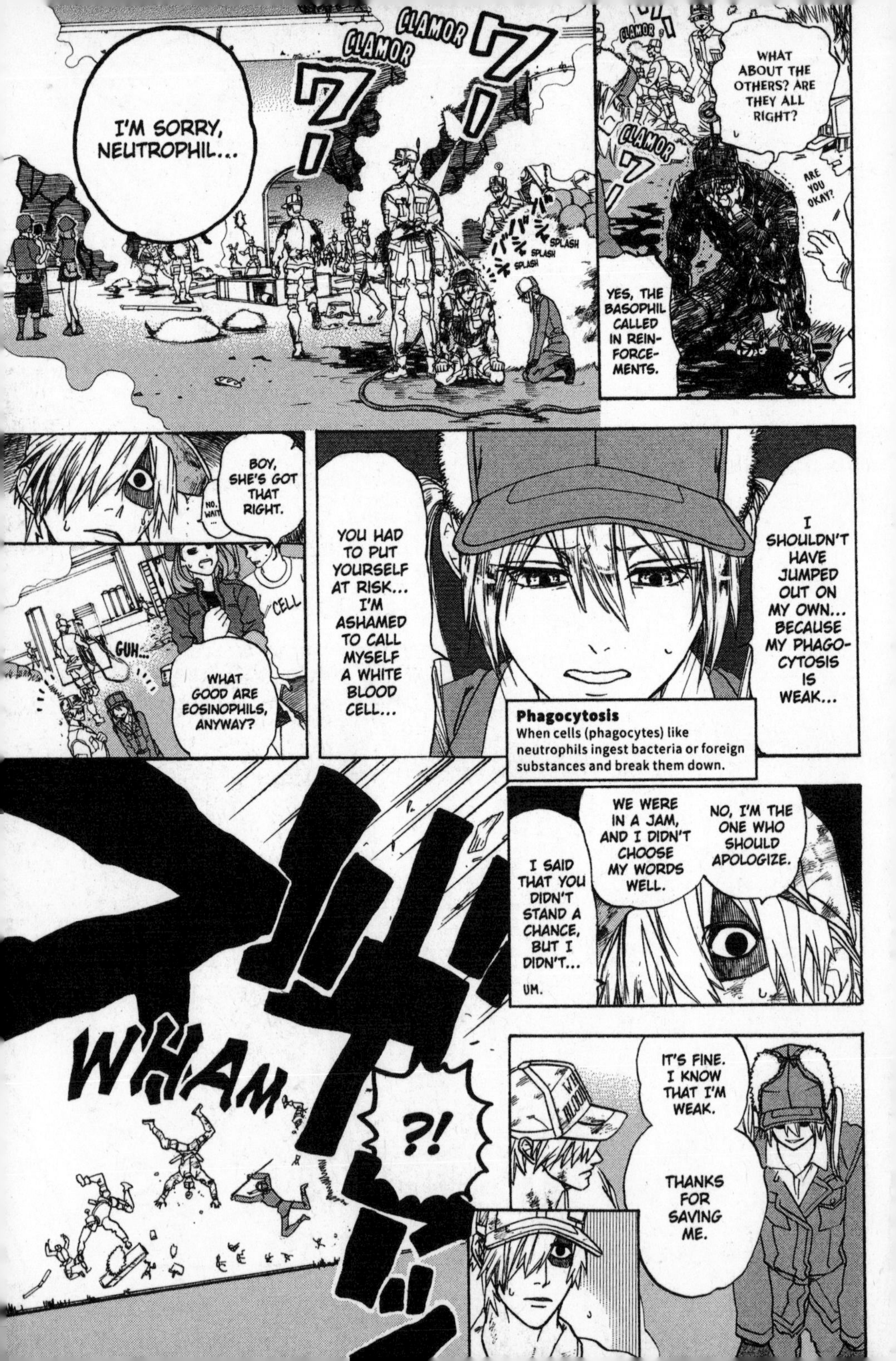
CLAMOR
WHAT ABOUT THE OTHERS? ARE THEY ALL RIGHT?
CLAMOR
ARE YOU OKAY?
YES, THE BASOPHIL CALLED IN REINFORCEMENTS.
CLAMOR
CLAMOR
I'M SORRY, NEUTROPHIL...
SPLASH
SPLASH
SPLASH
I SHOULDN'T HAVE JUMPED OUT ON MY OWN... BECAUSE MY PHAGOCYTOSIS IS WEAK...
YOU HAD TO PUT YOURSELF AT RISK... I'M ASHAMED TO CALL MYSELF A WHITE BLOOD CELL...
Phagocytosis
When cells (phagocytes) like neutrophils ingest bacteria or foreign substances and break them down.
BOY, SHE'S GOT THAT RIGHT.
NO, WAIT...
CELL
GUH...
WHAT GOOD ARE EOSINOPHILS, ANYWAY?
NO, I'M THE ONE WHO SHOULD APOLOGIZE.
WE WERE IN A JAM, AND I DIDN'T CHOOSE MY WORDS WELL.
I SAID THAT YOU DIDN'T STAND A CHANCE, BUT I DIDN'T...
UM.
IT'S FINE. I KNOW THAT I'M WEAK.
THANKS FOR SAVING ME.
WHAM
?!

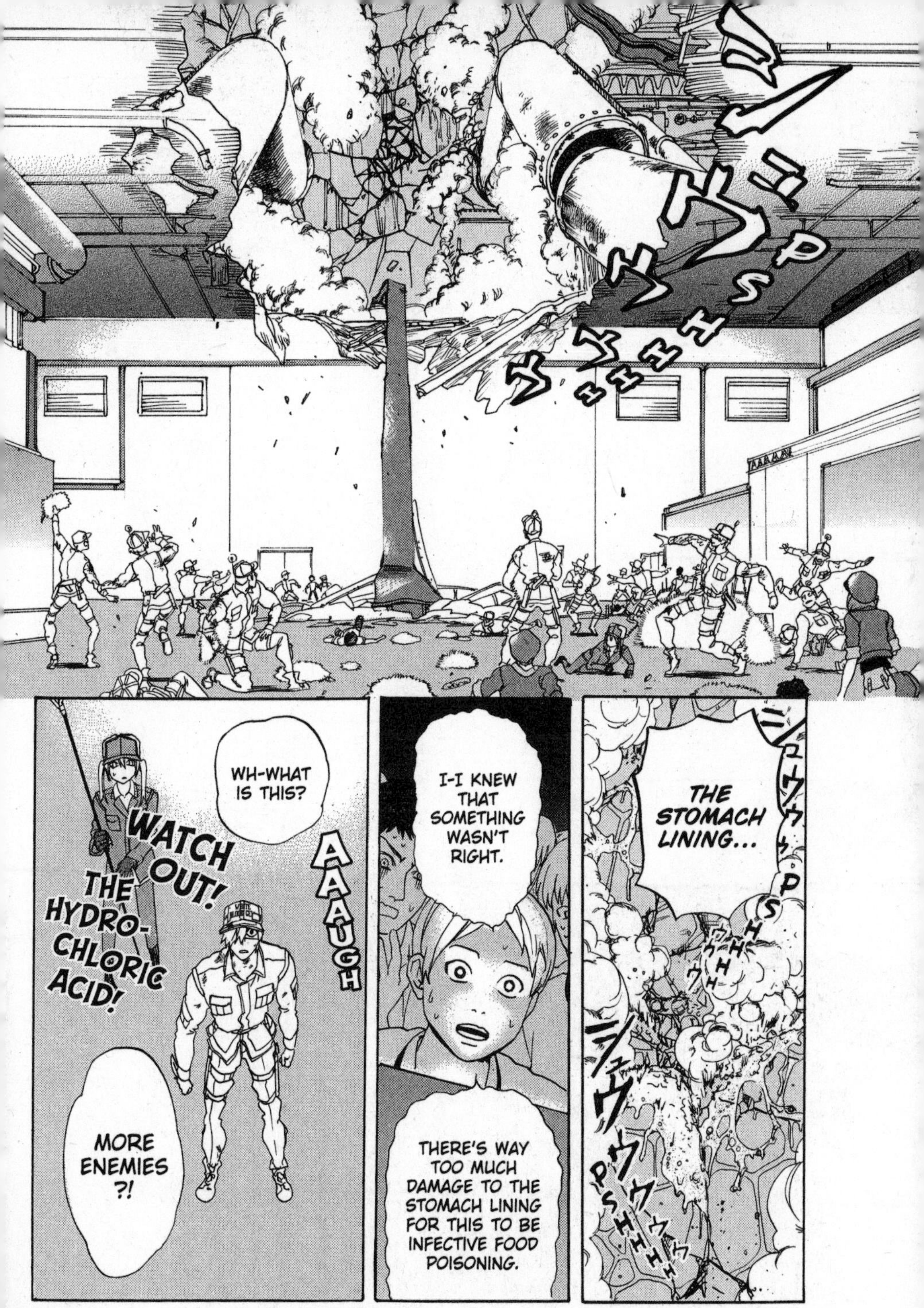
PSHHH
THE STOMACH LINING...
PSHHH
PSHHHH
I-I KNEW THAT SOMETHING WASN'T RIGHT.
THERE'S WAY TOO MUCH DAMAGE TO THE STOMACH LINING FOR THIS TO BE INFECTIVE FOOD POISONING.
WH-WHAT IS THIS?
AAAUGH
WATCH OUT! THE HYDRO-CHLORIC ACID!
MORE ENEMIES ?!

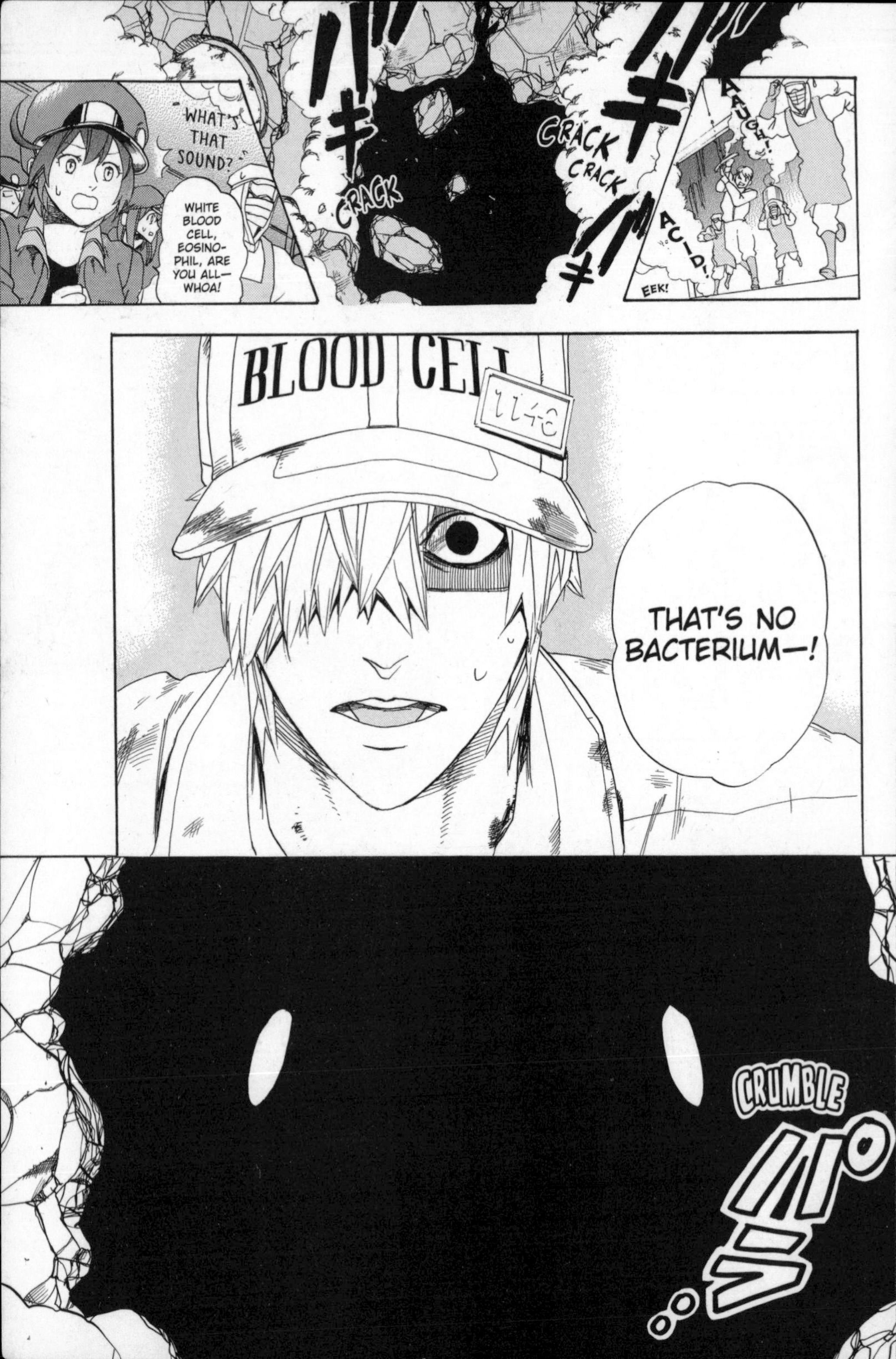
AAUGH!
ACID!
EEK!
CRACK CRACK
CRACK
WHAT'S THAT SOUND?
WHITE BLOOD CELL, EOSINO-PHIL, ARE YOU ALL—WHOA!
BLOOD CELL
THAT'S NO BACTERIUM—!
CRUMBLE

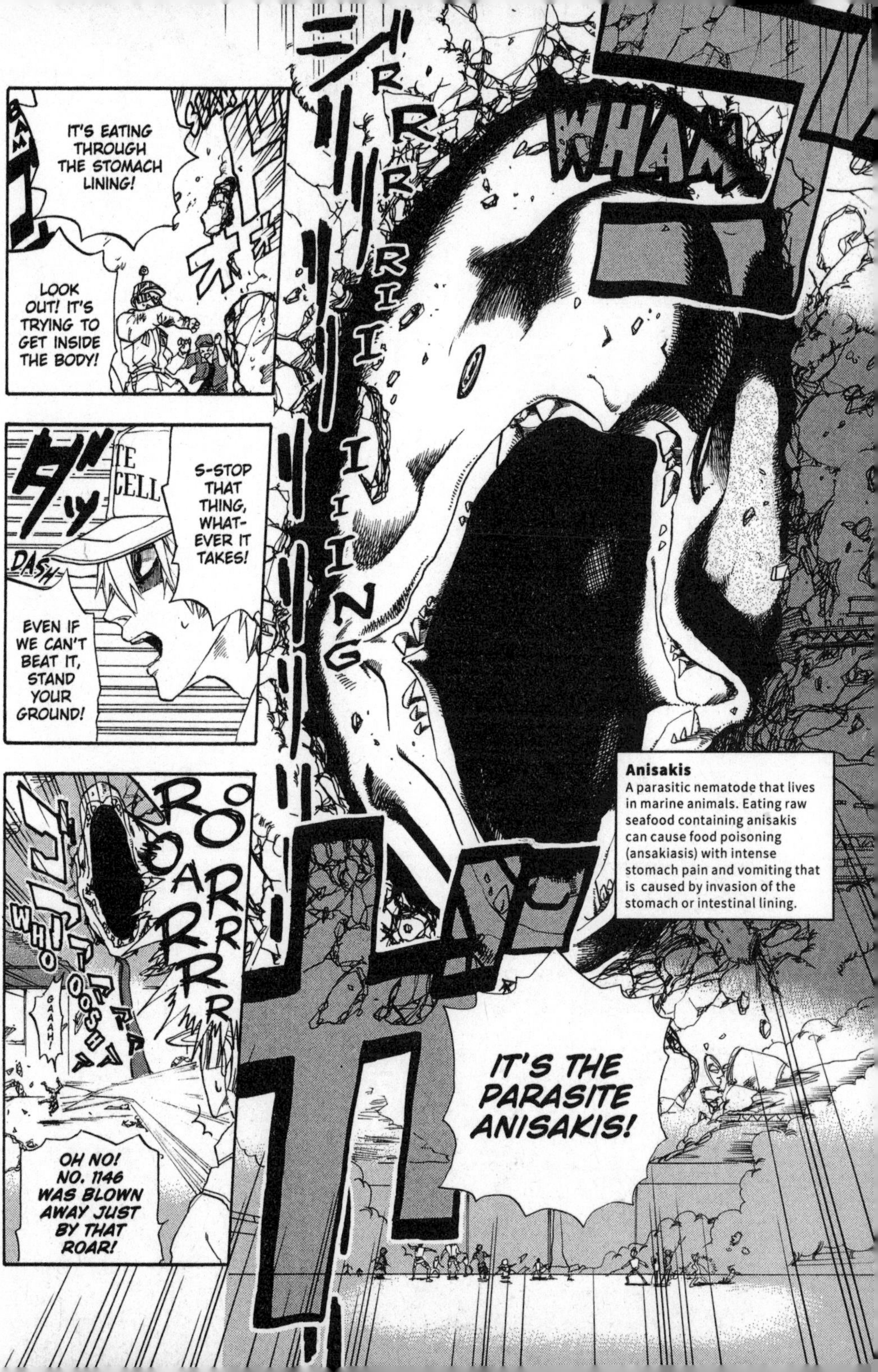
WHAM
RRRRIIIIING
IT'S THE PARASITE ANISAKIS!
BAM
IT'S EATING THROUGH THE STOMACH LINING!
LOOK OUT! IT'S TRYING TO GET INSIDE THE BODY!
DASH
S-STOP THAT THING, WHAT-EVER IT TAKES!
EVEN IF WE CAN'T BEAT IT, STAND YOUR GROUND!
ROOOARRRRRRR
WHOOOSH
GAAAH!
OH NO! NO. 1146 WAS BLOWN AWAY JUST BY THAT ROAR!

Anisakis
A parasitic nematode that lives in marine animals. Eating raw seafood containing anisakis can cause food poisoning (ansakiasis) with intense stomach pain and vomiting that is caused by invasion of the stomach or intestinal lining.

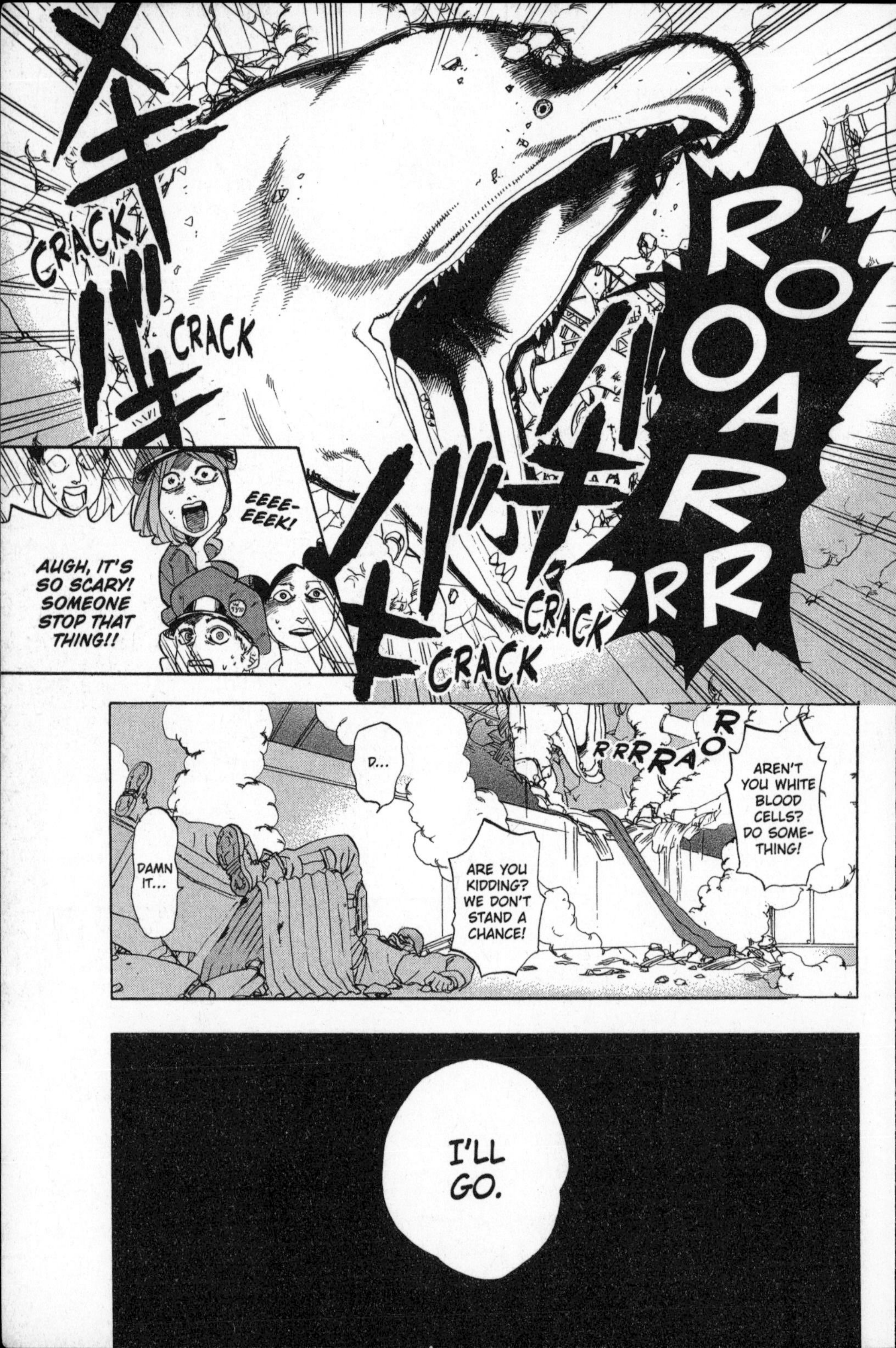
ROOARRRR
CRACK
CRACK
CRACK
CRACK
EEEE-EEEK!
AUGH, IT'S SO SCARY! SOMEONE STOP THAT THING!!
AREN'T YOU WHITE BLOOD CELLS? DO SOME-THING!
RRRRRAOR
ARE YOU KIDDING? WE DON'T STAND A CHANCE!
D...
DAMN IT...
I'LL GO.

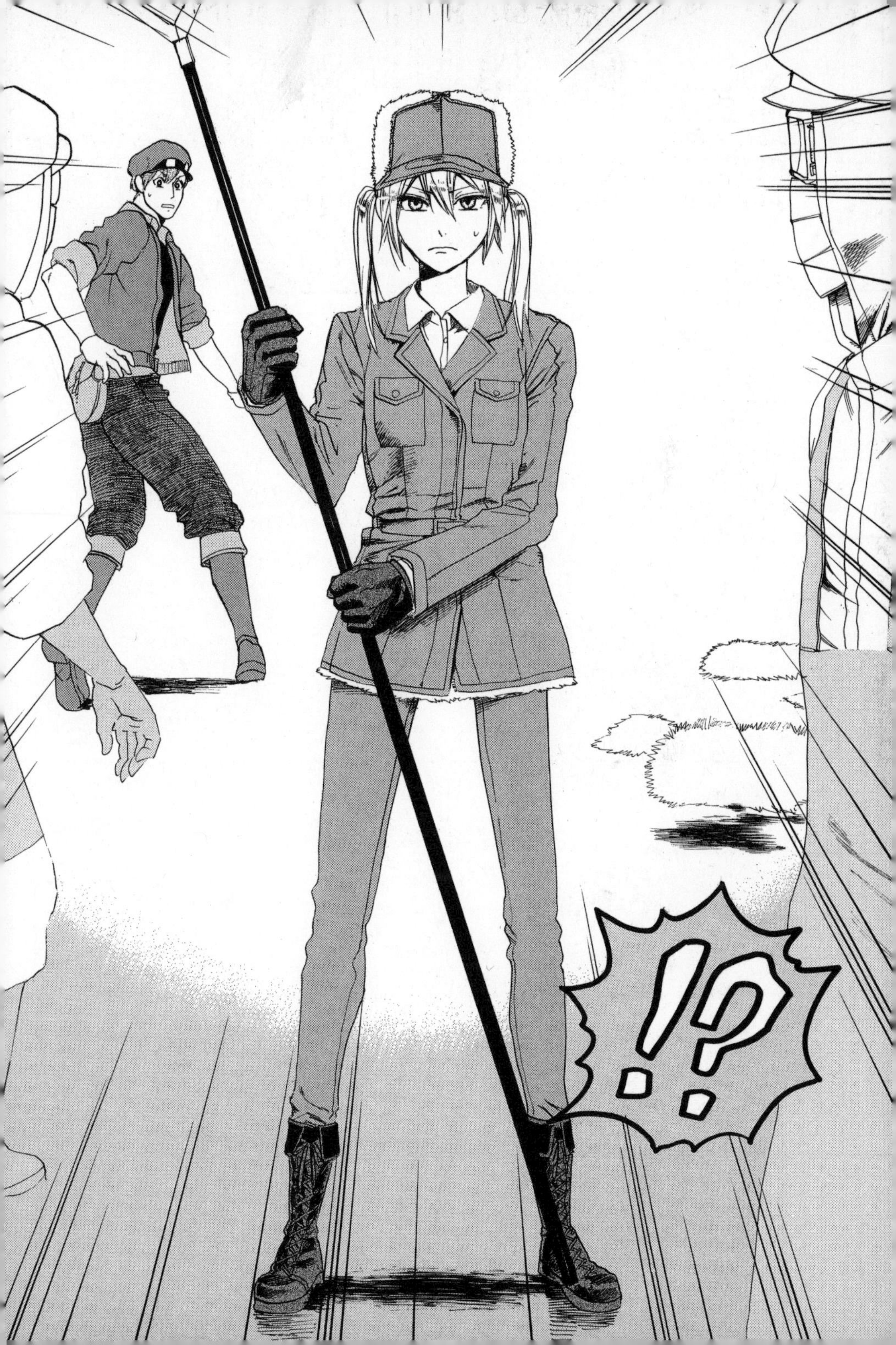
!?

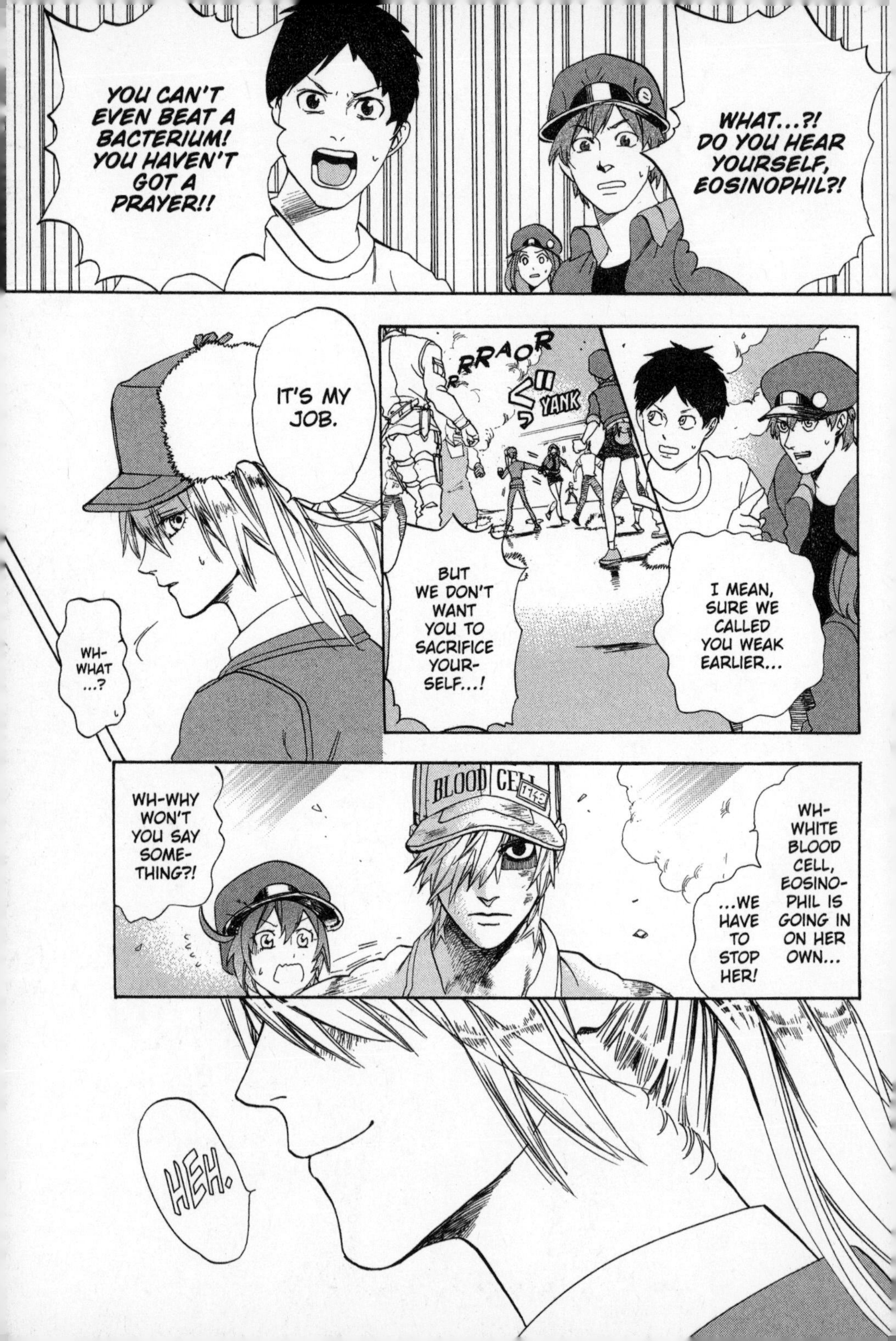
WHAT...?! DO YOU HEAR YOURSELF, EOSINOPHIL?!
YOU CAN'T EVEN BEAT A BACTERIUM! YOU HAVEN'T GOT A PRAYER!!
I MEAN, SURE WE CALLED YOU WEAK EARLIER...
RRRAOR
YANK
BUT WE DON'T WANT YOU TO SACRIFICE YOUR-SELF...!
IT'S MY JOB.
WH-WHAT...?
WH-WHITE BLOOD CELL, EOSINOPHIL IS GOING IN ON HER OWN...
...WE HAVE TO STOP HER!
WH-WHY WON'T YOU SAY SOME-THING?!
HEH.

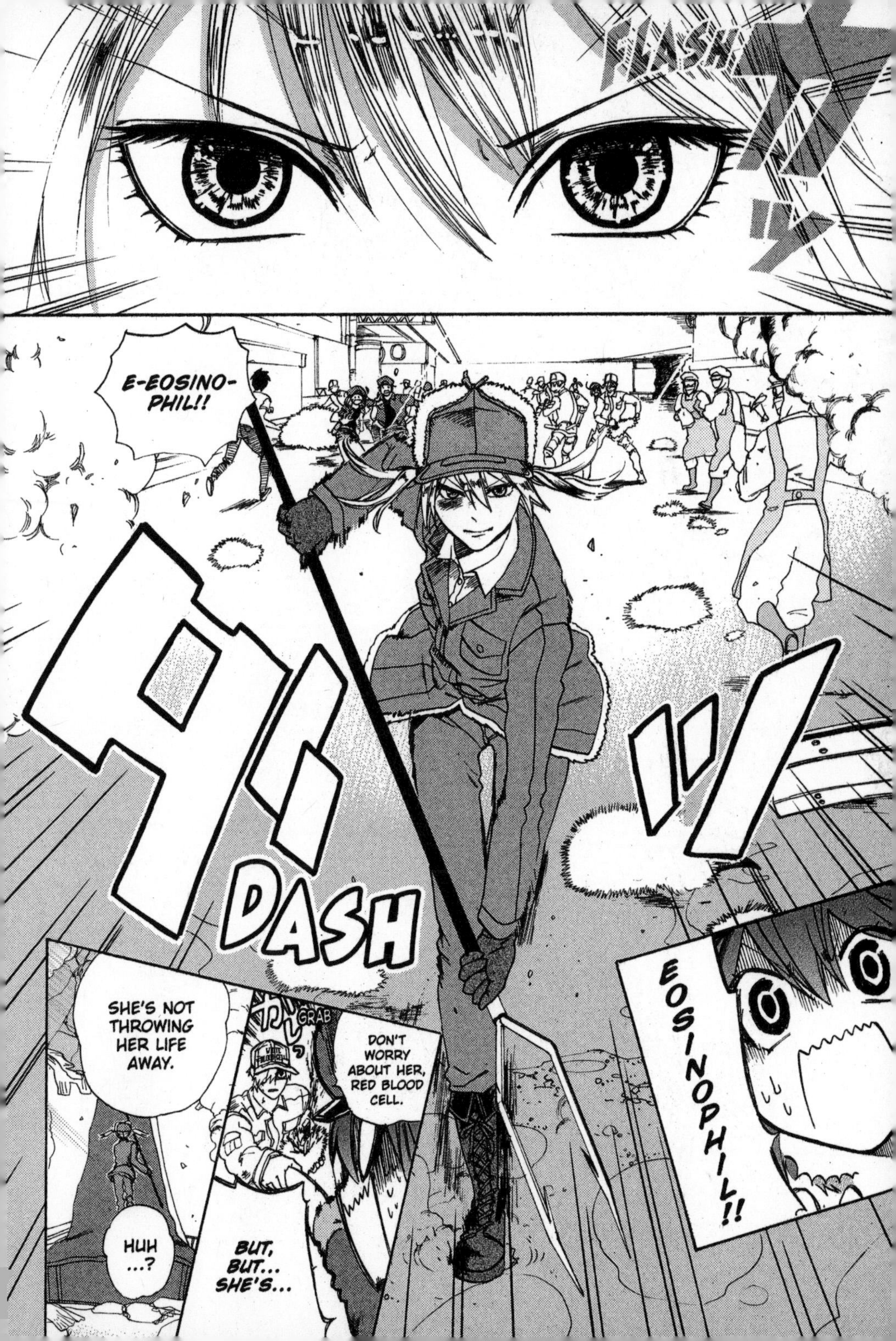
FLASH
E-EOSINO-PHIL!!
DASH
EOSINOPHIL!!
GRAB
DON'T WORRY ABOUT HER, RED BLOOD CELL.
BUT, BUT... SHE'S...
SHE'S NOT THROWING HER LIFE AWAY.
HUH ...?

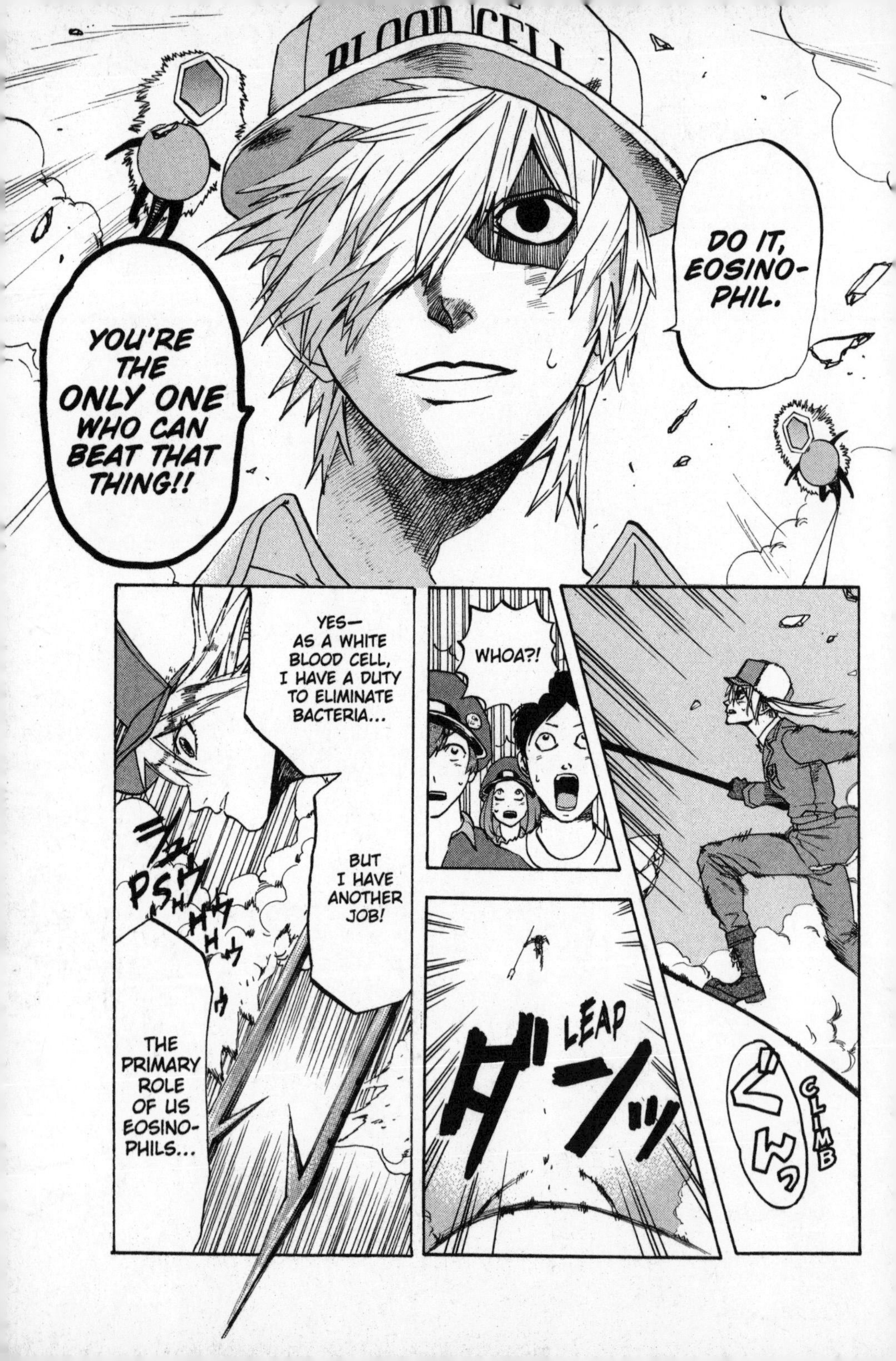
DO IT, EOSINOPHIL.
YOU'RE THE ONLY ONE WHO CAN BEAT THAT THING!!
CLIMB
WHOA?!
LEAP
YES— AS A WHITE BLOOD CELL, I HAVE A DUTY TO ELIMINATE BACTERIA...
BUT I HAVE ANOTHER JOB!
PSHHHH
THE PRIMARY ROLE OF US EOSINOPHILS...

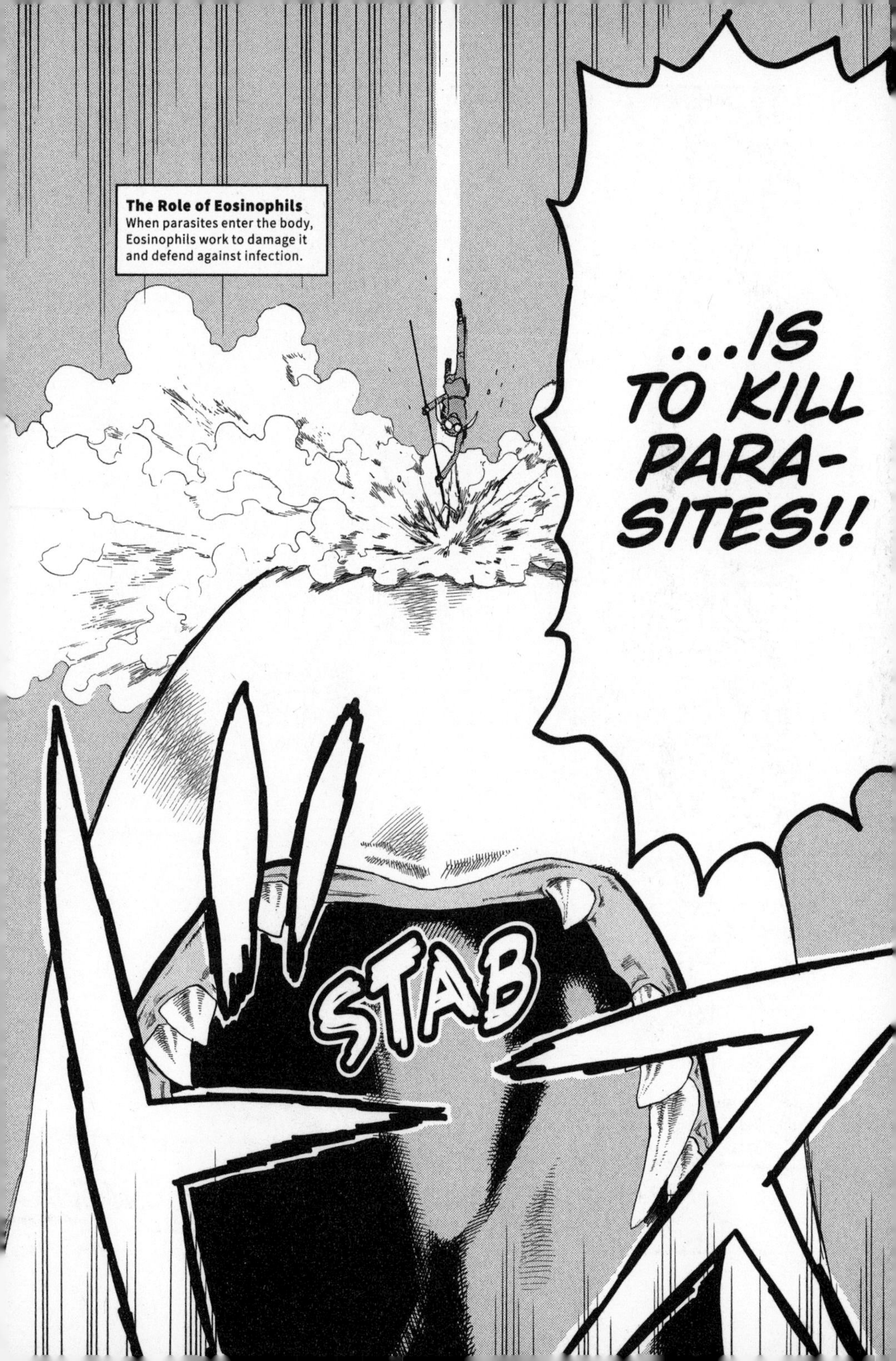
...IS TO KILL PARA-SITES!!
The Role of Eosinophils
When parasites enter the body, Eosinophils work to damage it and defend against infection.
STAB

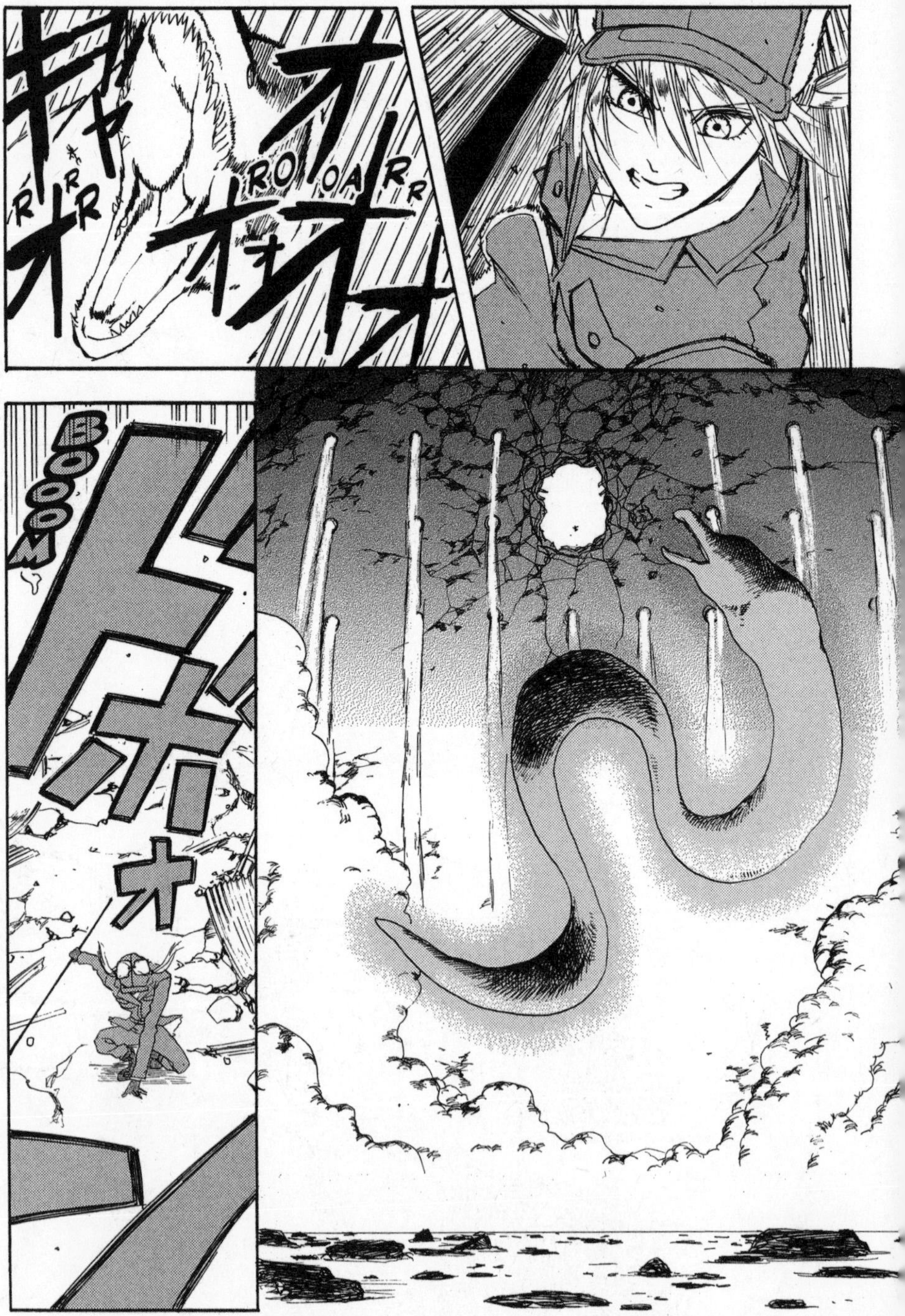
ROARR
BOOOOM

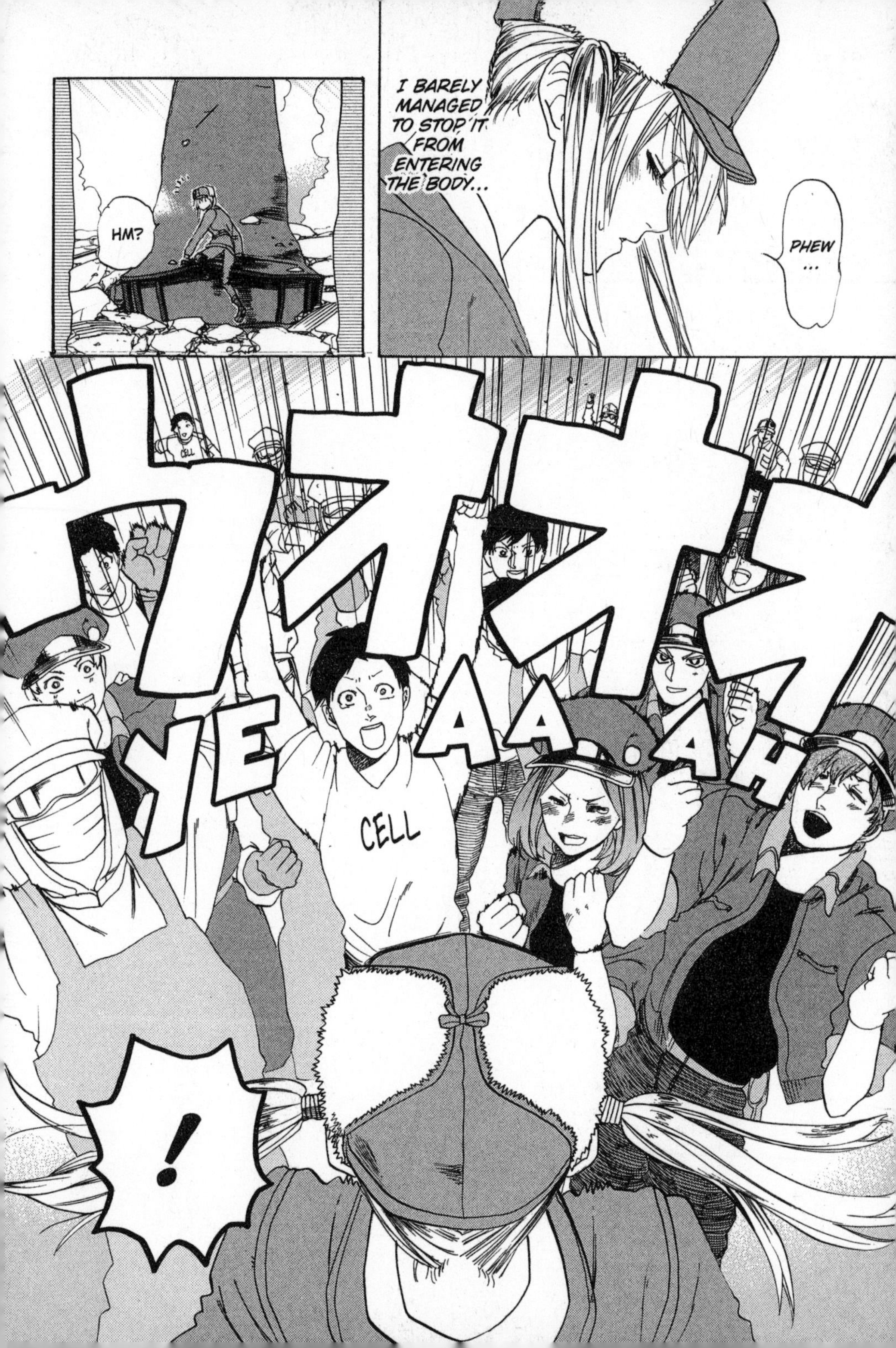
I BARELY MANAGED TO STOP IT FROM ENTERING THE BODY...
PHEW ...
HM?
ウオオオ
YEAAAH
CELL
!

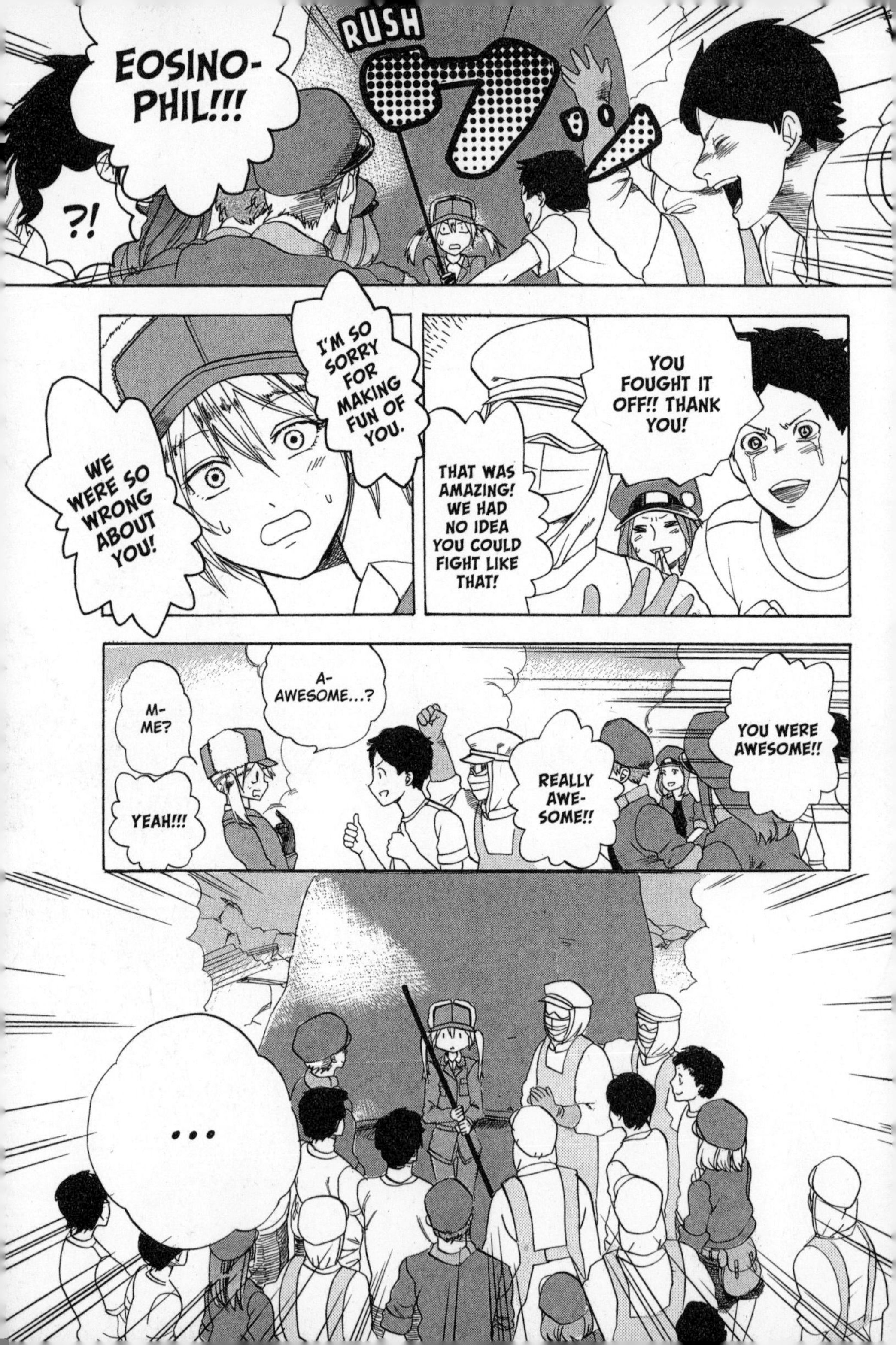
RUSH
EOSINO-PHIL!!!
?!
YOU FOUGHT IT OFF!! THANK YOU!
THAT WAS AMAZING! WE HAD NO IDEA YOU COULD FIGHT LIKE THAT!
I'M SO SORRY FOR MAKING FUN OF YOU.
WE WERE SO WRONG ABOUT YOU!
YOU WERE AWESOME!!
REALLY AWE-SOME!!
A- AWESOME...?
M- ME?
YEAH!!!
...

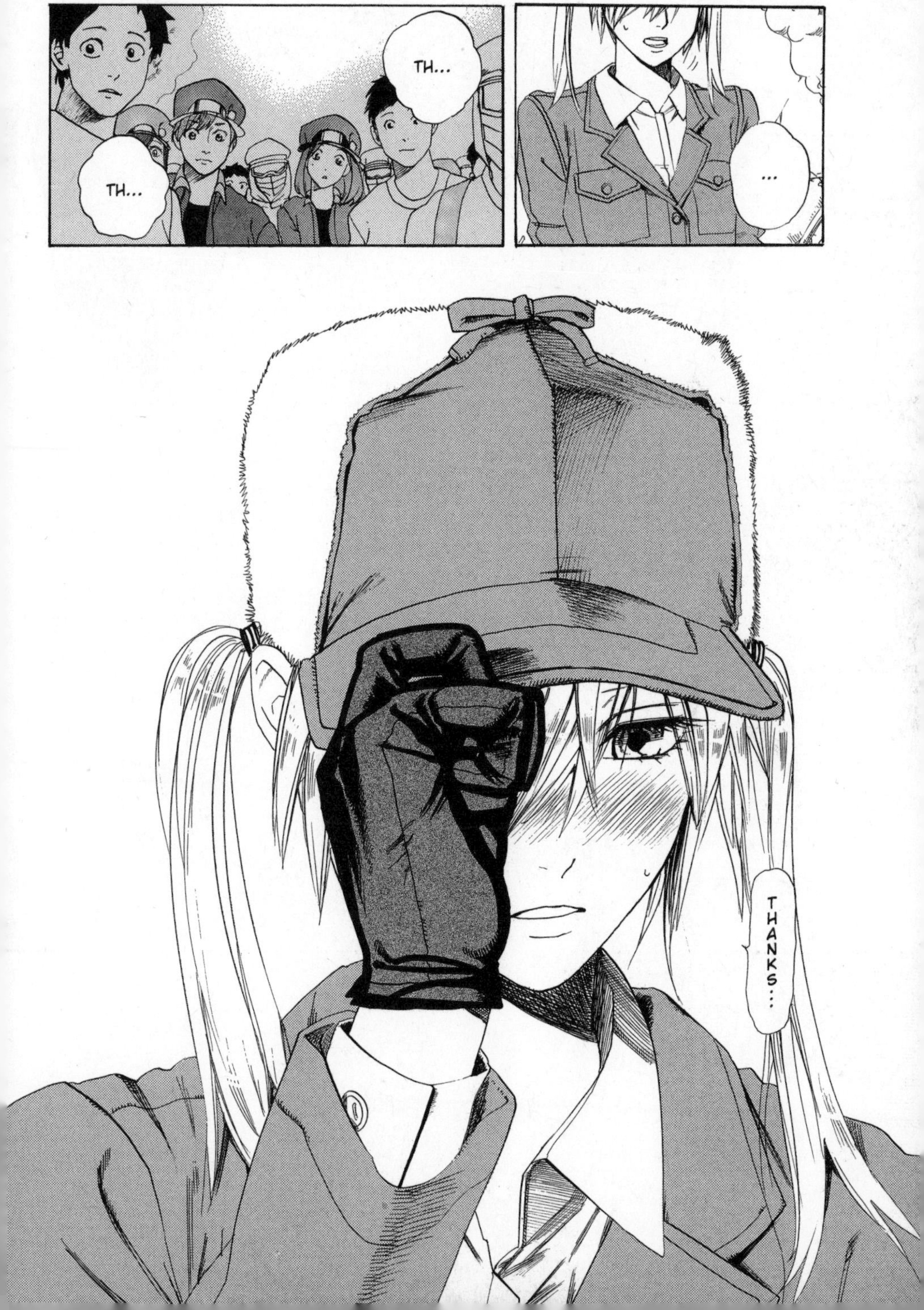
...
TH...
TH...
THANKS...

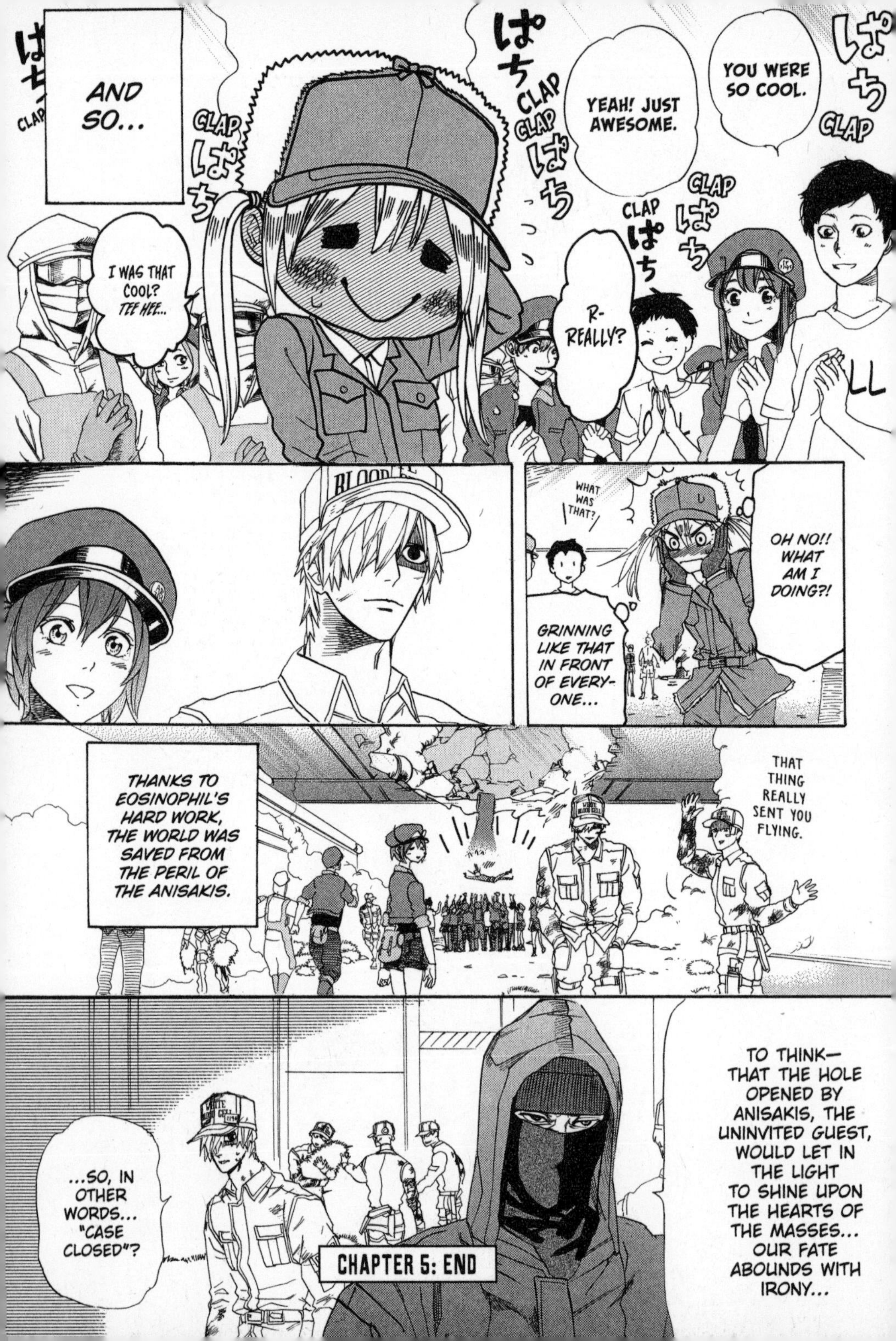

ぱち
CLAP
YOU WERE SO COOL.
YEAH! JUST AWESOME.
ぱち
CLAP
CLAP
ぱち
CLAP ぱち
CLAP ぱち
R-REALLY?
CLAP ぱち
AND SO...
ぱち
CLAP
I WAS THAT COOL? TEE HEE...
OH NO!! WHAT AM I DOING?!
WHAT WAS THAT?
GRINNING LIKE THAT IN FRONT OF EVERY-ONE...
THAT THING REALLY SENT YOU FLYING.
THANKS TO EOSINOPHIL'S HARD WORK, THE WORLD WAS SAVED FROM THE PERIL OF THE ANISAKIS.
TO THINK— THAT THE HOLE OPENED BY ANISAKIS, THE UNINVITED GUEST, WOULD LET IN THE LIGHT TO SHINE UPON THE HEARTS OF THE MASSES... OUR FATE ABOUNDS WITH IRONY...
CHAPTER 5: END
...SO, IN OTHER WORDS... "CASE CLOSED"?

Cells at Work!
はたらく細胞

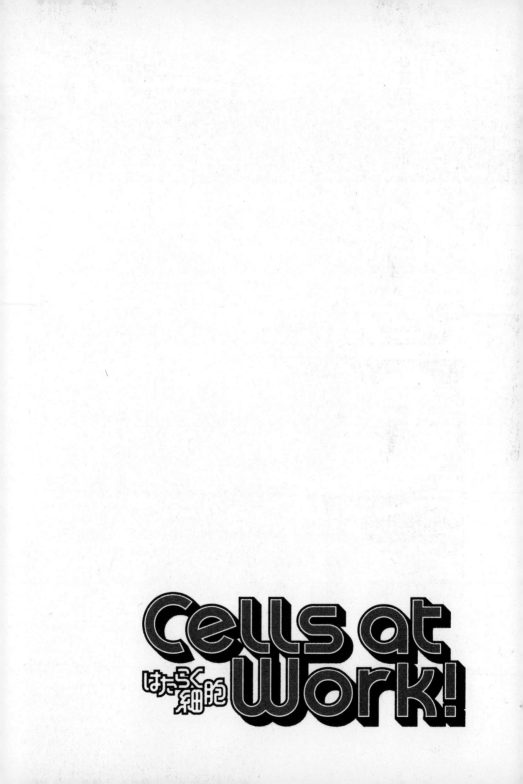

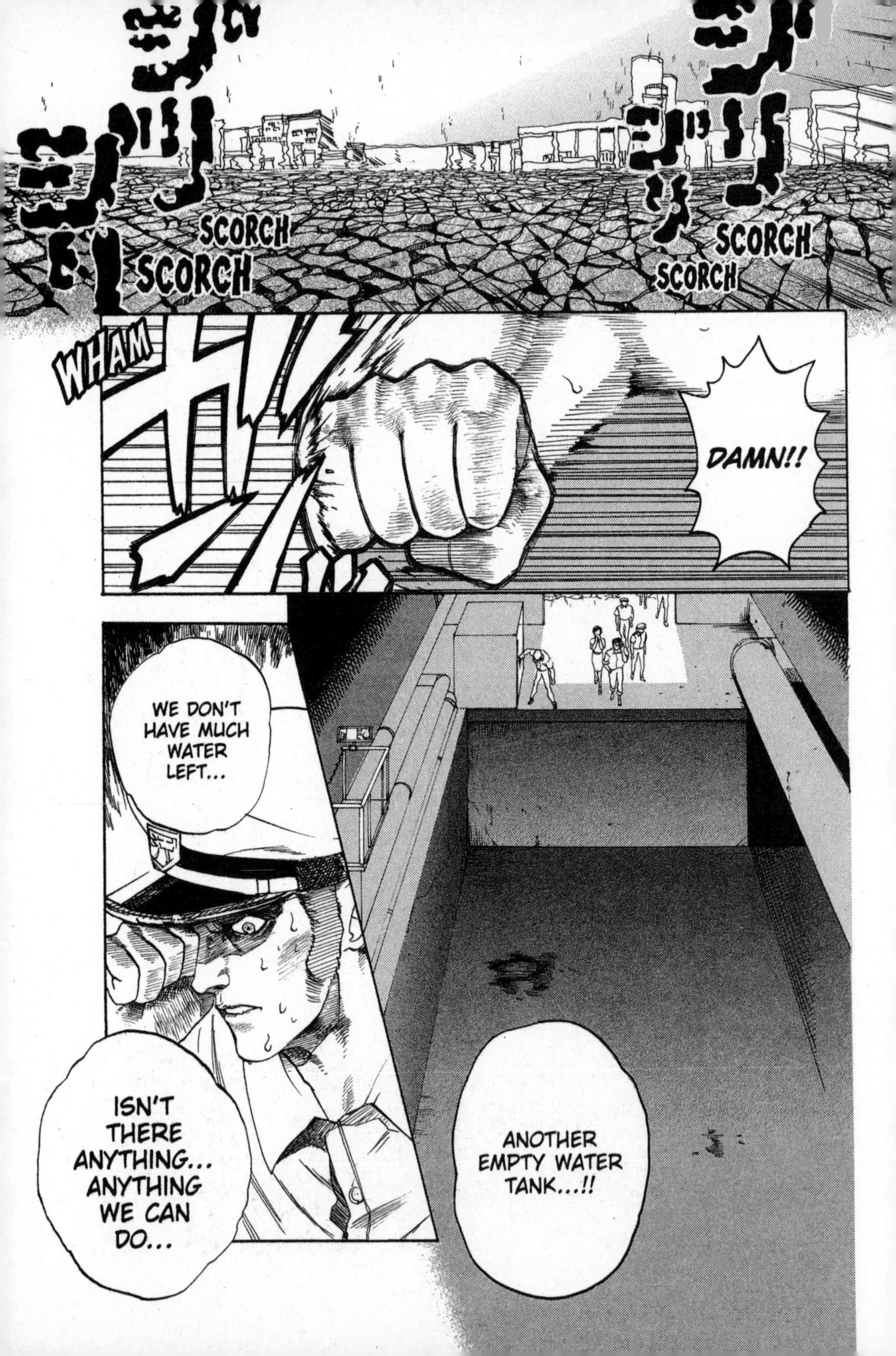
SCORCH
SCORCH
SCORCH
SCORCH
DAMN!!
WHAM
ANOTHER EMPTY WATER TANK...!!
WE DON'T HAVE MUCH WATER LEFT...
ISN'T THERE ANYTHING... ANYTHING WE CAN DO...

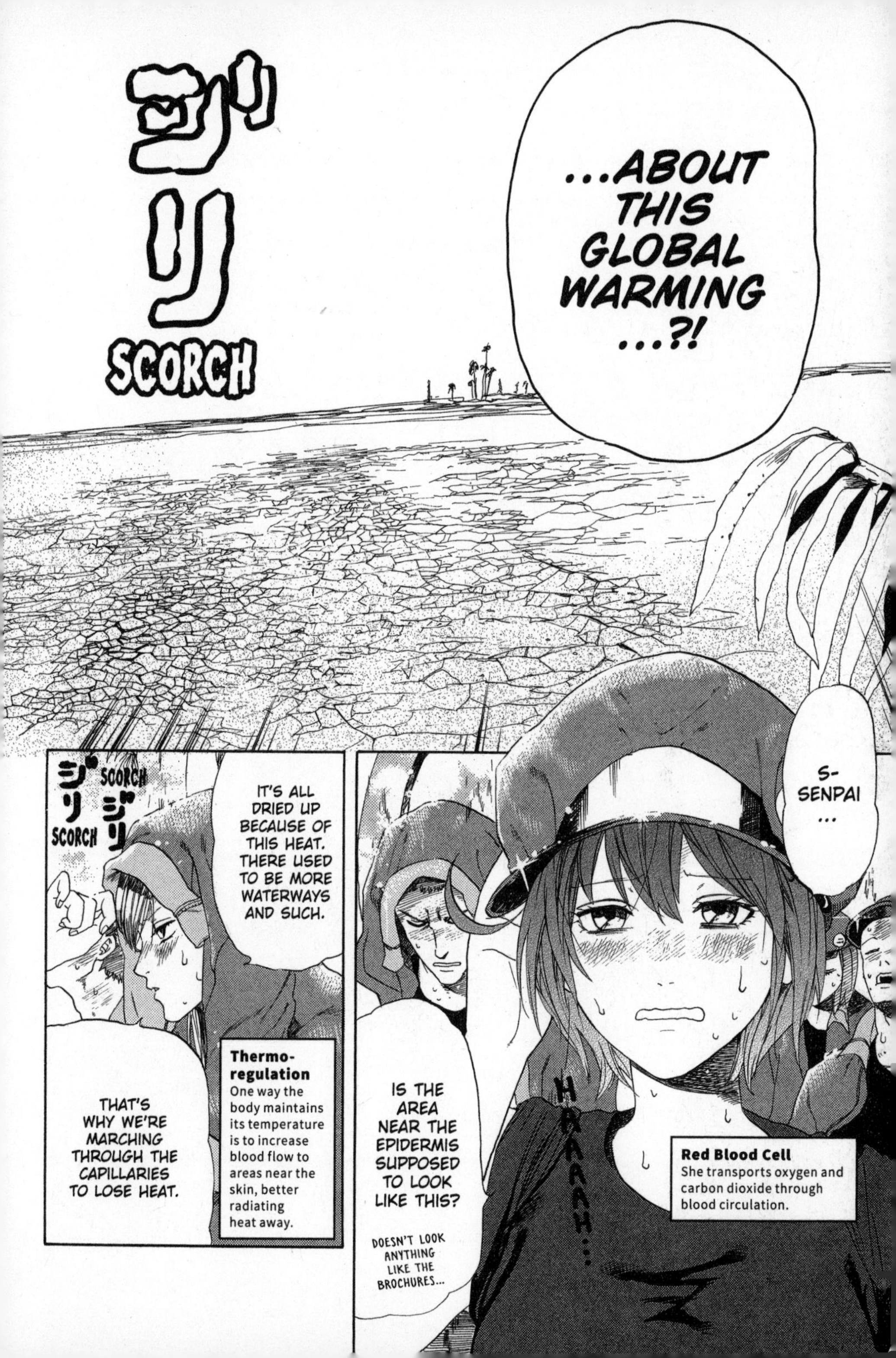
...ABOUT THIS GLOBAL WARMING...?!
ジリ
SCORCH
S-SENPAI...
Red Blood Cell
She transports oxygen and carbon dioxide through blood circulation.
HAAAAH...
IS THE AREA NEAR THE EPIDERMIS SUPPOSED TO LOOK LIKE THIS?
DOESN'T LOOK ANYTHING LIKE THE BROCHURES...
ジリ SCORCH ジリ SCORCH
IT'S ALL DRIED UP BECAUSE OF THIS HEAT. THERE USED TO BE MORE WATERWAYS AND SUCH.
Thermo-regulation
One way the body maintains its temperature is to increase blood flow to areas near the skin, better radiating heat away.
THAT'S WHY WE'RE MARCHING THROUGH THE CAPILLARIES TO LOSE HEAT.

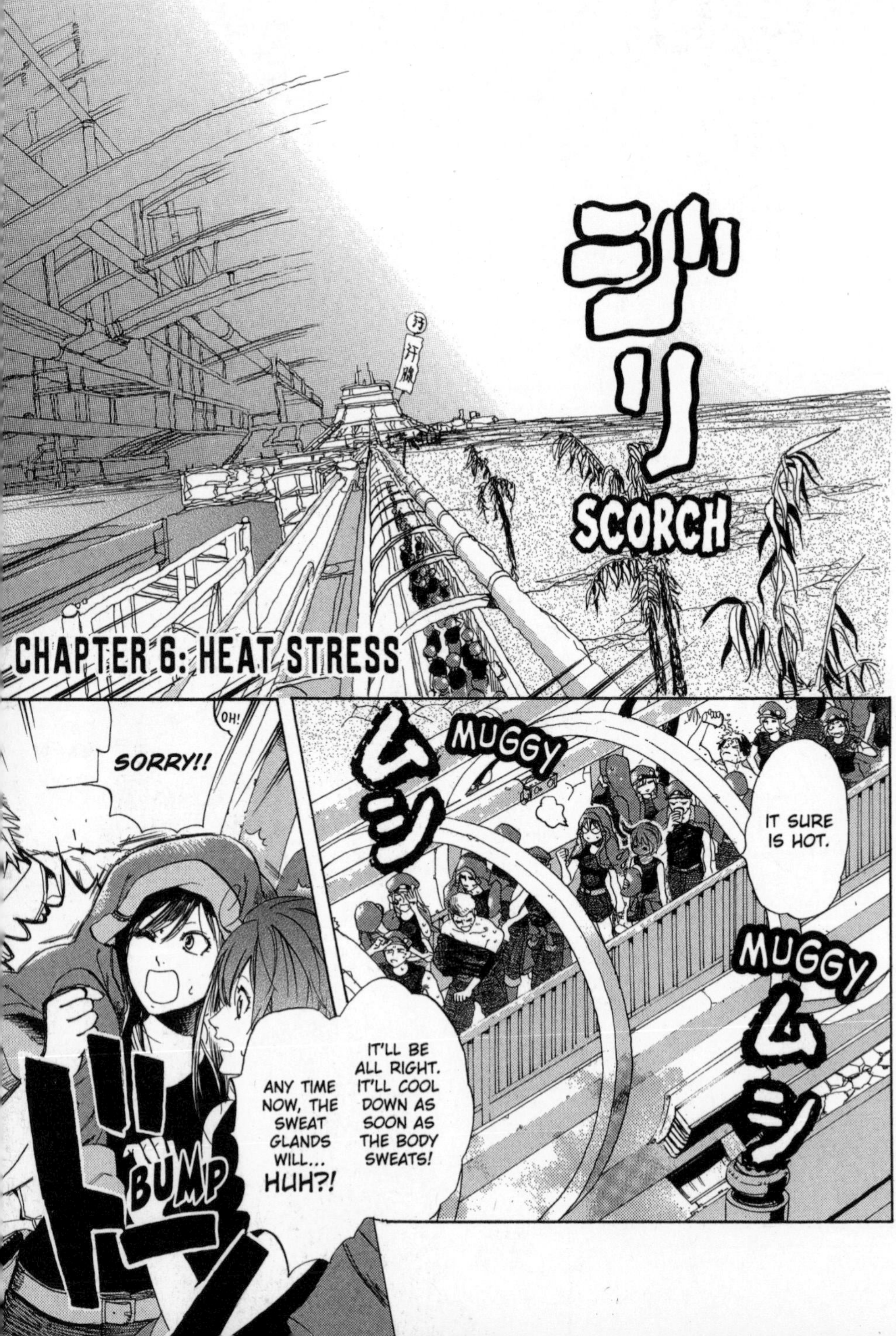
ジリ
SCORCH
CHAPTER 6: HEAT STRESS
ムシ
MUGGY
IT SURE IS HOT.
MUGGY
ムシ
OH!
SORRY!!
IT'LL BE ALL RIGHT. IT'LL COOL DOWN AS SOON AS THE BODY SWEATS!
ANY TIME NOW, THE SWEAT GLANDS WILL... HUH?!
BUMP

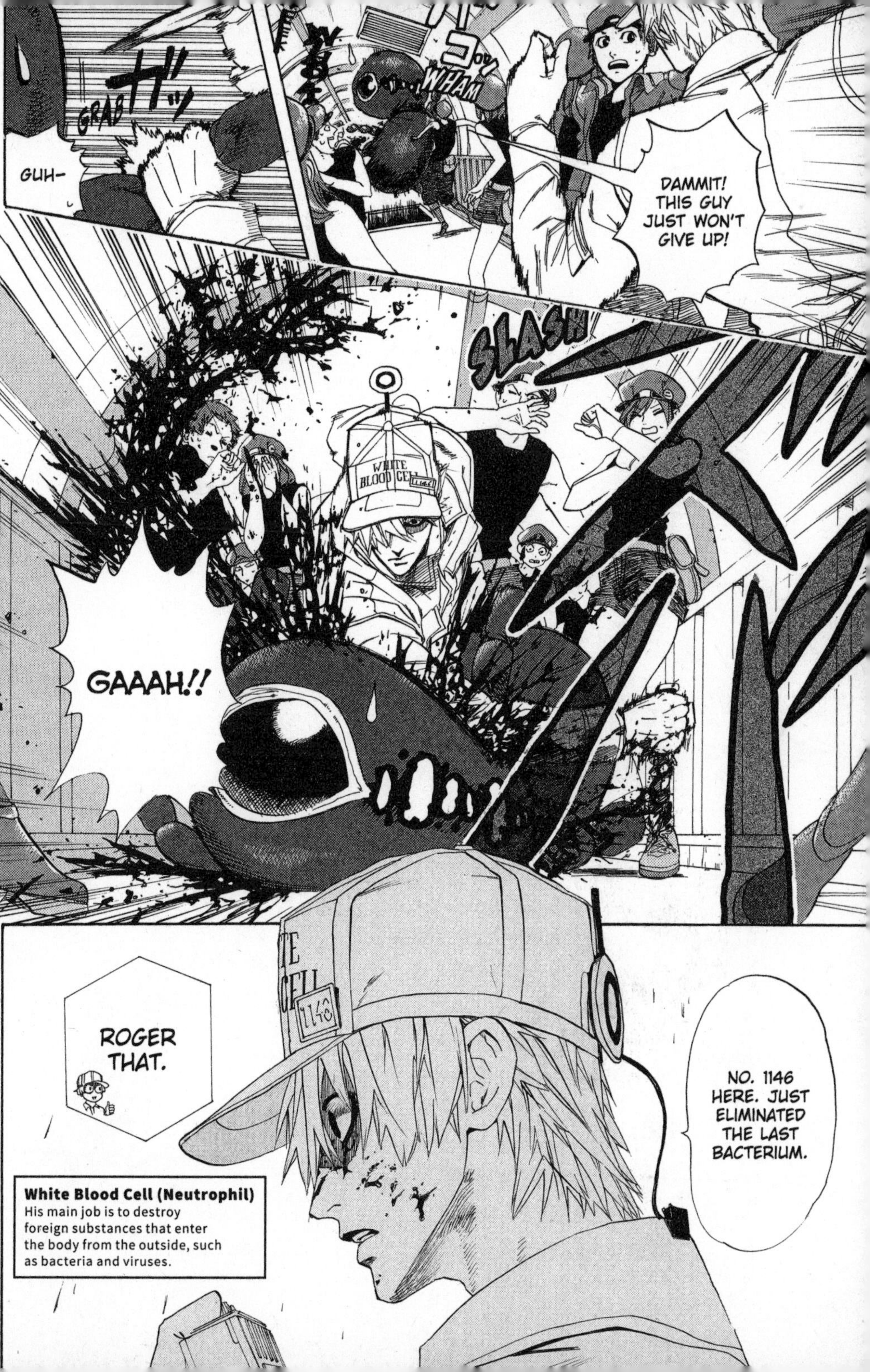
WHAM
DAMMIT! THIS GUY JUST WON'T GIVE UP!
GRAB
GUH-
SLASH
GAAAH!!
NO. 1146 HERE. JUST ELIMINATED THE LAST BACTERIUM.
ROGER THAT.
White Blood Cell (Neutrophil)
His main job is to destroy foreign substances that enter the body from the outside, such as bacteria and viruses.

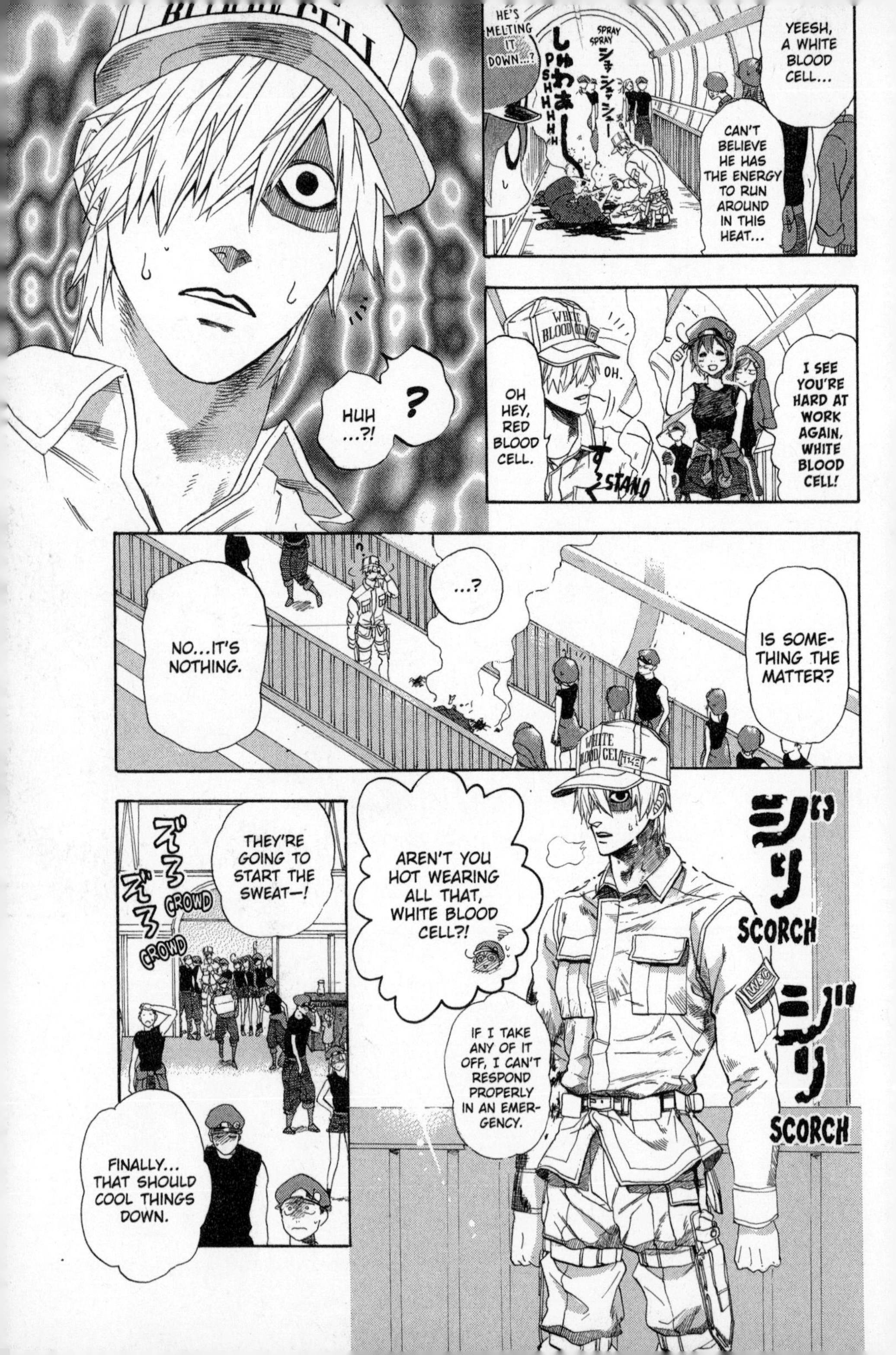
YEESH, A WHITE BLOOD CELL...
CAN'T BELIEVE HE HAS THE ENERGY TO RUN AROUND IN THIS HEAT...
SPRAY SPRAY
PSHHHHH
HE'S MELTING IT DOWN...?
I SEE YOU'RE HARD AT WORK AGAIN, WHITE BLOOD CELL!
OH.
OH HEY, RED BLOOD CELL.
STAND
?
HUH ...?!
IS SOME-THING THE MATTER?
...?
NO...IT'S NOTHING.
SCORCH
SCORCH
AREN'T YOU HOT WEARING ALL THAT, WHITE BLOOD CELL?!
IF I TAKE ANY OF IT OFF, I CAN'T RESPOND PROPERLY IN AN EMER-GENCY.
THEY'RE GOING TO START THE SWEAT—!
CROWD
CROWD
FINALLY... THAT SHOULD COOL THINGS DOWN.

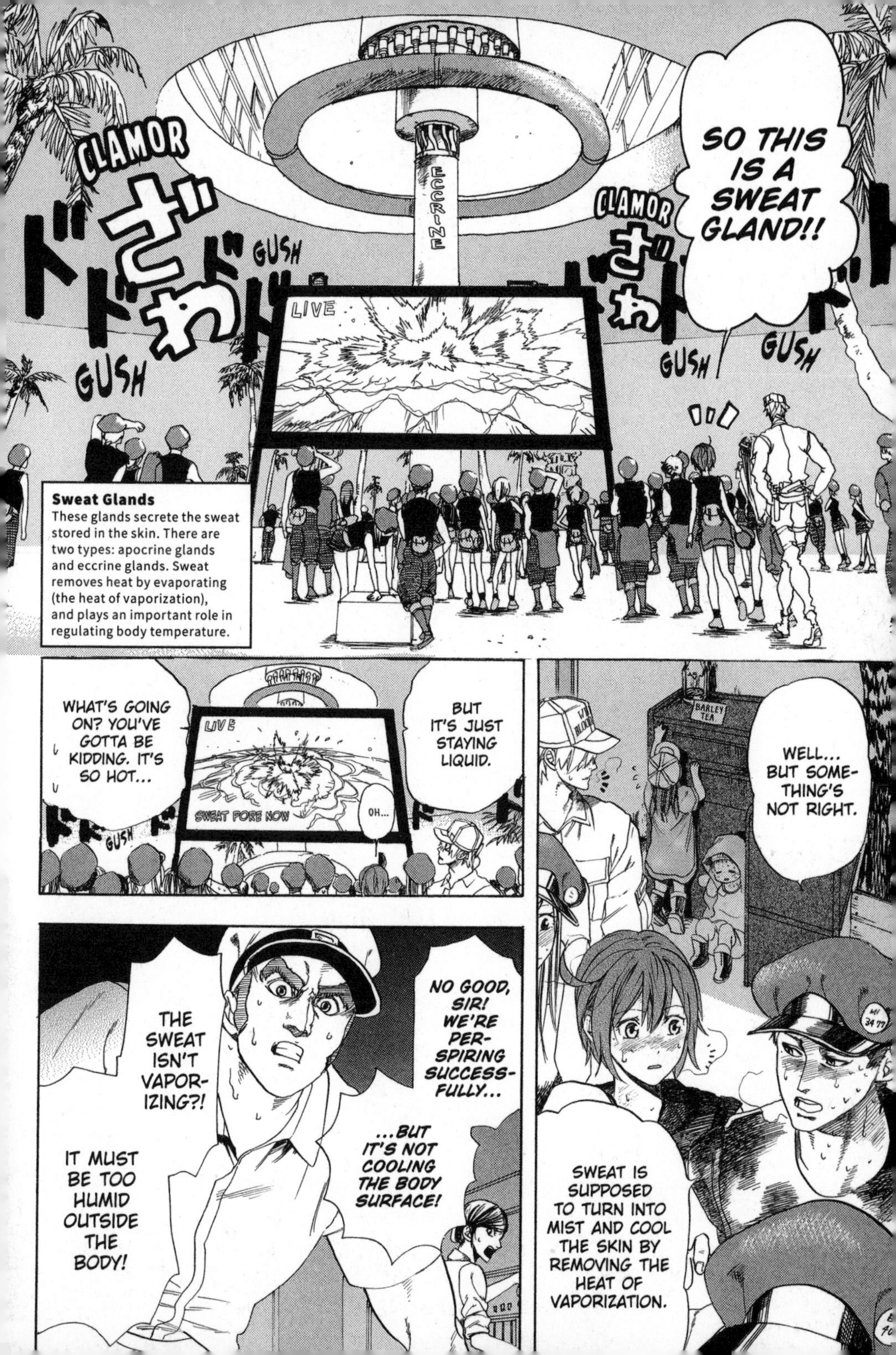
SO THIS IS A SWEAT GLAND!!
CLAMOR
ざわ
GUSH
GUSH
ドド
ECCRINE
LIVE
CLAMOR
ざわ
ドドド
GUSH
GUSH
Sweat Glands
These glands secrete the sweat stored in the skin. There are two types: apocrine glands and eccrine glands. Sweat removes heat by evaporating (the heat of vaporization), and plays an important role in regulating body temperature.
WELL... BUT SOME-THING'S NOT RIGHT.
BARLEY TEA
SWEAT IS SUPPOSED TO TURN INTO MIST AND COOL THE SKIN BY REMOVING THE HEAT OF VAPORIZATION.
BUT IT'S JUST STAYING LIQUID.
WHAT'S GOING ON? YOU'VE GOTTA BE KIDDING. IT'S SO HOT...
LIVE
SWEAT PORE NOW
OH...
GUSH
NO GOOD, SIR! WE'RE PER-SPIRING SUCCESS-FULLY...
...BUT IT'S NOT COOLING THE BODY SURFACE!
THE SWEAT ISN'T VAPOR-IZING?!
IT MUST BE TOO HUMID OUTSIDE THE BODY!

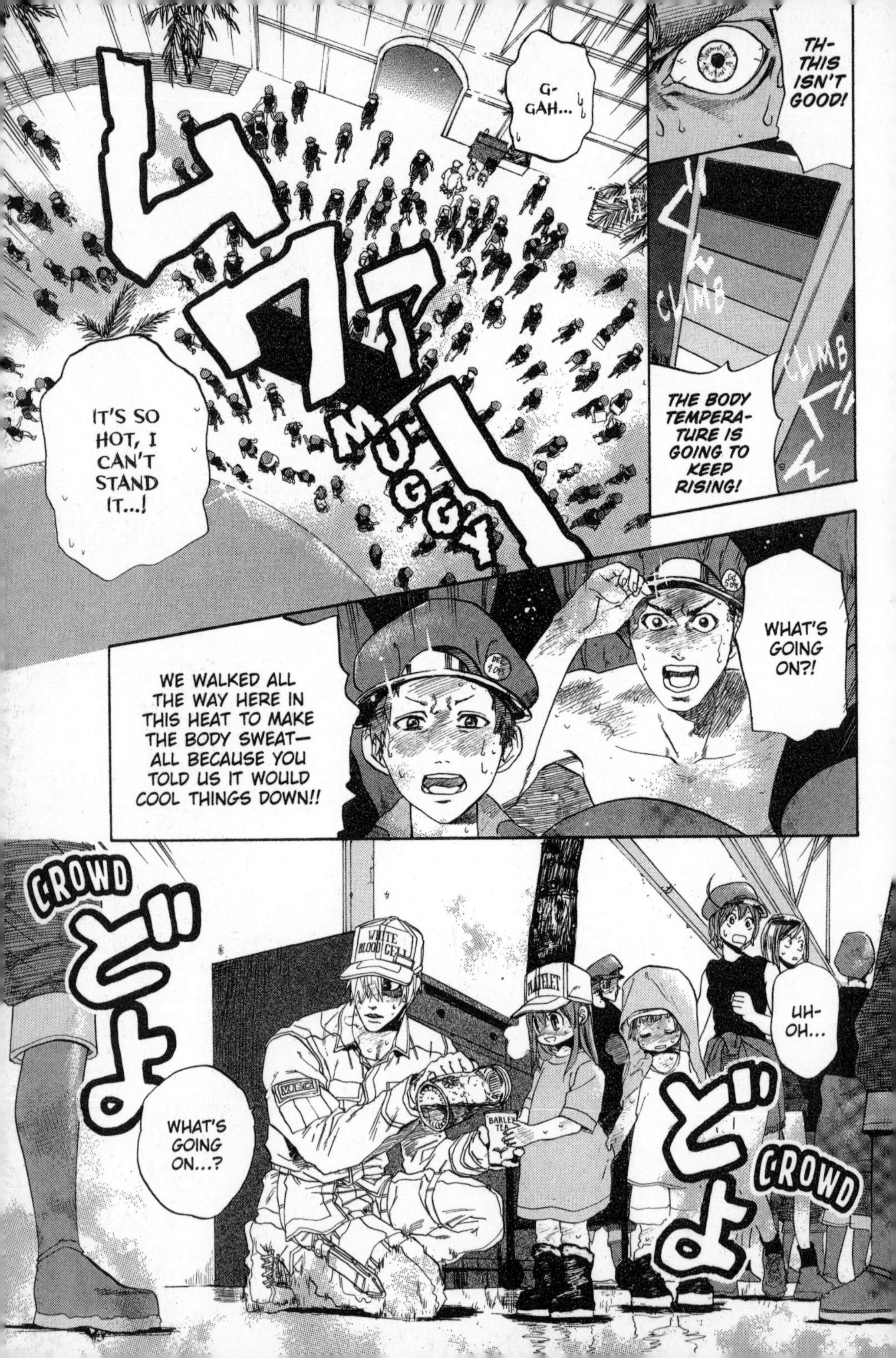
TH-THIS ISN'T GOOD!
CLIMB
CLIMB
THE BODY TEMPERATURE IS GOING TO KEEP RISING!
G-GAH...
MUGGY
IT'S SO HOT, I CAN'T STAND IT...!
WHAT'S GOING ON?!
WE WALKED ALL THE WAY HERE IN THIS HEAT TO MAKE THE BODY SWEAT—ALL BECAUSE YOU TOLD US IT WOULD COOL THINGS DOWN!!
CROWD
UH-OH...
PLATELET
WHITE BLOOD CELL
BARLEY TEA
WHAT'S GOING ON...?
CROWD

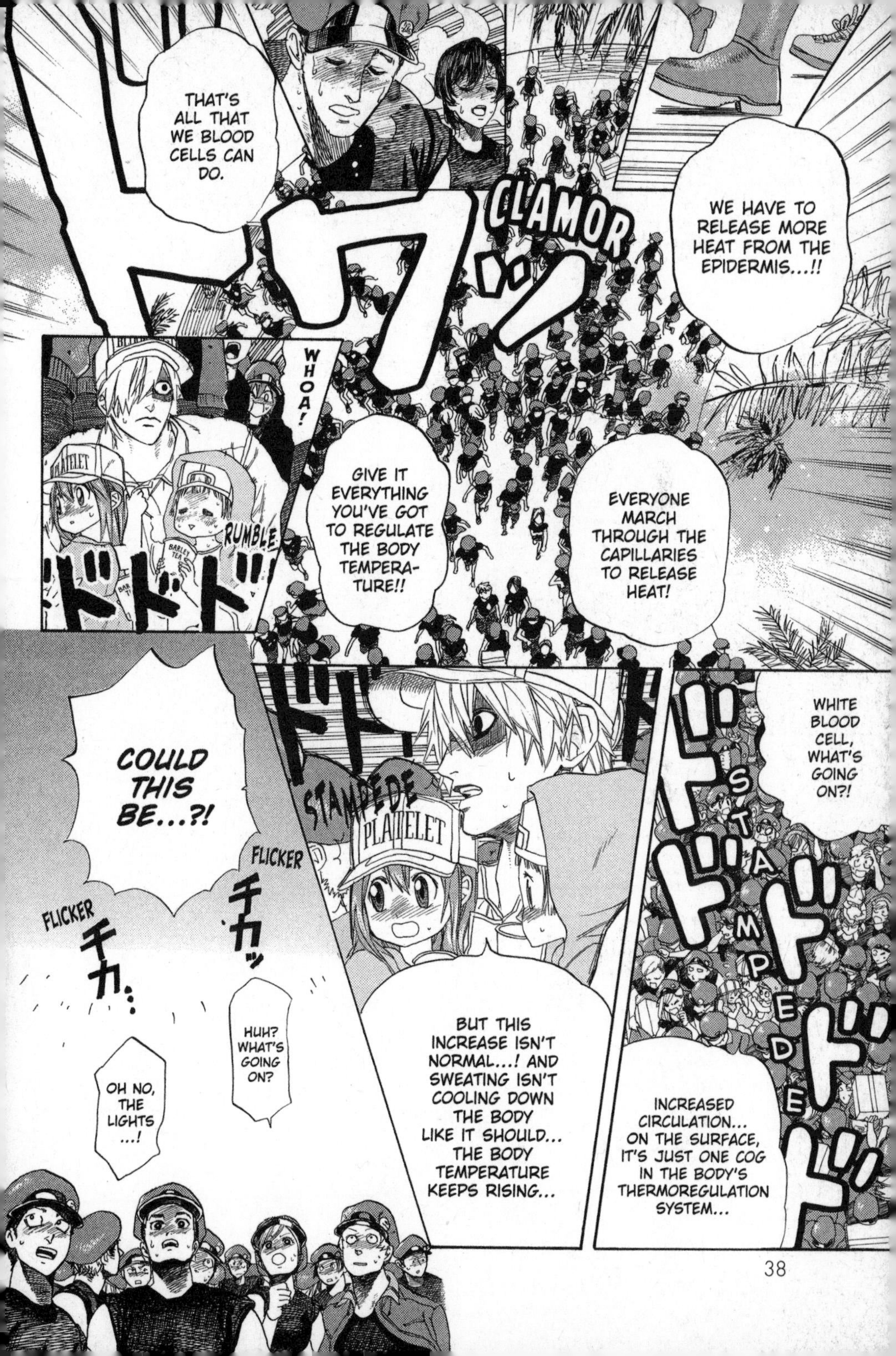
WE HAVE TO RELEASE MORE HEAT FROM THE EPIDERMIS...!!
THAT'S ALL THAT WE BLOOD CELLS CAN DO.
CLAMOR
EVERYONE MARCH THROUGH THE CAPILLARIES TO RELEASE HEAT!
GIVE IT EVERYTHING YOU'VE GOT TO REGULATE THE BODY TEMPERA-TURE!!
WHOA!
PLATELET
BARLEY TEA
RUMBLE
WHITE BLOOD CELL, WHAT'S GOING ON?!
STAMPEDE
INCREASED CIRCULATION... ON THE SURFACE, IT'S JUST ONE COG IN THE BODY'S THERMOREGULATION SYSTEM...
STAMPEDE
PLATELET
BUT THIS INCREASE ISN'T NORMAL...! AND SWEATING ISN'T COOLING DOWN THE BODY LIKE IT SHOULD... THE BODY TEMPERATURE KEEPS RISING...
COULD THIS BE...?!
FLICKER
FLICKER
HUH? WHAT'S GOING ON?
OH NO, THE LIGHTS ...!

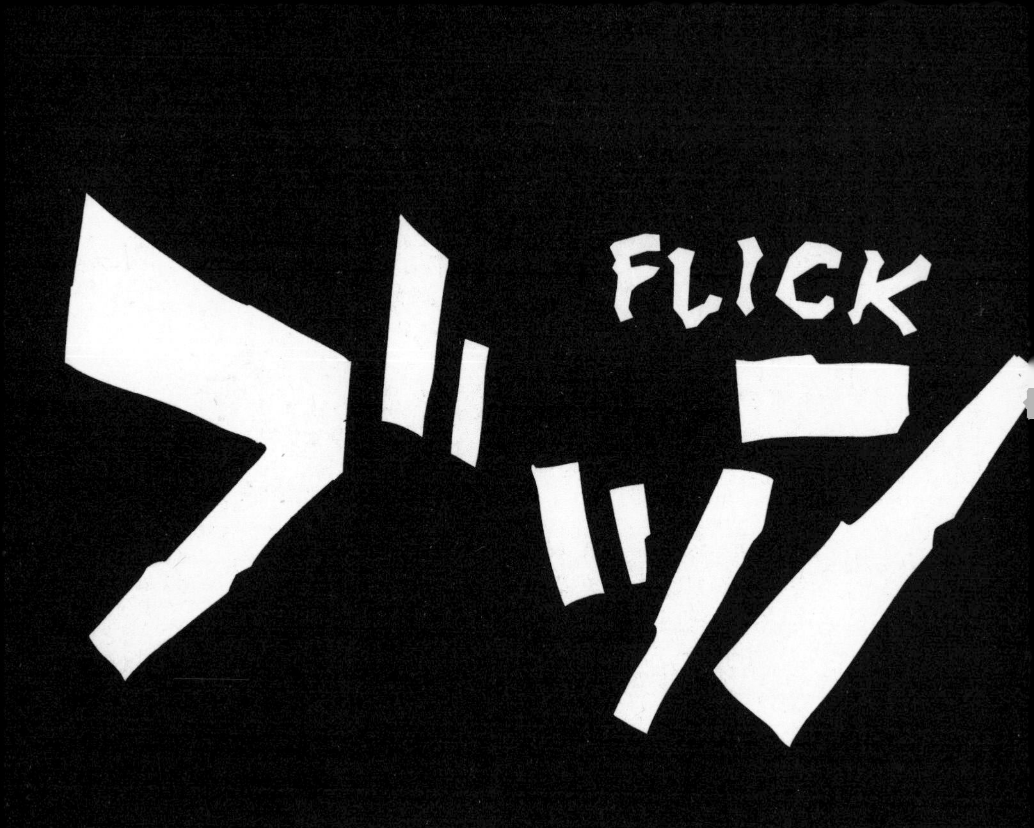
FLICK

Heat Stress
A general term for health disorders resulting from the malfunction of thermoregulatory processes, or from the breakdown in the balance of water or electrolytes in the body. It is divided into three levels based on severity. Heat syncope, characterized by symptoms such as dizziness, lightheadedness and numbness in the lips, is considered the lightest level of heat stress. It is caused when blood vessels near the skin dilate to increase blood flow, leading to low blood pressure and reduced circulation to the brain.

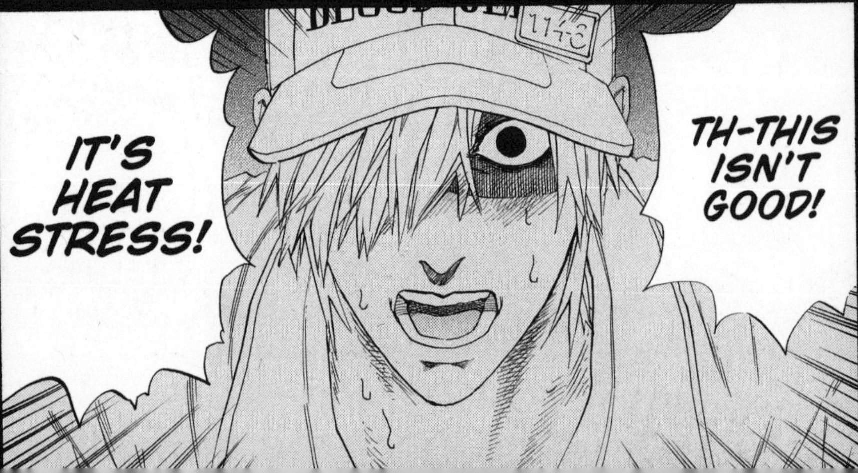
TH-THIS ISN'T GOOD!
IT'S HEAT STRESS!

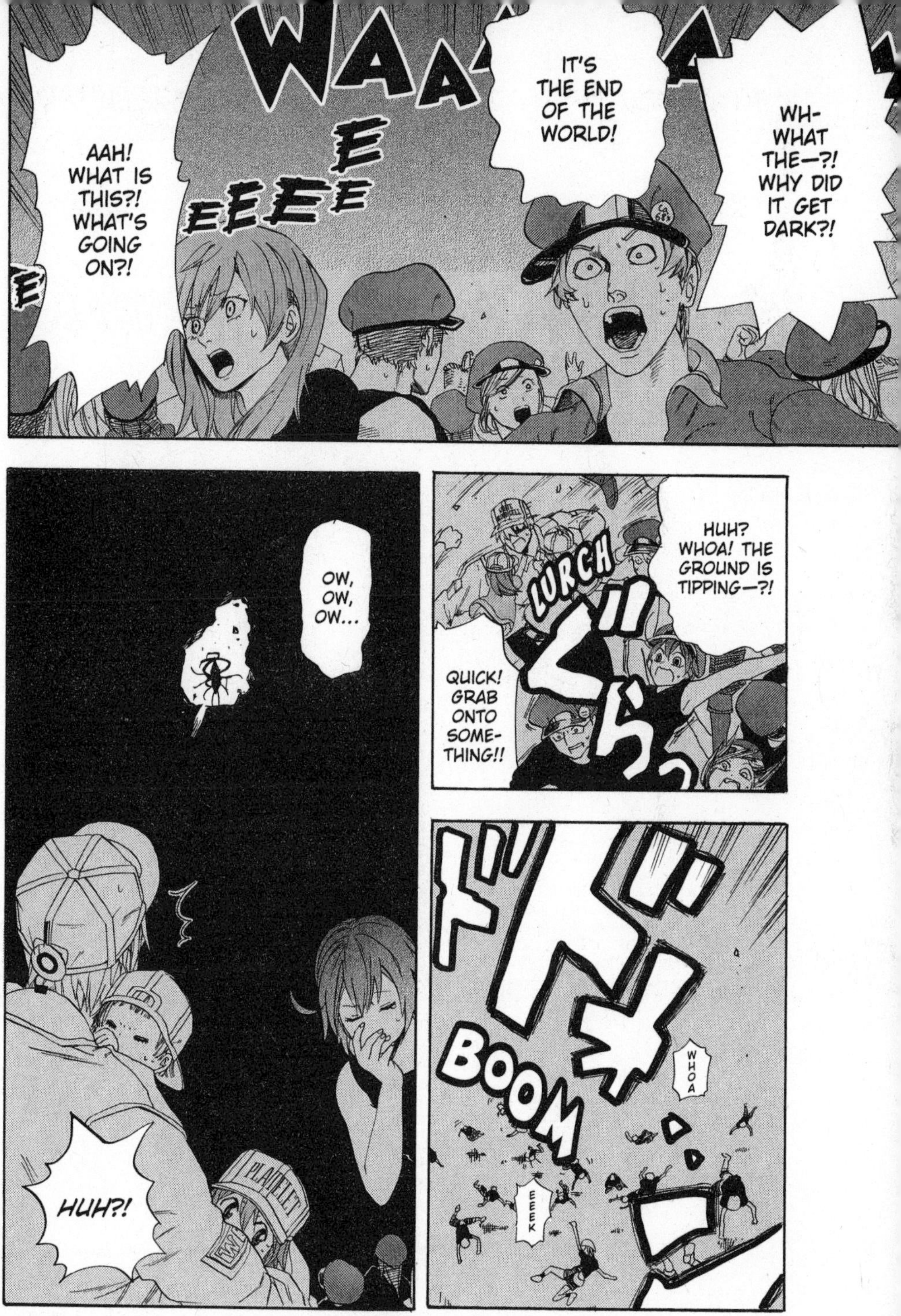
WH- WHAT THE—?! WHY DID IT GET DARK?!
IT'S THE END OF THE WORLD!
WAAA
EEEEE
AAH! WHAT IS THIS?! WHAT'S GOING ON?!
HUH? WHOA! THE GROUND IS TIPPING—?!
LURCH
QUICK! GRAB ONTO SOMETHING!!
BOOM
WHOA
EEEK
OW, OW, OW...
HUH?!

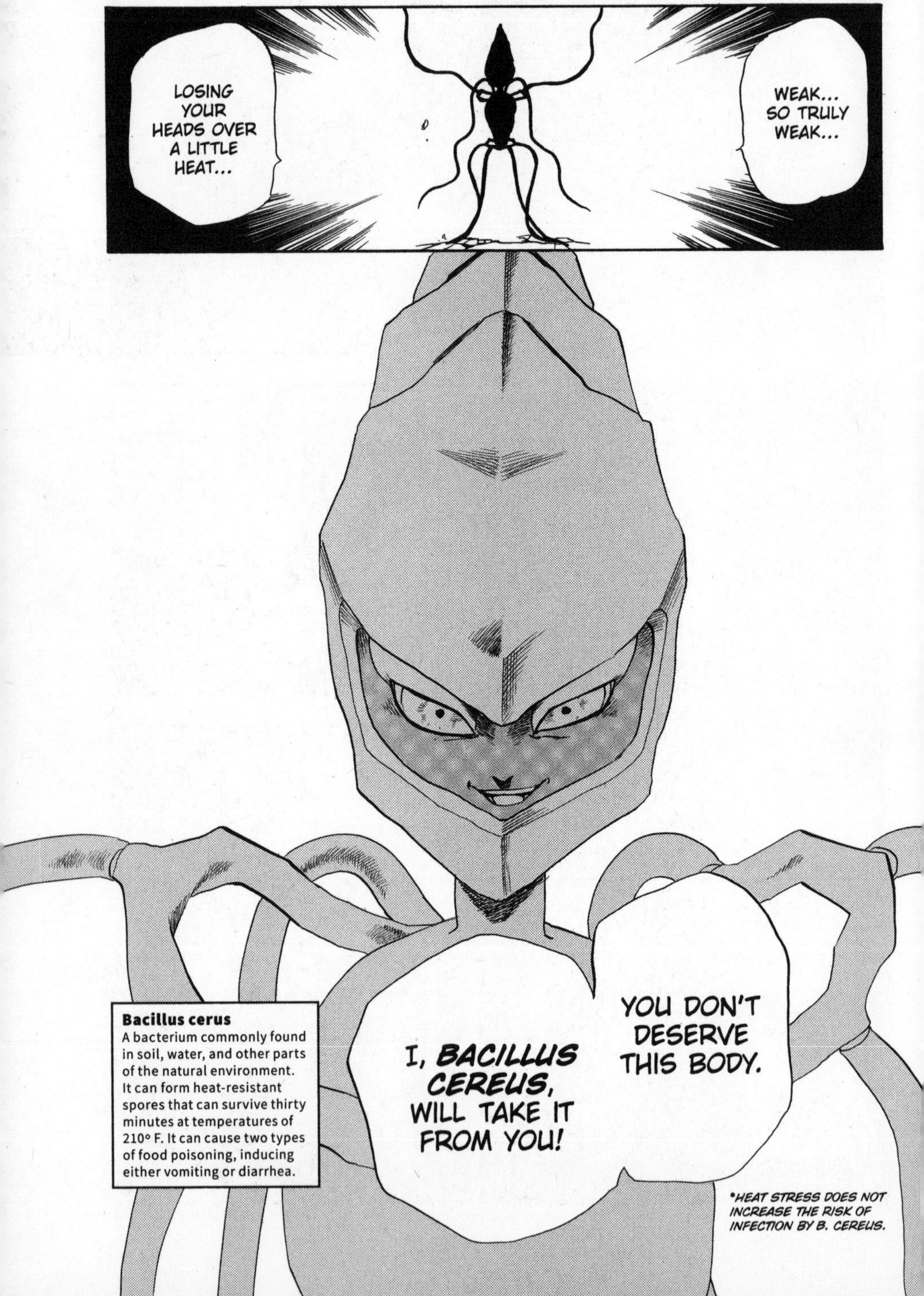
WEAK... SO TRULY WEAK...
LOSING YOUR HEADS OVER A LITTLE HEAT...
YOU DON'T DESERVE THIS BODY.
I, *BACILLUS CEREUS*, WILL TAKE IT FROM YOU!
Bacillus cerus
A bacterium commonly found in soil, water, and other parts of the natural environment. It can form heat-resistant spores that can survive thirty minutes at temperatures of 210° F. It can cause two types of food poisoning, inducing either vomiting or diarrhea.
*HEAT STRESS DOES NOT INCREASE THE RISK OF INFECTION BY B. CEREUS.

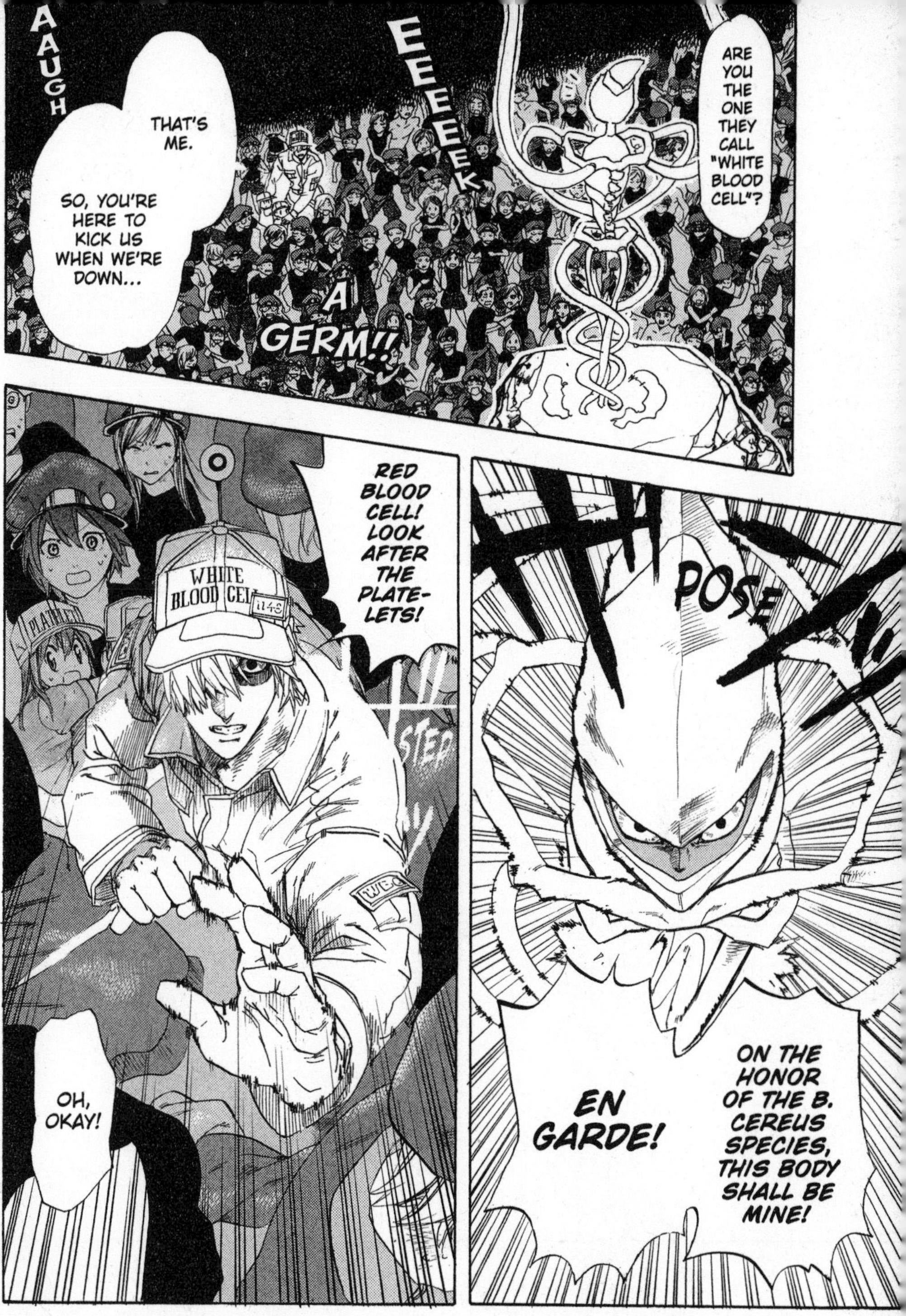
ARE YOU THE ONE THEY CALL "WHITE BLOOD CELL"?
EEEEEEK
A GERM!!
THAT'S ME.
SO, YOU'RE HERE TO KICK US WHEN WE'RE DOWN...
AAUGH
POSE
ON THE HONOR OF THE B. CEREUS SPECIES, THIS BODY SHALL BE MINE!
EN GARDE!
RED BLOOD CELL! LOOK AFTER THE PLATE-LETS!
WHITE BLOOD CELL
STEP
OH, OKAY!

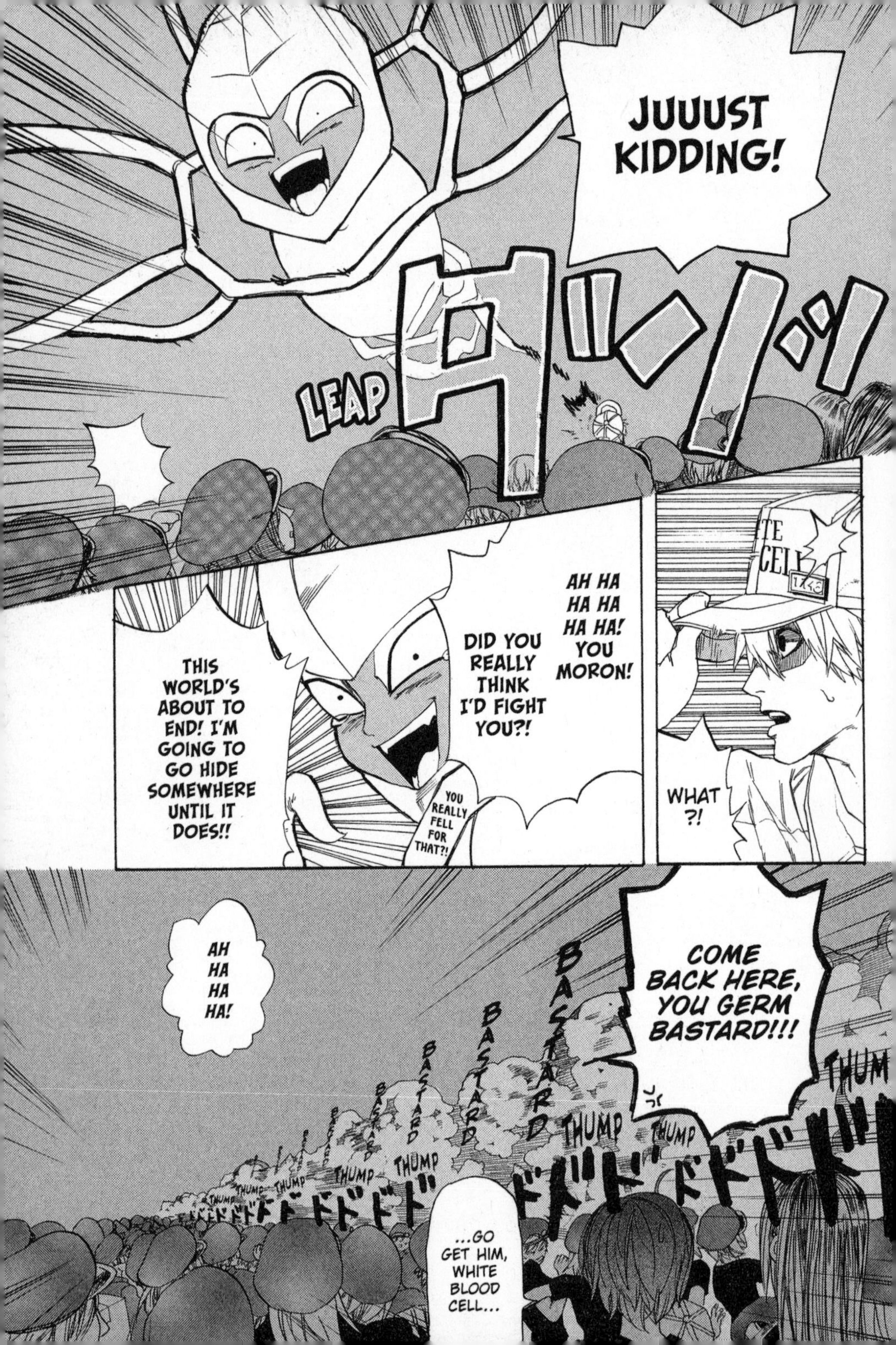
JUUUST KIDDING!
LEAP
WHAT ?!
AH HA HA HA HA HA! YOU MORON!
DID YOU REALLY THINK I'D FIGHT YOU?!
YOU REALLY FELL FOR THAT?!
THIS WORLD'S ABOUT TO END! I'M GOING TO GO HIDE SOMEWHERE UNTIL IT DOES!!
COME BACK HERE, YOU GERM BASTARD!!!
AH HA HA HA!
BASTARD
BASTARD
BASTARD
THUMP
THUMP
THUMP
THUMP
THUMP
THUMP
...GO GET HIM, WHITE BLOOD CELL...

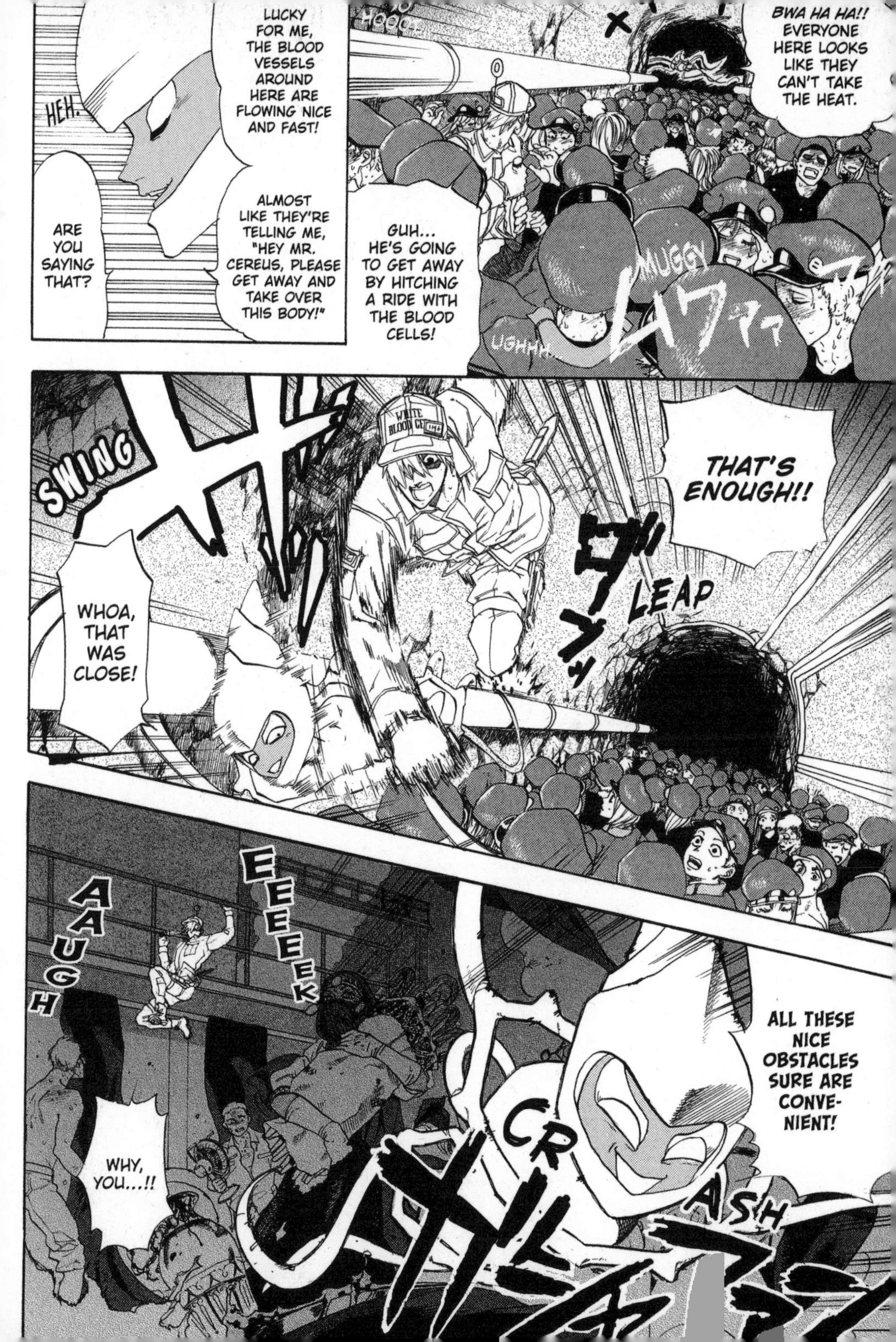
BWA HA HA!! EVERYONE HERE LOOKS LIKE THEY CAN'T TAKE THE HEAT.
MUGGY
UGHHH
GUH... HE'S GOING TO GET AWAY BY HITCHING A RIDE WITH THE BLOOD CELLS!
HEH.
LUCKY FOR ME, THE BLOOD VESSELS AROUND HERE ARE FLOWING NICE AND FAST!
ALMOST LIKE THEY'RE TELLING ME, "HEY MR. CEREUS, PLEASE GET AWAY AND TAKE OVER THIS BODY!"
ARE YOU SAYING THAT?
THAT'S ENOUGH!!
LEAP
SWING
WHOA, THAT WAS CLOSE!
ALL THESE NICE OBSTACLES SURE ARE CONVE-NIENT!
CRASH
EEEEEK
AAAUGH
WHY, YOU...!!

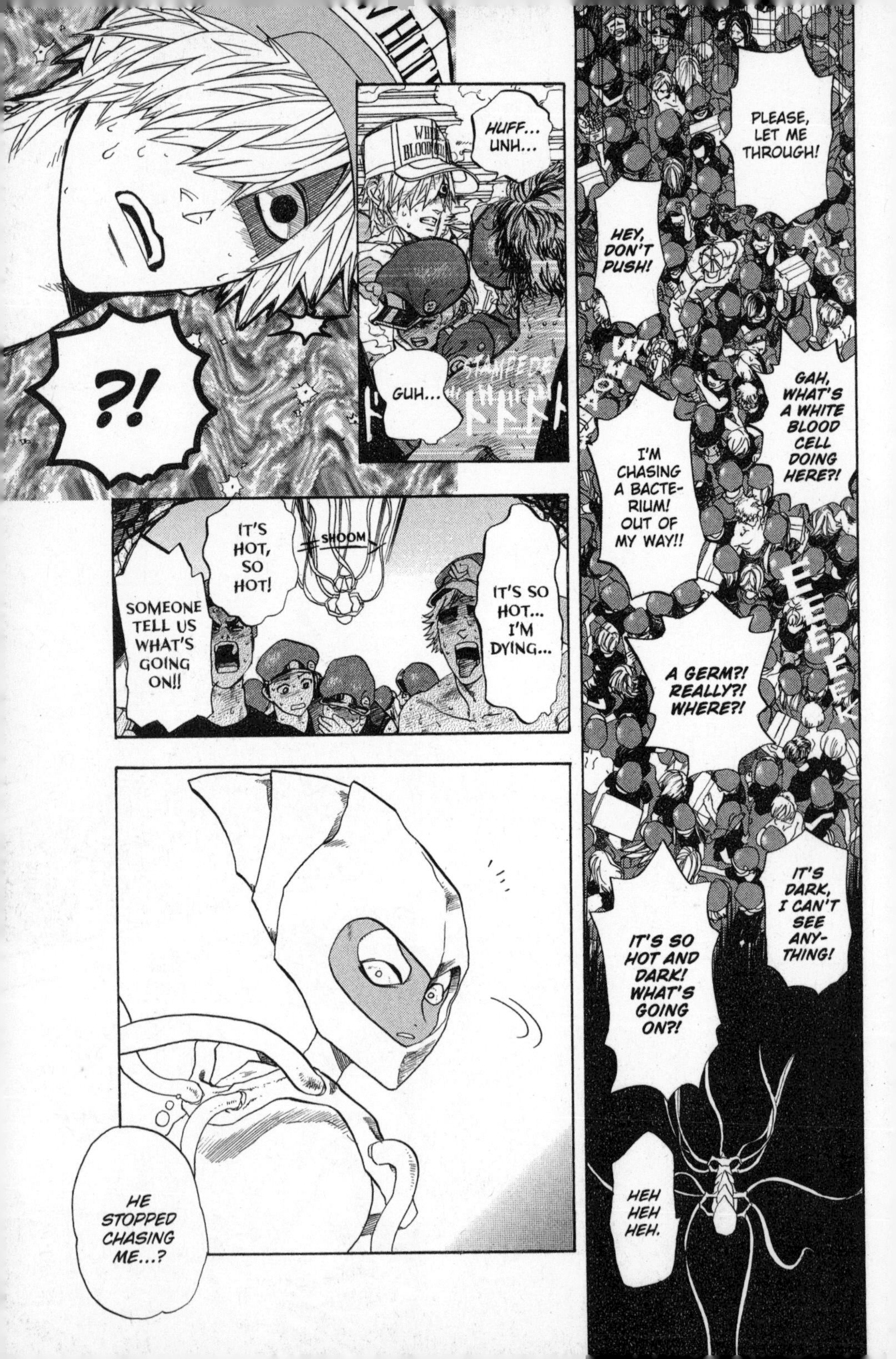
PLEASE, LET ME THROUGH!
HEY, DON'T PUSH!
GAH, WHAT'S A WHITE BLOOD CELL DOING HERE?!
I'M CHASING A BACTERIUM! OUT OF MY WAY!!
A GERM?! REALLY?! WHERE?!
IT'S DARK, I CAN'T SEE ANYTHING!
IT'S SO HOT AND DARK! WHAT'S GOING ON?!
HEH HEH HEH.
HUFF... UNH...
STAMPEDE
GUH...
?!
IT'S SO HOT... I'M DYING...
SHOOM
IT'S HOT, SO HOT!
SOMEONE TELL US WHAT'S GOING ON!!
HE STOPPED CHASING ME...?

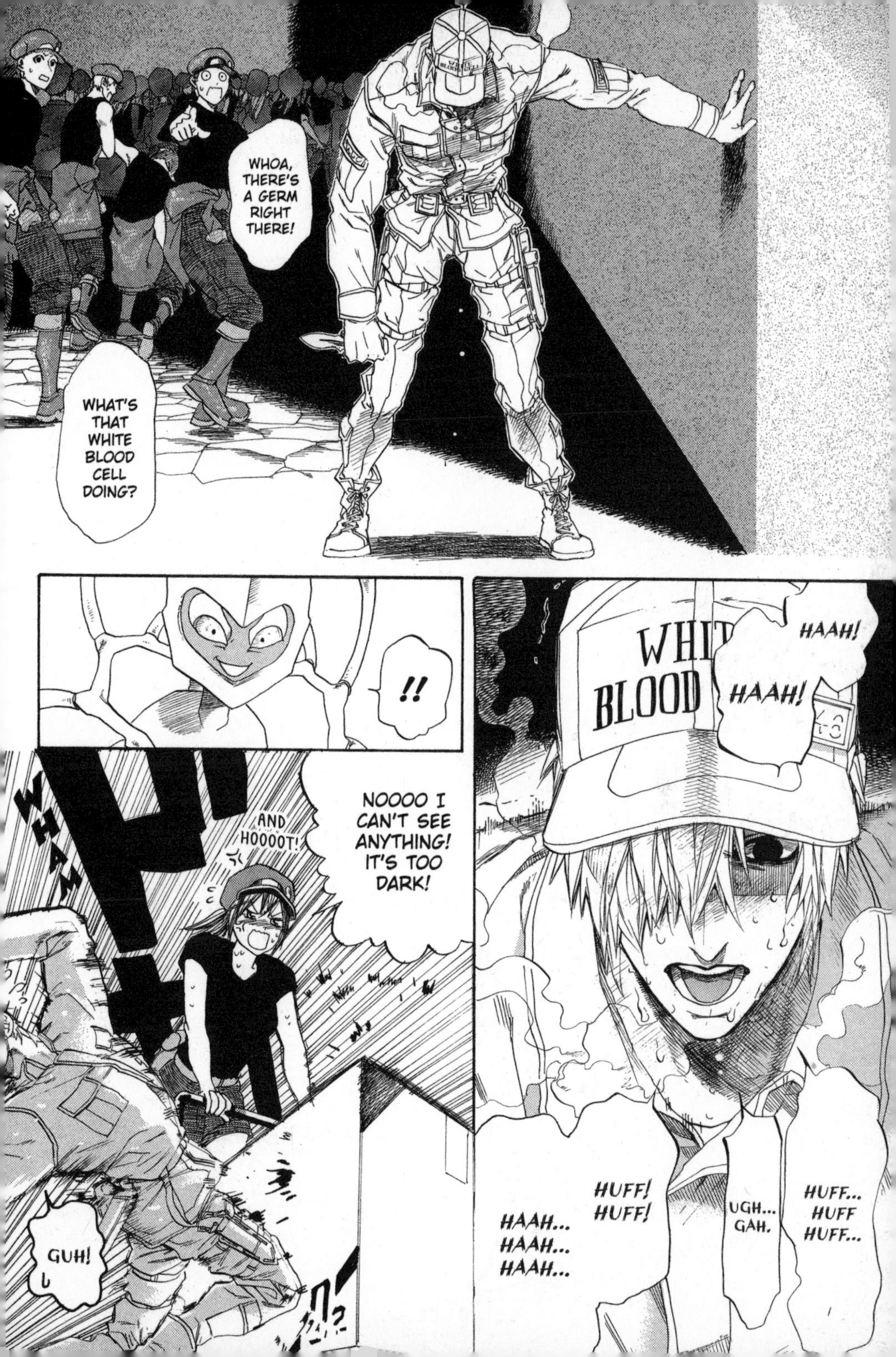
WHOA, THERE'S A GERM RIGHT THERE!
WHAT'S THAT WHITE BLOOD CELL DOING?
HAAH!
HAAH!
HUFF... HUFF HUFF...
UGH... GAH.
HUFF! HUFF!
HAAH... HAAH... HAAH...
!!
NOOOO I CAN'T SEE ANYTHING! IT'S TOO DARK!
AND HOOOOT!
WHAM
GUH!

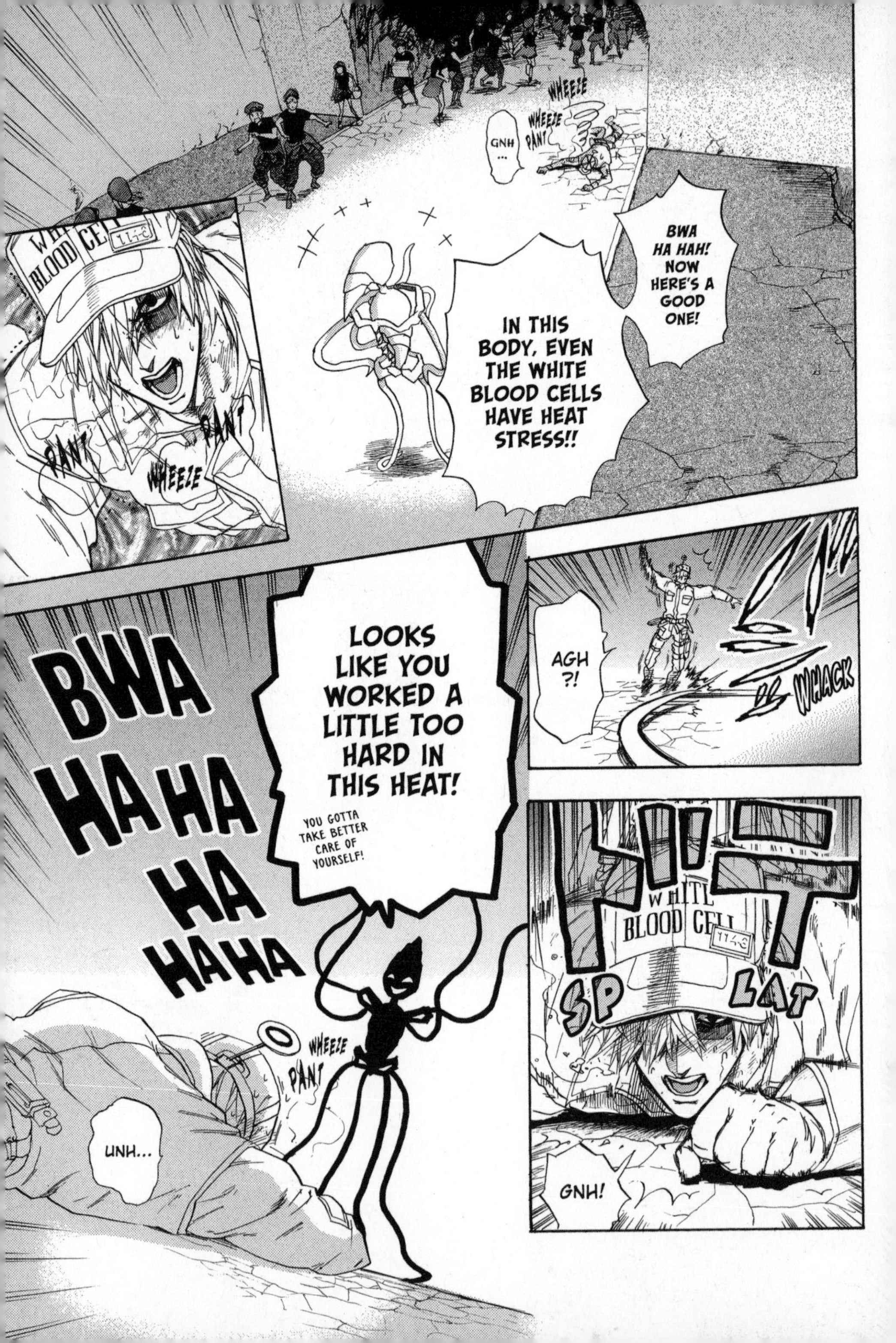
WHEEZE
WHEEZE PANT
GNH ...
BWA HA HAH! NOW HERE'S A GOOD ONE!
IN THIS BODY, EVEN THE WHITE BLOOD CELLS HAVE HEAT STRESS!!
PANT PANT
WHEEZE
AGH ?!
WHACK
SPLAT
GNH!
LOOKS LIKE YOU WORKED A LITTLE TOO HARD IN THIS HEAT!
YOU GOTTA TAKE BETTER CARE OF YOURSELF!
BWA HA HA HA HA HAHA
WHEEZE PANT
UNH...

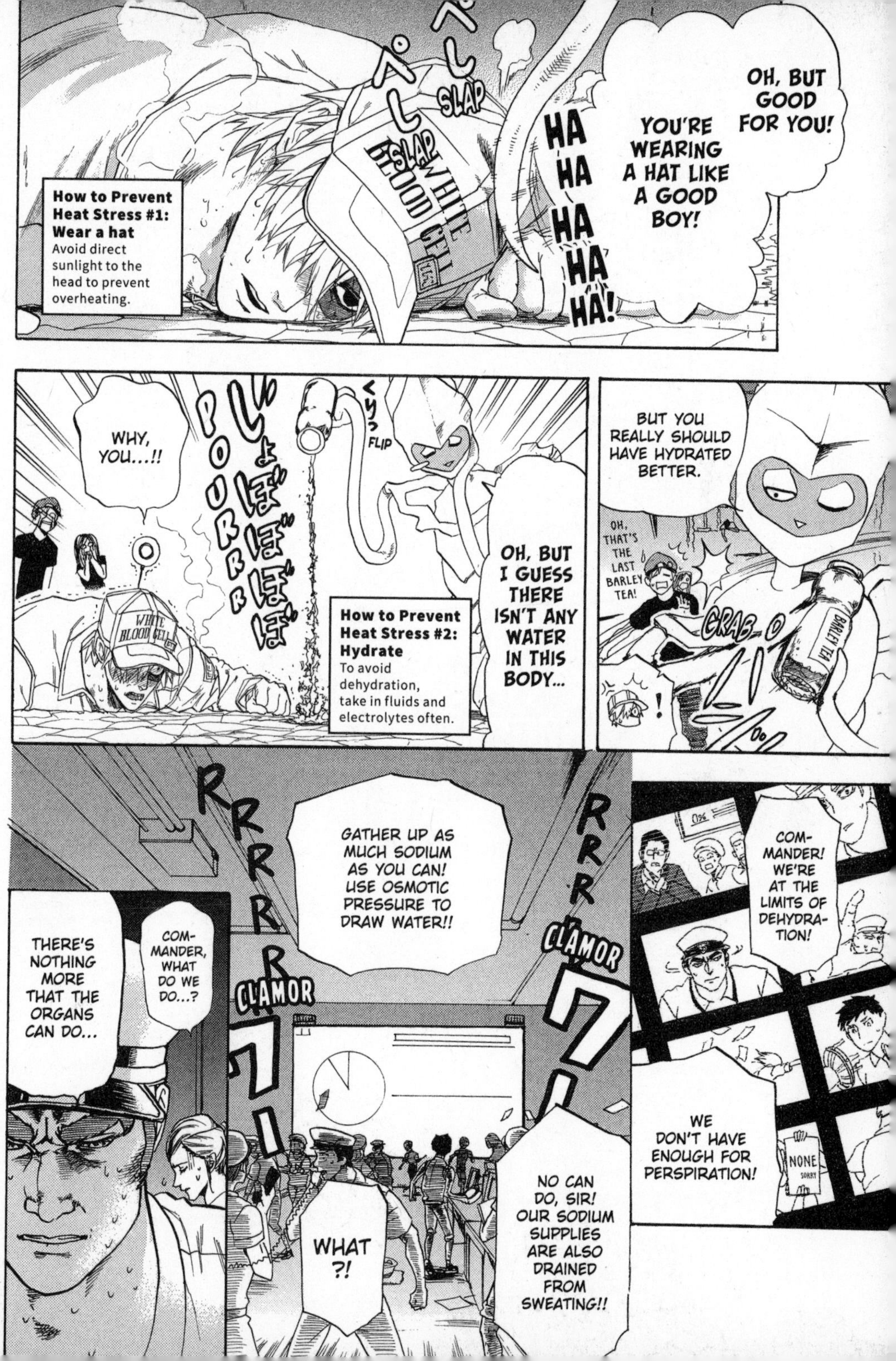

OH, BUT GOOD FOR YOU!
YOU'RE WEARING A HAT LIKE A GOOD BOY!
HA HA HA HA HA!
ぺし ぺし
SLAP SLAP SLAP
WHITE BLOOD CELL
How to Prevent Heat Stress #1: Wear a hat
Avoid direct sunlight to the head to prevent overheating.
BUT YOU REALLY SHOULD HAVE HYDRATED BETTER.
OH, THAT'S THE LAST BARLEY TEA!
GRAB
BARLEY TEA
!
OH, BUT I GUESS THERE ISN'T ANY WATER IN THIS BODY...
くりっ
FLIP
How to Prevent Heat Stress #2: Hydrate
To avoid dehydration, take in fluids and electrolytes often.
じょぼぼぼぼ
POURRR
WHY, YOU...!!
WHITE BLOOD CELL
COM-MANDER! WE'RE AT THE LIMITS OF DEHYDRA-TION!
WE DON'T HAVE ENOUGH FOR PERSPIRATION!
NONE
SORRY
RRRR
CLAMOR
GATHER UP AS MUCH SODIUM AS YOU CAN! USE OSMOTIC PRESSURE TO DRAW WATER!!
RRRRR
NO CAN DO, SIR! OUR SODIUM SUPPLIES ARE ALSO DRAINED FROM SWEATING!!
CLAMOR
WHAT ?!
COM-MANDER, WHAT DO WE DO...?
THERE'S NOTHING MORE THAT THE ORGANS CAN DO...

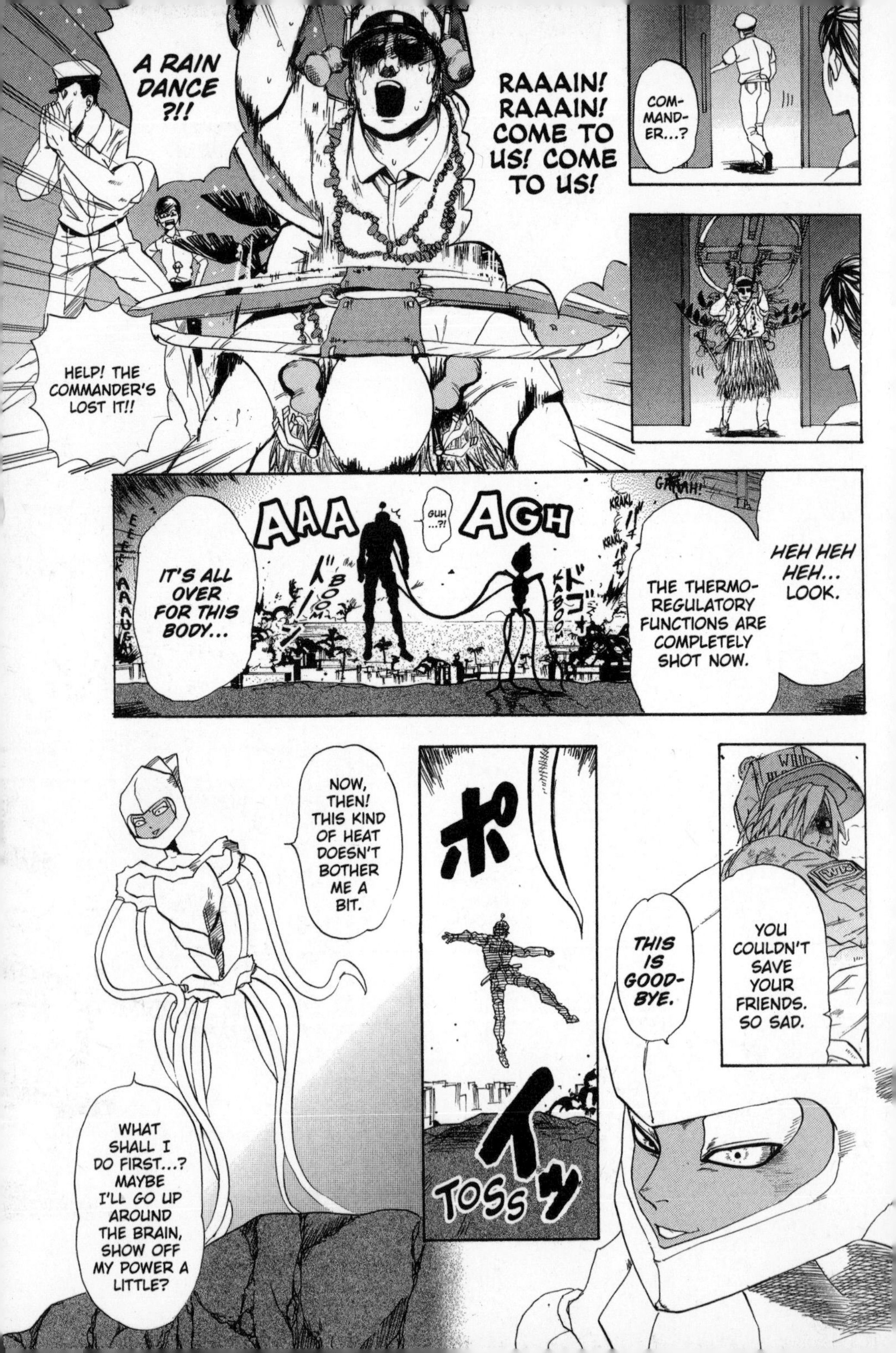

COM-MANDER...?
RAAAIN! RAAAIN! COME TO US! COME TO US!
A RAIN DANCE?!!
HELP! THE COMMANDER'S LOST IT!!
HEH HEH HEH... LOOK.
THE THERMO-REGULATORY FUNCTIONS ARE COMPLETELY SHOT NOW.
KRAKL
KRAKL
KABOOM
AAA AGH
GUH ...?!
BOOM
IT'S ALL OVER FOR THIS BODY...
YOU COULDN'T SAVE YOUR FRIENDS. SO SAD.
THIS IS GOOD-BYE.
ポイッ
TOSS
NOW, THEN! THIS KIND OF HEAT DOESN'T BOTHER ME A BIT.
WHAT SHALL I DO FIRST...? MAYBE I'LL GO UP AROUND THE BRAIN, SHOW OFF MY POWER A LITTLE?

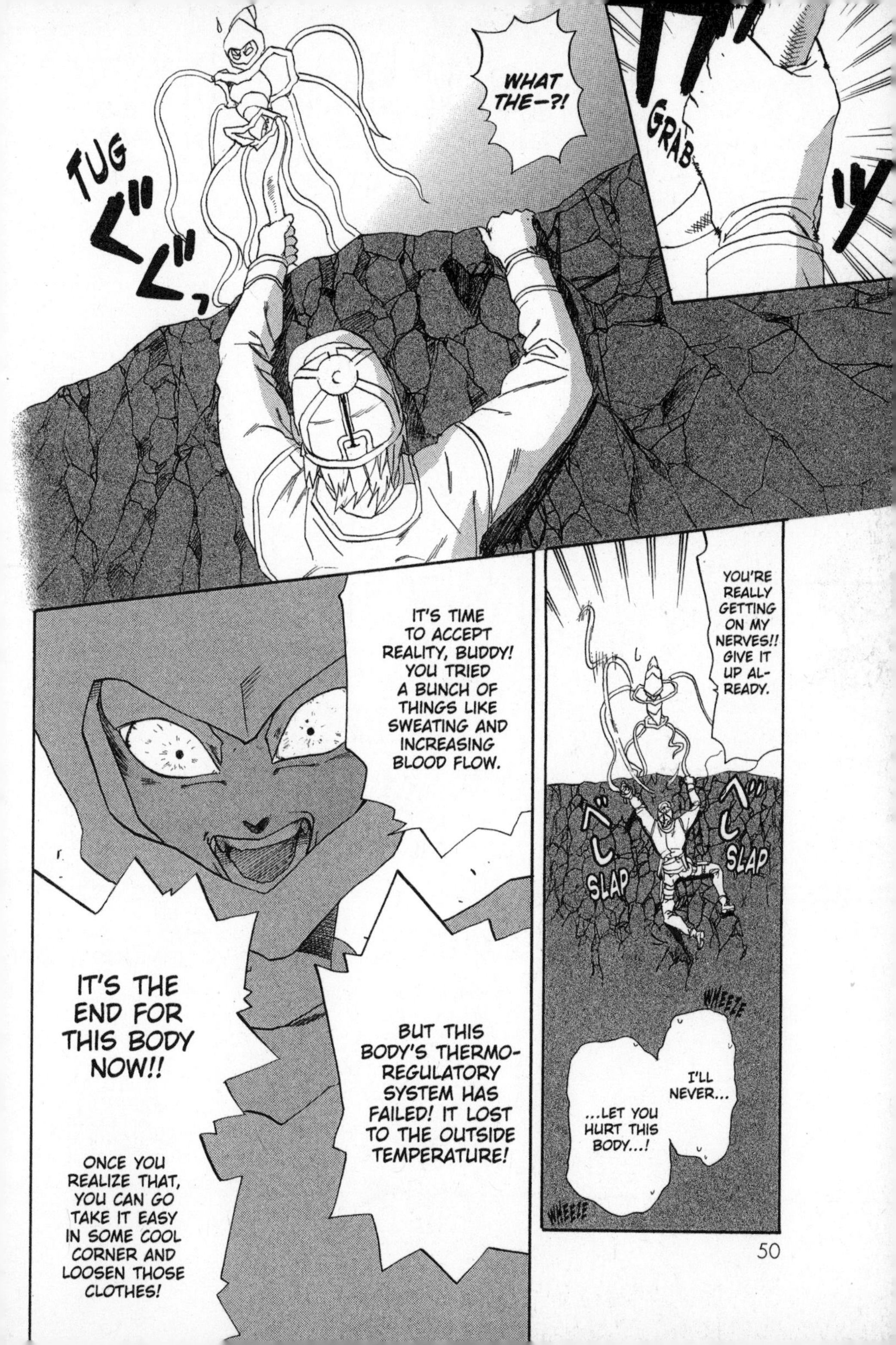
GRAB
WHAT THE—?!
TUG
YOU'RE REALLY GETTING ON MY NERVES!! GIVE IT UP AL-READY.
SLAP
SLAP
WHEEZE
I'LL NEVER...
...LET YOU HURT THIS BODY...!
WHEEZE
IT'S TIME TO ACCEPT REALITY, BUDDY! YOU TRIED A BUNCH OF THINGS LIKE SWEATING AND INCREASING BLOOD FLOW.
BUT THIS BODY'S THERMO-REGULATORY SYSTEM HAS FAILED! IT LOST TO THE OUTSIDE TEMPERATURE!
IT'S THE END FOR THIS BODY NOW!!
ONCE YOU REALIZE THAT, YOU CAN GO TAKE IT EASY IN SOME COOL CORNER AND LOOSEN THOSE CLOTHES!

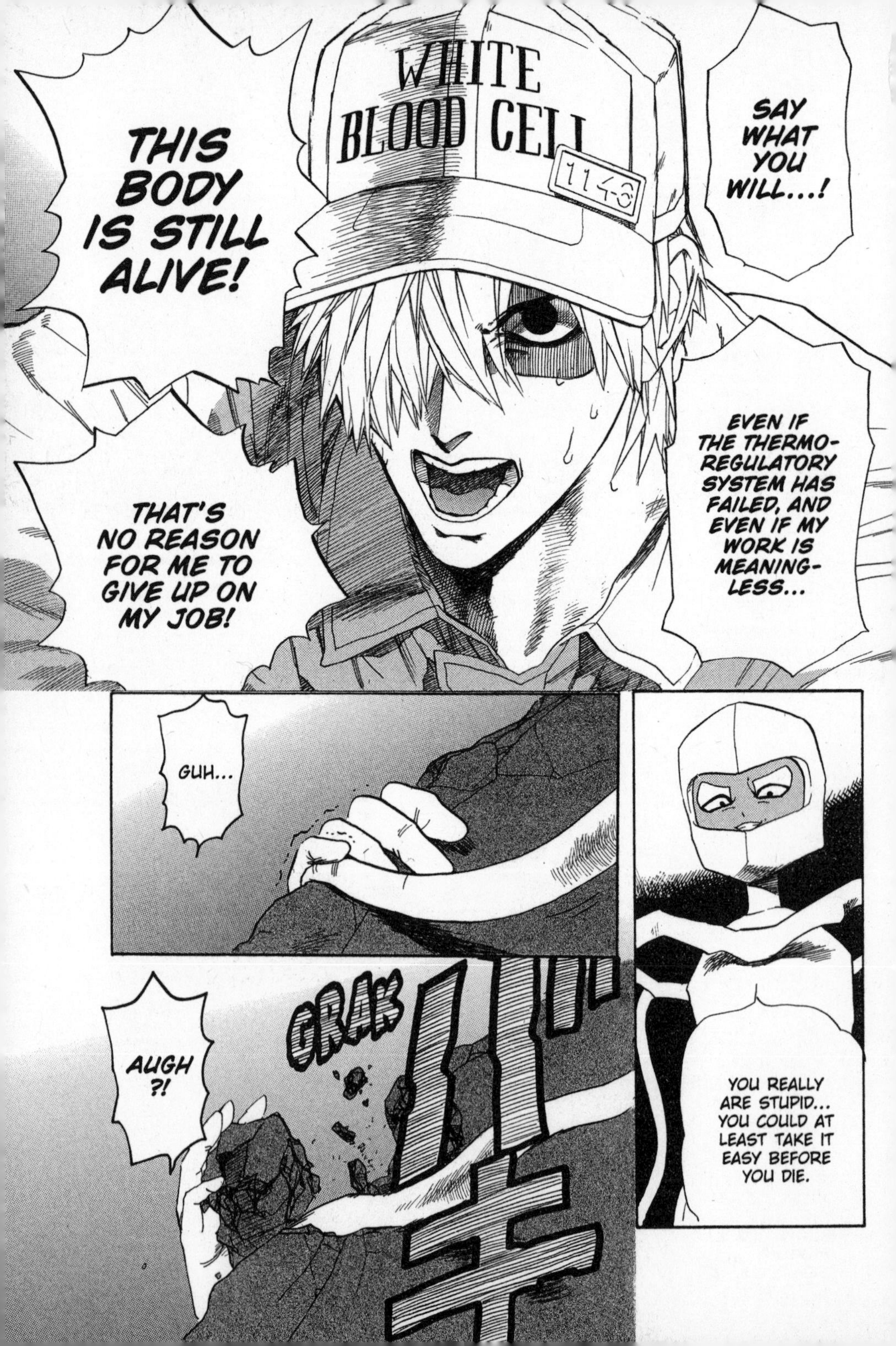
WHITE BLOOD CELL
SAY WHAT YOU WILL...!
THIS BODY IS STILL ALIVE!
EVEN IF THE THERMO-REGULATORY SYSTEM HAS FAILED, AND EVEN IF MY WORK IS MEANING-LESS...
THAT'S NO REASON FOR ME TO GIVE UP ON MY JOB!
YOU REALLY ARE STUPID... YOU COULD AT LEAST TAKE IT EASY BEFORE YOU DIE.
GUH...
CRAK
AUGH ?!

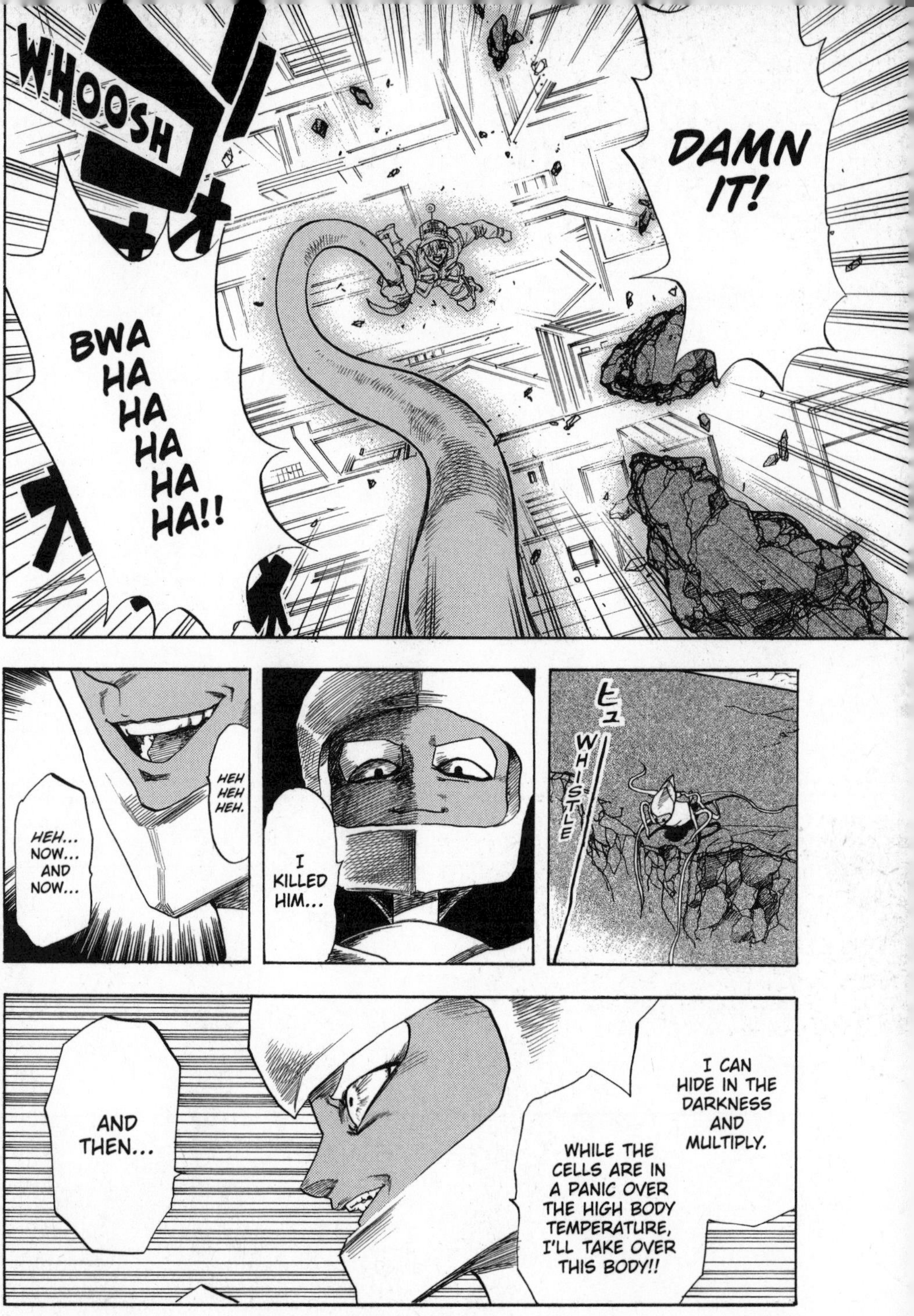

DAMN IT!
WHOOSH
BWA HA HA HA HA HA HA!!
WHISTLE
I KILLED HIM...
HEH HEH HEH.
HEH... NOW... AND NOW...
I CAN HIDE IN THE DARKNESS AND MULTIPLY.
WHILE THE CELLS ARE IN A PANIC OVER THE HIGH BODY TEMPERATURE, I'LL TAKE OVER THIS BODY!!
AND THEN...

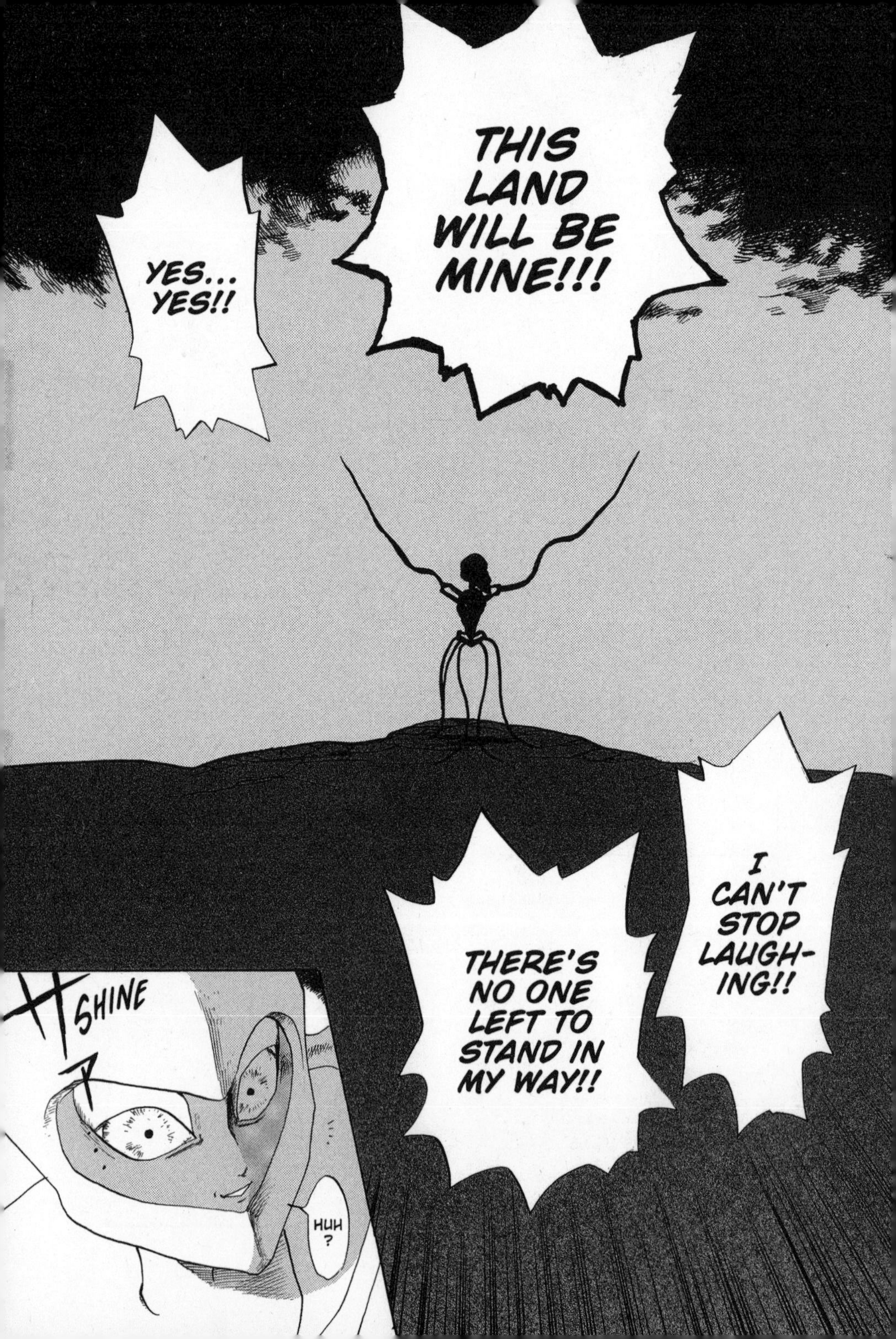
THIS LAND WILL BE MINE!!!
YES... YES!!
I CAN'T STOP LAUGH-ING!!
THERE'S NO ONE LEFT TO STAND IN MY WAY!!
SHINE
HUH ?

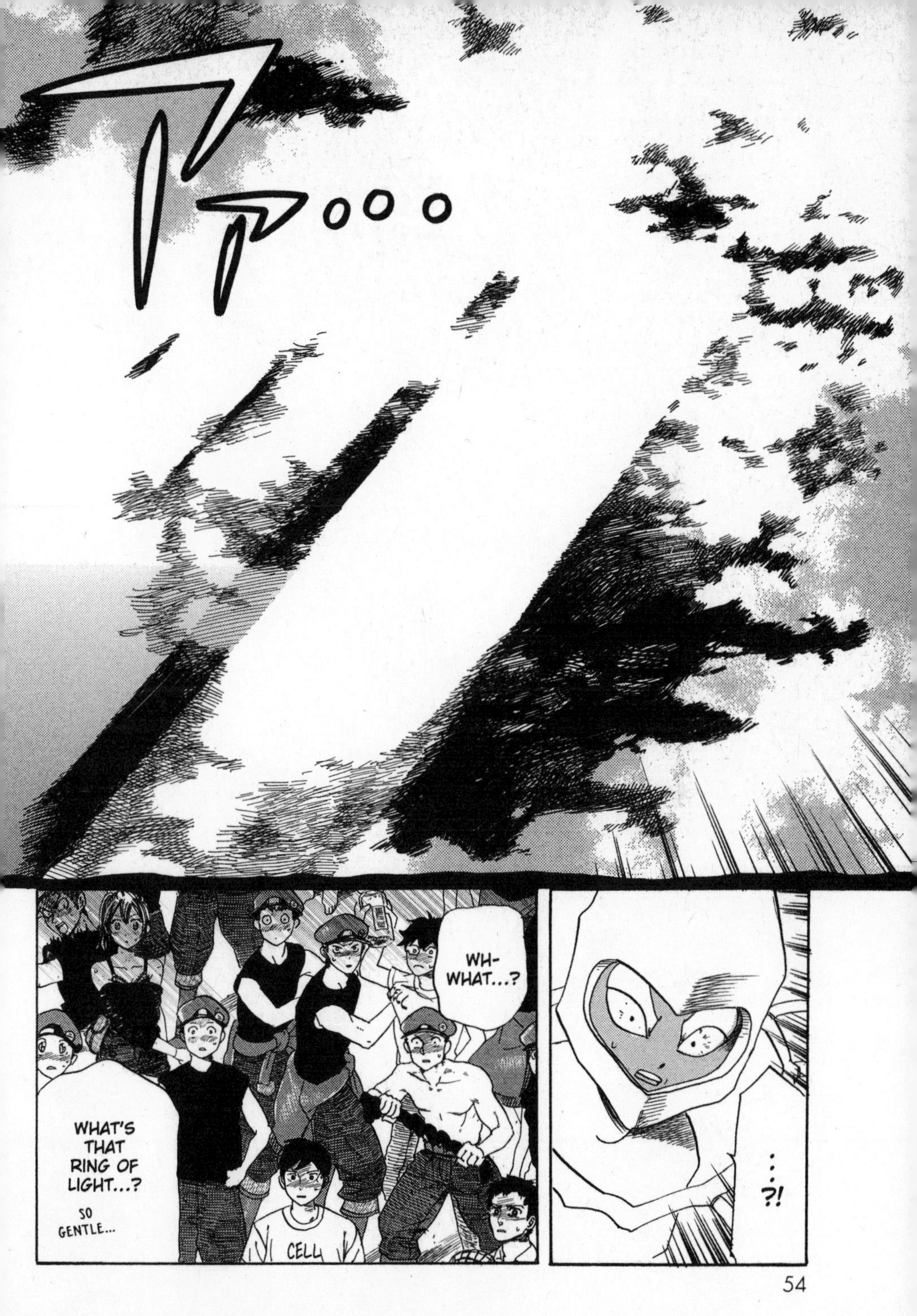
...?!
WH- WHAT...?
WHAT'S THAT RING OF LIGHT...?
SO GENTLE...

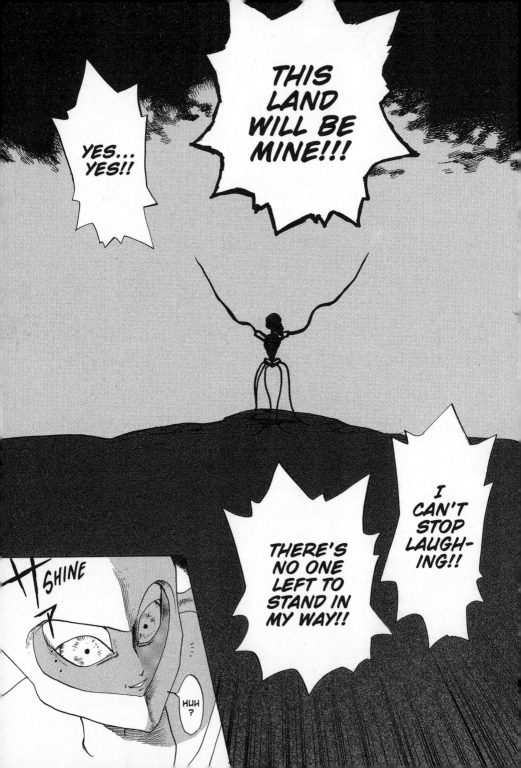

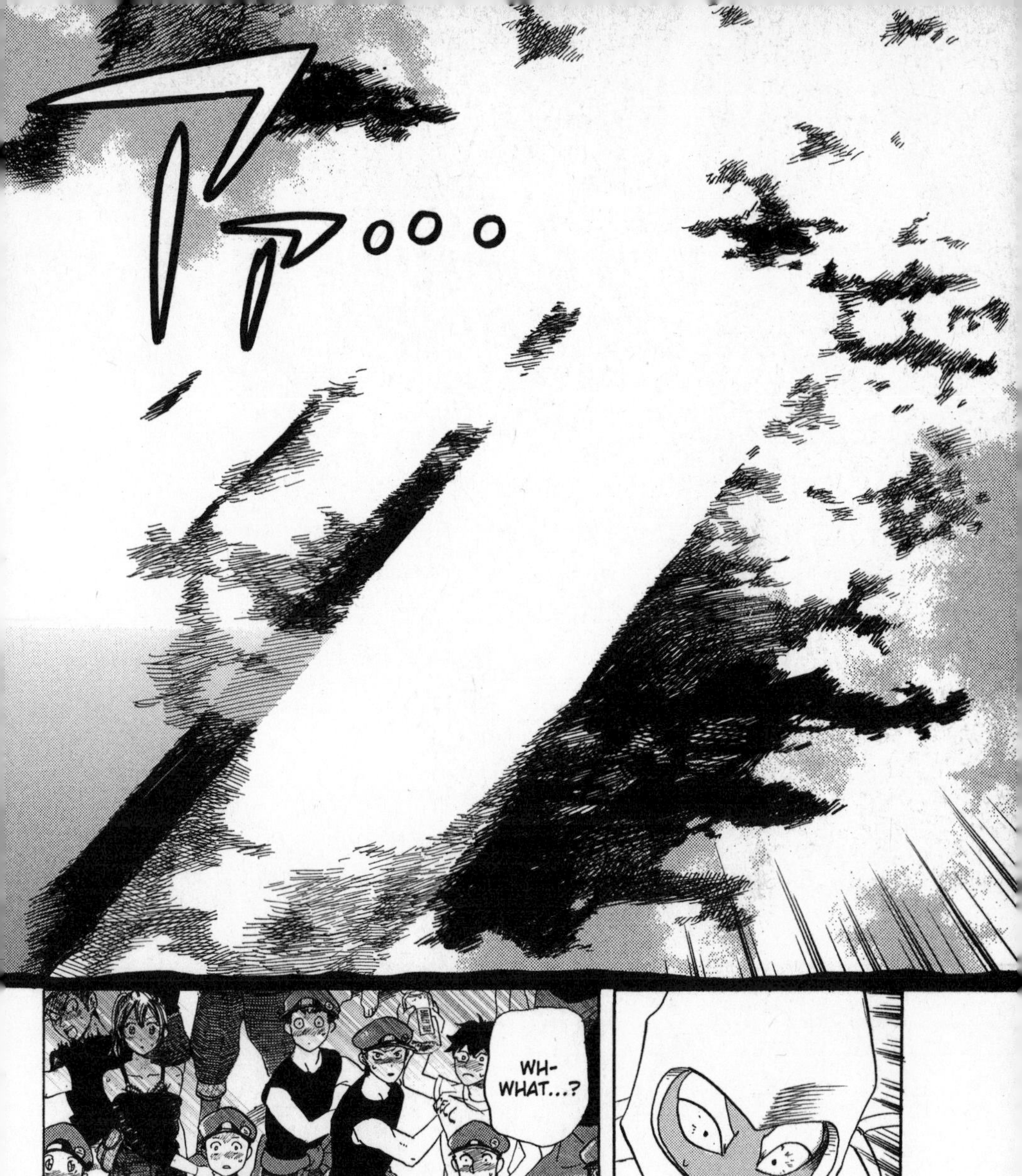

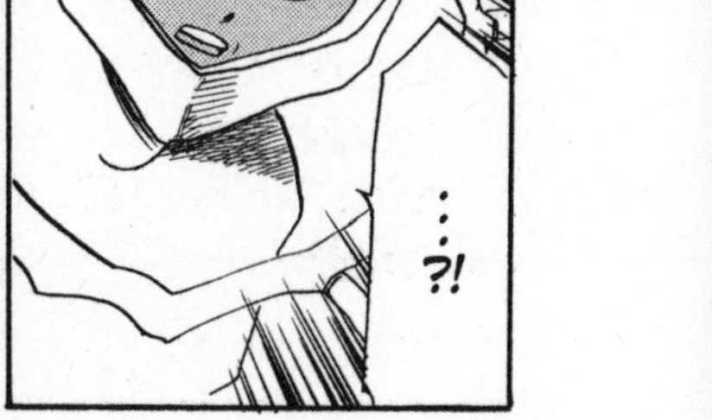
...?!

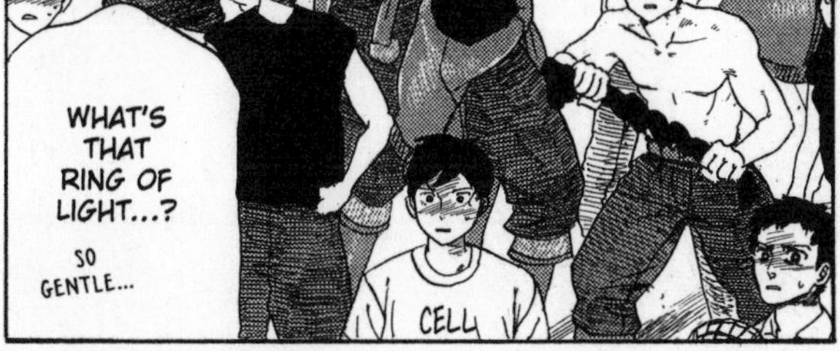
WH- WHAT...?
WHAT'S THAT RING OF LIGHT...?
SO GENTLE...

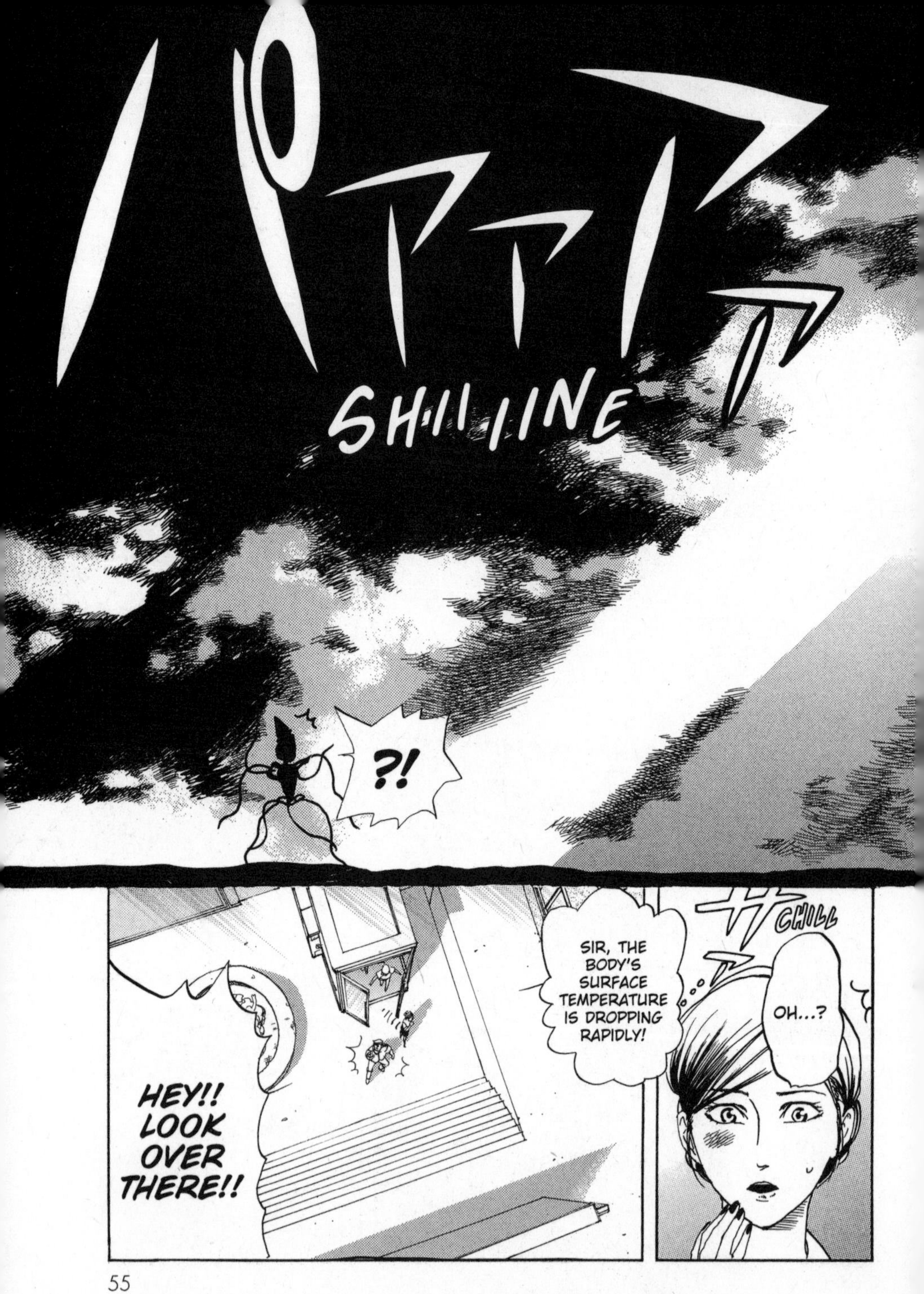
パァァァ
SHIIIINE
?!
CHILL
OH...?
SIR, THE BODY'S SURFACE TEMPERATURE IS DROPPING RAPIDLY!
HEY!! LOOK OVER THERE!!

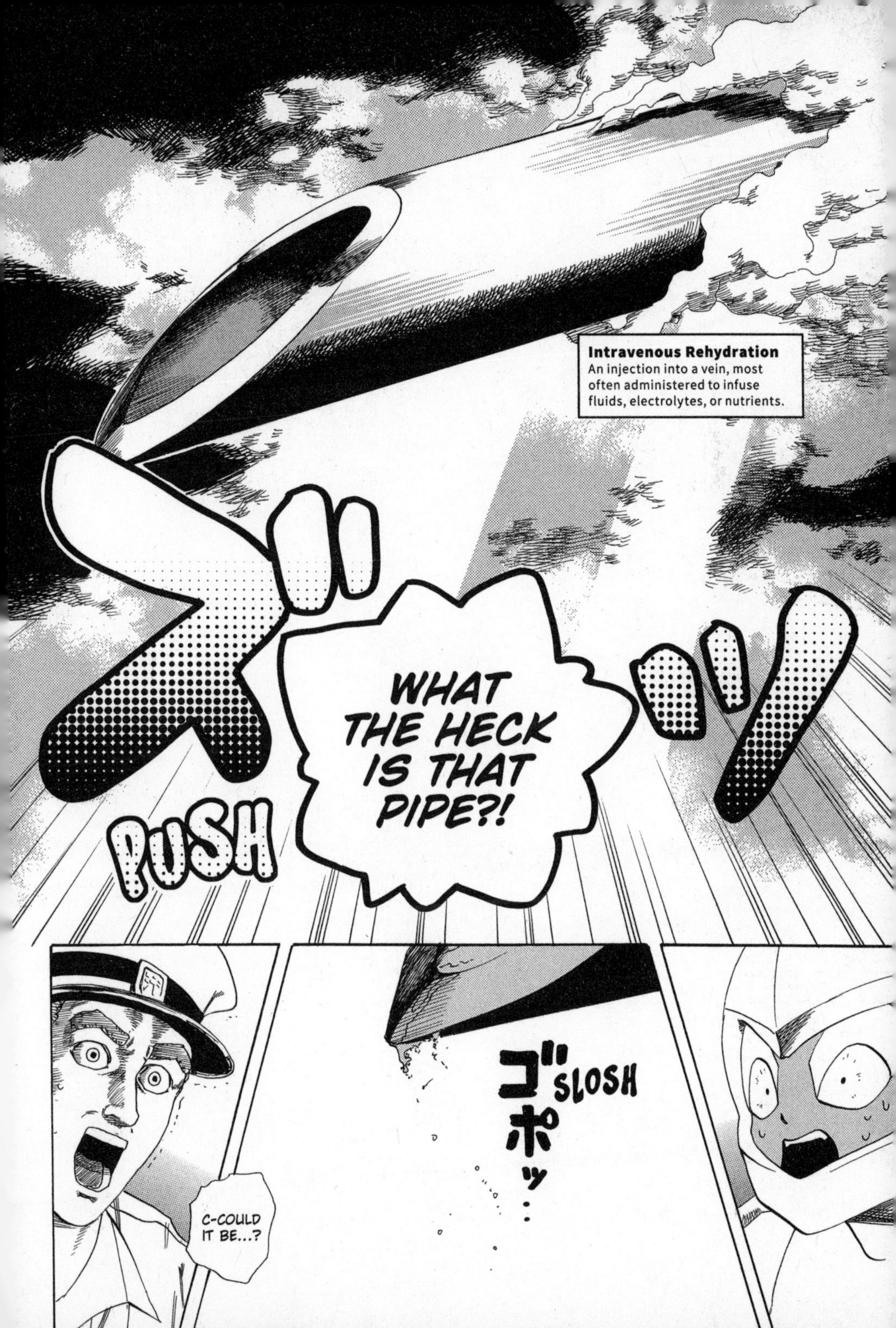
Intravenous Rehydration
An injection into a vein, most often administered to infuse fluids, electrolytes, or nutrients.
ズッ
PUSH
WHAT THE HECK IS THAT PIPE?!
ゴポッ
SLOSH
C-COULD IT BE...?

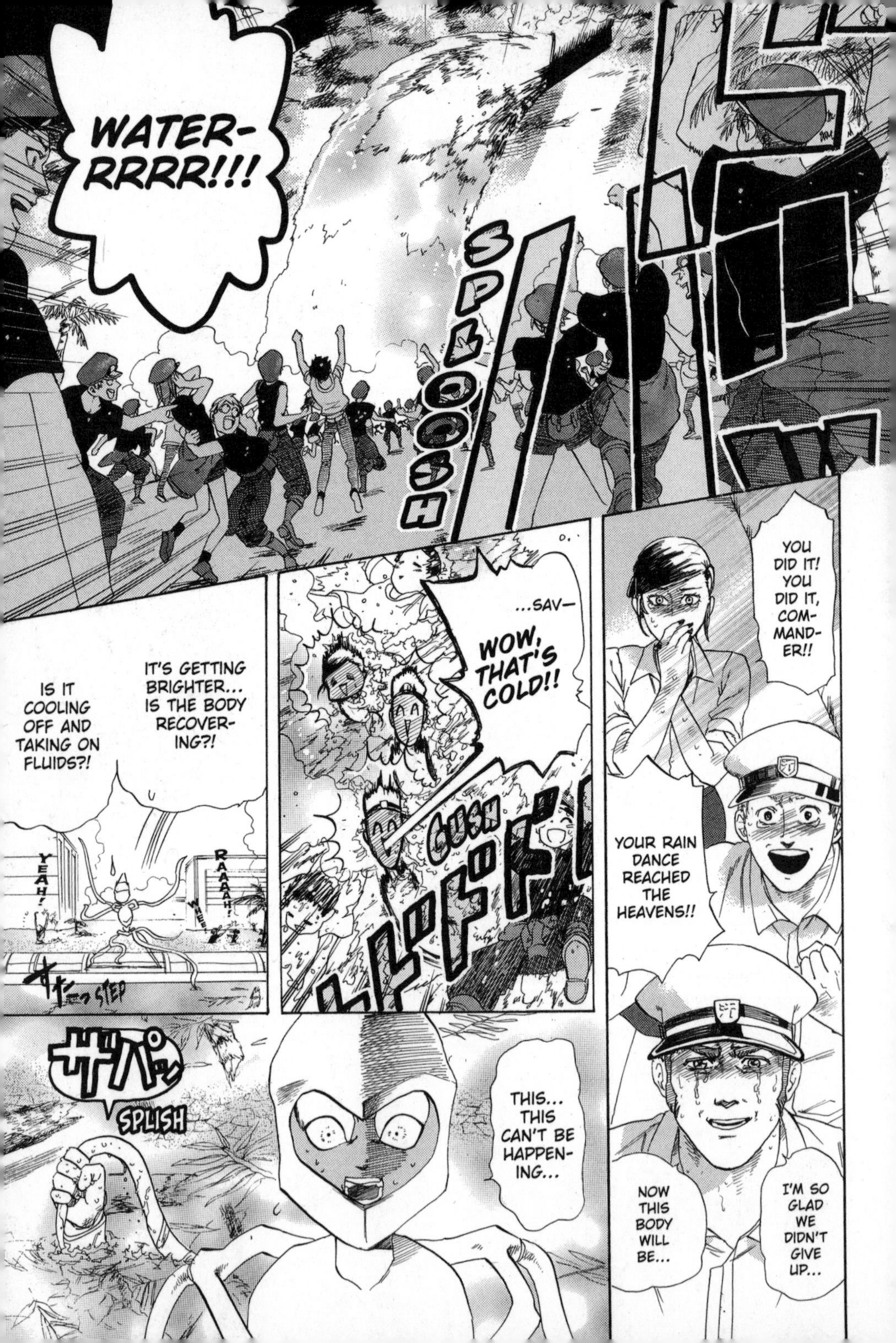
WATER-RRRR!!!
SPLOOSH
YOU DID IT! YOU DID IT, COMMANDER!!
YOUR RAIN DANCE REACHED THE HEAVENS!!
I'M SO GLAD WE DIDN'T GIVE UP...
NOW THIS BODY WILL BE...
...SAV—
WOW, THAT'S COLD!!
GUSH
IT'S GETTING BRIGHTER... IS THE BODY RECOVERING?!
IS IT COOLING OFF AND TAKING ON FLUIDS?!
RAAAAH!
WHEE!
YEAH!
STEP
THIS... THIS CAN'T BE HAPPENING...
SPLISH

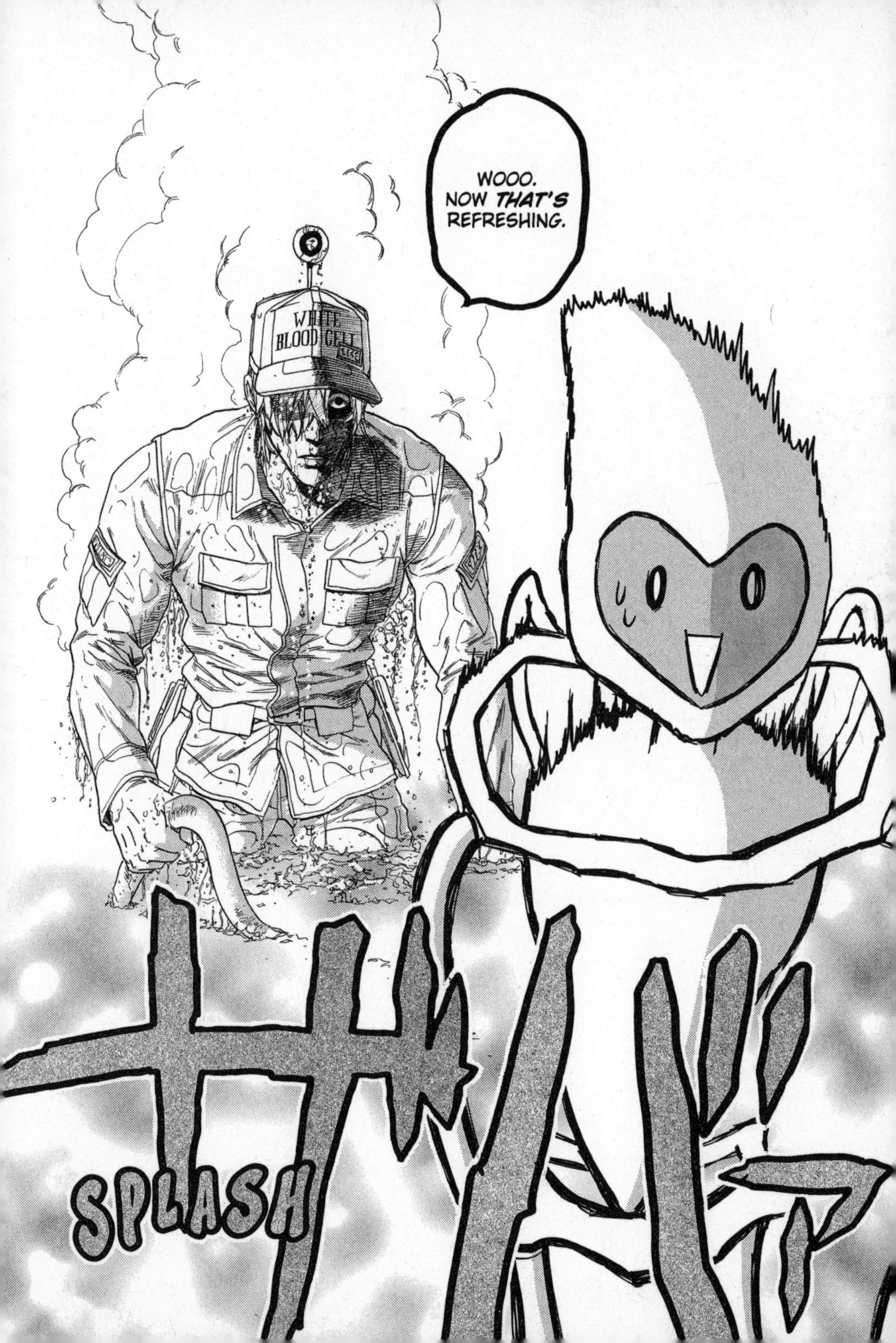
WOOO. NOW THAT'S REFRESHING.
WHITE BLOOD CELL
SPLASH

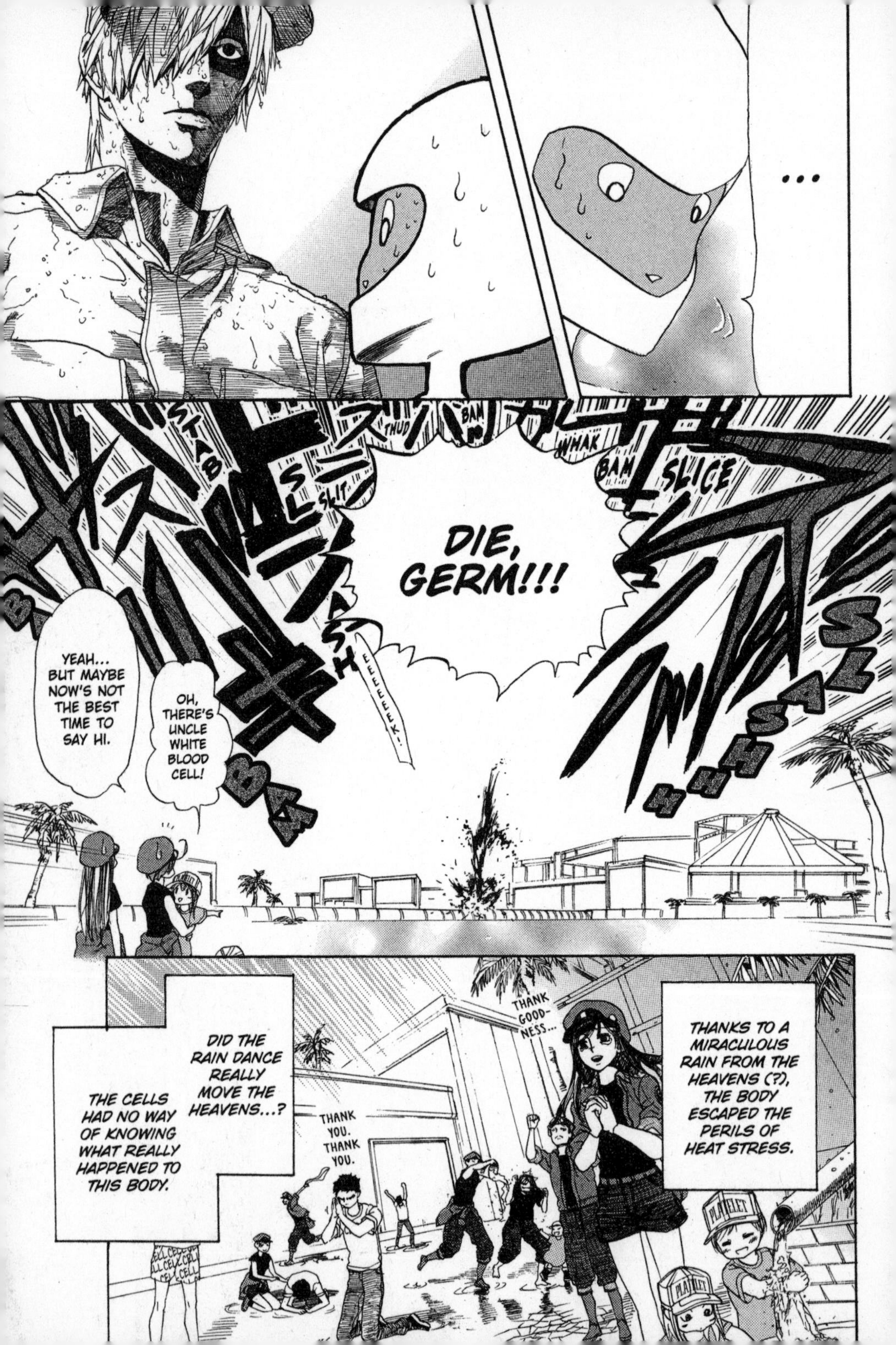
...
SLICE
WHAK
BAM
THUD
SLIT
STAB
DIE, GERM!!!
EEEEEEEEK!
OH, THERE'S UNCLE WHITE BLOOD CELL!
YEAH... BUT MAYBE NOW'S NOT THE BEST TIME TO SAY HI.
THANKS TO A MIRACULOUS RAIN FROM THE HEAVENS (?), THE BODY ESCAPED THE PERILS OF HEAT STRESS.
THANK GOODNESS...
THANK YOU. THANK YOU.
DID THE RAIN DANCE REALLY MOVE THE HEAVENS...?
THE CELLS HAD NO WAY OF KNOWING WHAT REALLY HAPPENED TO THIS BODY.

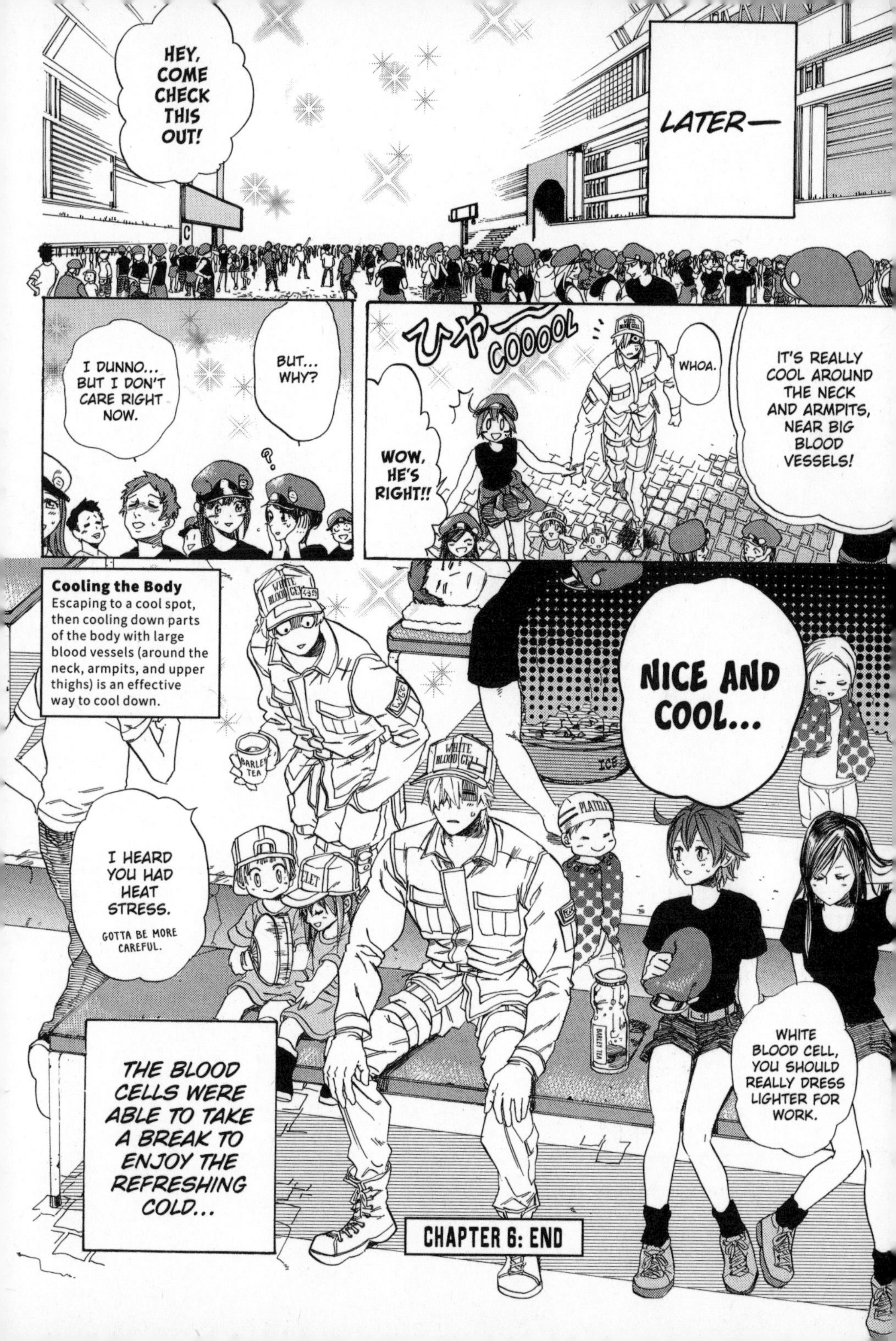
LATER—
HEY, COME CHECK THIS OUT!
ひゃ— COOOOL
WHOA.
IT'S REALLY COOL AROUND THE NECK AND ARMPITS, NEAR BIG BLOOD VESSELS!
WOW, HE'S RIGHT!!
BUT... WHY?
I DUNNO... BUT I DON'T CARE RIGHT NOW.
NICE AND COOL...
Cooling the Body
Escaping to a cool spot, then cooling down parts of the body with large blood vessels (around the neck, armpits, and upper thighs) is an effective way to cool down.
WHITE BLOOD CELL, YOU SHOULD REALLY DRESS LIGHTER FOR WORK.
I HEARD YOU HAD HEAT STRESS.
GOTTA BE MORE CAREFUL.
THE BLOOD CELLS WERE ABLE TO TAKE A BREAK TO ENJOY THE REFRESHING COLD...
CHAPTER 6: END

WHITE
BLOOD CELL
1146

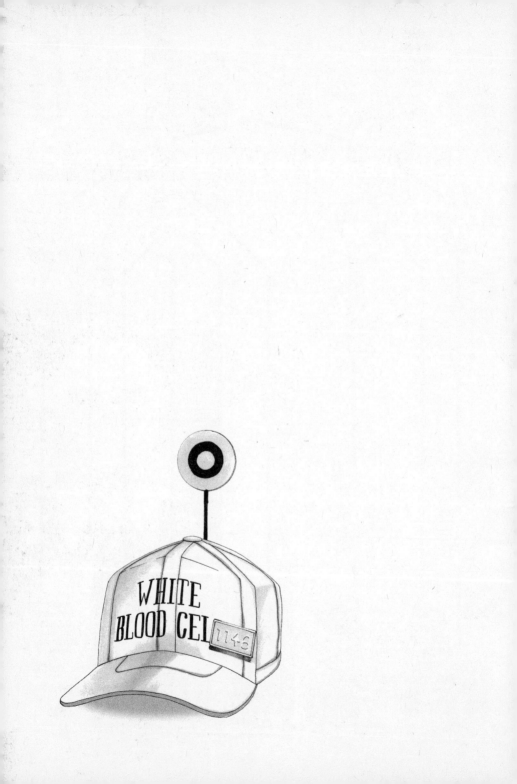

THE DIFFERENTIATION OF BLOOD CELLS
(ABBREVIATED)

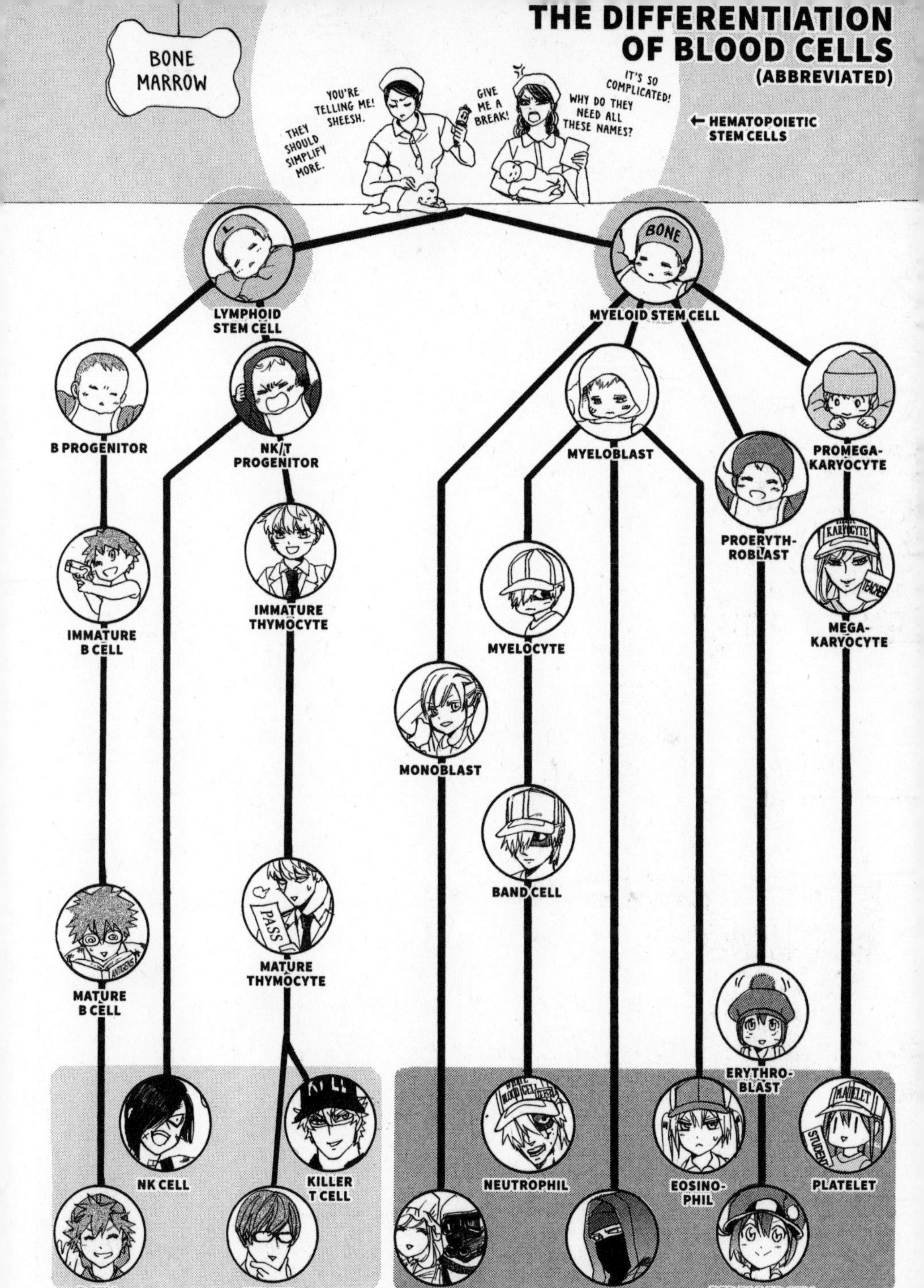

BONE MARROW
IT'S SO COMPLICATED!
WHY DO THEY NEED ALL THESE NAMES?
GIVE ME A BREAK!
YOU'RE TELLING ME! SHEESH.
THEY SHOULD SIMPLIFY MORE.
← HEMATOPOIETIC STEM CELLS
BONE
LYMPHOID STEM CELL
MYELOID STEM CELL
B PROGENITOR
NK/T PROGENITOR
MYELOBLAST
PROMEGA-KARYOCYTE
PROERYTH-ROBLAST
KARYOCYTE
TEACHER
MEGA-KARYOCYTE
IMMATURE B CELL
IMMATURE THYMOCYTE
MYELOCYTE
MONOBLAST
BAND CELL
PASS
MATURE THYMOCYTE
ANTIGENS
MATURE B CELL
ERYTHRO-BLAST
PLATELET
STUDENT
NK CELL
KILLER T CELL
NEUTROPHIL
EOSINO-PHIL
PLATELET
B CELL
HELPER T CELL
MACROPHAGE/ MONOCYTE
BASOPHIL
RED BLOOD CELL

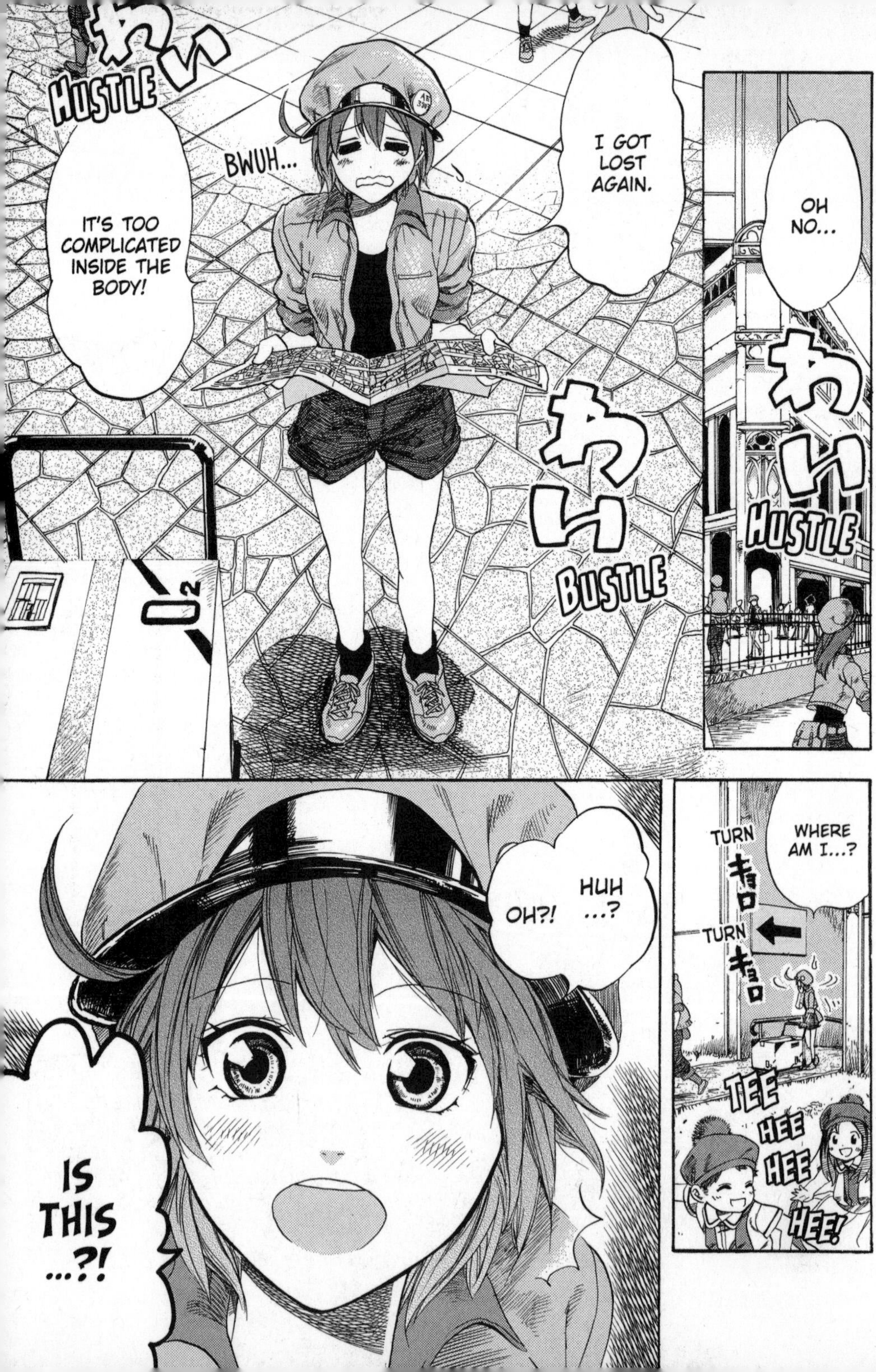
OH NO...
わい
HUSTLE
I GOT LOST AGAIN.
BWUH...
IT'S TOO COMPLICATED INSIDE THE BODY!
わい
HUSTLE
わい
BUSTLE
WHERE AM I...?
TURN
キョロ
TURN
キョロ
TEE HEE HEE HEE!
HUH ...?
OH?!
IS THIS ...?!

CHAPTER 7: ERYTHROBLASTS AND MYELOCYTES

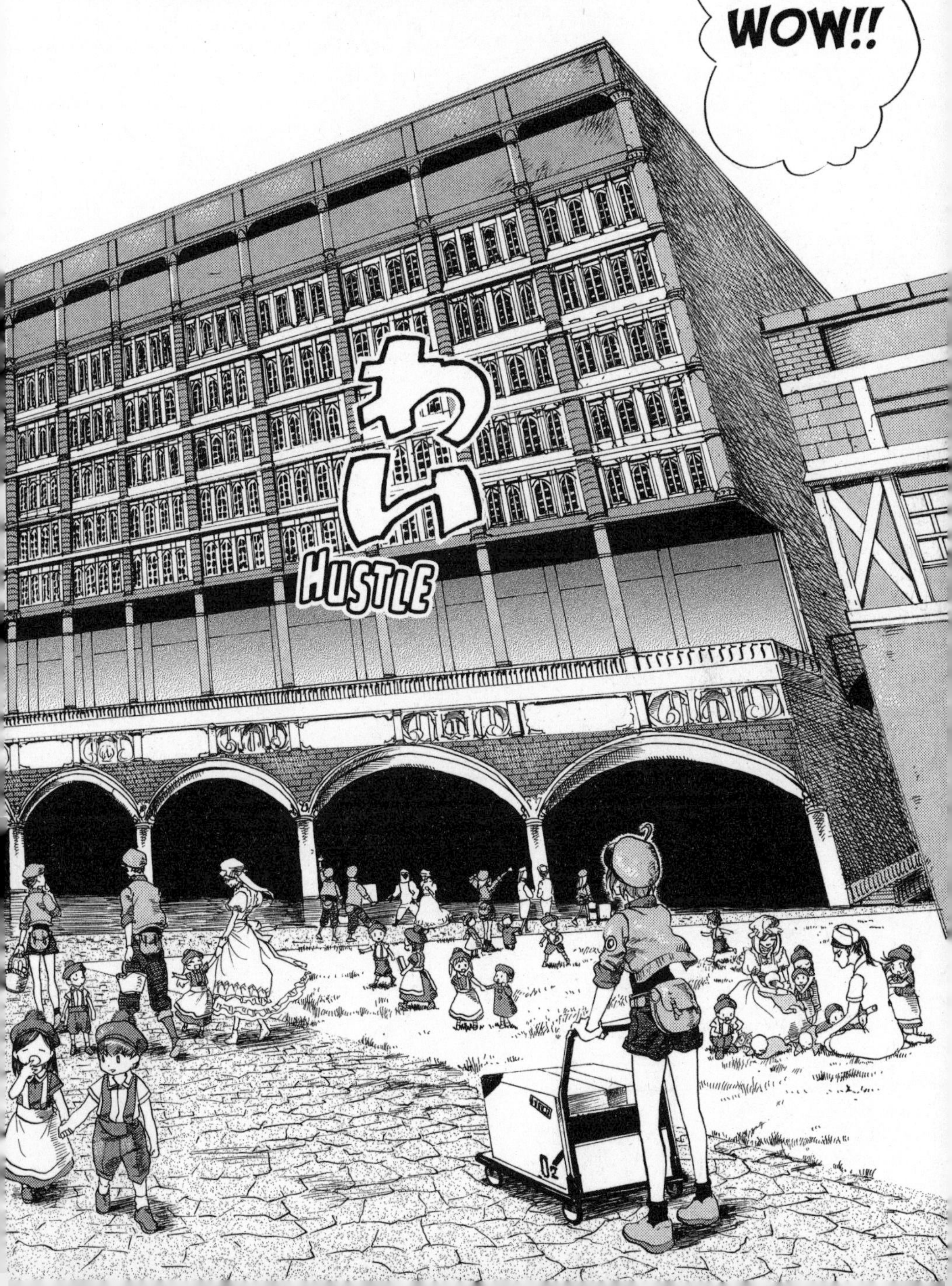
WOW!!
HUSTLE

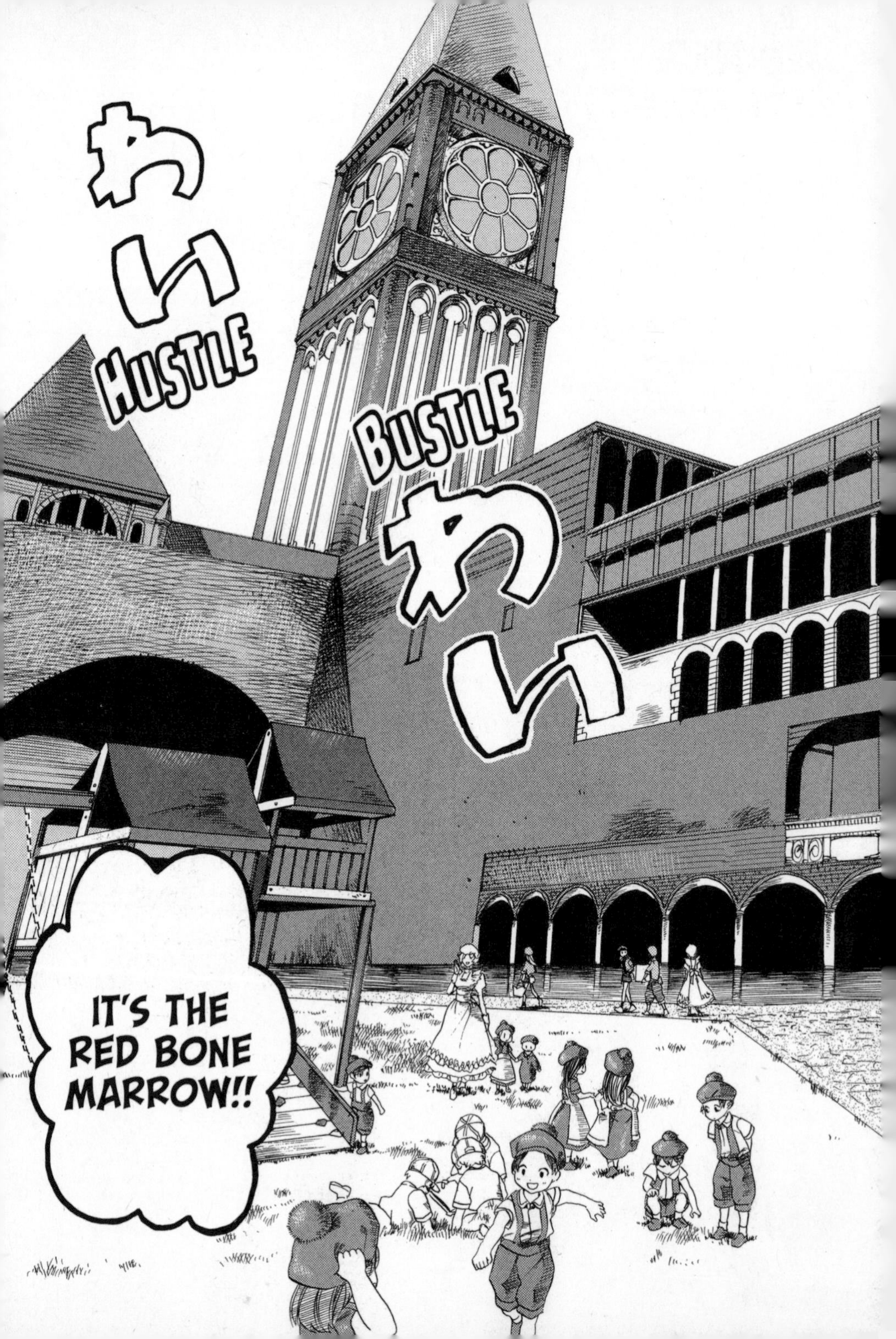
わい
HUSTLE
BUSTLE
わい
IT'S THE RED BONE MARROW!!

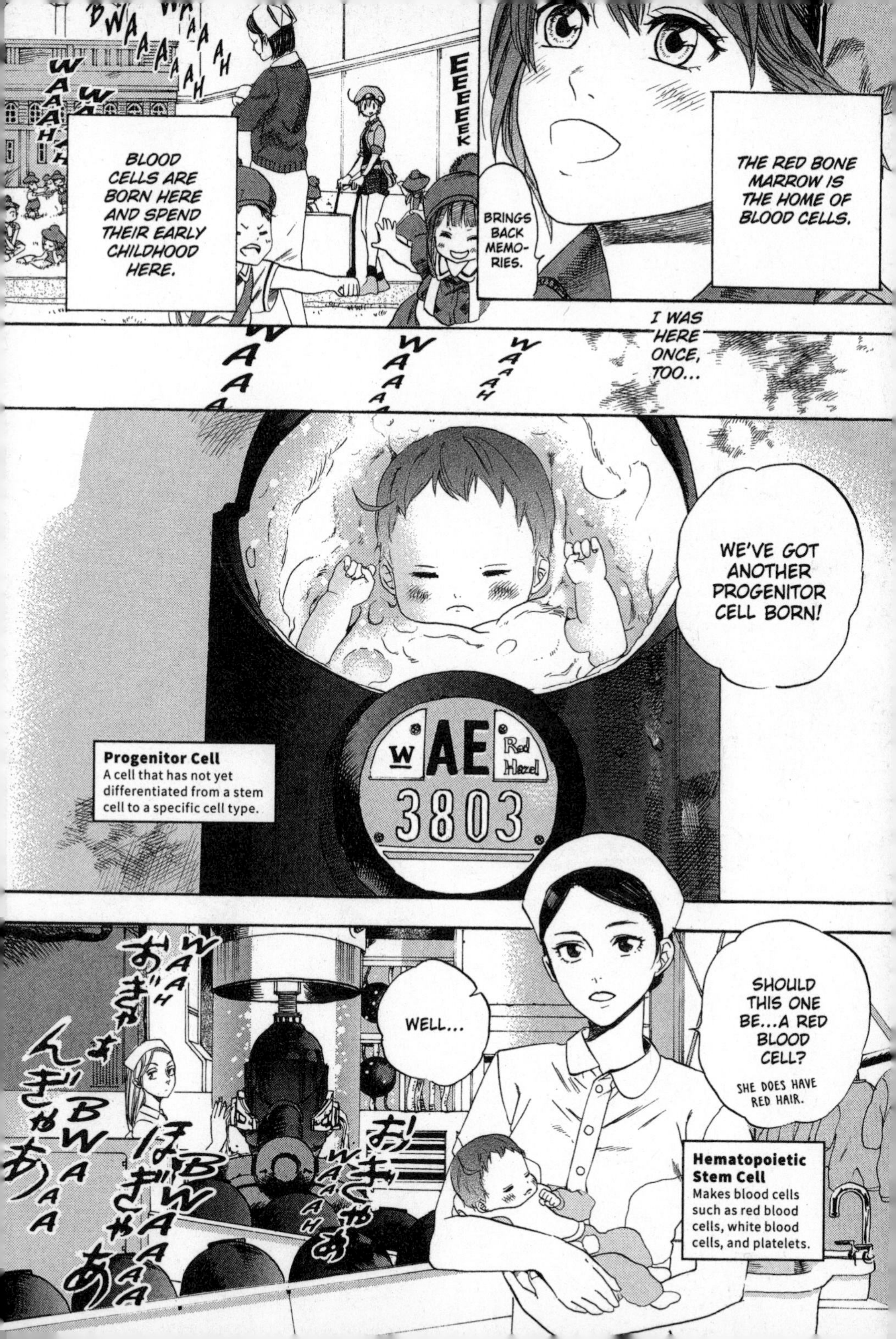
THE RED BONE MARROW IS THE HOME OF BLOOD CELLS.
BRINGS BACK MEMORIES.
EEEEEK
WAAAAH
BWAAAAH
WAAAAH
BLOOD CELLS ARE BORN HERE AND SPEND THEIR EARLY CHILDHOOD HERE.
I WAS HERE ONCE, TOO...
WAAAH
WAAA
WAAA
WE'VE GOT ANOTHER PROGENITOR CELL BORN!
W AE Red Hazel 3803
Progenitor Cell
A cell that has not yet differentiated from a stem cell to a specific cell type.
SHOULD THIS ONE BE...A RED BLOOD CELL?
SHE DOES HAVE RED HAIR.
Hematopoietic Stem Cell
Makes blood cells such as red blood cells, white blood cells, and platelets.
WELL...
おぎゃあ WAAAH
ほぎゃあ BWAAAAA
おぎゃあ WAAAH
んぎゃあ BWAAA

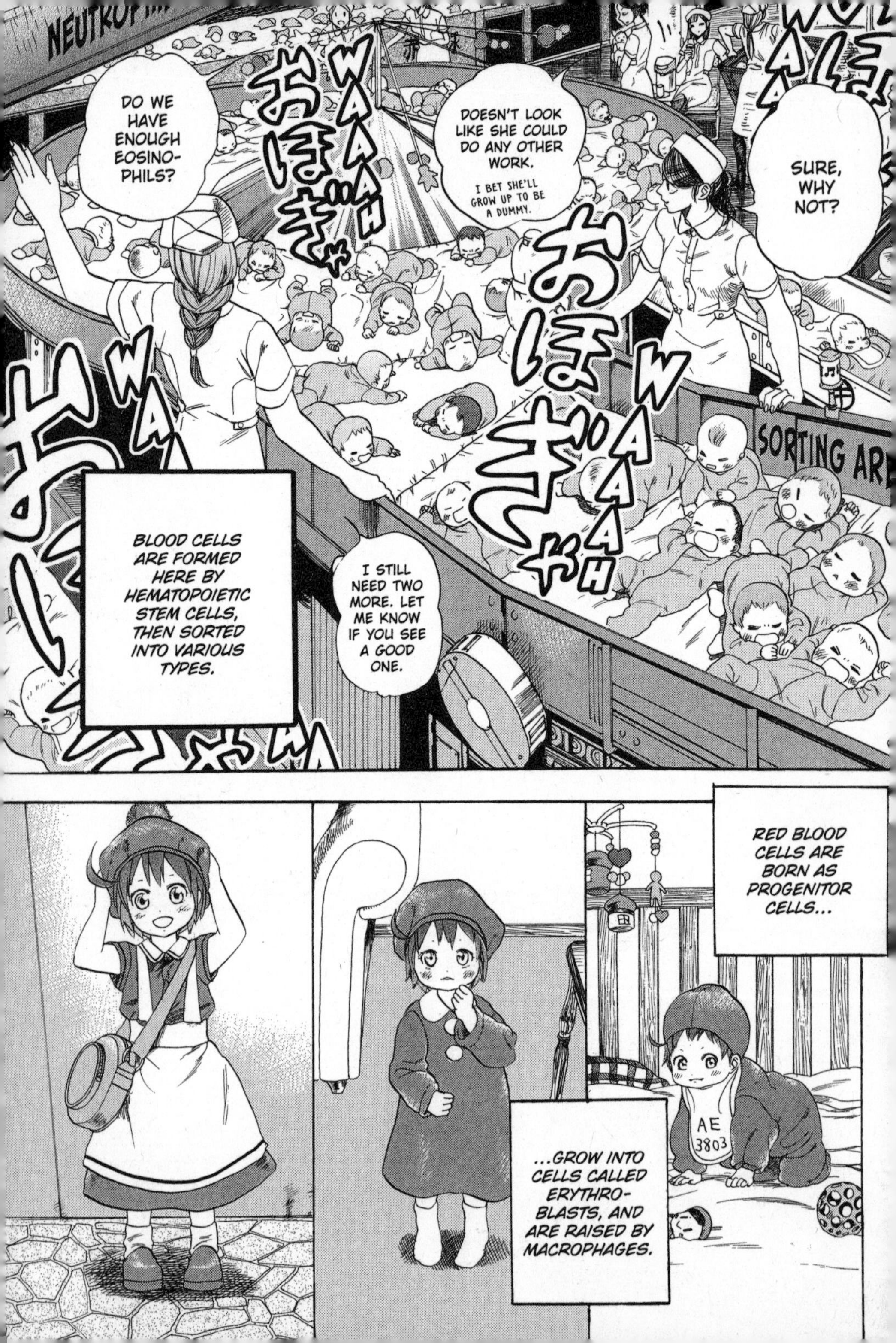
SURE, WHY NOT?
DOESN'T LOOK LIKE SHE COULD DO ANY OTHER WORK.
I BET SHE'LL GROW UP TO BE A DUMMY.
WAAAAH おほぎゃ
DO WE HAVE ENOUGH EOSINO-PHILS?
WAAAAH おほぎゃ
I STILL NEED TWO MORE. LET ME KNOW IF YOU SEE A GOOD ONE.
BLOOD CELLS ARE FORMED HERE BY HEMATOPOIETIC STEM CELLS, THEN SORTED INTO VARIOUS TYPES.
RED BLOOD CELLS ARE BORN AS PROGENITOR CELLS...
AE 3803
...GROW INTO CELLS CALLED ERYTHRO-BLASTS, AND ARE RAISED BY MACROPHAGES.

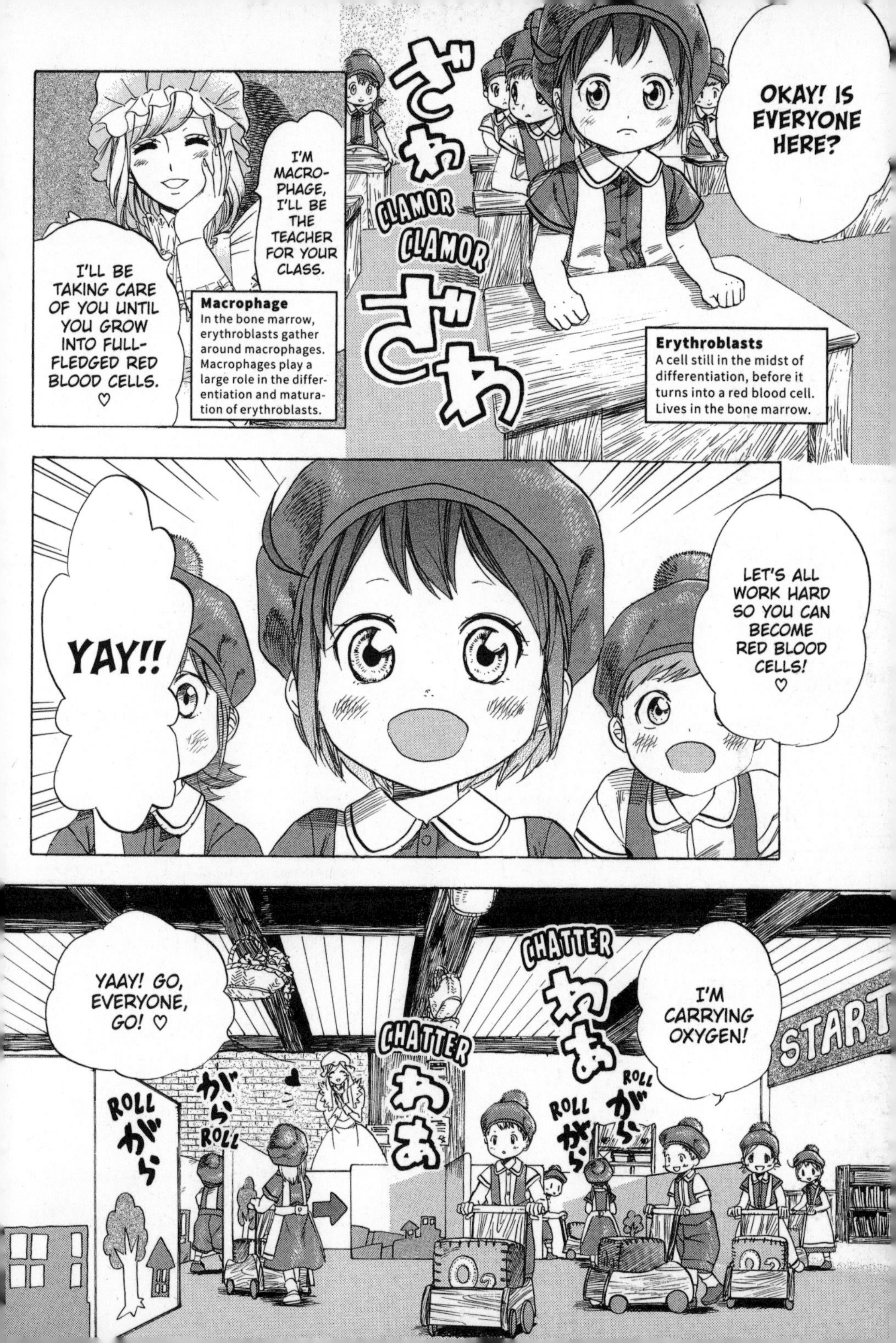
OKAY! IS EVERYONE HERE?
ざわ CLAMOR CLAMOR ざわ
Erythroblasts
A cell still in the midst of differentiation, before it turns into a red blood cell. Lives in the bone marrow.
I'M MACROPHAGE, I'LL BE THE TEACHER FOR YOUR CLASS.
I'LL BE TAKING CARE OF YOU UNTIL YOU GROW INTO FULL-FLEDGED RED BLOOD CELLS. ♡
Macrophage
In the bone marrow, erythroblasts gather around macrophages. Macrophages play a large role in the differentiation and maturation of erythroblasts.
LET'S ALL WORK HARD SO YOU CAN BECOME RED BLOOD CELLS! ♡
YAY!!
START
I'M CARRYING OXYGEN!
CHATTER わあ
CHATTER わあ
ROLL がら ROLL がら
YAAY! GO, EVERYONE, GO! ♡
がら ROLL
ROLL がら

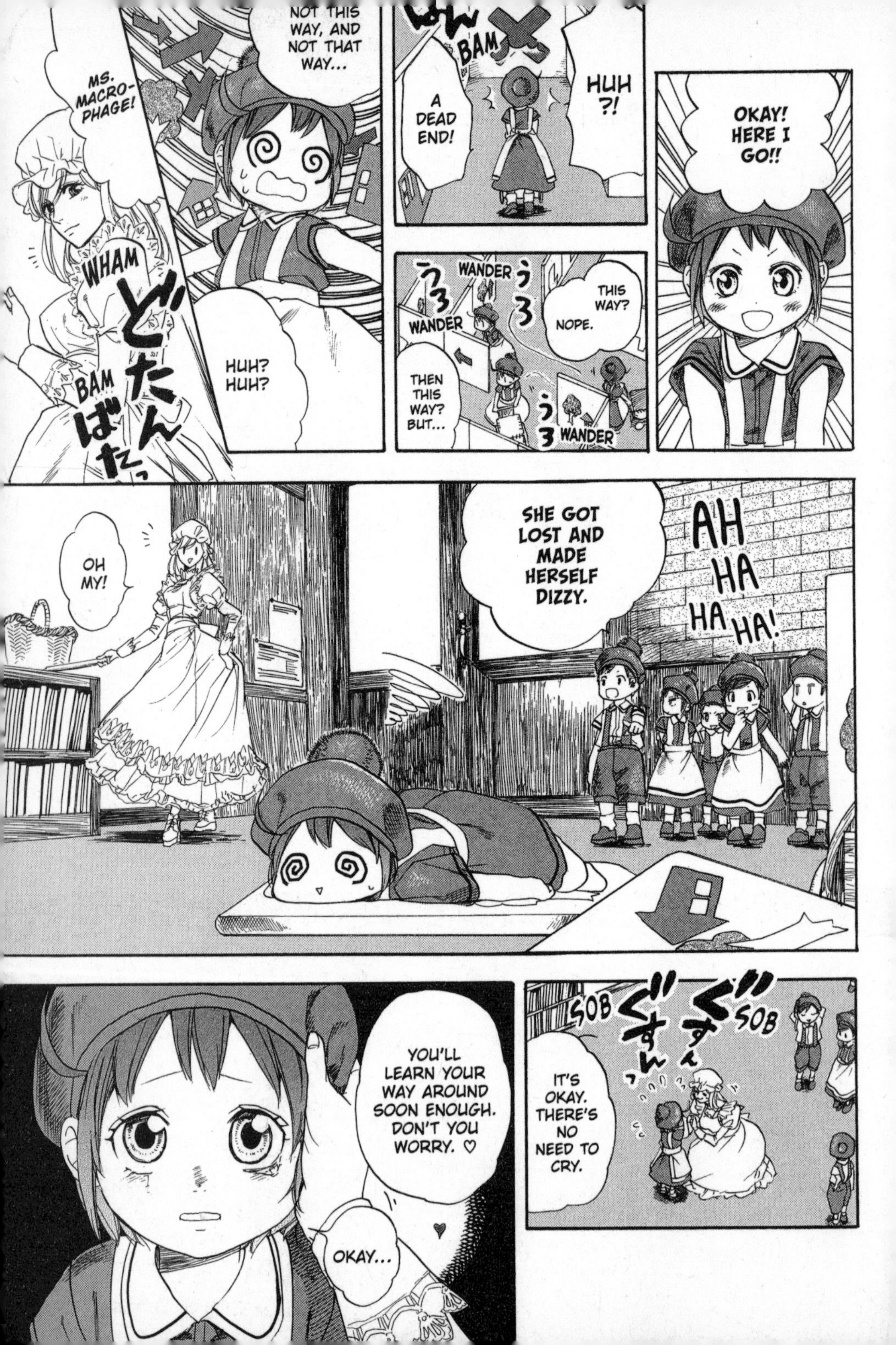
OKAY! HERE I GO!!
HUH ?!
BAM
A DEAD END!
THIS WAY?
NOPE.
WANDER
WANDER
THEN THIS WAY? BUT...
WANDER
NOT THIS WAY, AND NOT THAT WAY...
HUH? HUH?
MS. MACRO-PHAGE!
WHAM
BAM
SHE GOT LOST AND MADE HERSELF DIZZY.
AH HA HA HA!
OH MY!
SOB
SOB
IT'S OKAY. THERE'S NO NEED TO CRY.
YOU'LL LEARN YOUR WAY AROUND SOON ENOUGH. DON'T YOU WORRY. ♡
OKAY...

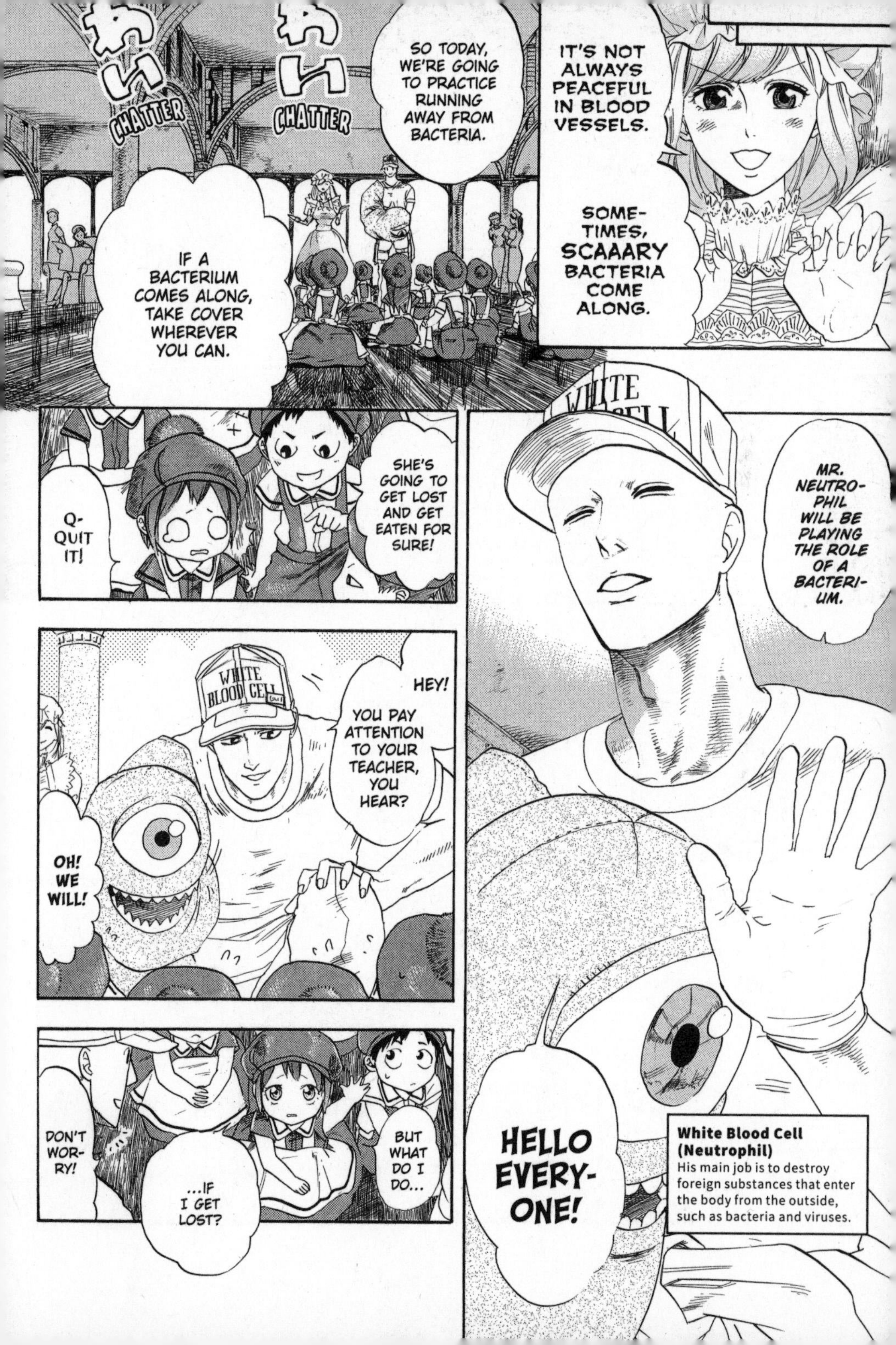
IT'S NOT ALWAYS PEACEFUL IN BLOOD VESSELS.
SOMETIMES, SCAAARY BACTERIA COME ALONG.
わい CHATTER
わい CHATTER
SO TODAY, WE'RE GOING TO PRACTICE RUNNING AWAY FROM BACTERIA.
IF A BACTERIUM COMES ALONG, TAKE COVER WHEREVER YOU CAN.
MR. NEUTROPHIL WILL BE PLAYING THE ROLE OF A BACTERIUM.
HELLO EVERYONE!
White Blood Cell (Neutrophil)
His main job is to destroy foreign substances that enter the body from the outside, such as bacteria and viruses.
SHE'S GOING TO GET LOST AND GET EATEN FOR SURE!
Q-QUIT IT!
HEY! YOU PAY ATTENTION TO YOUR TEACHER, YOU HEAR?
OH! WE WILL!
BUT WHAT DO I DO...
...IF I GET LOST?
DON'T WORRY!

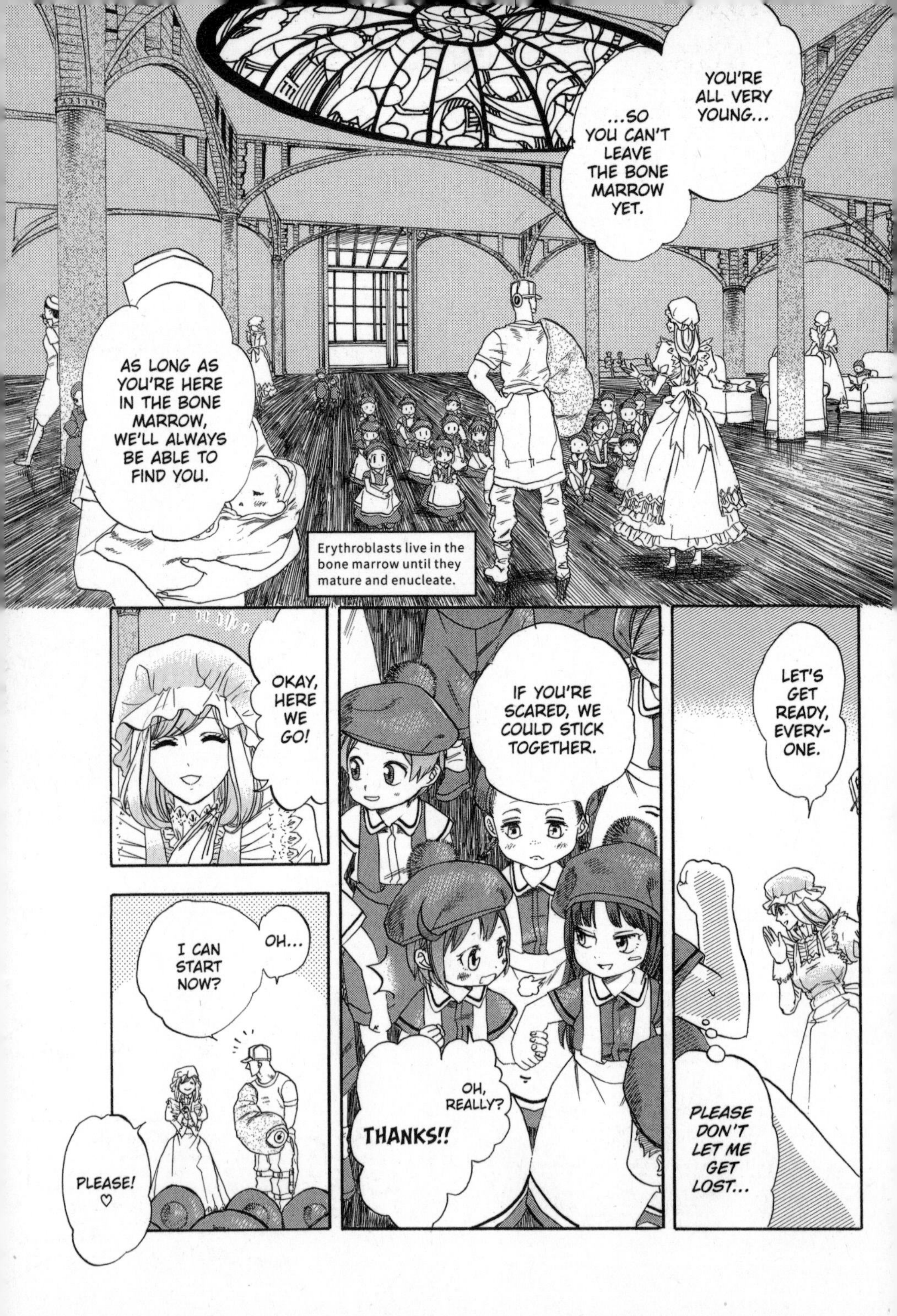
YOU'RE ALL VERY YOUNG...
...SO YOU CAN'T LEAVE THE BONE MARROW YET.
AS LONG AS YOU'RE HERE IN THE BONE MARROW, WE'LL ALWAYS BE ABLE TO FIND YOU.
Erythroblasts live in the bone marrow until they mature and enucleate.
LET'S GET READY, EVERYONE.
PLEASE DON'T LET ME GET LOST...
IF YOU'RE SCARED, WE COULD STICK TOGETHER.
OH, REALLY?
THANKS!!
OKAY, HERE WE GO!
OH...
I CAN START NOW?
PLEASE! ♡

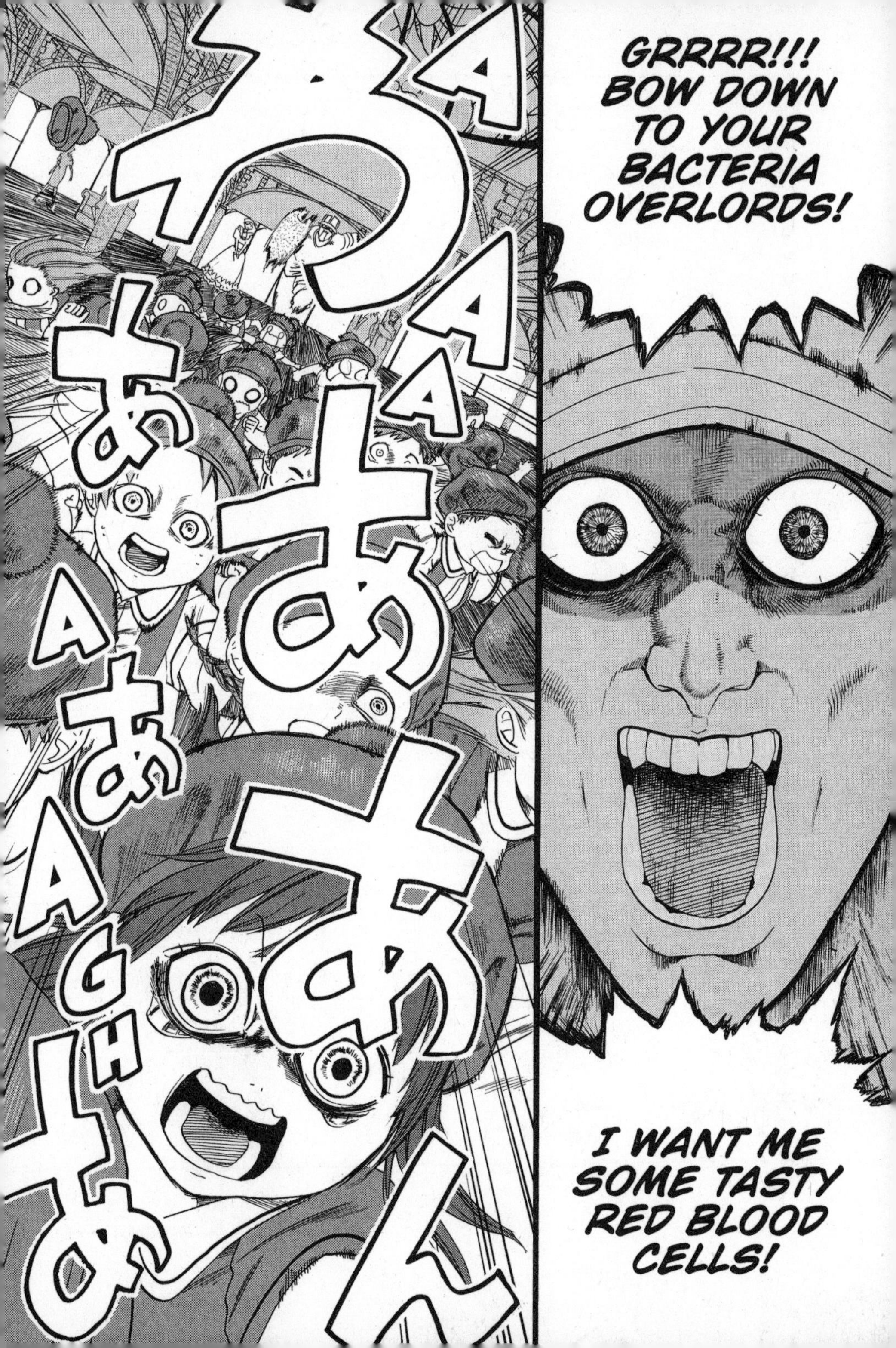
GRRRR!!! BOW DOWN TO YOUR BACTERIA OVERLORDS!
I WANT ME SOME TASTY RED BLOOD CELLS!
AAA
AAGH

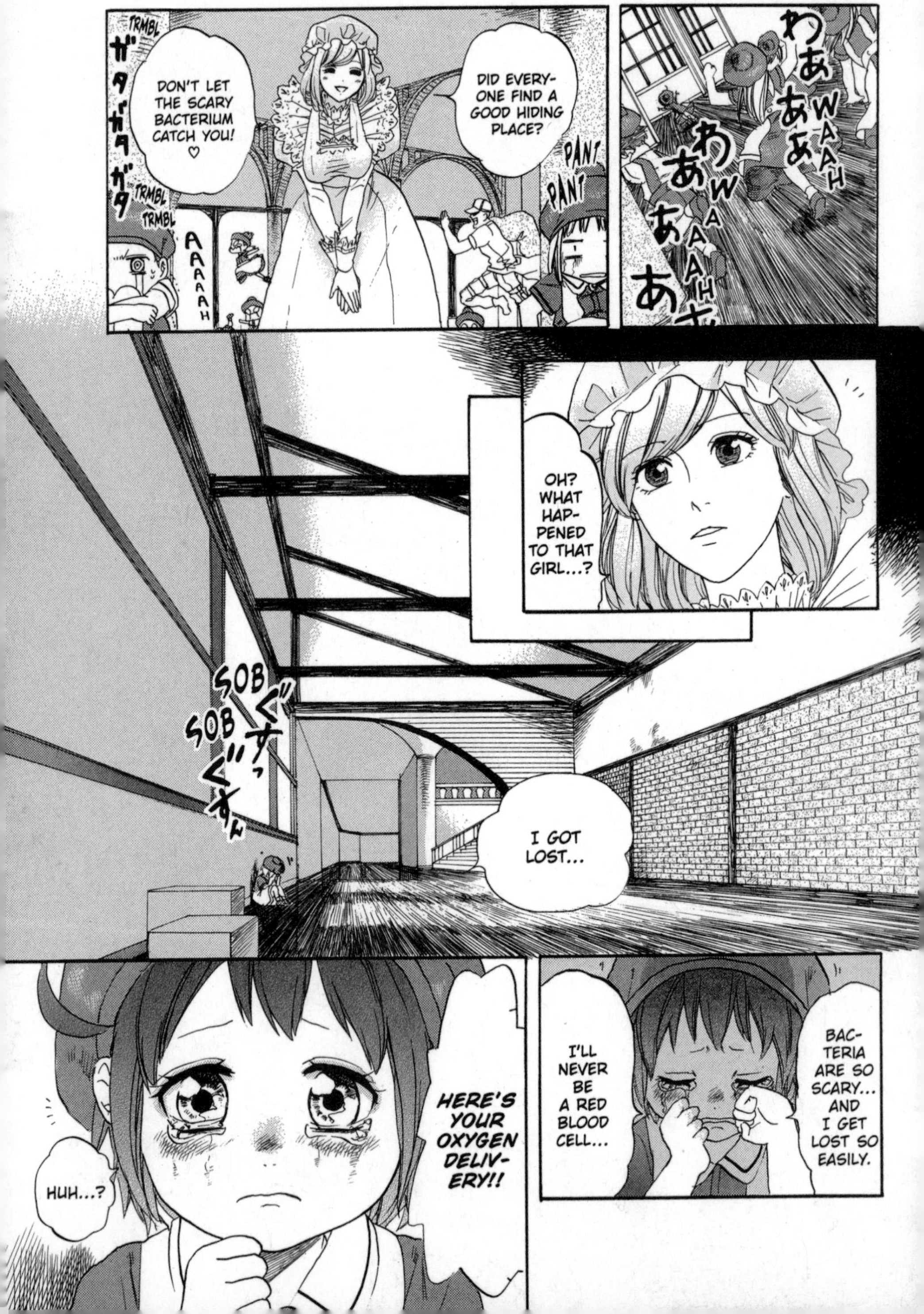
わあぁ
WAAH
わあ
WAAAH
DID EVERY-ONE FIND A GOOD HIDING PLACE?
PANT PANT
DON'T LET THE SCARY BACTERIUM CATCH YOU! ♡
TRMBL
ガタガタガタ
TRMBL TRMBL
AAAAAH
OH? WHAT HAP-PENED TO THAT GIRL...?
SOB SOB
ぐすっ ぐすん
I GOT LOST...
BAC-TERIA ARE SO SCARY... AND I GET LOST SO EASILY.
I'LL NEVER BE A RED BLOOD CELL...
HERE'S YOUR OXYGEN DELIV-ERY!!
HUH...?

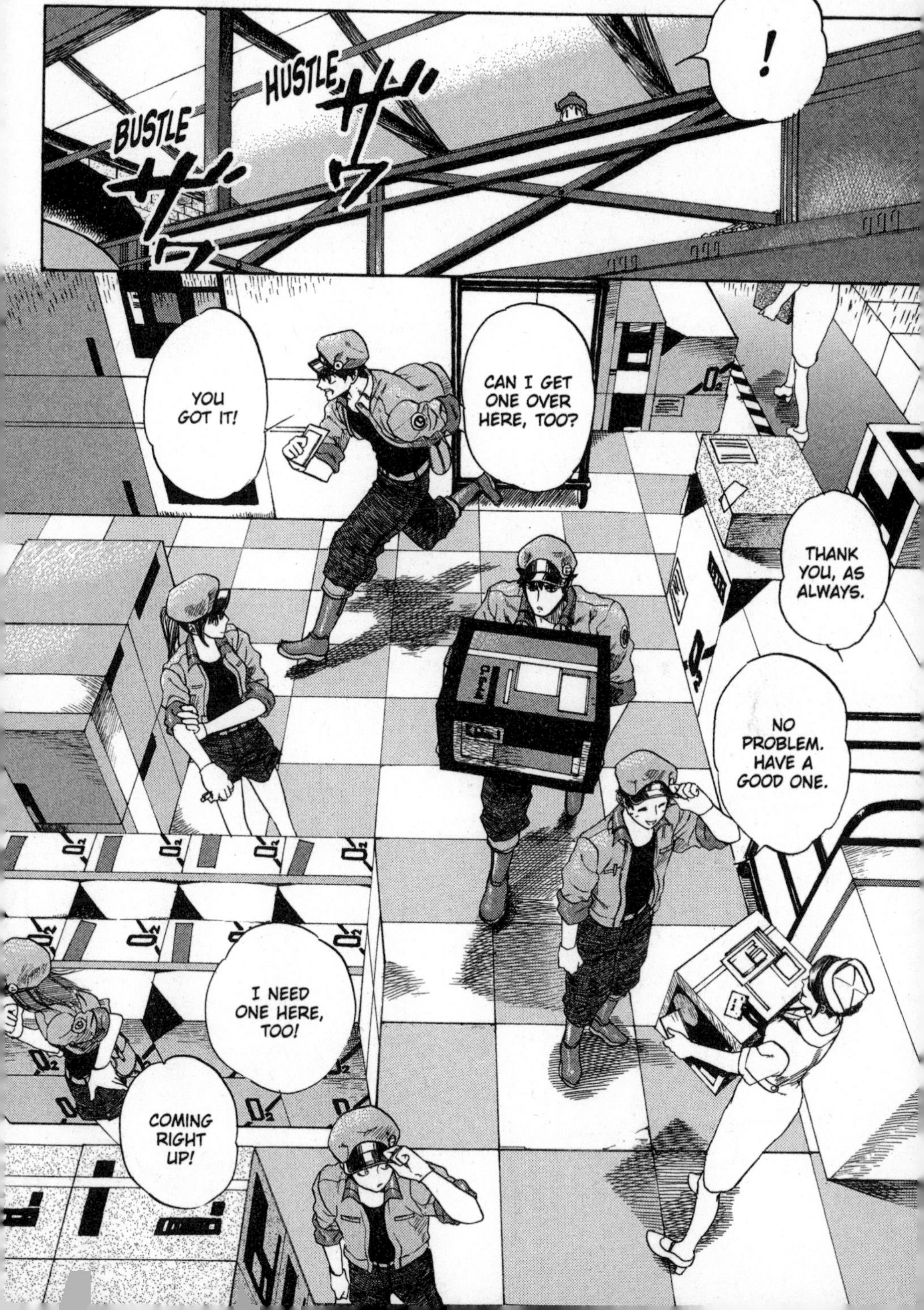

!
HUSTLE
ザワ
BUSTLE
ザワ
CAN I GET ONE OVER HERE, TOO?
YOU GOT IT!
THANK YOU, AS ALWAYS.
NO PROBLEM. HAVE A GOOD ONE.
I NEED ONE HERE, TOO!
COMING RIGHT UP!

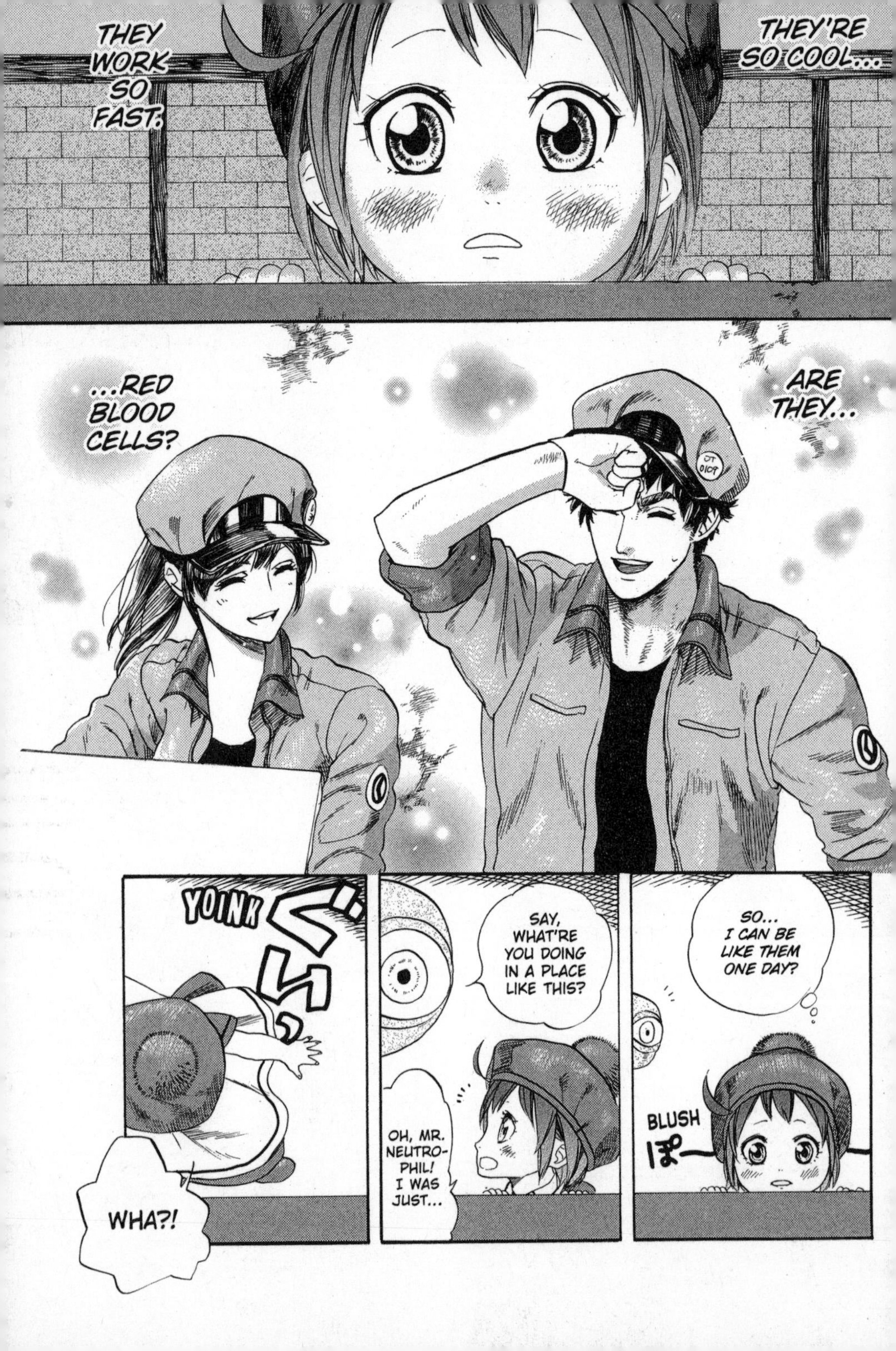
THEY'RE SO COOL...
THEY WORK SO FAST.
ARE THEY...
...RED BLOOD CELLS?
SO... I CAN BE LIKE THEM ONE DAY?
BLUSH
ぽ—
SAY, WHAT'RE YOU DOING IN A PLACE LIKE THIS?
OH, MR. NEUTROPHIL! I WAS JUST...
YOINK
WHA?!

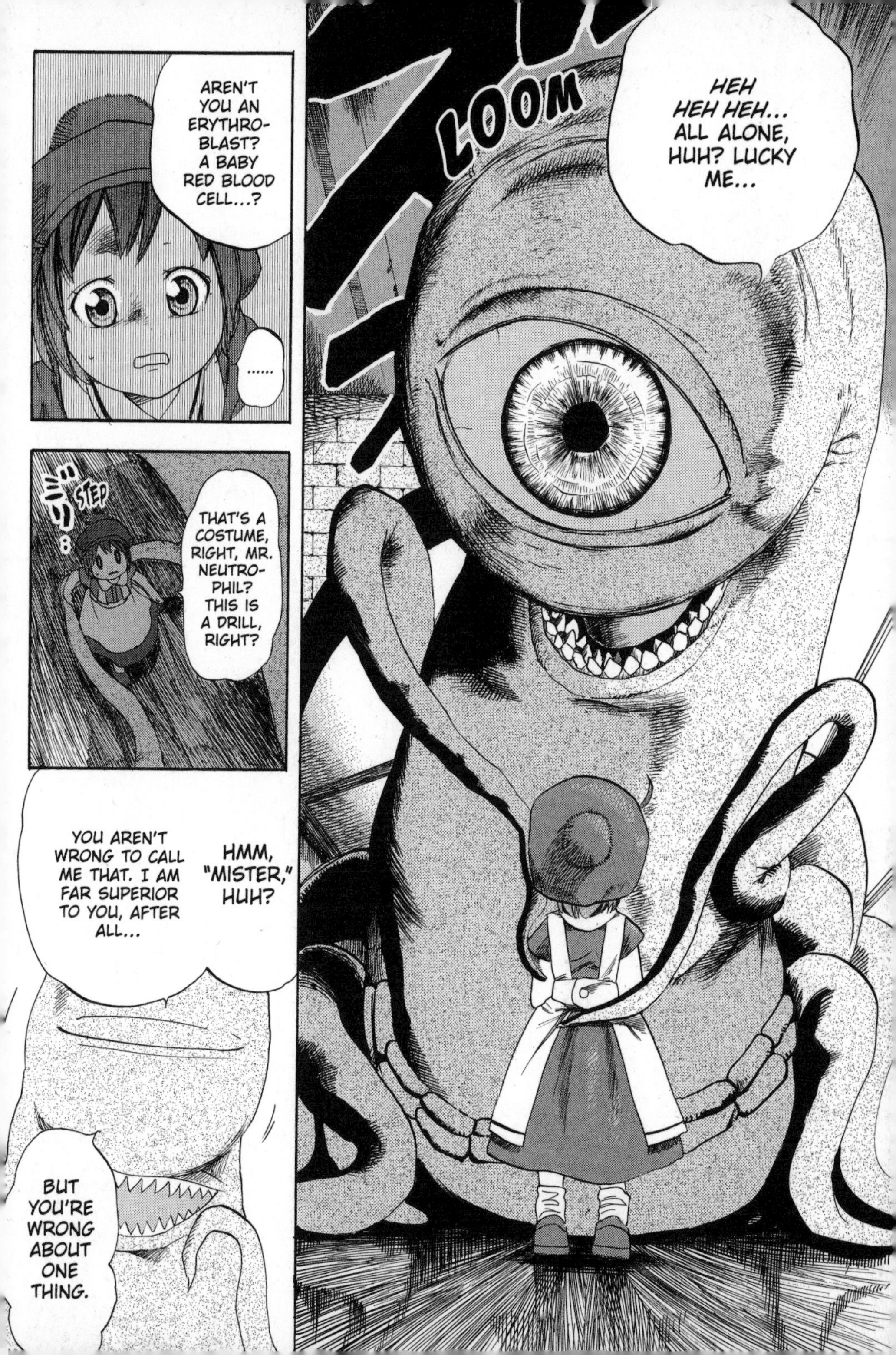
LOOM
HEH HEH HEH... ALL ALONE, HUH? LUCKY ME...
AREN'T YOU AN ERYTHRO-BLAST? A BABY RED BLOOD CELL...?
......
STEP
THAT'S A COSTUME, RIGHT, MR. NEUTRO-PHIL? THIS IS A DRILL, RIGHT?
HMM, "MISTER," HUH?
YOU AREN'T WRONG TO CALL ME THAT. I AM FAR SUPERIOR TO YOU, AFTER ALL...
BUT YOU'RE WRONG ABOUT ONE THING.

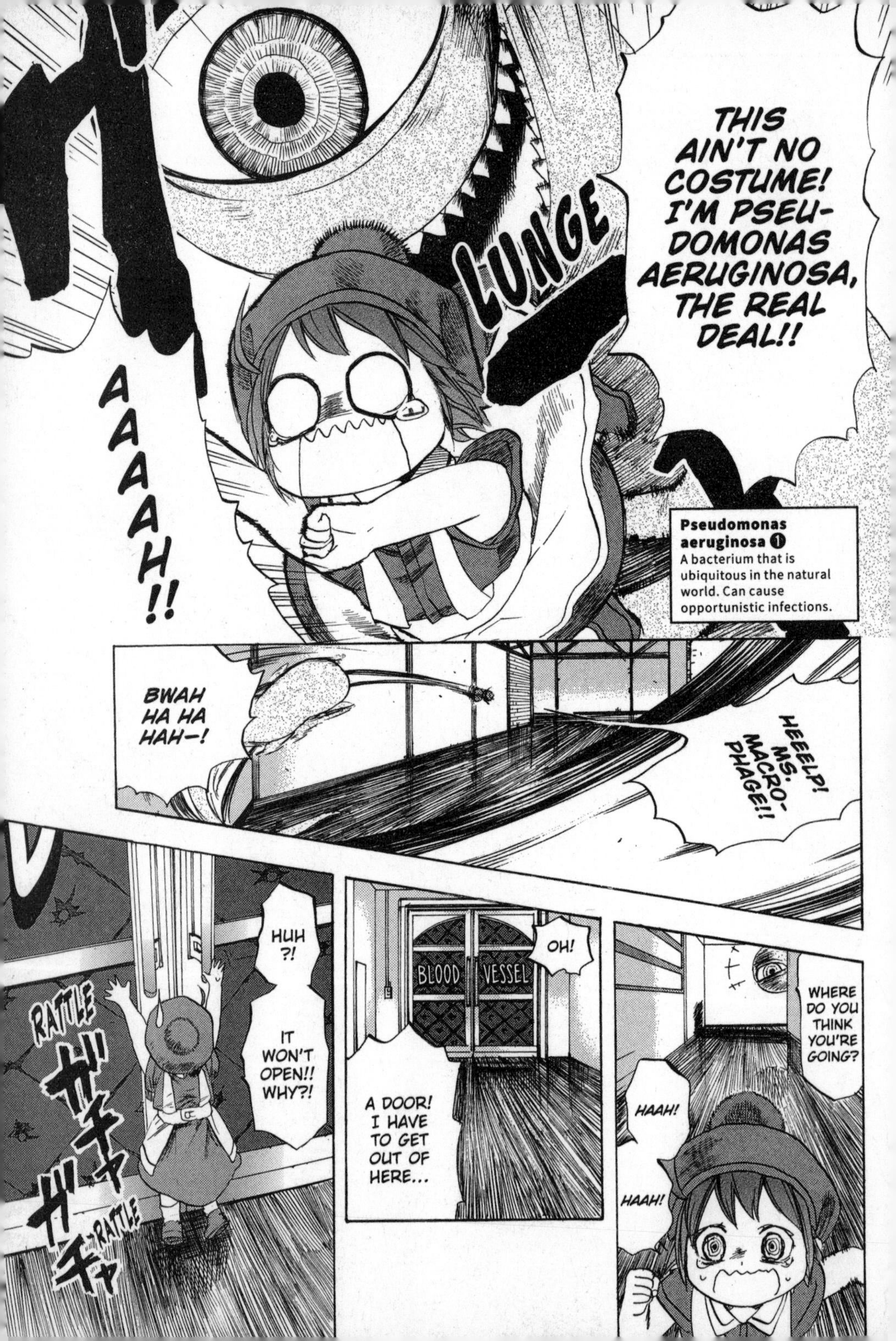
THIS AIN'T NO COSTUME! I'M PSEUDOMONAS AERUGINOSA, THE REAL DEAL!!
LUNGE
AAAAAH!!
Pseudomonas aeruginosa ①
A bacterium that is ubiquitous in the natural world. Can cause opportunistic infections.
HEEELP! MS. MACROPHAGE!!
BWAH HA HA HAH—!
WHERE DO YOU THINK YOU'RE GOING?
HAAH!
HAAH!
OH!
BLOOD VESSEL
A DOOR! I HAVE TO GET OUT OF HERE...
HUH?!
IT WON'T OPEN!! WHY?!
RATTLE
ガチャ
ガチャ
RATTLE

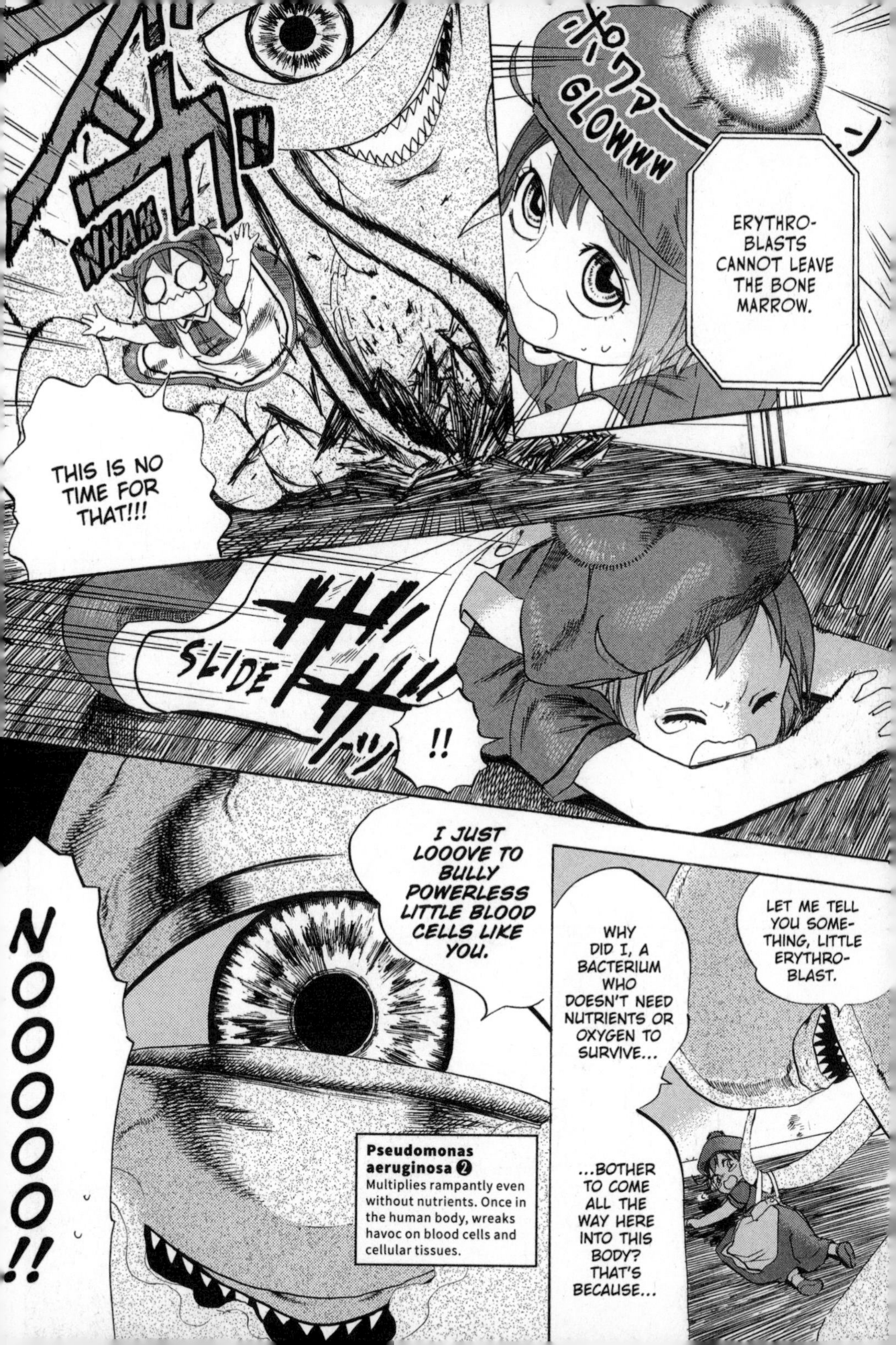
GLOWWW
ERYTHRO-BLASTS CANNOT LEAVE THE BONE MARROW.
WHAM
THIS IS NO TIME FOR THAT!!!
SLIDE
!!
LET ME TELL YOU SOME-THING, LITTLE ERYTHRO-BLAST.
WHY DID I, A BACTERIUM WHO DOESN'T NEED NUTRIENTS OR OXYGEN TO SURVIVE...
...BOTHER TO COME ALL THE WAY HERE INTO THIS BODY? THAT'S BECAUSE...
I JUST LOOOVE TO BULLY POWERLESS LITTLE BLOOD CELLS LIKE YOU.
NOOOOOO!!
Pseudomonas aeruginosa ❷
Multiplies rampantly even without nutrients. Once in the human body, wreaks havoc on blood cells and cellular tissues.

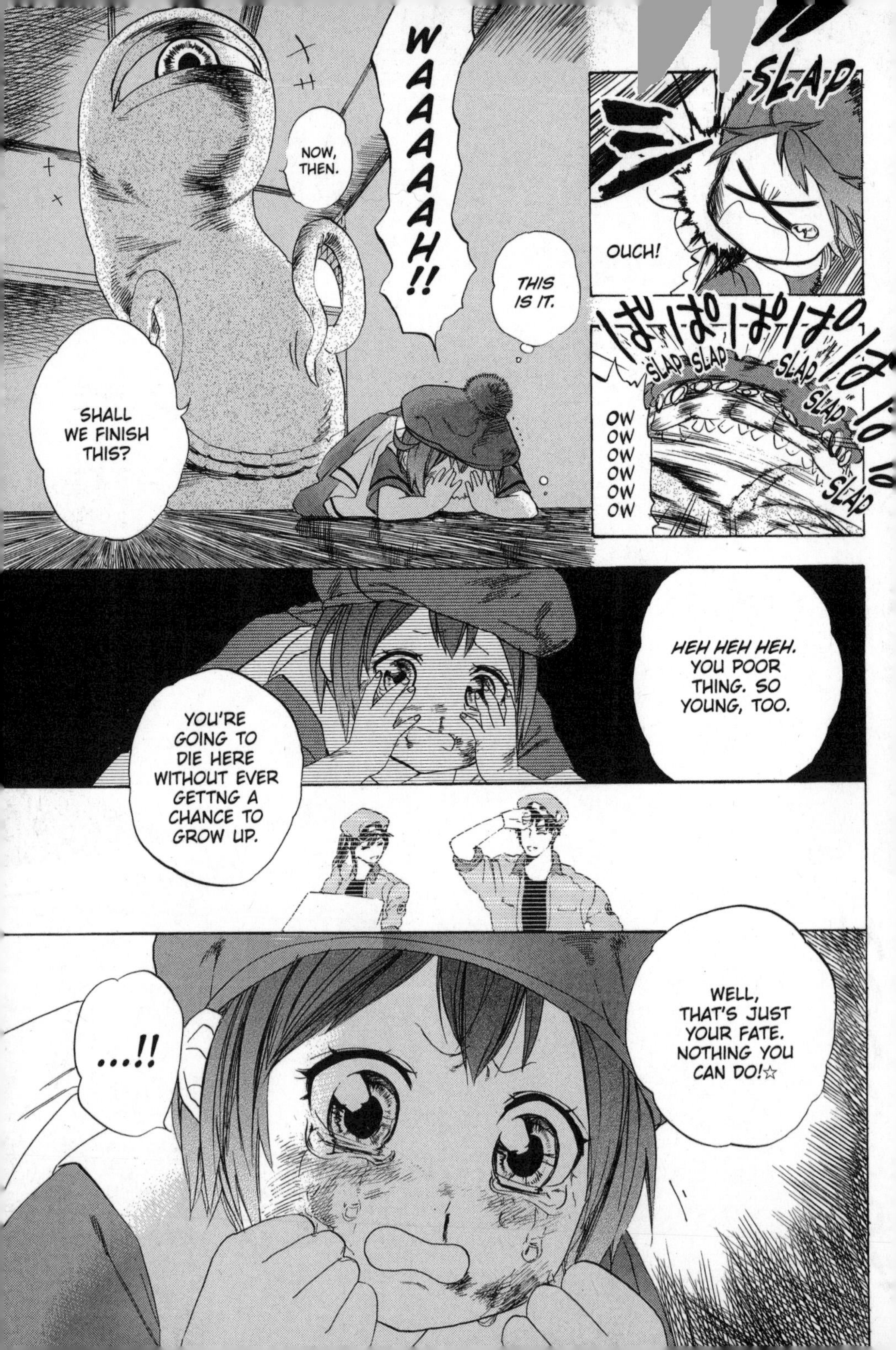
SLAP
OUCH!
SLAP SLAP SLAP SLAP SLAP
OW OW OW OW OW OW
WAAAAAAH!!
THIS IS IT.
NOW, THEN.
SHALL WE FINISH THIS?
HEH HEH HEH. YOU POOR THING. SO YOUNG, TOO.
YOU'RE GOING TO DIE HERE WITHOUT EVER GETTNG A CHANCE TO GROW UP.
WELL, THAT'S JUST YOUR FATE. NOTHING YOU CAN DO!☆
...!!

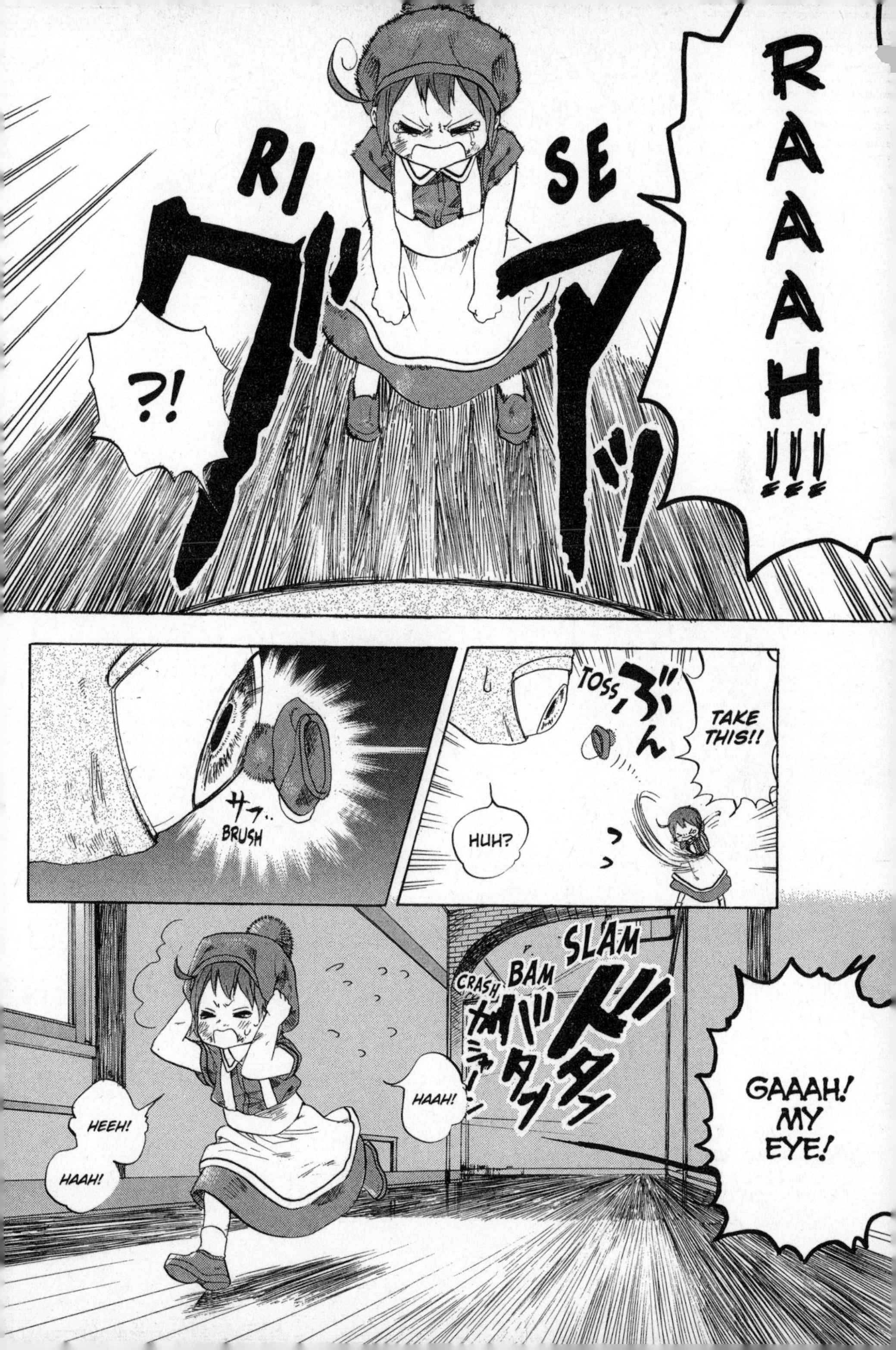
RAAAH!!!
RI SE
?!
TOSS
ぶん
TAKE THIS!!
HUH?
サッ..
BRUSH
GAAAH! MY EYE!
SLAM
BAM
CRASH
HAAH!
HEEH!
HAAH!

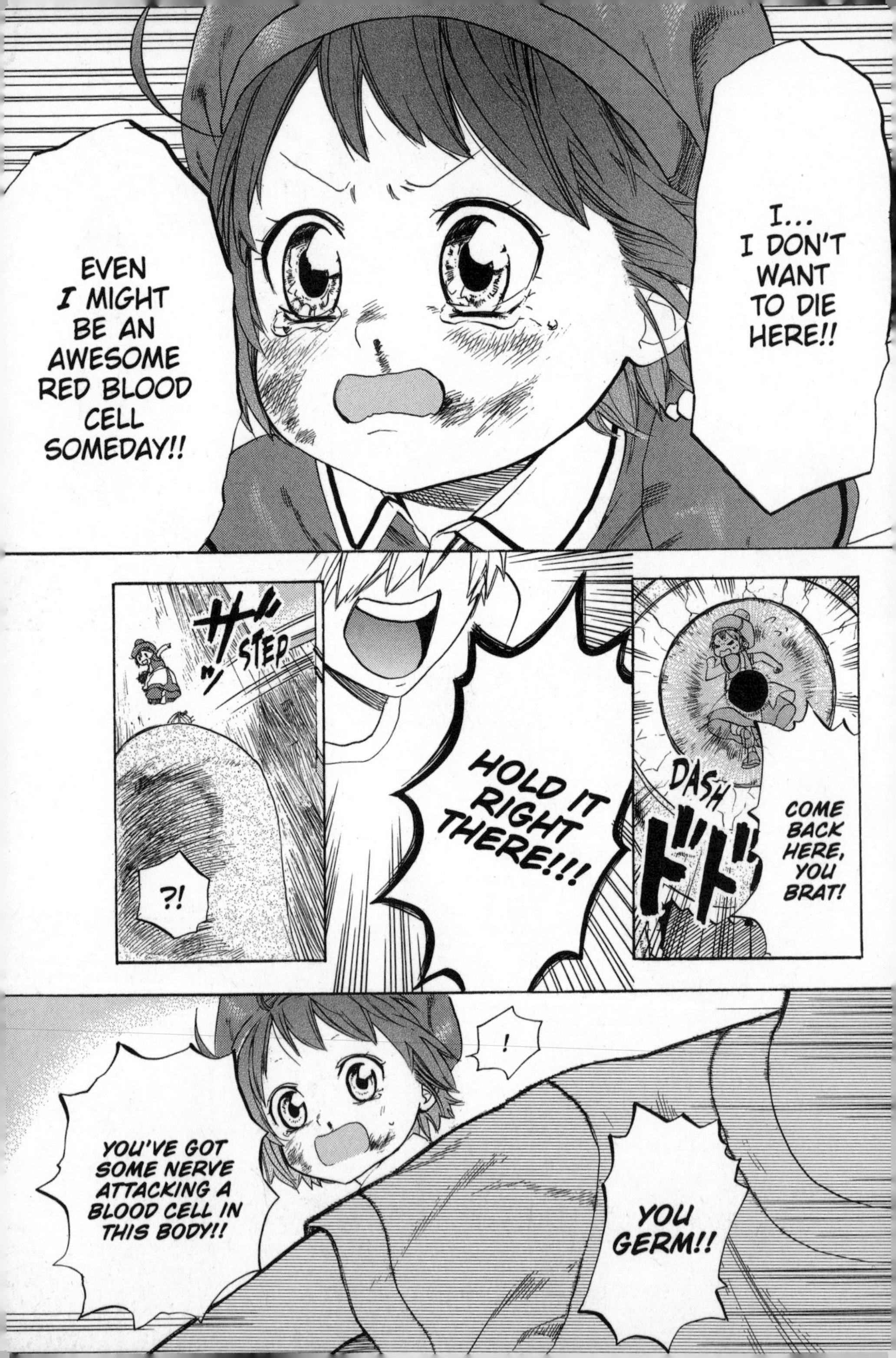
I... I DON'T WANT TO DIE HERE!!
EVEN I MIGHT BE AN AWESOME RED BLOOD CELL SOMEDAY!!
DASH
ドド
COME BACK HERE, YOU BRAT!
HOLD IT RIGHT THERE!!!
ザッ
STEP
?!
!
YOU'VE GOT SOME NERVE ATTACKING A BLOOD CELL IN THIS BODY!!
YOU GERM!!

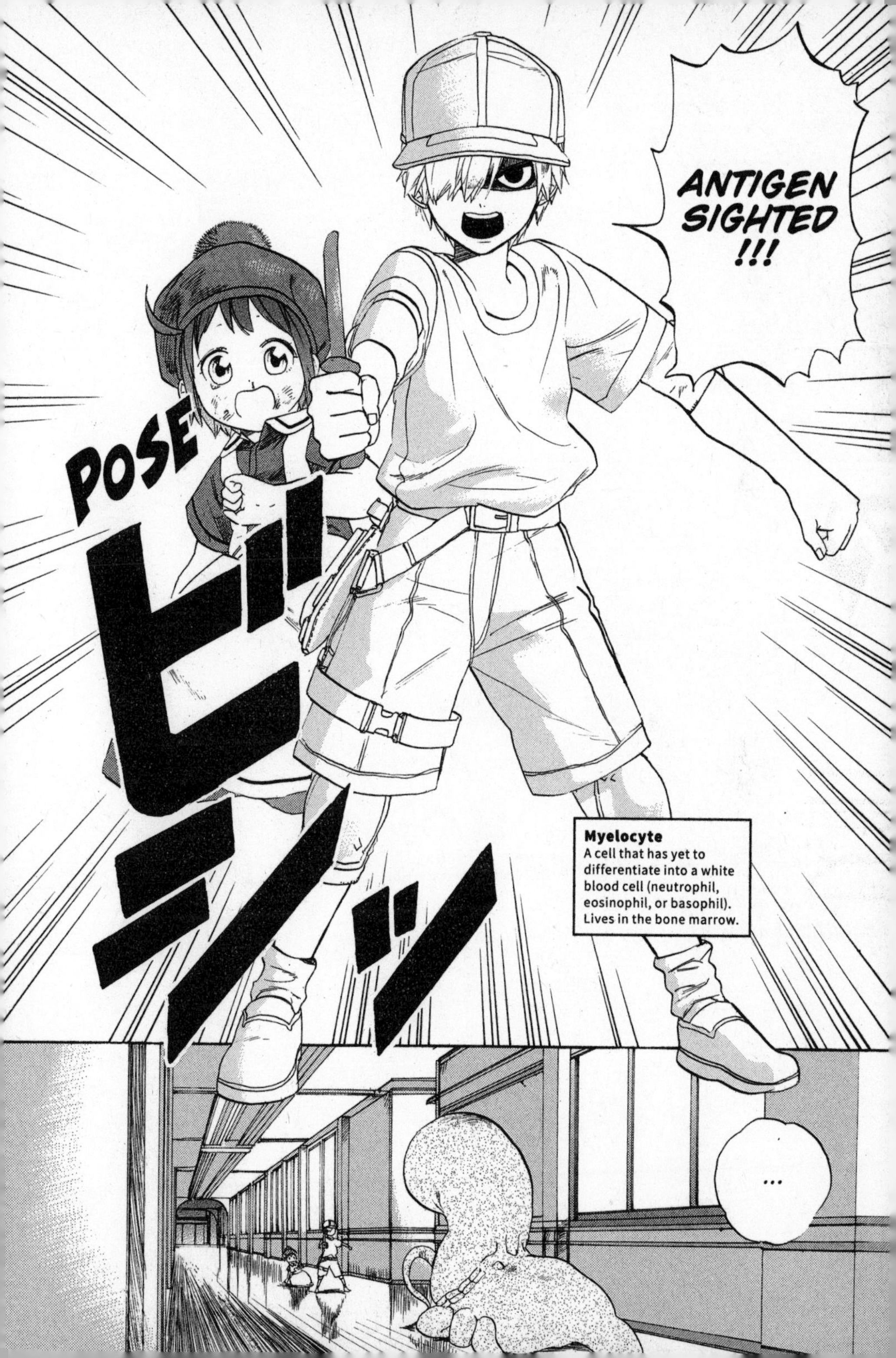
ANTIGEN SIGHTED !!!
POSE
Myelocyte
A cell that has yet to differentiate into a white blood cell (neutrophil, eosinophil, or basophil). Lives in the bone marrow.
...

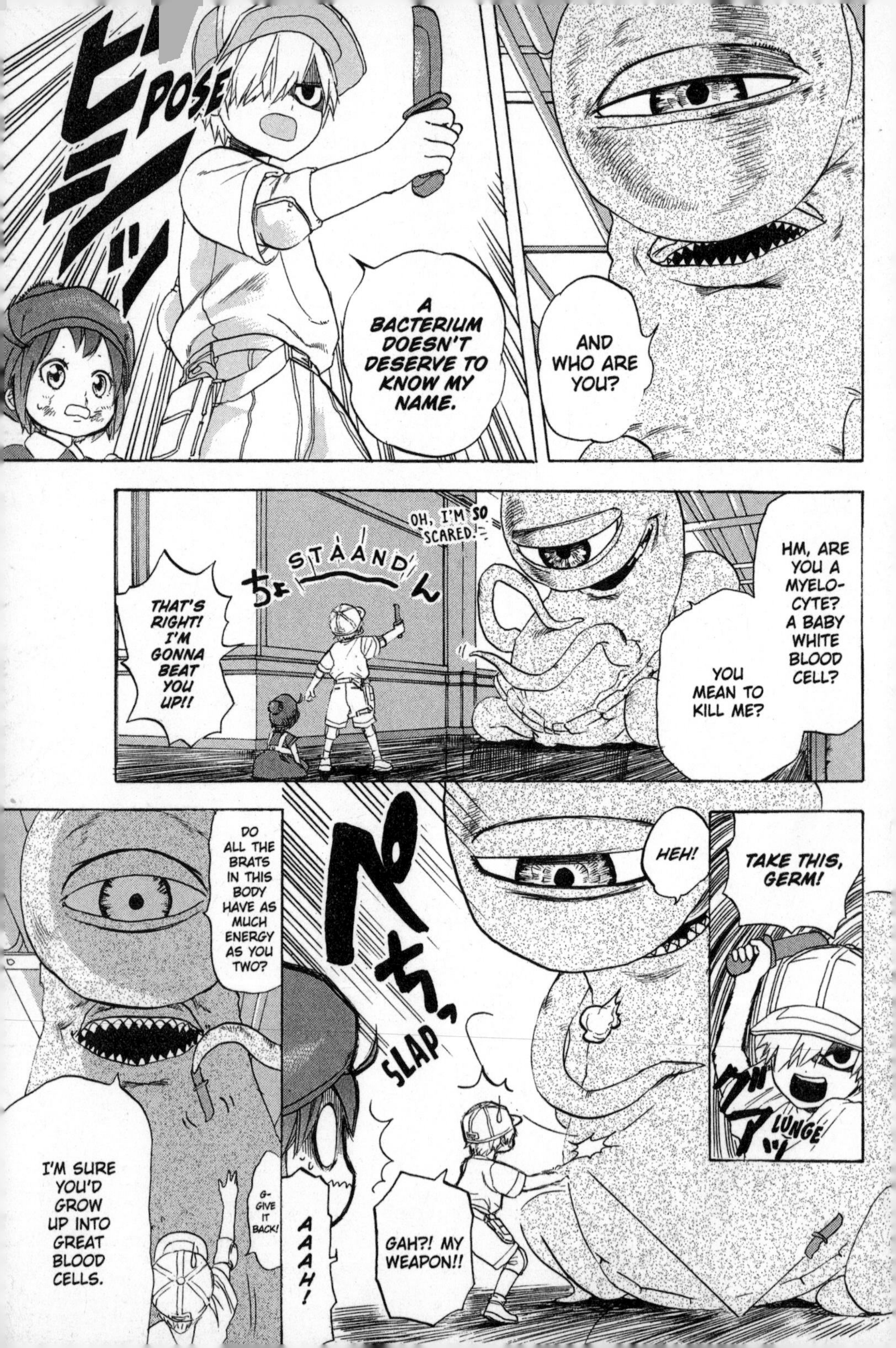
AND WHO ARE YOU?
POSE
A BACTERIUM DOESN'T DESERVE TO KNOW MY NAME.
HM, ARE YOU A MYELOCYTE? A BABY WHITE BLOOD CELL?
YOU MEAN TO KILL ME?
OH, I'M SO SCARED.
STAAND
THAT'S RIGHT! I'M GONNA BEAT YOU UP!!
TAKE THIS, GERM!
LUNGE
HEH!
SLAP
GAH?! MY WEAPON!!
AAAAH!
G-GIVE IT BACK!
DO ALL THE BRATS IN THIS BODY HAVE AS MUCH ENERGY AS YOU TWO?
I'M SURE YOU'D GROW UP INTO GREAT BLOOD CELLS.

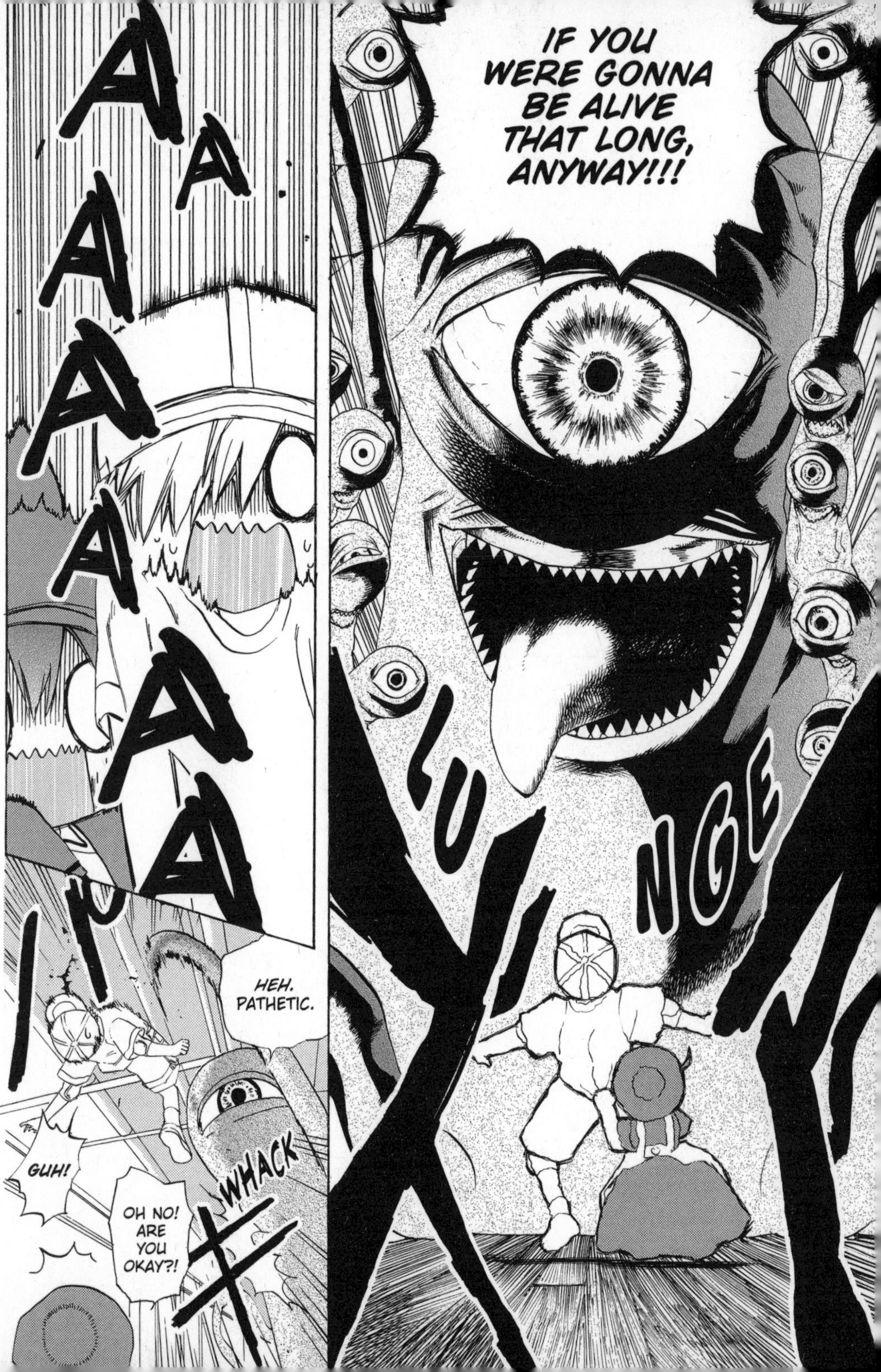
IF YOU WERE GONNA BE ALIVE THAT LONG, ANYWAY!!!
LUNGE
AAAAAAAAAAAH!
HEH. PATHETIC.
WHACK
GUH!
OH NO! ARE YOU OKAY?!

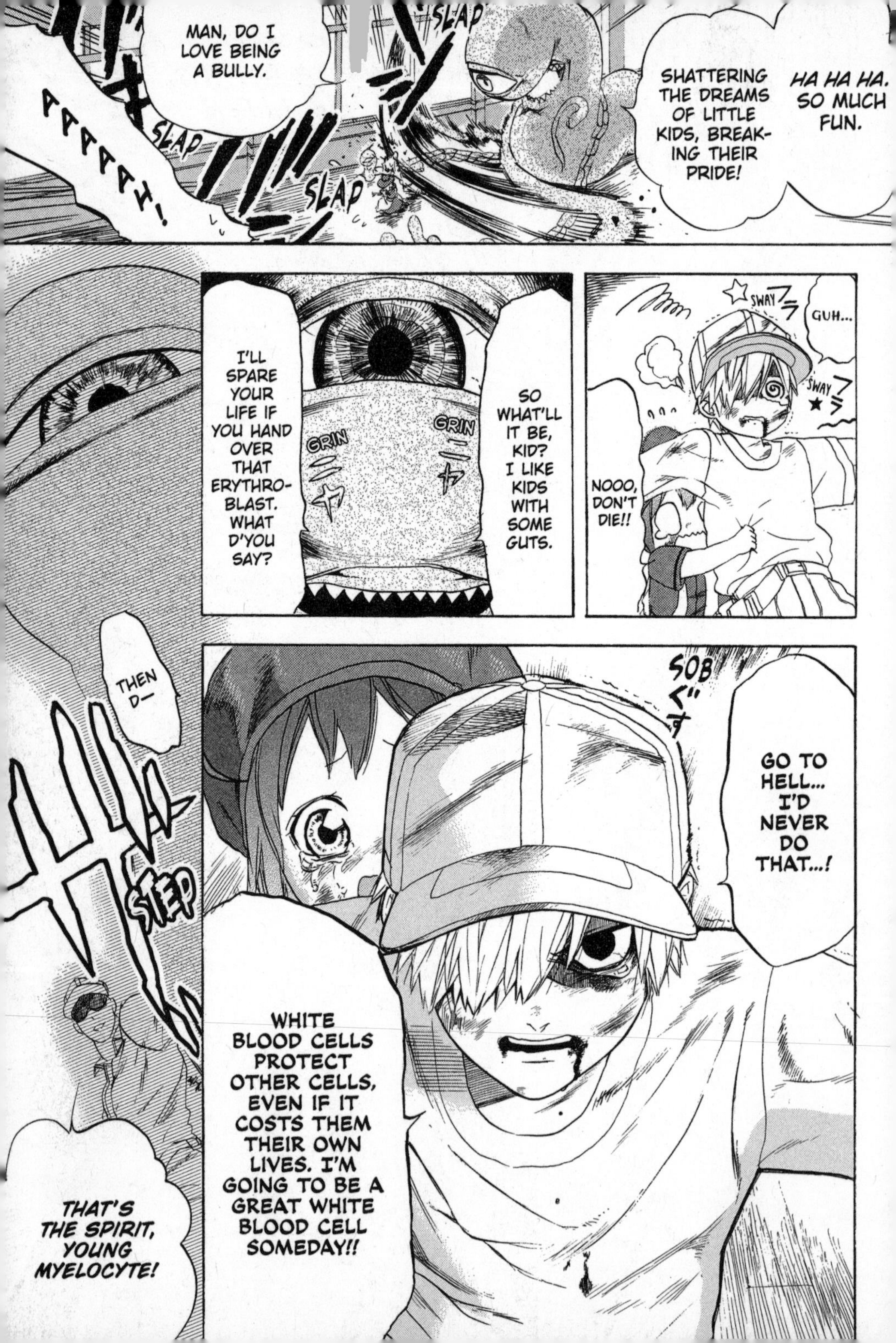
HA HA HA. SO MUCH FUN.
SHATTERING THE DREAMS OF LITTLE KIDS, BREAKING THEIR PRIDE!
SLAP
SLAP
MAN, DO I LOVE BEING A BULLY.
SLAP
SLAP
AAAAAAH!
SWAY
GUH...
SWAY
NOOO, DON'T DIE!!
SO WHAT'LL IT BE, KID? I LIKE KIDS WITH SOME GUTS.
GRIN
GRIN
I'LL SPARE YOUR LIFE IF YOU HAND OVER THAT ERYTHROBLAST. WHAT D'YOU SAY?
SOB
GO TO HELL... I'D NEVER DO THAT...!
WHITE BLOOD CELLS PROTECT OTHER CELLS, EVEN IF IT COSTS THEM THEIR OWN LIVES. I'M GOING TO BE A GREAT WHITE BLOOD CELL SOMEDAY!!
THEN D—
STEP
THAT'S THE SPIRIT, YOUNG MYELOCYTE!

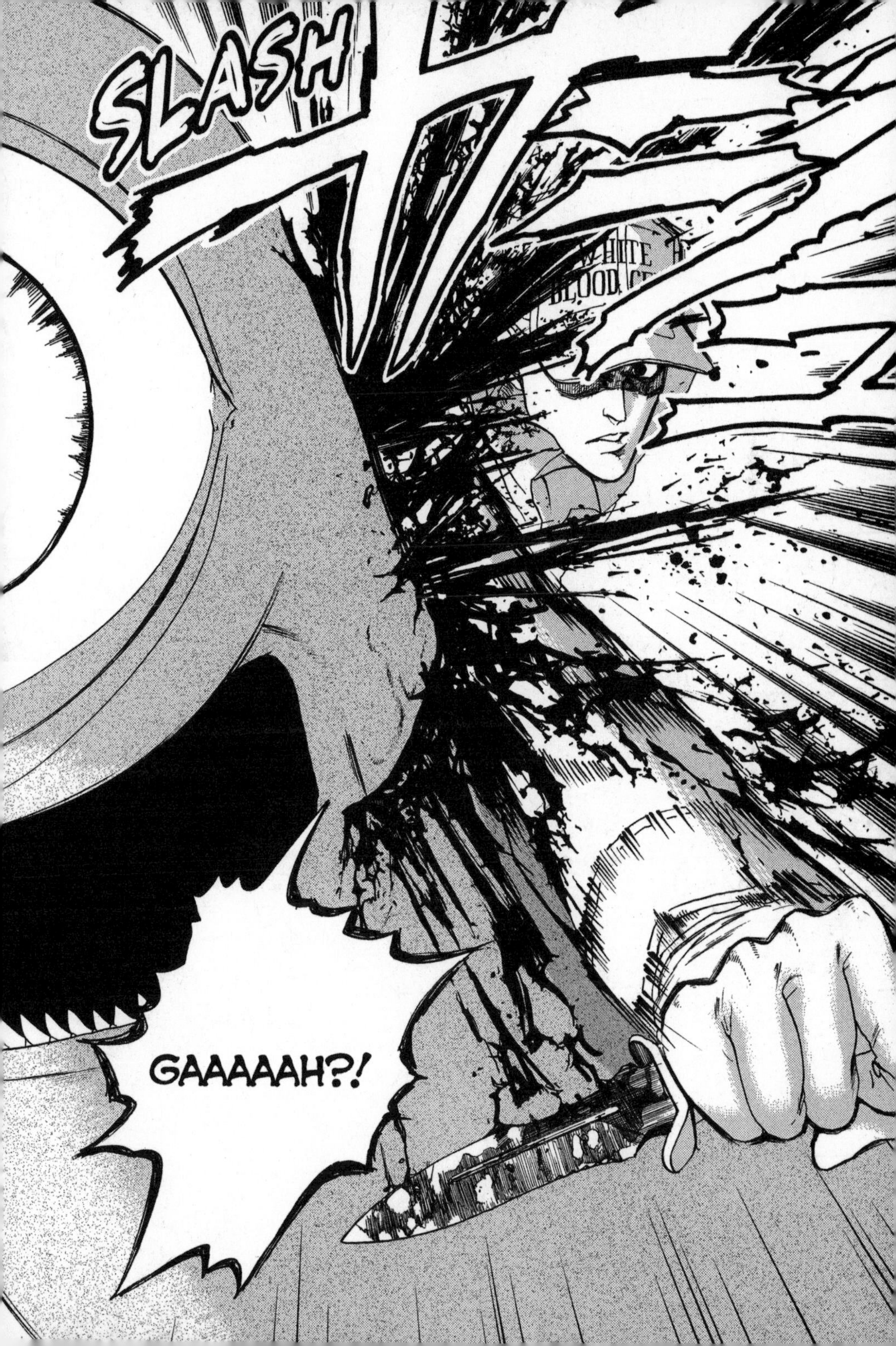
SLASH
GAAAAAH?!

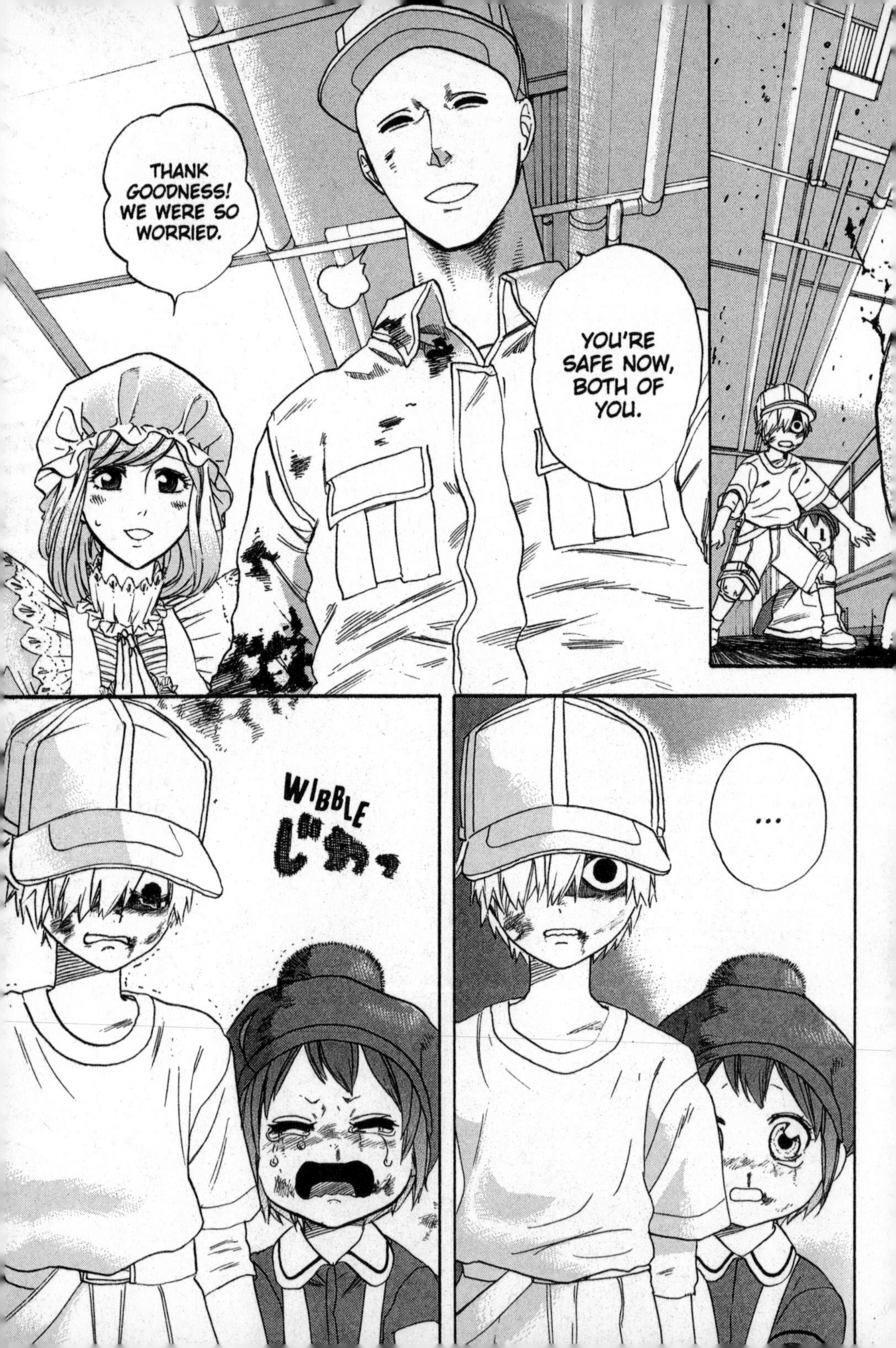

YOU'RE SAFE NOW, BOTH OF YOU.
THANK GOODNESS! WE WERE SO WORRIED.
...
WIBBLE
じわっ

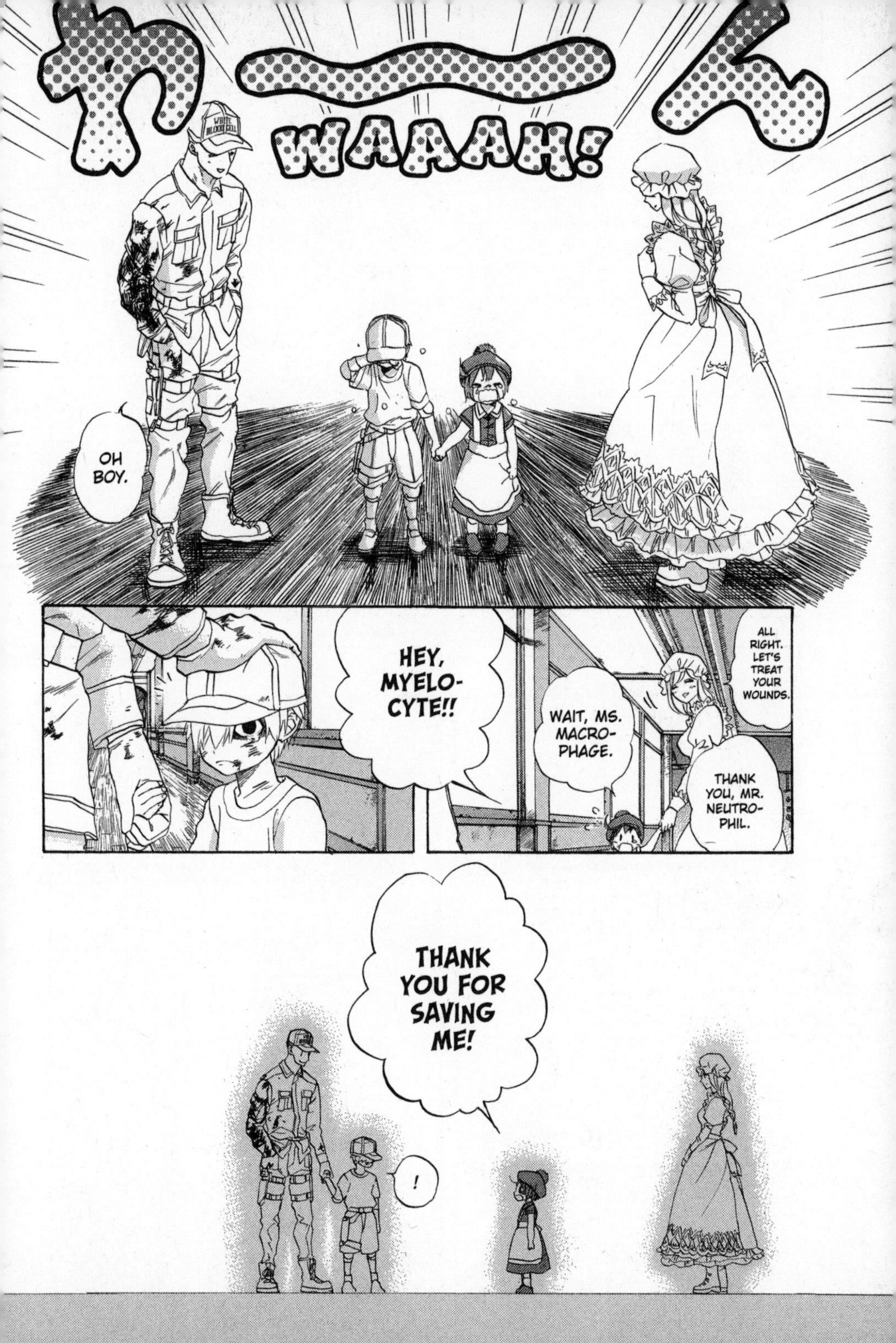
わーーん
WAAAAH!
OH BOY.
ALL RIGHT. LET'S TREAT YOUR WOUNDS.
THANK YOU, MR. NEUTRO-PHIL.
WAIT, MS. MACRO-PHAGE.
HEY, MYELO-CYTE!!
THANK YOU FOR SAVING ME!
!

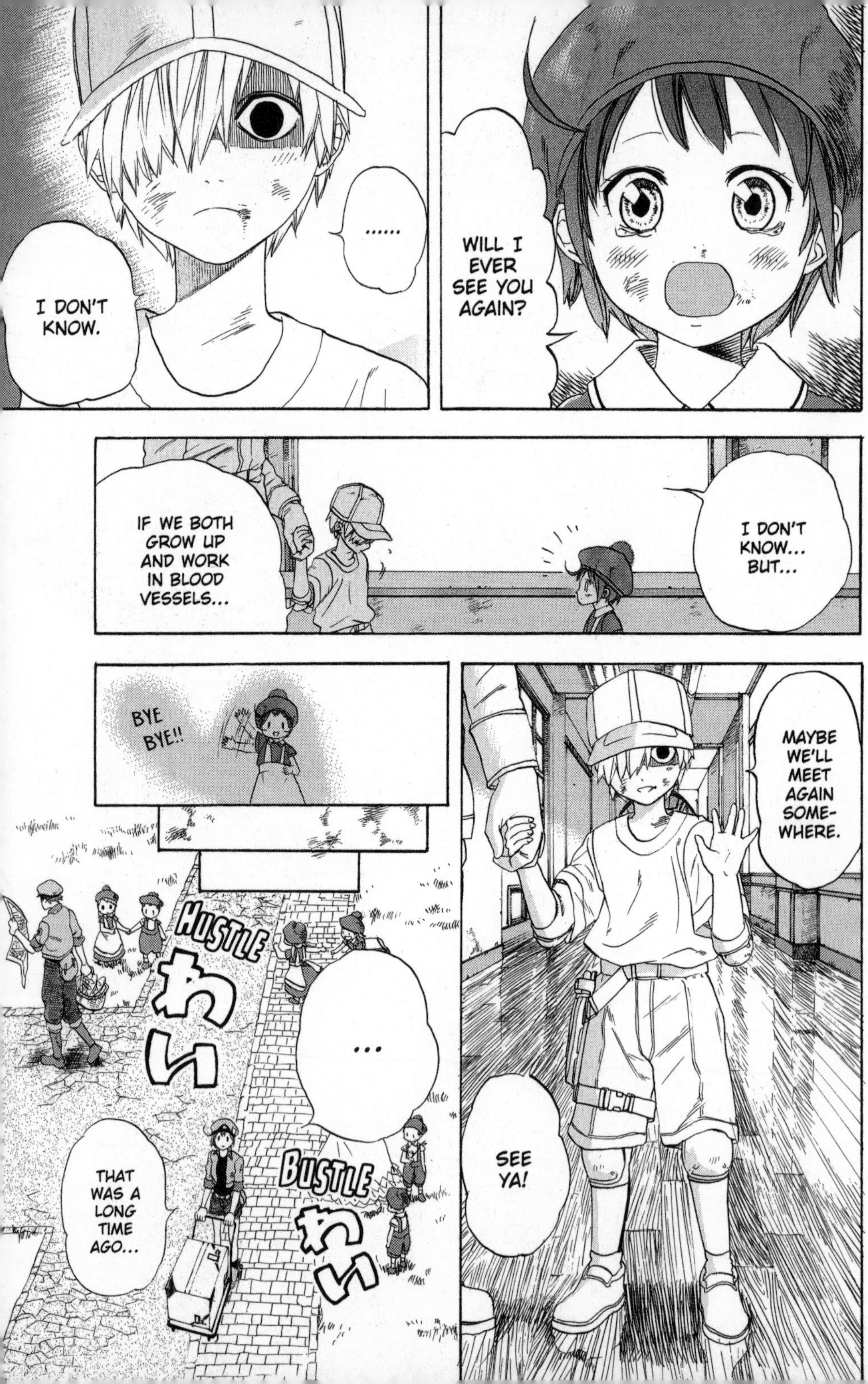
WILL I EVER SEE YOU AGAIN?
......
I DON'T KNOW.
I DON'T KNOW... BUT...
IF WE BOTH GROW UP AND WORK IN BLOOD VESSELS...
MAYBE WE'LL MEET AGAIN SOME-WHERE.
SEE YA!
BYE BYE!!
...
HUSTLE わい
BUSTLE わい
THAT WAS A LONG TIME AGO...

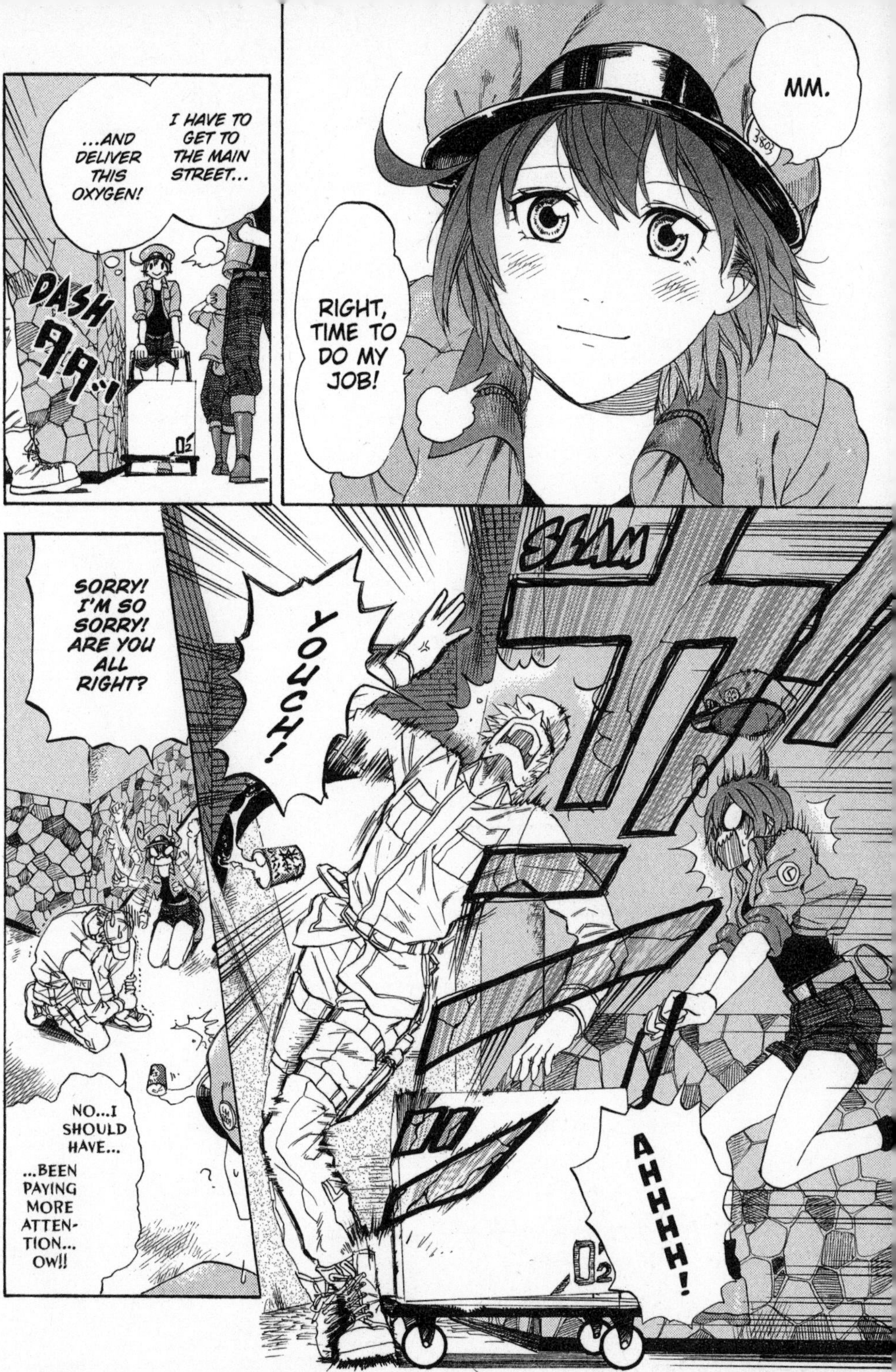
MM.
RIGHT, TIME TO DO MY JOB!
I HAVE TO GET TO THE MAIN STREET...
...AND DELIVER THIS OXYGEN!
DASH
SLAM
YOUCH!
AHHHH!
SORRY! I'M SO SORRY! ARE YOU ALL RIGHT?
NO...I SHOULD HAVE...
...BEEN PAYING MORE ATTENTION... OW!!

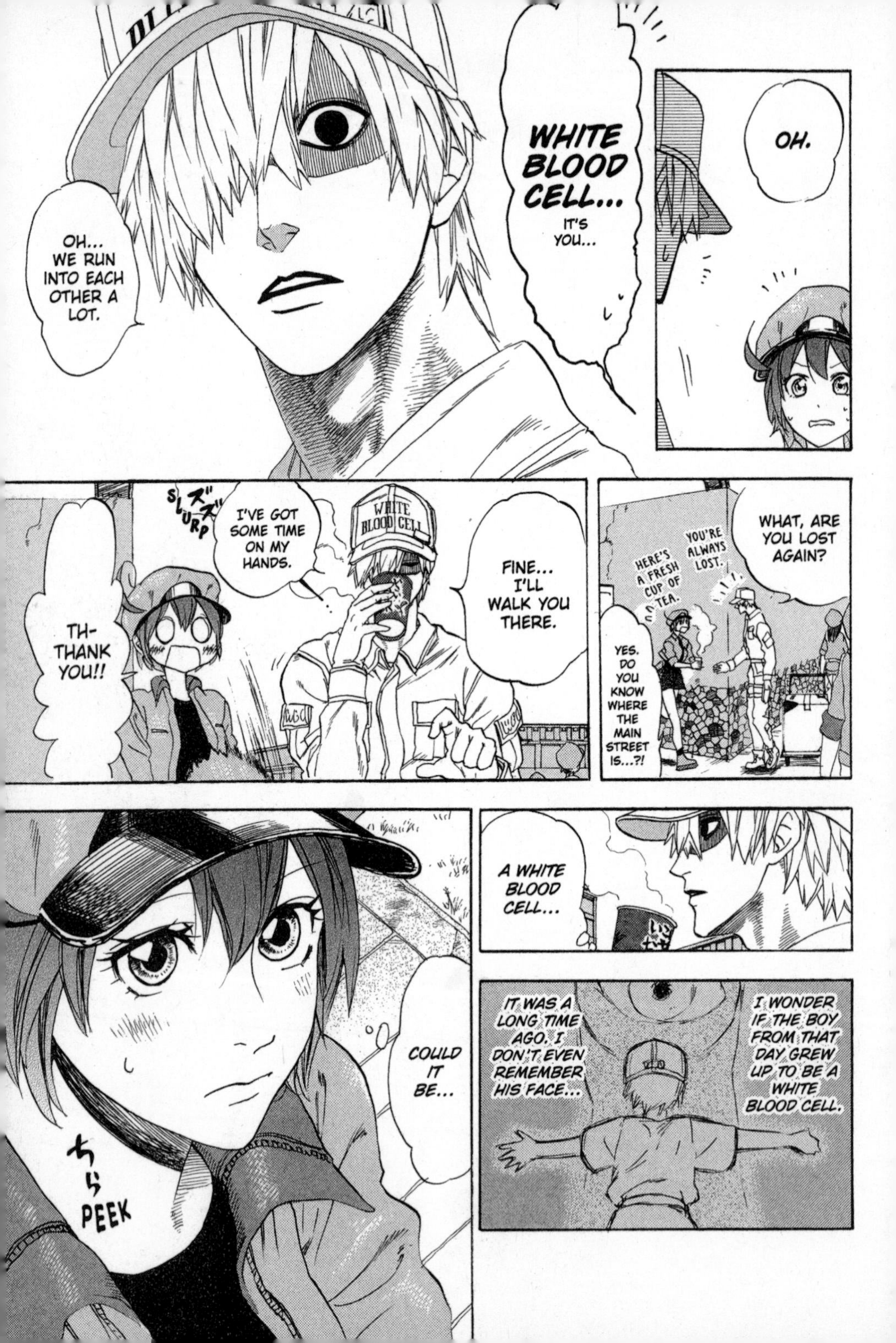
OH.
WHITE BLOOD CELL...
IT'S YOU...
OH... WE RUN INTO EACH OTHER A LOT.
WHAT, ARE YOU LOST AGAIN?
YOU'RE ALWAYS LOST.
HERE'S A FRESH CUP OF TEA.
YES. DO YOU KNOW WHERE THE MAIN STREET IS...?!
FINE... I'LL WALK YOU THERE.
I'VE GOT SOME TIME ON MY HANDS.
ズズ SLURP
TH-THANK YOU!!
A WHITE BLOOD CELL...
I WONDER IF THE BOY FROM THAT DAY GREW UP TO BE A WHITE BLOOD CELL.
IT WAS A LONG TIME AGO. I DON'T EVEN REMEMBER HIS FACE...
COULD IT BE...
ちら PEEK

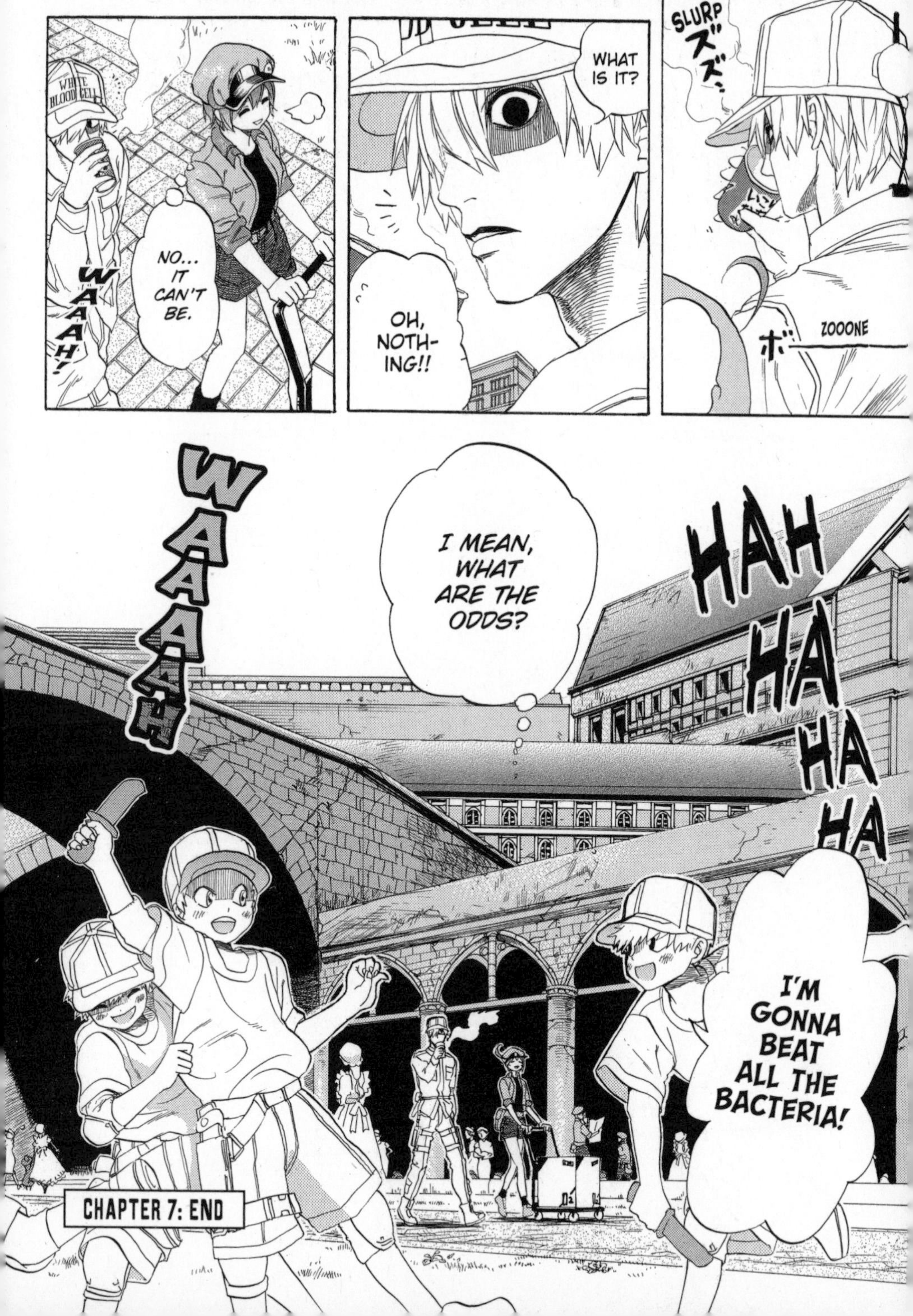
SLURP
ズズ…
ボ
ZOOONE
WHAT IS IT?
OH, NOTHING!!
NO... IT CAN'T BE.
WAAAAH!
HAH HA HA HA HA
I'M GONNA BEAT ALL THE BACTERIA!
I MEAN, WHAT ARE THE ODDS?
WAAAAAH
CHAPTER 7: END

ENUCLEATION OF ERYTHROBLASTS

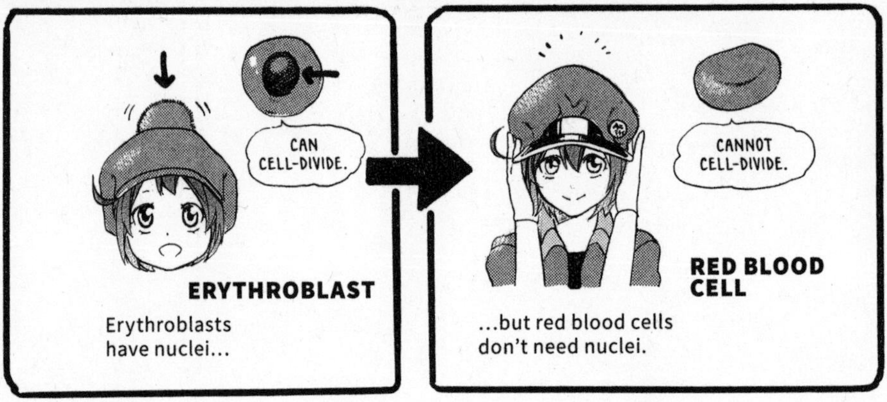
CAN CELL-DIVIDE.
ERYTHROBLAST
Erythroblasts have nuclei...
CANNOT CELL-DIVIDE.
RED BLOOD CELL
...but red blood cells don't need nuclei.

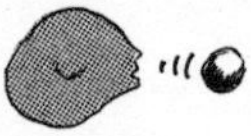

This is called **enucleation.**

This is a mark of becoming a full-fledged red blood cell.

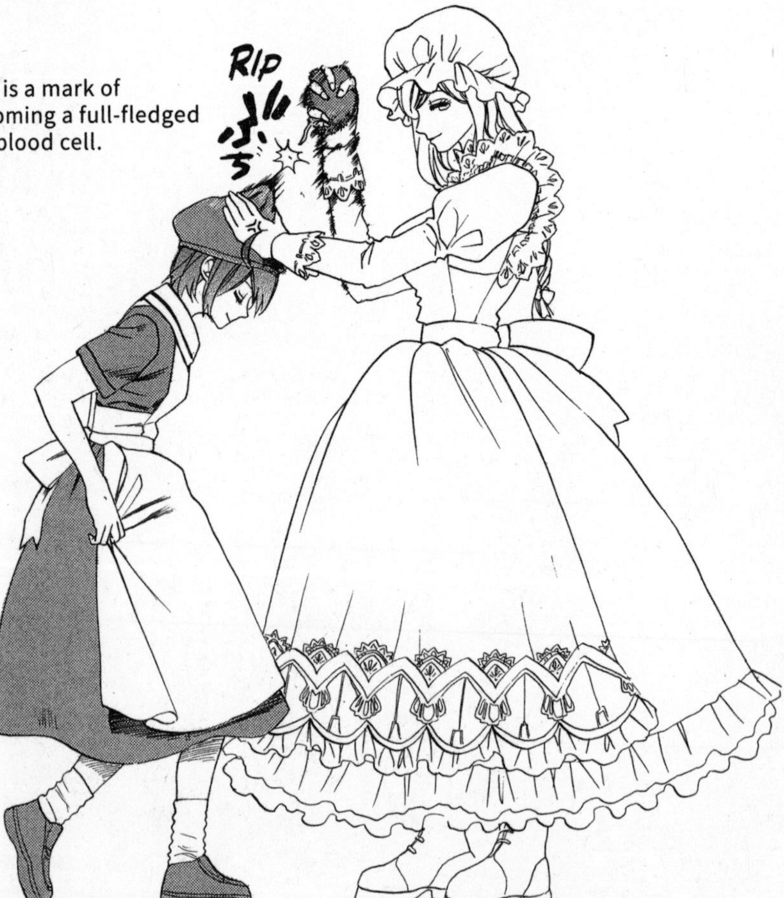
RIP
ぶち

Cells at Work!

はたらく細胞

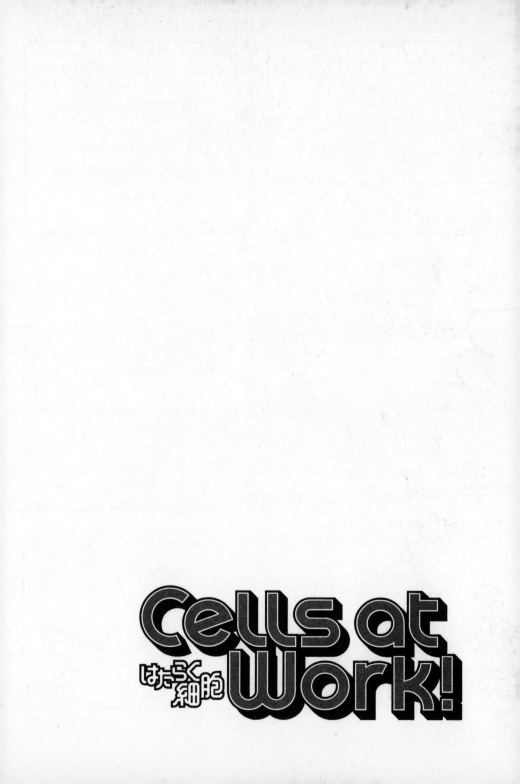

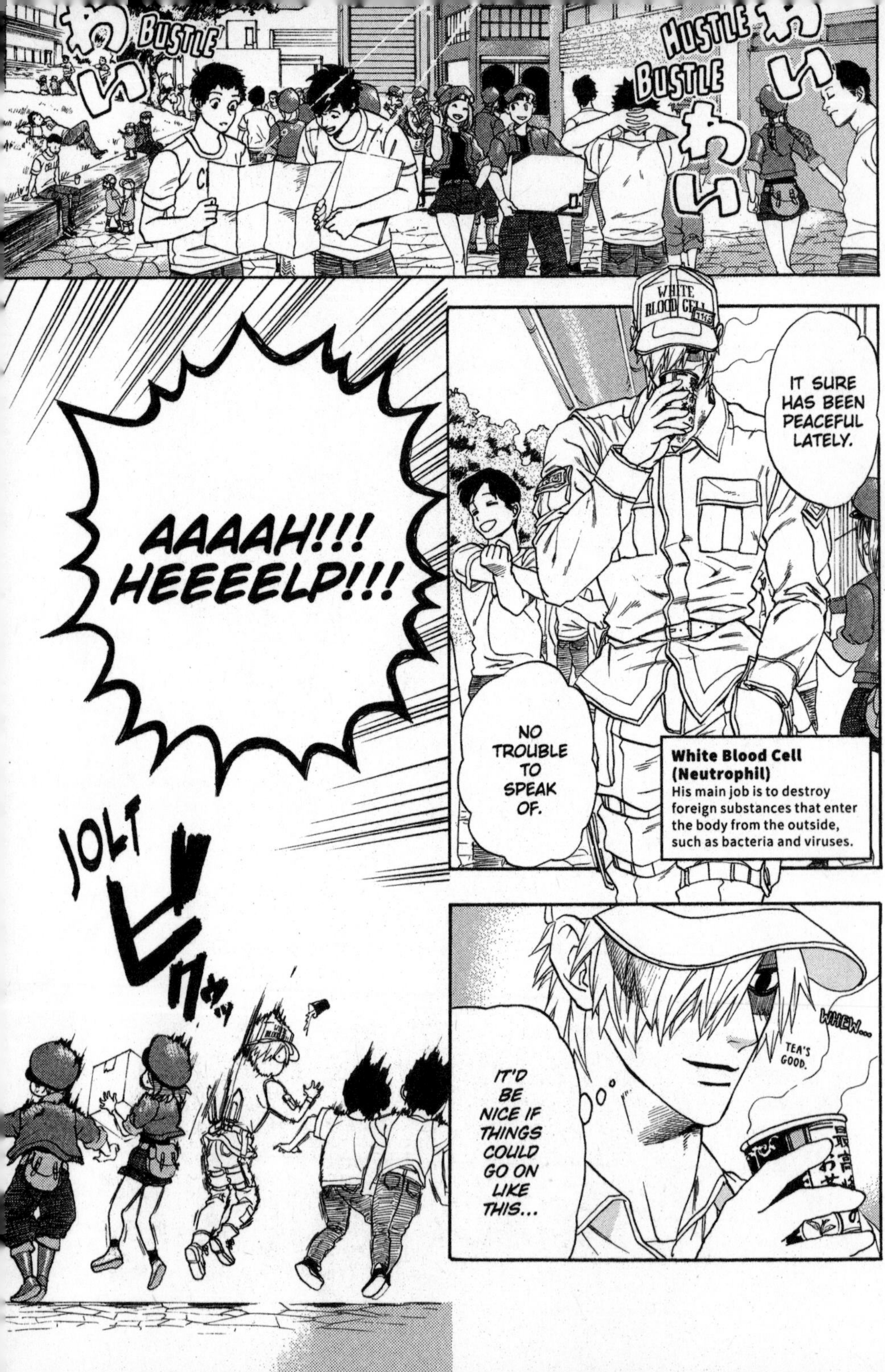
わい わい
HUSTLE BUSTLE
わい わい
BUSTLE
IT SURE HAS BEEN PEACEFUL LATELY.
NO TROUBLE TO SPEAK OF.
White Blood Cell (Neutrophil)
His main job is to destroy foreign substances that enter the body from the outside, such as bacteria and viruses.
WHEW...
TEA'S GOOD.
IT'D BE NICE IF THINGS COULD GO ON LIKE THIS...
AAAAH!!! HEEEEELP!!!
JOLT
ビクッ

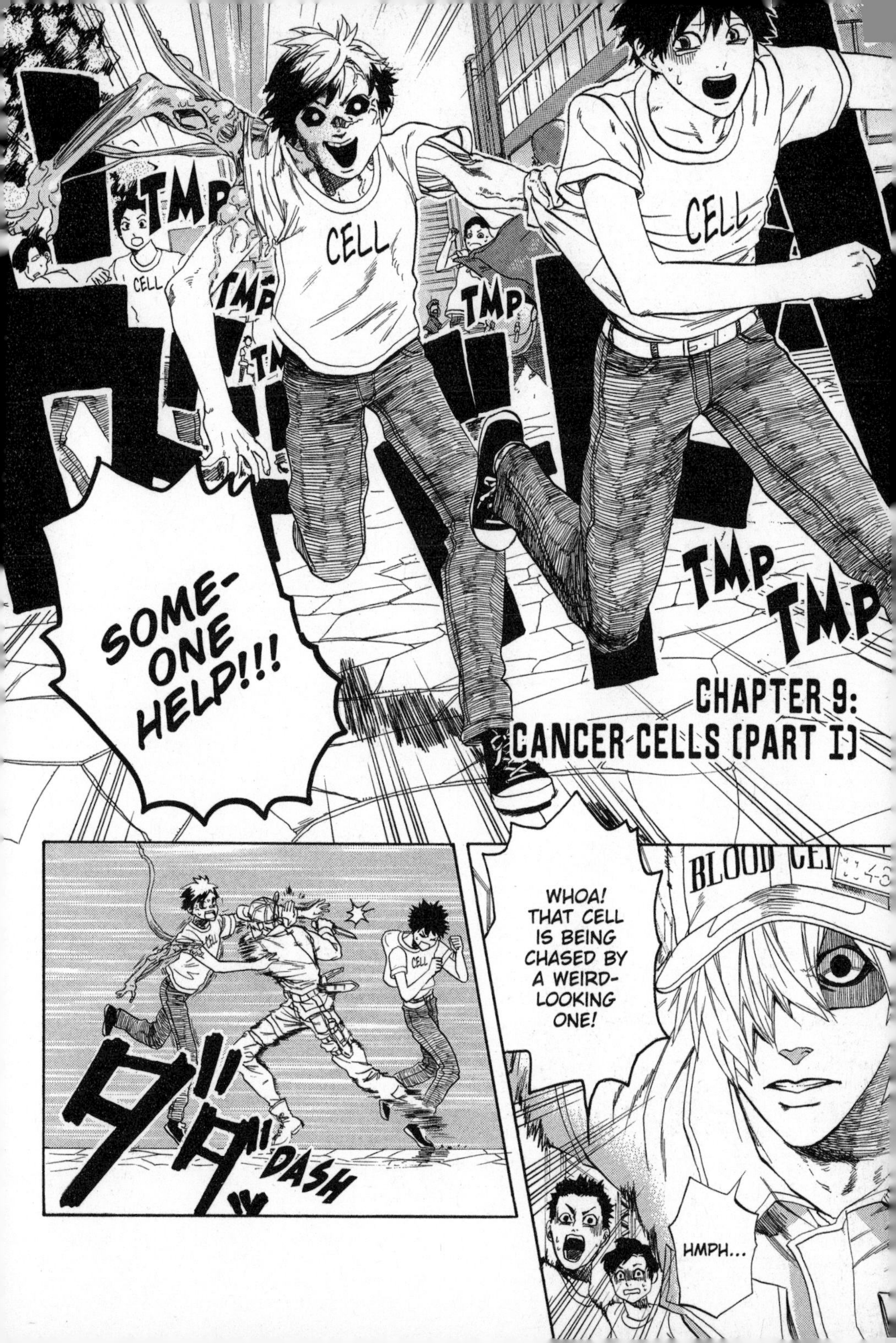
TMP
TMP
TMP
TMP
CELL
CELL
CELL
SOME-ONE HELP!!!
TMP TMP
CHAPTER 9: CANCER CELLS (PART I)
WHOA! THAT CELL IS BEING CHASED BY A WEIRD-LOOKING ONE!
HMPH...
CELL
CELL
DASH

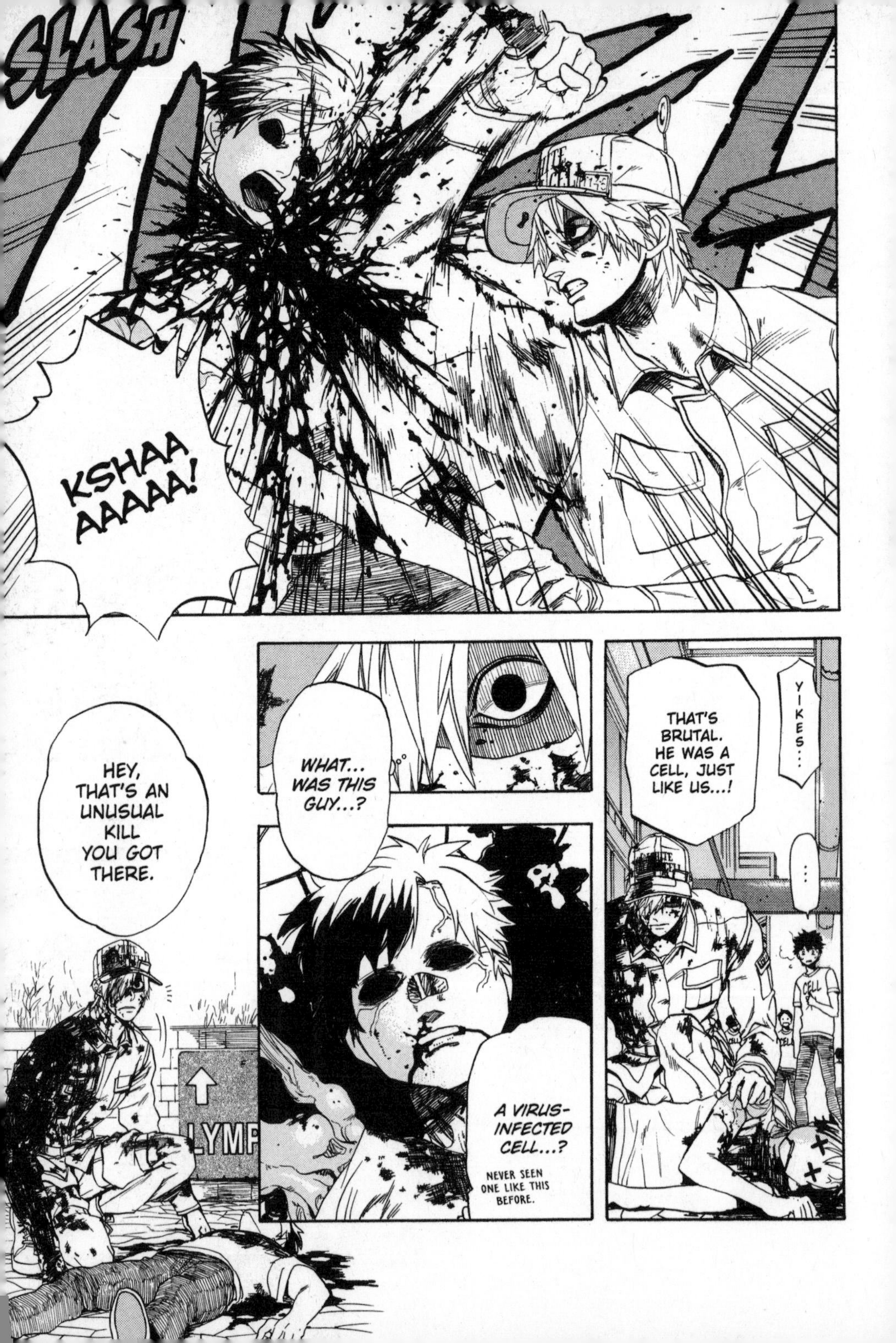
SLASH
KSHAA AAAAA!
YIKES...
THAT'S BRUTAL. HE WAS A CELL, JUST LIKE US...!
...
WHAT... WAS THIS GUY...?
A VIRUS-INFECTED CELL...?
NEVER SEEN ONE LIKE THIS BEFORE.
HEY, THAT'S AN UNUSUAL KILL YOU GOT THERE.
LYMP

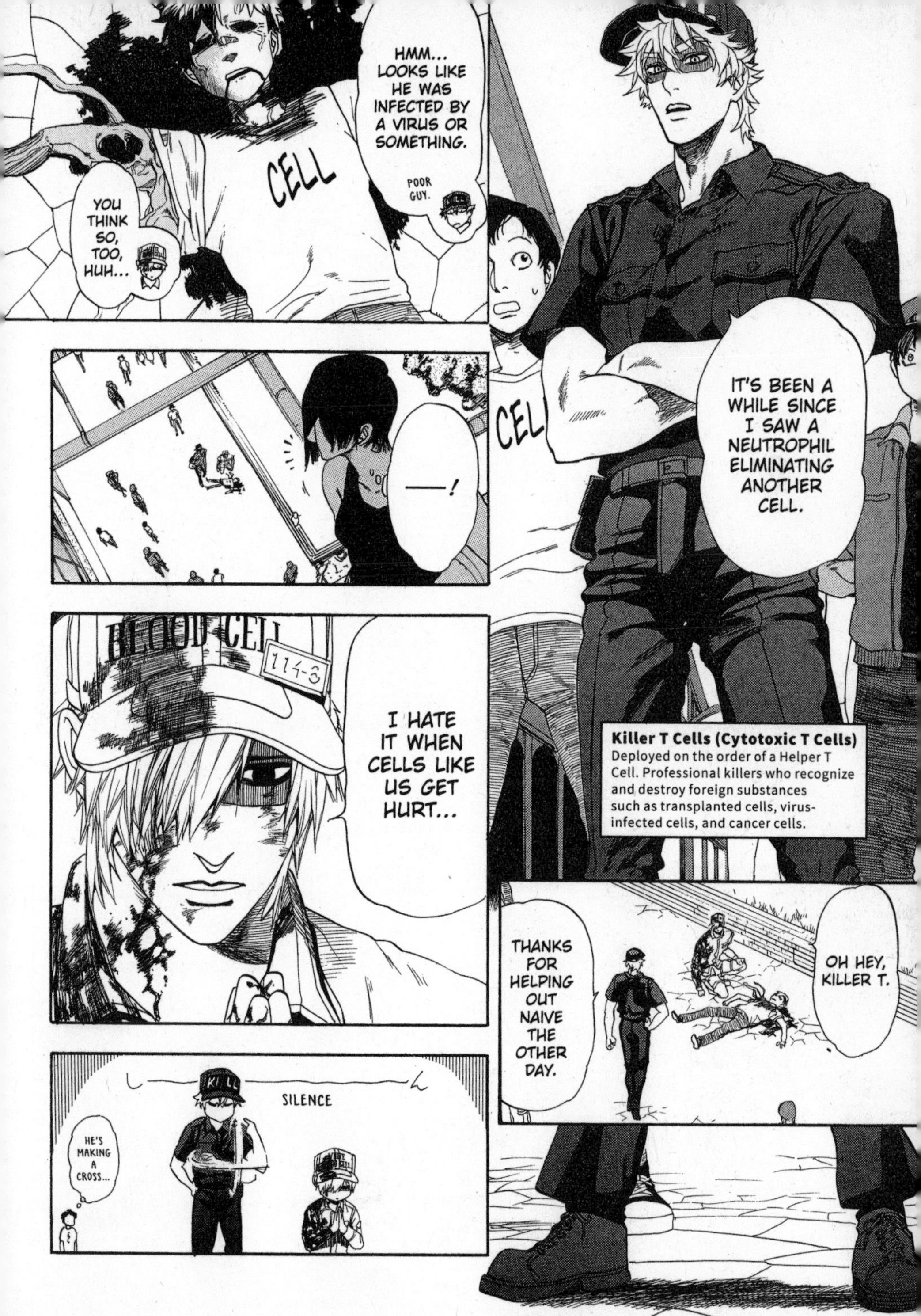
IT'S BEEN A WHILE SINCE I SAW A NEUTROPHIL ELIMINATING ANOTHER CELL.
Killer T Cells (Cytotoxic T Cells)
Deployed on the order of a Helper T Cell. Professional killers who recognize and destroy foreign substances such as transplanted cells, virus-infected cells, and cancer cells.
OH HEY, KILLER T.
THANKS FOR HELPING OUT NAIVE THE OTHER DAY.
HMM... LOOKS LIKE HE WAS INFECTED BY A VIRUS OR SOMETHING.
POOR GUY.
CELL
YOU THINK SO, TOO, HUH...
—!
CELL
BLOOD CELL
1146
I HATE IT WHEN CELLS LIKE US GET HURT...
SILENCE
KILL
HE'S MAKING A CROSS...

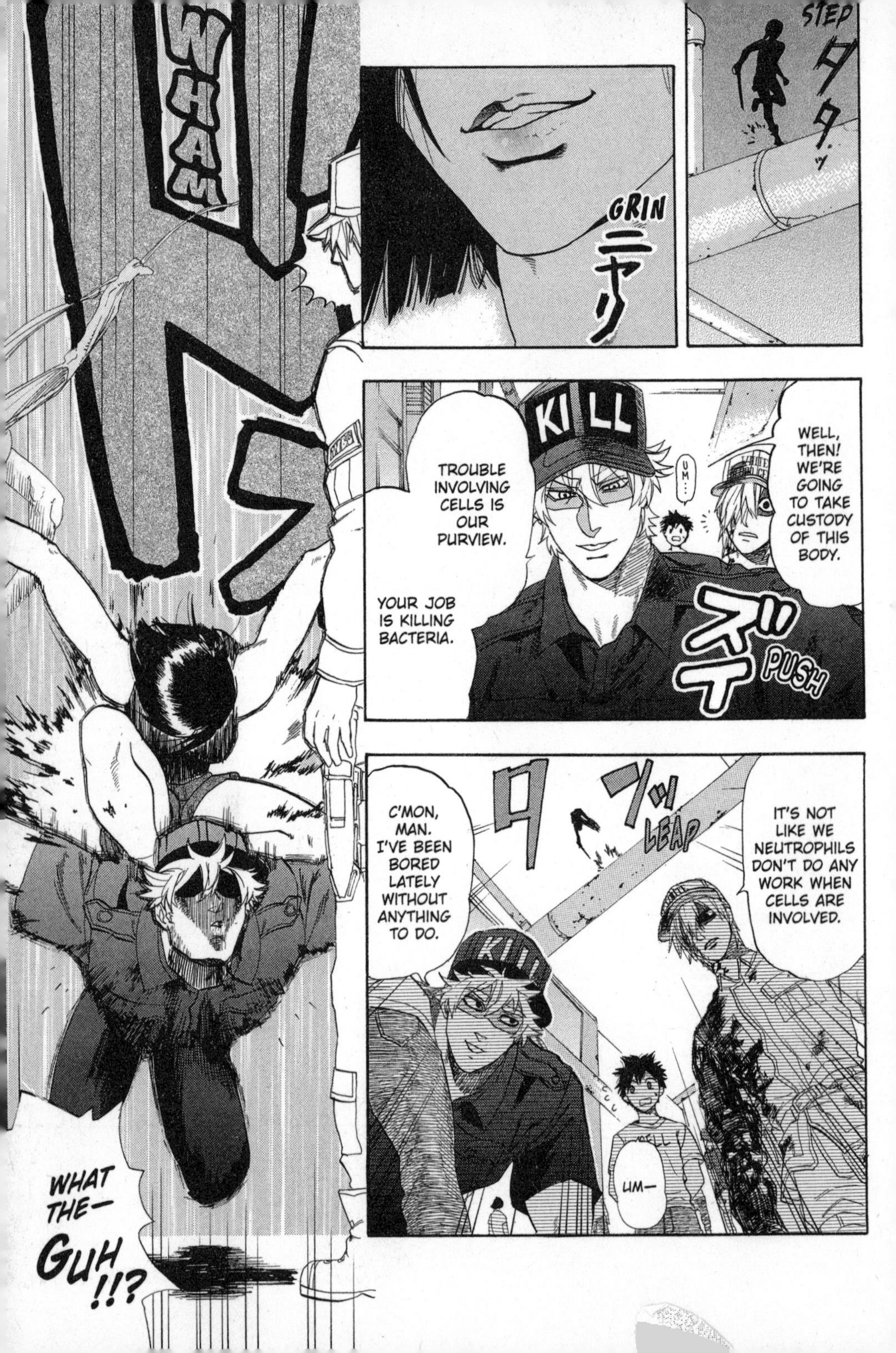
STEP
タタッ
GRIN
ニヤリ
WELL, THEN! WE'RE GOING TO TAKE CUSTODY OF THIS BODY.
UM...
TROUBLE INVOLVING CELLS IS OUR PURVIEW.
YOUR JOB IS KILLING BACTERIA.
ズイ
PUSH
IT'S NOT LIKE WE NEUTROPHILS DON'T DO ANY WORK WHEN CELLS ARE INVOLVED.
タッ
LEAP
C'MON, MAN. I'VE BEEN BORED LATELY WITHOUT ANYTHING TO DO.
UM—
WHAM
WHAT THE—
GUH!!?

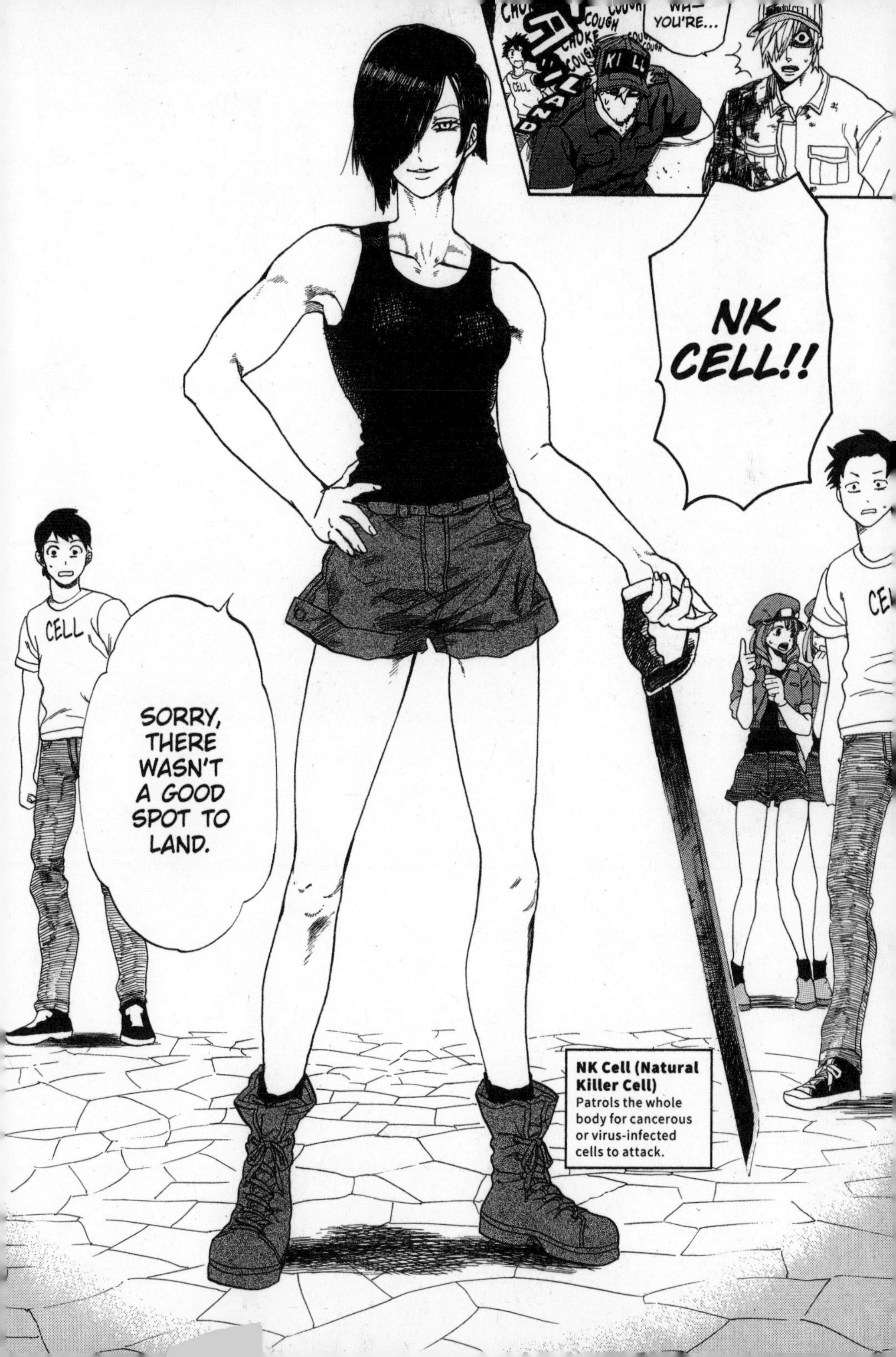
WH— YOU'RE...
COUGH COUGH COUGH COUGH
CHOKE CHOKE COUGH COUGH
NK CELL!!
SORRY, THERE WASN'T A GOOD SPOT TO LAND.
NK Cell (Natural Killer Cell)
Patrols the whole body for cancerous or virus-infected cells to attack.

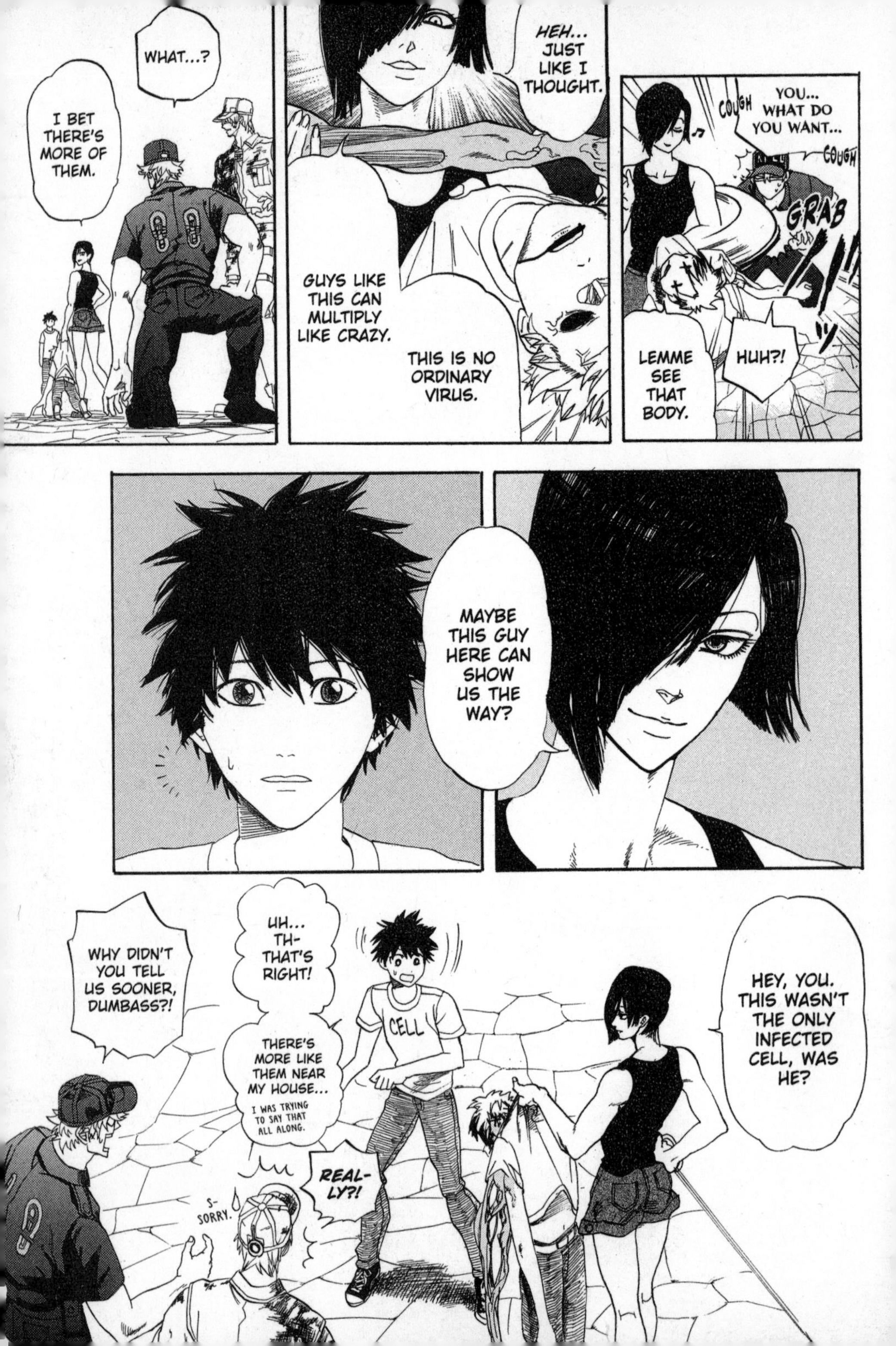

YOU... WHAT DO YOU WANT...
COUGH
COUGH
GRAB
HUH?!
LEMME SEE THAT BODY.
HEH... JUST LIKE I THOUGHT.
THIS IS NO ORDINARY VIRUS.
GUYS LIKE THIS CAN MULTIPLY LIKE CRAZY.
WHAT...?
I BET THERE'S MORE OF THEM.
MAYBE THIS GUY HERE CAN SHOW US THE WAY?
HEY, YOU. THIS WASN'T THE ONLY INFECTED CELL, WAS HE?
CELL
UH... TH-THAT'S RIGHT!
THERE'S MORE LIKE THEM NEAR MY HOUSE...
I WAS TRYING TO SAY THAT ALL ALONG.
REAL-LY?!
WHY DIDN'T YOU TELL US SOONER, DUMBASS?!
S-SORRY.

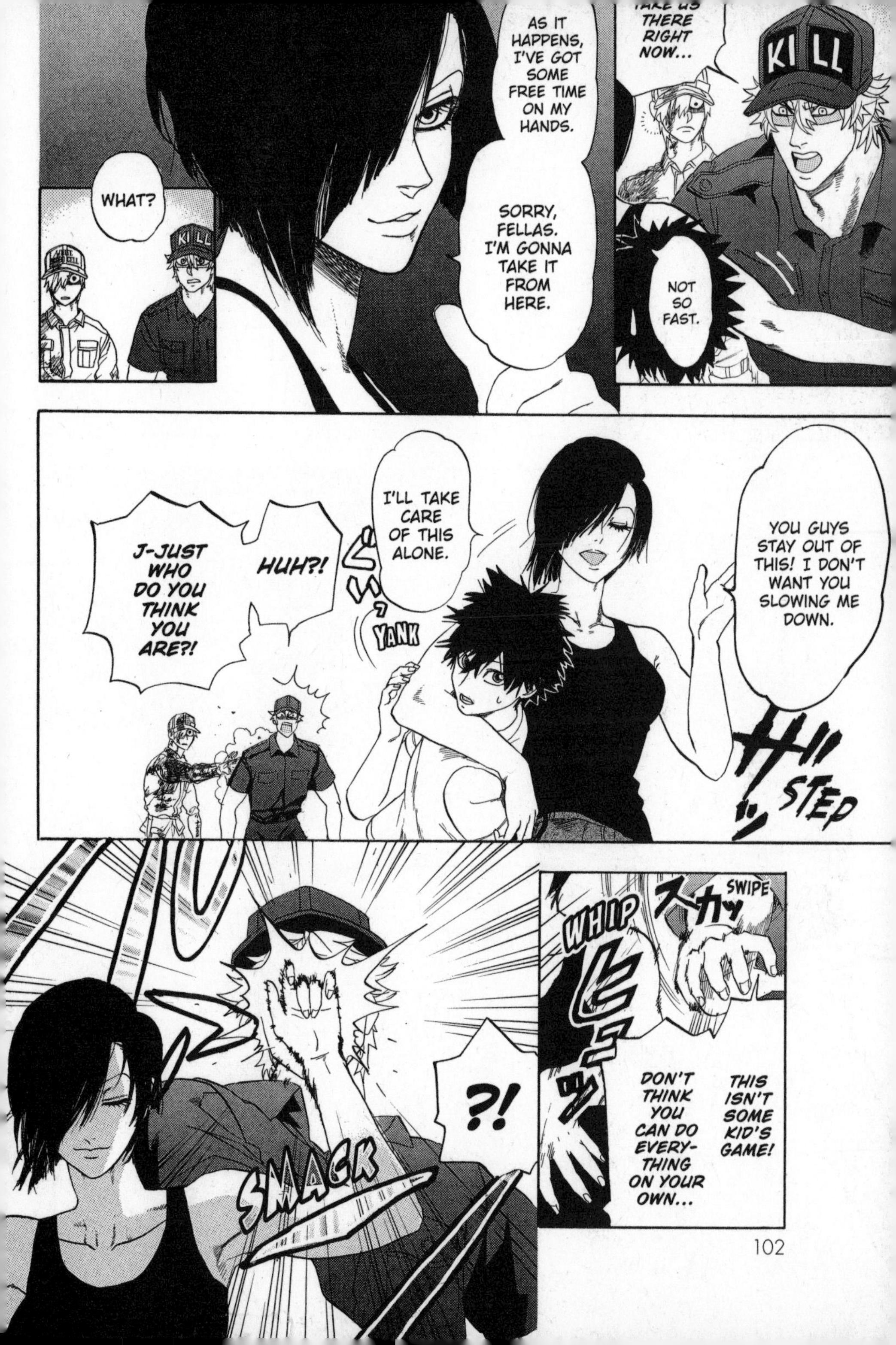
THERE RIGHT NOW…
NOT SO FAST.
AS IT HAPPENS, I'VE GOT SOME FREE TIME ON MY HANDS.
SORRY, FELLAS. I'M GONNA TAKE IT FROM HERE.
WHAT?
YOU GUYS STAY OUT OF THIS! I DON'T WANT YOU SLOWING ME DOWN.
STEP
I'LL TAKE CARE OF THIS ALONE.
YANK
HUH?!
J-JUST WHO DO YOU THINK YOU ARE?!
SWIPE
スカッ
WHIP
THIS ISN'T SOME KID'S GAME!
DON'T THINK YOU CAN DO EVERY-THING ON YOUR OWN…
?!
SMACK

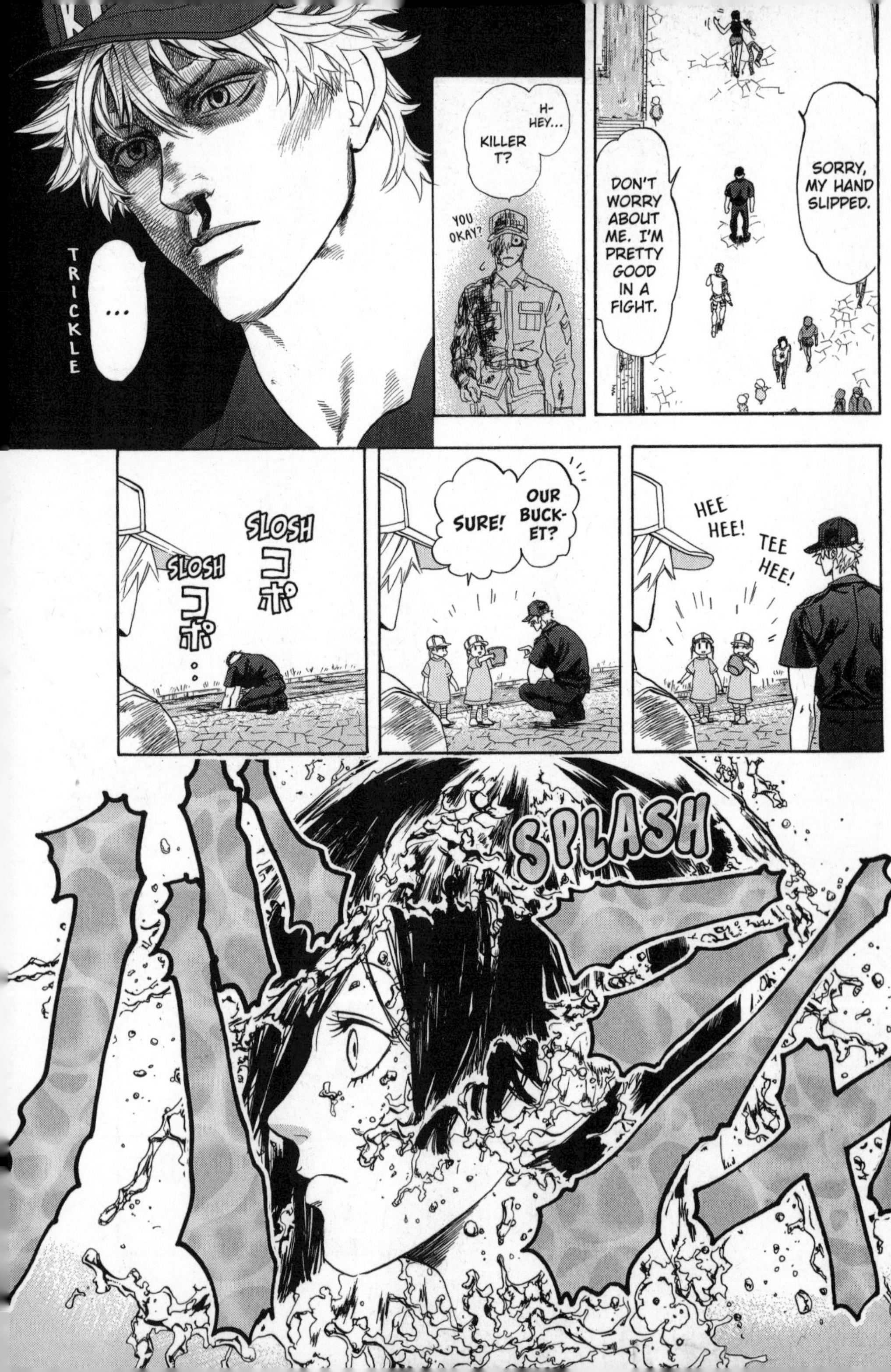
SORRY, MY HAND SLIPPED.
DON'T WORRY ABOUT ME. I'M PRETTY GOOD IN A FIGHT.
H-HEY... KILLER T?
YOU OKAY?
TRICKLE
...
HEE HEE!
TEE HEE!
OUR BUCK-ET?
SURE!
SLOSH
コポ
SLOSH
コポ
SPLASH

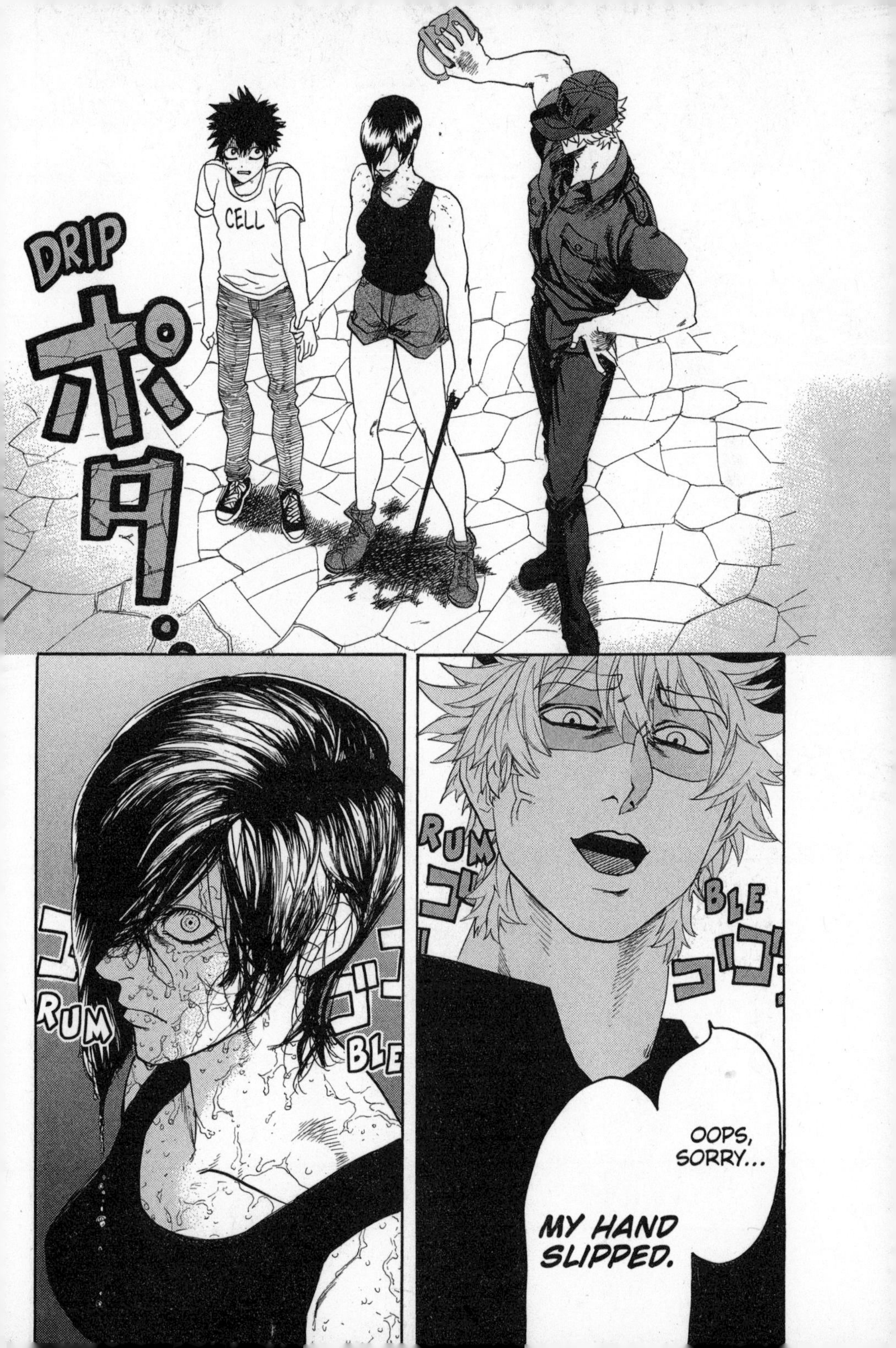
DRIP
ポタ
RUM
BLE
OOPS, SORRY...
MY HAND SLIPPED.
RUM
BLE

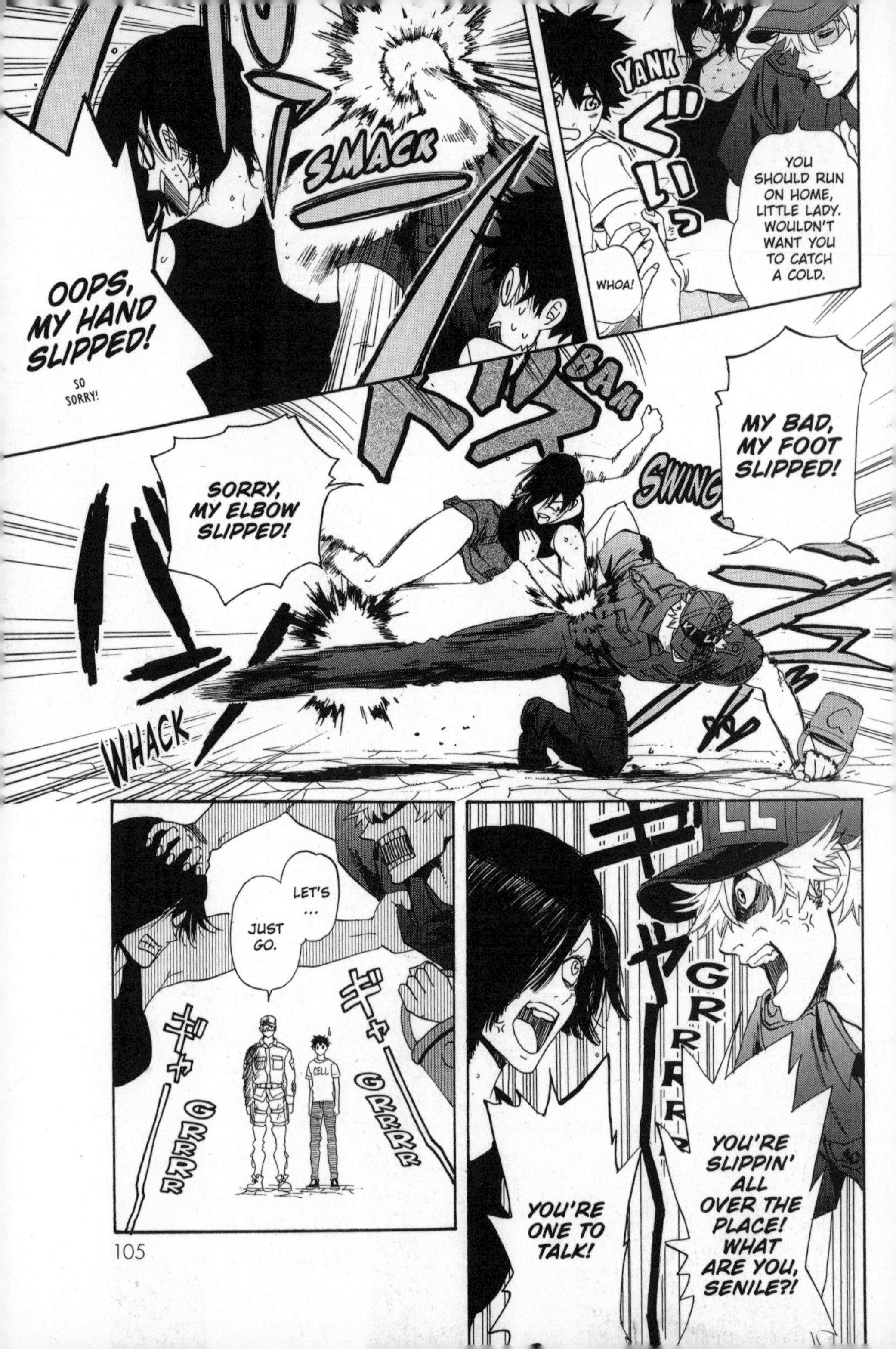

YANK
YOU SHOULD RUN ON HOME, LITTLE LADY. WOULDN'T WANT YOU TO CATCH A COLD.
WHOA!
SMACK
OOPS, MY HAND SLIPPED!
SO SORRY!
BAM
MY BAD, MY FOOT SLIPPED!
SWING
SORRY, MY ELBOW SLIPPED!
WHACK
GRRRR
YOU'RE SLIPPIN' ALL OVER THE PLACE! WHAT ARE YOU, SENILE?!
YOU'RE ONE TO TALK!
LET'S... JUST GO.
CELL
GRRRR
GRRRR

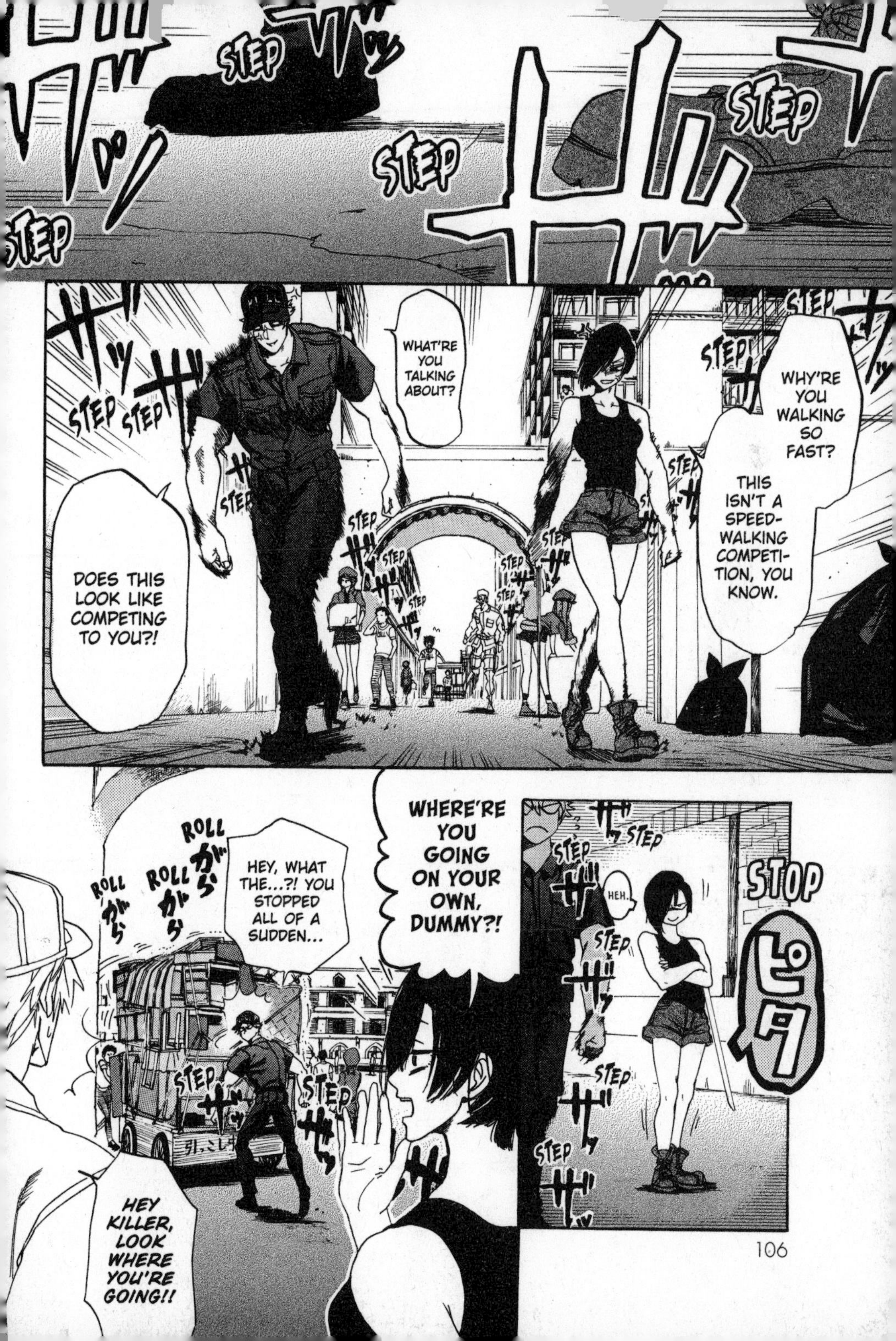
STEP
STEP
STEP
STEP
WHY'RE YOU WALKING SO FAST?
THIS ISN'T A SPEED-WALKING COMPETITION, YOU KNOW.
WHAT'RE YOU TALKING ABOUT?
DOES THIS LOOK LIKE COMPETING TO YOU?!
STEP
STEP
STOP
HEH.
STEP
STEP
STEP
WHERE'RE YOU GOING ON YOUR OWN, DUMMY?!
HEY, WHAT THE...?! YOU STOPPED ALL OF A SUDDEN...
ROLL
ROLL
STEP
STEP
HEY KILLER, LOOK WHERE YOU'RE GOING!!

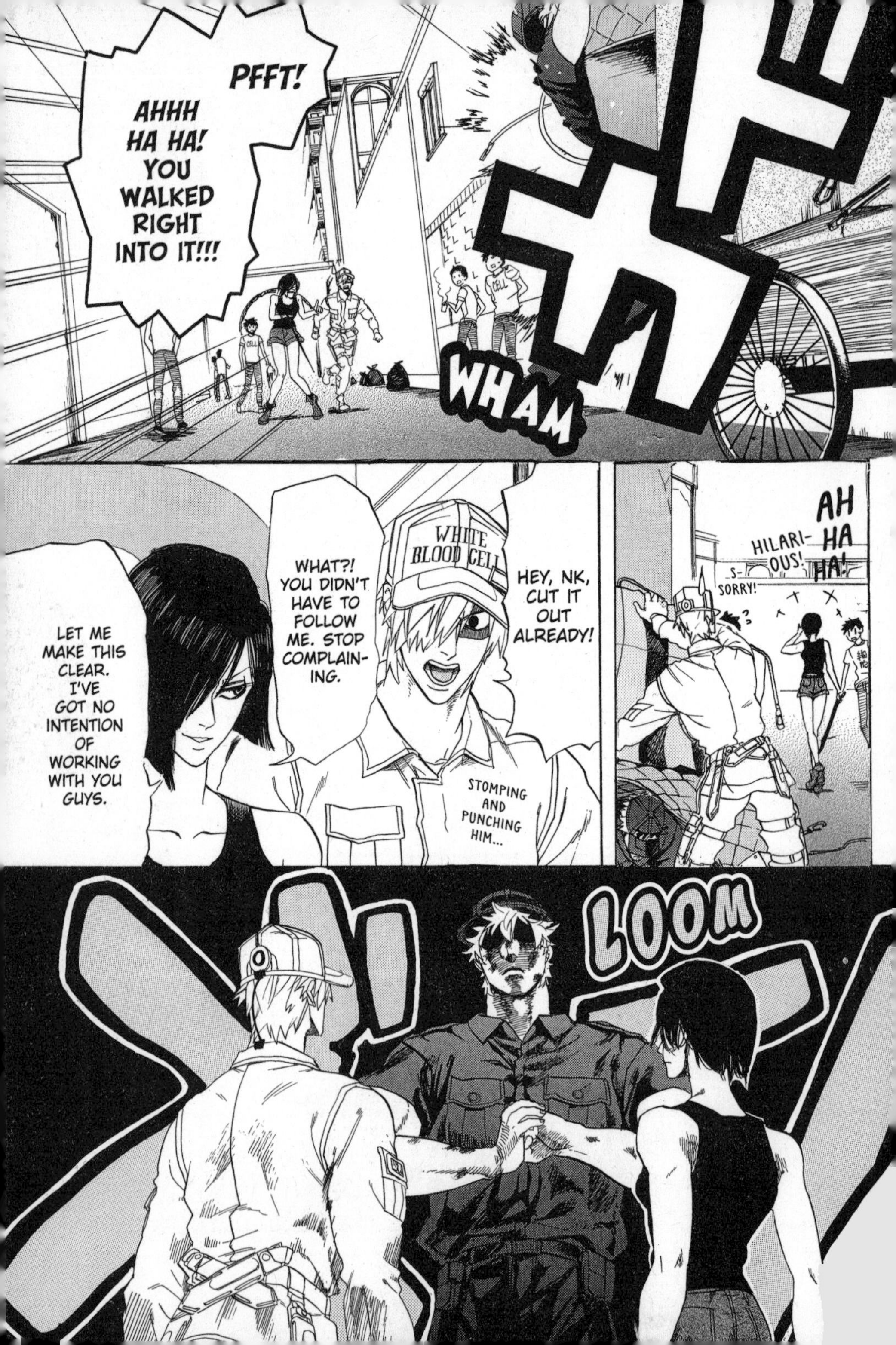
PFFT!
AHHH HA HA! YOU WALKED RIGHT INTO IT!!!
WHAM
AH HA HA!
HILARIOUS!
S-SORRY!
HEY, NK, CUT IT OUT ALREADY!
WHAT?! YOU DIDN'T HAVE TO FOLLOW ME. STOP COMPLAINING.
WHITE BLOOD CELL
STOMPING AND PUNCHING HIM...
LET ME MAKE THIS CLEAR. I'VE GOT NO INTENTION OF WORKING WITH YOU GUYS.
LOOM

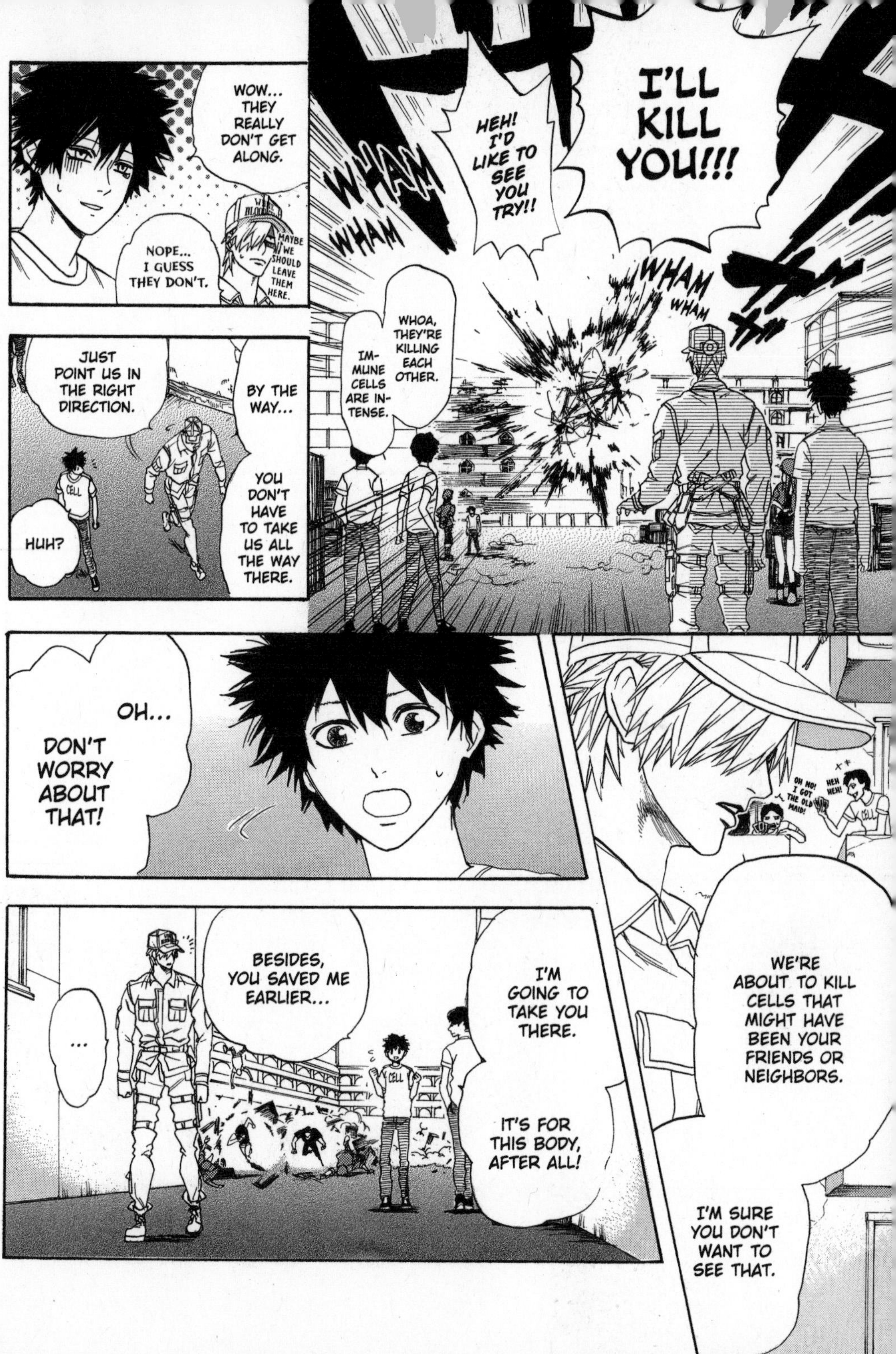
I'LL KILL YOU!!!
HEH! I'D LIKE TO SEE YOU TRY!!
WHAM WHAM
WHAM WHAM
WHOA, THEY'RE KILLING EACH OTHER.
IM-MUNE CELLS ARE IN-TENSE.
WOW... THEY REALLY DON'T GET ALONG.
MAYBE WE SHOULD LEAVE THEM HERE.
NOPE... I GUESS THEY DON'T.
BY THE WAY...
YOU DON'T HAVE TO TAKE US ALL THE WAY THERE.
JUST POINT US IN THE RIGHT DIRECTION.
HUH?
HEH HEH!
OH NO! I GOT THE OLD MAID!
WE'RE ABOUT TO KILL CELLS THAT MIGHT HAVE BEEN YOUR FRIENDS OR NEIGHBORS.
I'M SURE YOU DON'T WANT TO SEE THAT.
OH...
DON'T WORRY ABOUT THAT!
I'M GOING TO TAKE YOU THERE.
IT'S FOR THIS BODY, AFTER ALL!
BESIDES, YOU SAVED ME EARLIER...
...

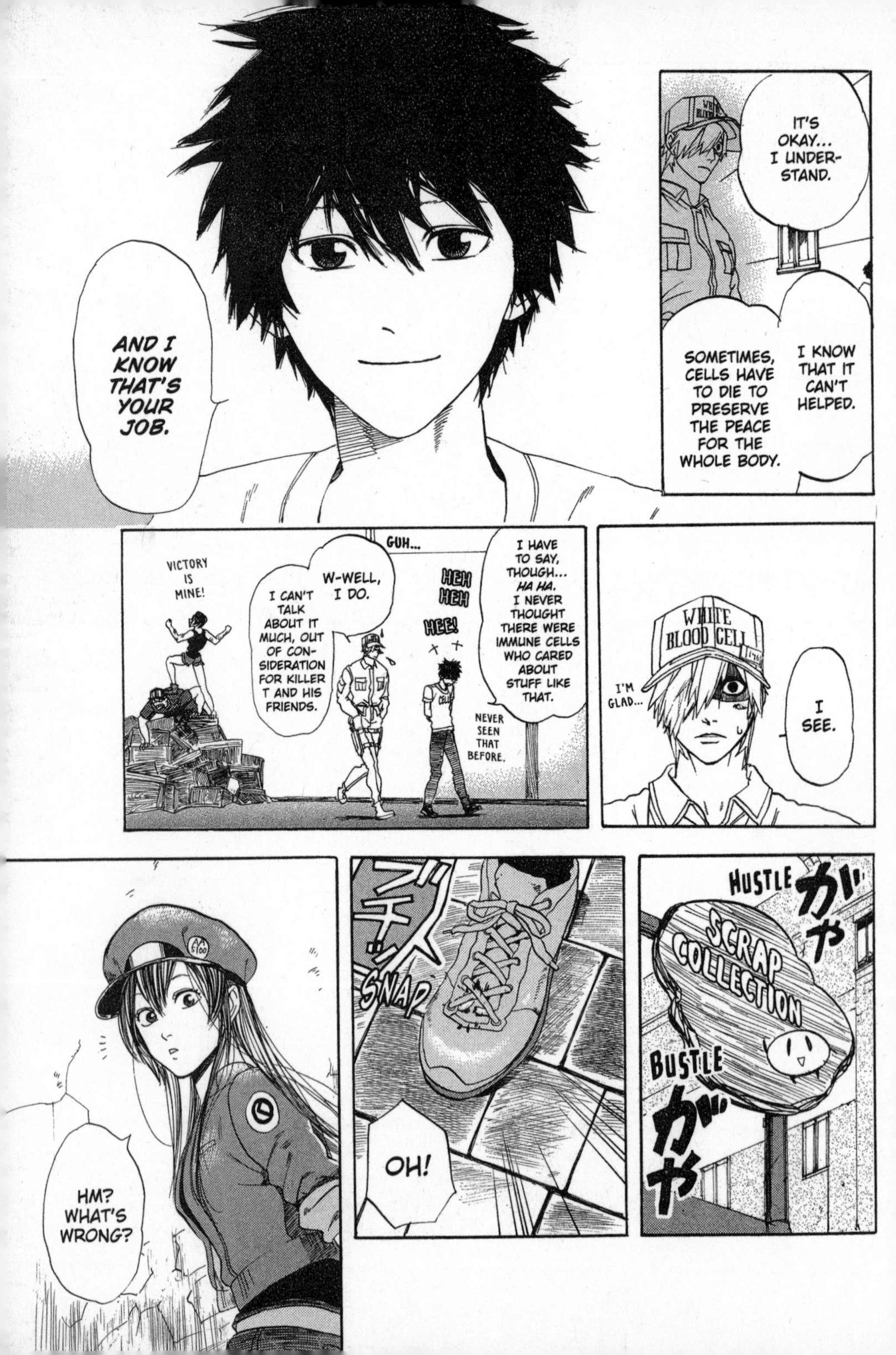
IT'S OKAY... I UNDERSTAND.
I KNOW THAT IT CAN'T HELPED.
SOMETIMES, CELLS HAVE TO DIE TO PRESERVE THE PEACE FOR THE WHOLE BODY.
AND I KNOW THAT'S YOUR JOB.
I SEE.
I'M GLAD...
I HAVE TO SAY, THOUGH... HA HA. I NEVER THOUGHT THERE WERE IMMUNE CELLS WHO CARED ABOUT STUFF LIKE THAT.
NEVER SEEN THAT BEFORE.
HEH HEH HEE!
GUH...
W-WELL, I DO.
I CAN'T TALK ABOUT IT MUCH, OUT OF CONSIDERATION FOR KILLER T AND HIS FRIENDS.
VICTORY IS MINE!
HUSTLE
がや
SCRAP COLLECTION
BUSTLE
がや
ブチッ
SNAP
OH!
HM? WHAT'S WRONG?

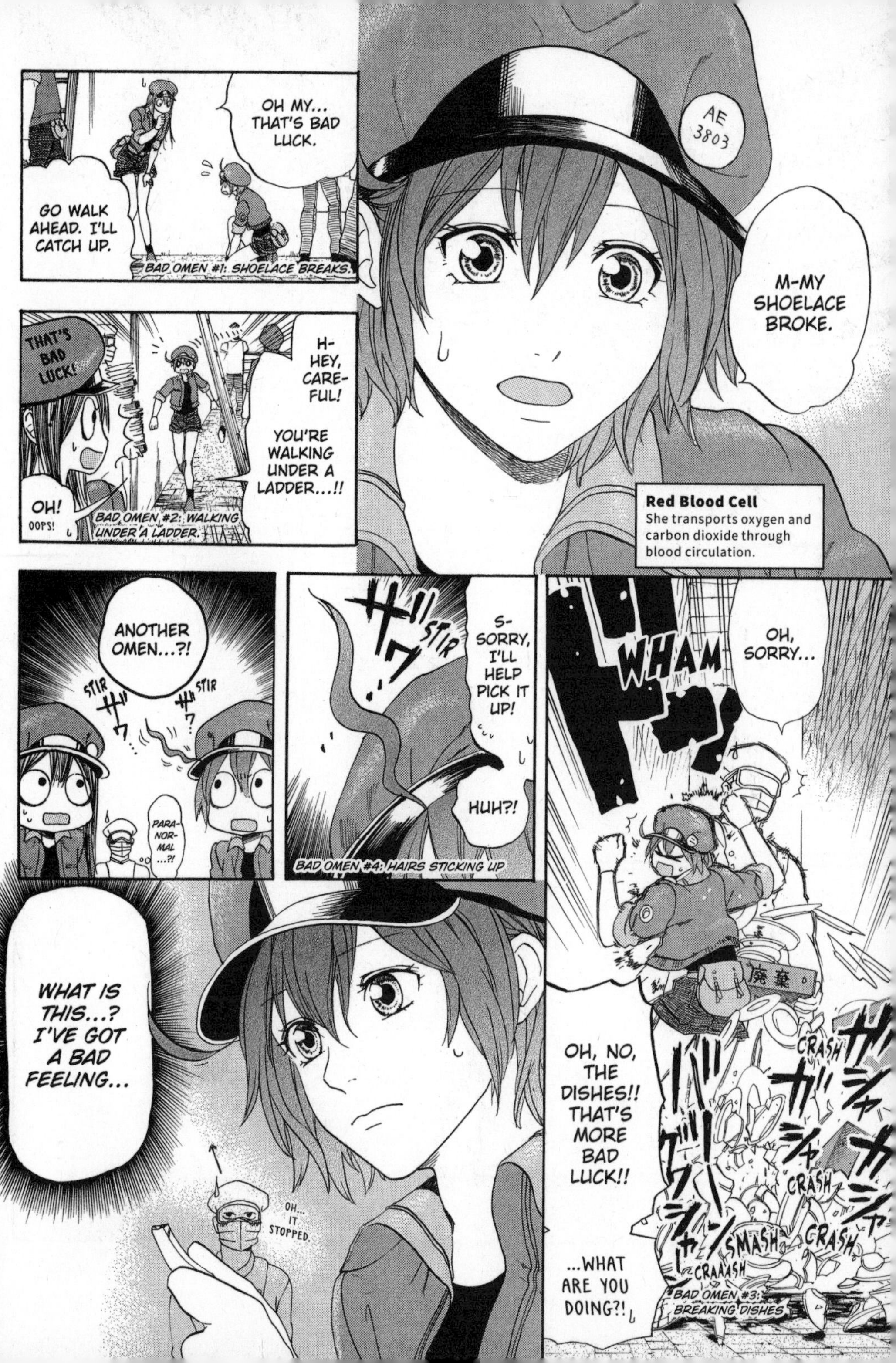
AE 3803
M-MY SHOELACE BROKE.
Red Blood Cell
She transports oxygen and carbon dioxide through blood circulation.
OH MY... THAT'S BAD LUCK.
GO WALK AHEAD. I'LL CATCH UP.
BAD OMEN #1: SHOELACE BREAKS.
H- HEY, CARE- FUL!
YOU'RE WALKING UNDER A LADDER...!!
THAT'S BAD LUCK!
OH!
OOPS!
BAD OMEN #2: WALKING UNDER A LADDER.
OH, SORRY...
WHAM
OH, NO, THE DISHES!! THAT'S MORE BAD LUCK!!
CRASH
CRASH
CRASH
SMASH
CRAAASH
...WHAT ARE YOU DOING?!
BAD OMEN #3: BREAKING DISHES
STIR
S- SORRY, I'LL HELP PICK IT UP!
HUH?!
BAD OMEN #4: HAIRS STICKING UP
ANOTHER OMEN...?!
STIR
STIR
PARA- NOR- MAL ...?!
WHAT IS THIS...? I'VE GOT A BAD FEELING...
OH... IT STOPPED.

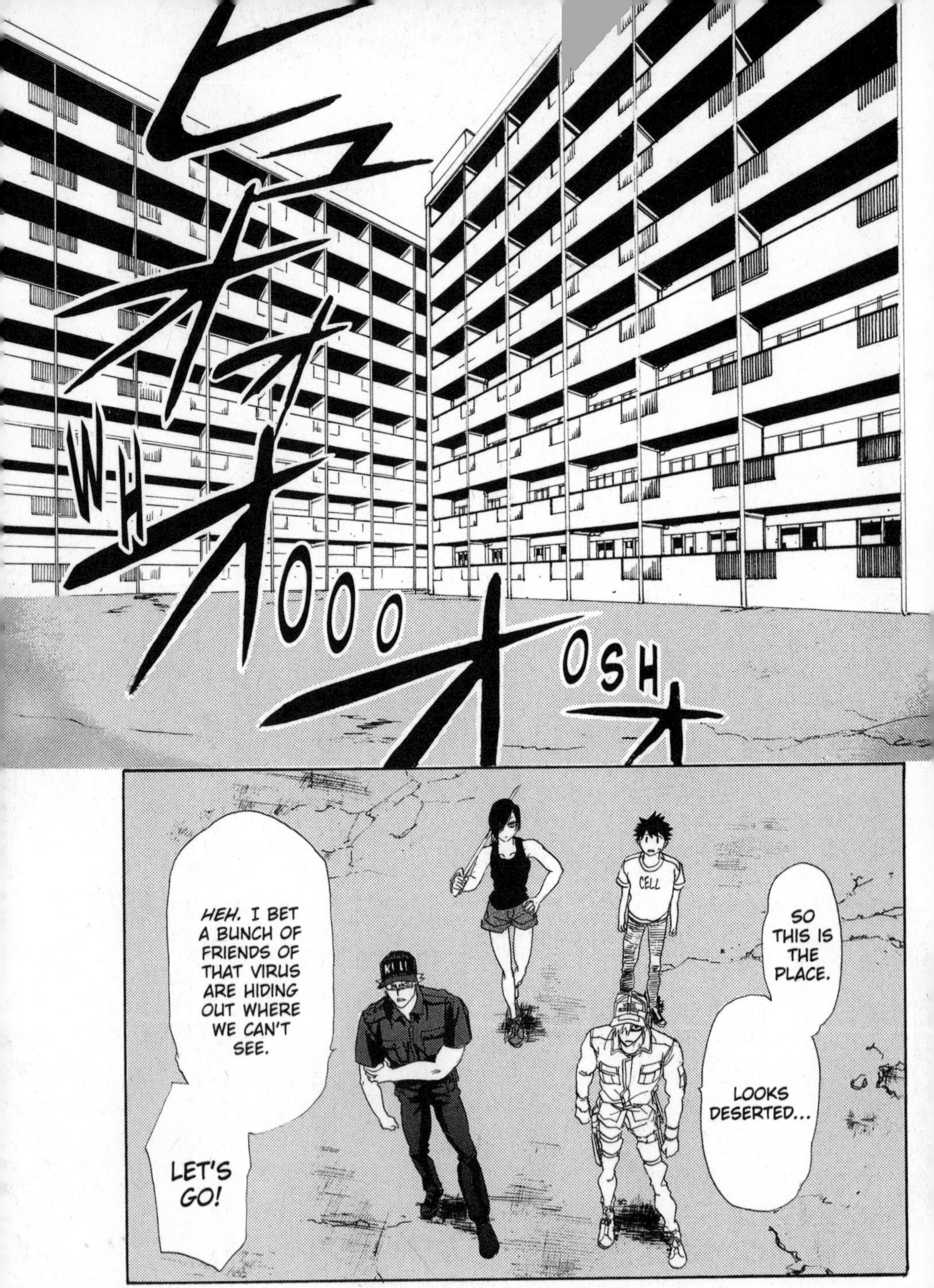
W-H
OOOO
OSH
SO THIS IS THE PLACE.
LOOKS DESERTED...
HEH. I BET A BUNCH OF FRIENDS OF THAT VIRUS ARE HIDING OUT WHERE WE CAN'T SEE.
LET'S GO!

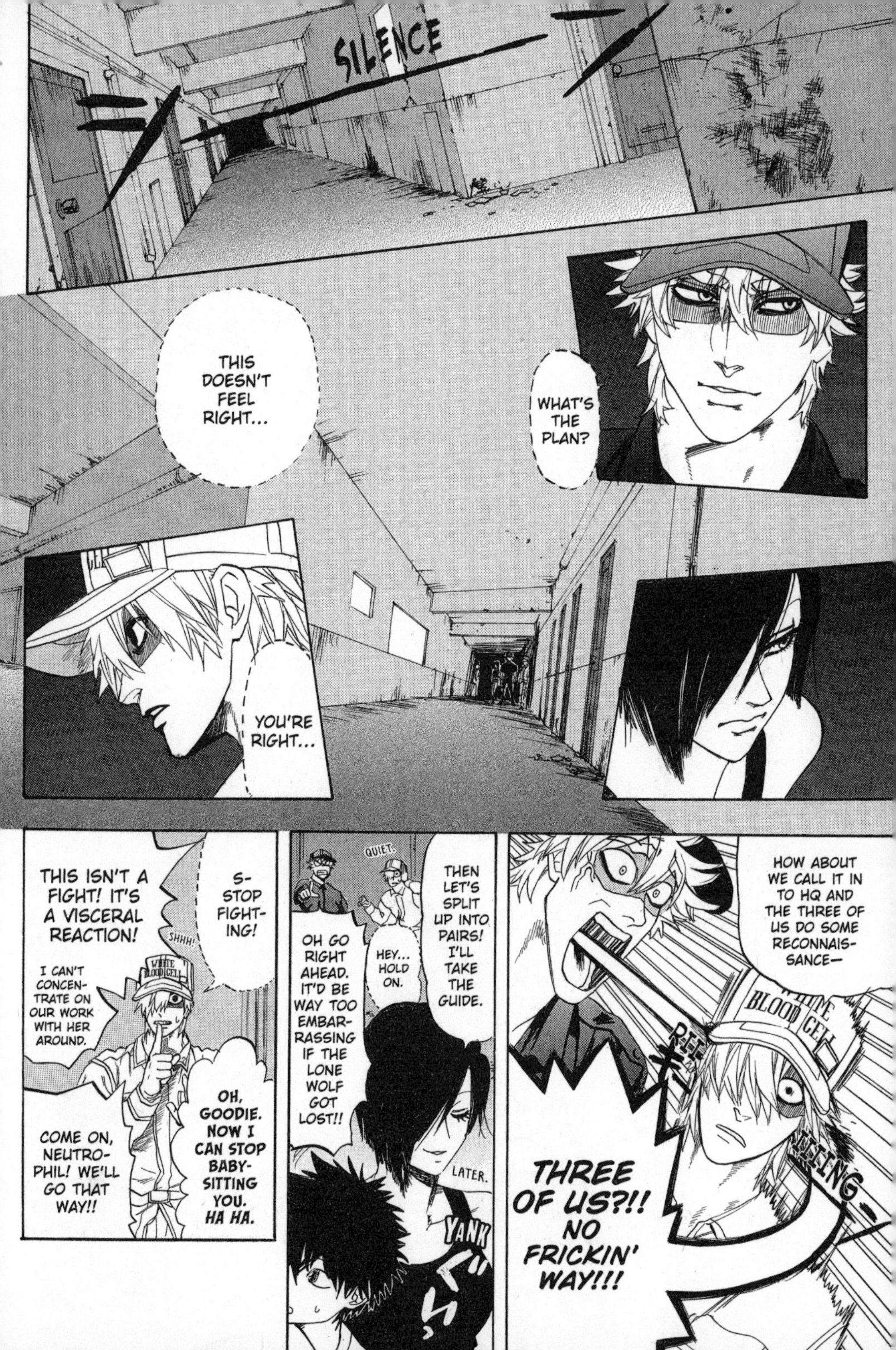
SILENCE
WHAT'S THE PLAN?
THIS DOESN'T FEEL RIGHT...
YOU'RE RIGHT...
HOW ABOUT WE CALL IT IN TO HQ AND THE THREE OF US DO SOME RECONNAIS-SANCE—
THREE OF US?!! NO FRICKIN' WAY!!!
THEN LET'S SPLIT UP INTO PAIRS! I'LL TAKE THE GUIDE.
QUIET.
HEY... HOLD ON.
OH GO RIGHT AHEAD. IT'D BE WAY TOO EMBARRASSING IF THE LONE WOLF GOT LOST!!
LATER.
YANK
S-STOP FIGHTING!
THIS ISN'T A FIGHT! IT'S A VISCERAL REACTION!
SHHH!
WHITE BLOOD CELL
I CAN'T CONCENTRATE ON OUR WORK WITH HER AROUND.
OH, GOODIE. NOW I CAN STOP BABYSITTING YOU. HA HA.
COME ON, NEUTROPHIL! WE'LL GO THAT WAY!!

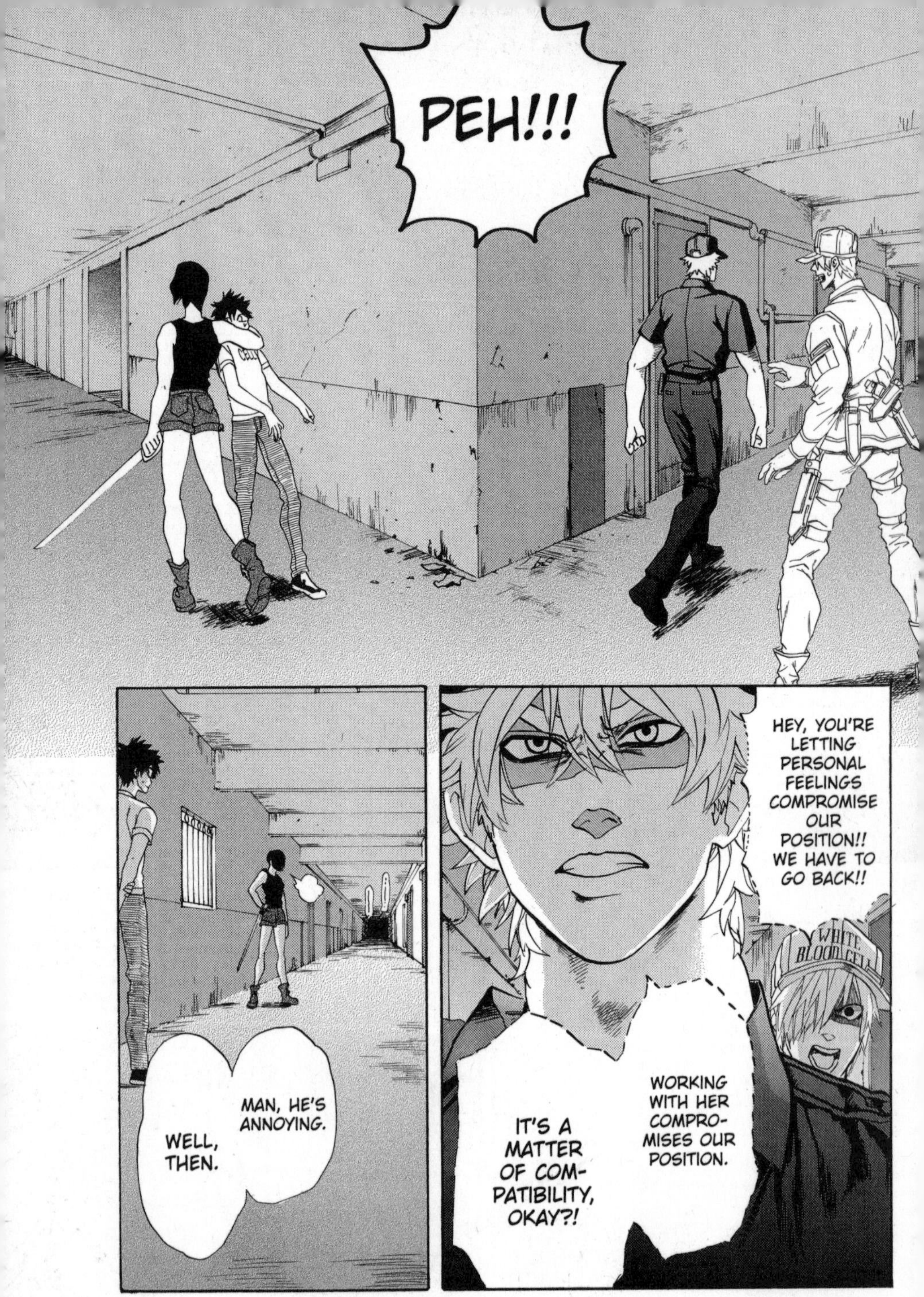
PEH!!!
HEY, YOU'RE LETTING PERSONAL FEELINGS COMPROMISE OUR POSITION!! WE HAVE TO GO BACK!!
WORKING WITH HER COMPRO- MISES OUR POSITION.
IT'S A MATTER OF COM- PATIBILITY, OKAY?!
MAN, HE'S ANNOYING.
WELL, THEN.

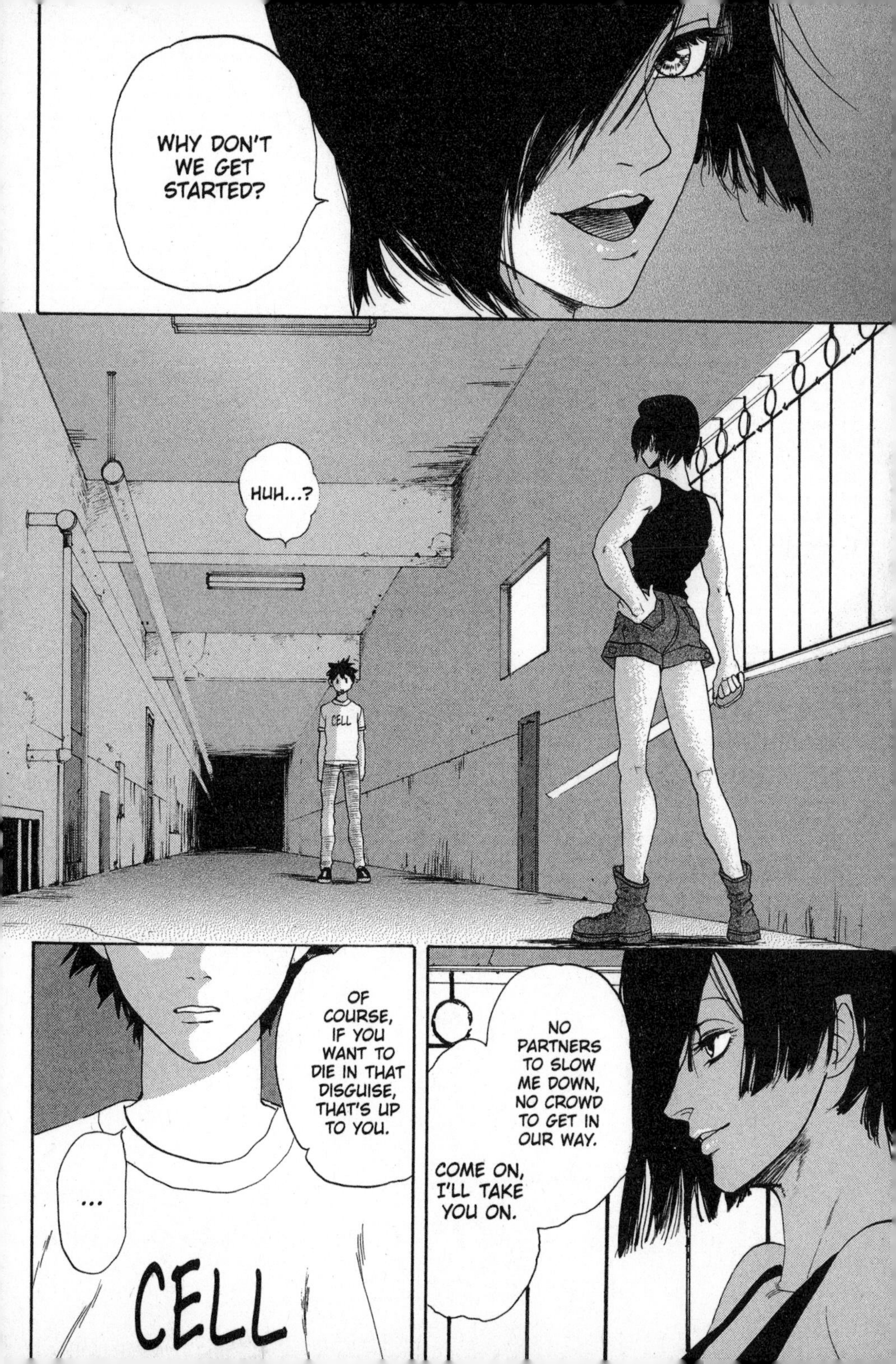
WHY DON'T WE GET STARTED?
HUH...?
NO PARTNERS TO SLOW ME DOWN, NO CROWD TO GET IN OUR WAY.
COME ON, I'LL TAKE YOU ON.
OF COURSE, IF YOU WANT TO DIE IN THAT DISGUISE, THAT'S UP TO YOU.
...
CELL

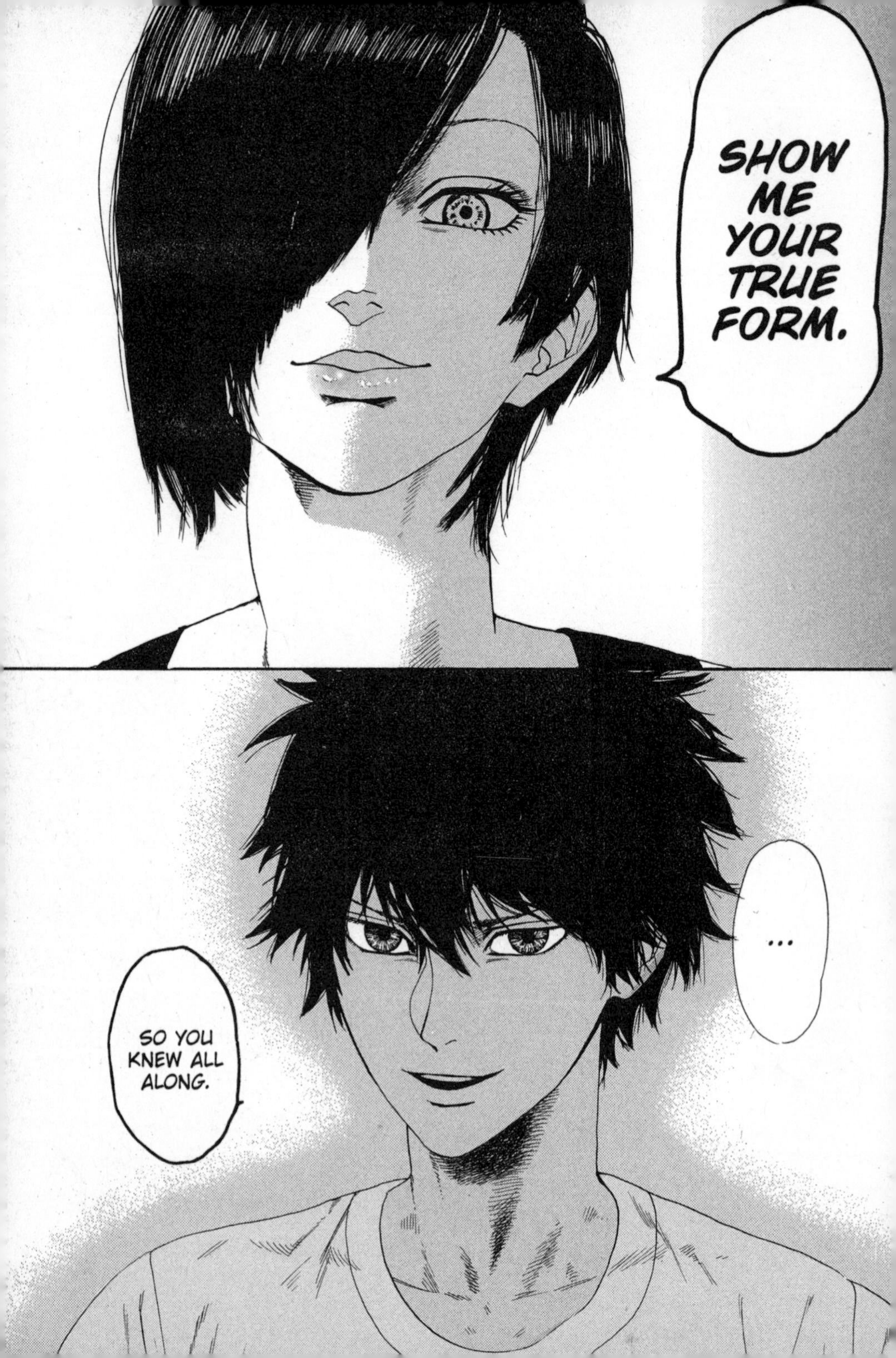
SHOW ME YOUR TRUE FORM.
...
SO YOU KNEW ALL ALONG.

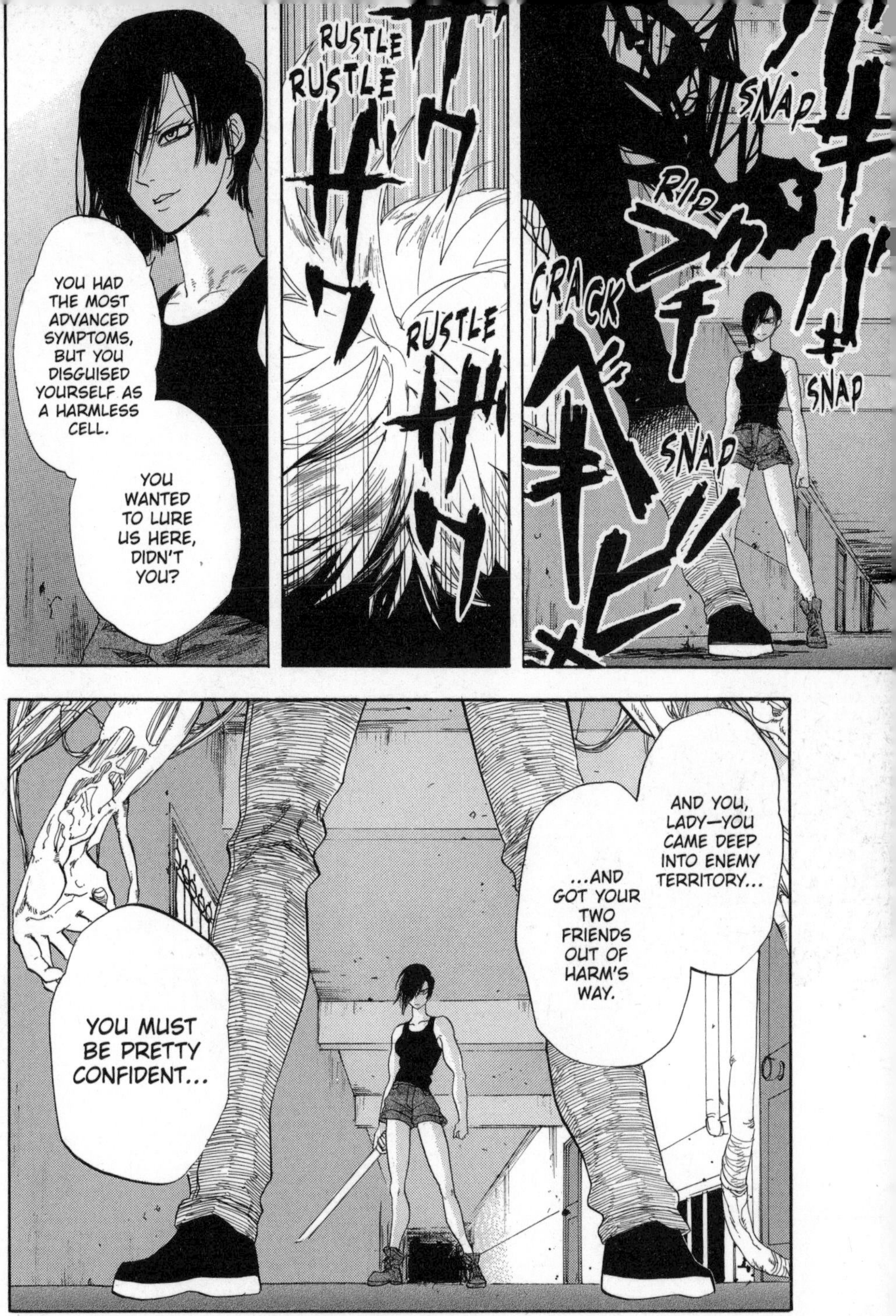
SNAP
RIP
CRACK
SNAP
SNAP
RUSTLE RUSTLE
RUSTLE
YOU HAD THE MOST ADVANCED SYMPTOMS, BUT YOU DISGUISED YOURSELF AS A HARMLESS CELL.
YOU WANTED TO LURE US HERE, DIDN'T YOU?
AND YOU, LADY—YOU CAME DEEP INTO ENEMY TERRITORY...
...AND GOT YOUR TWO FRIENDS OUT OF HARM'S WAY.
YOU MUST BE PRETTY CONFIDENT...

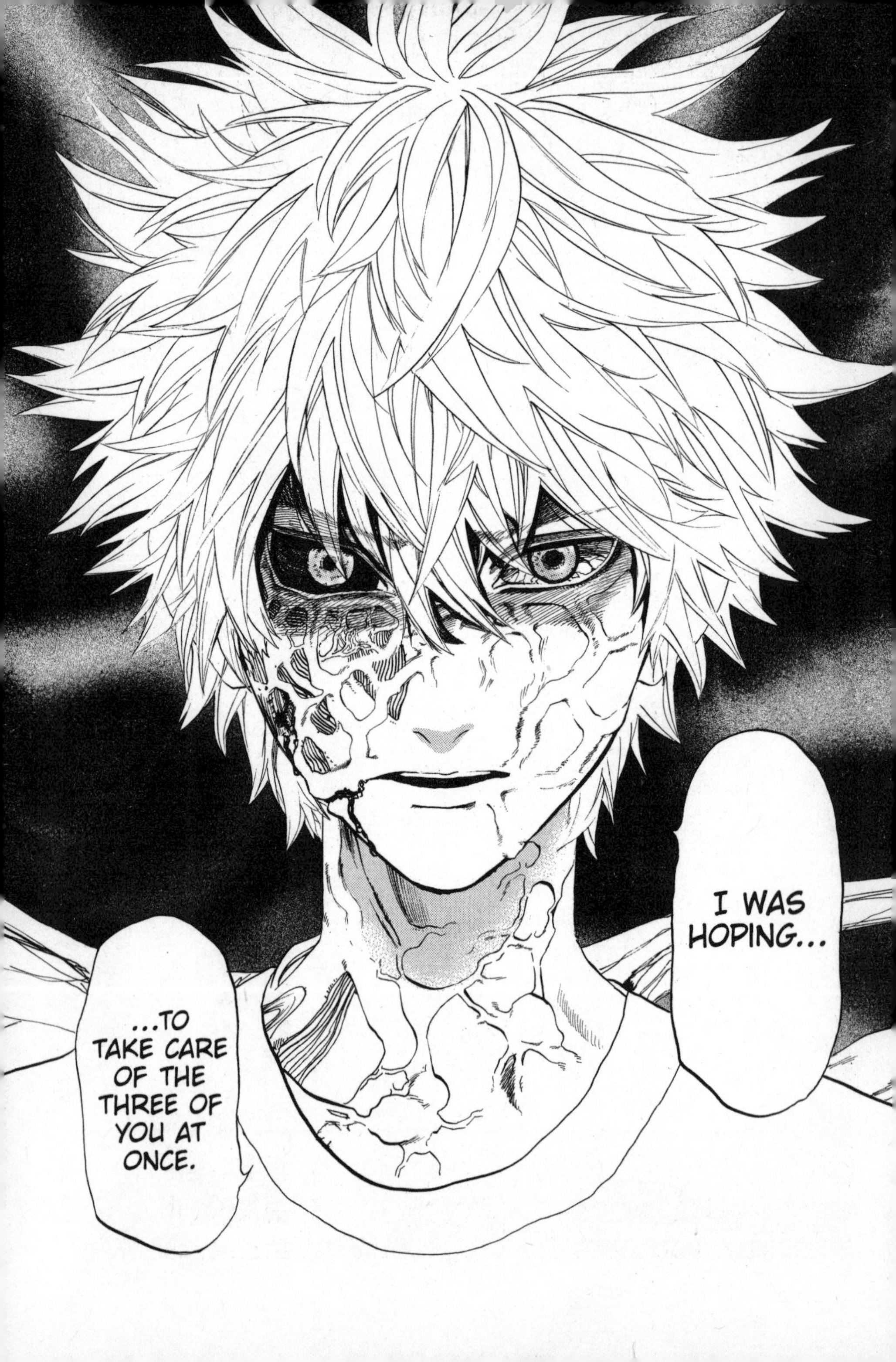
I WAS HOPING...
...TO TAKE CARE OF THE THREE OF YOU AT ONCE.

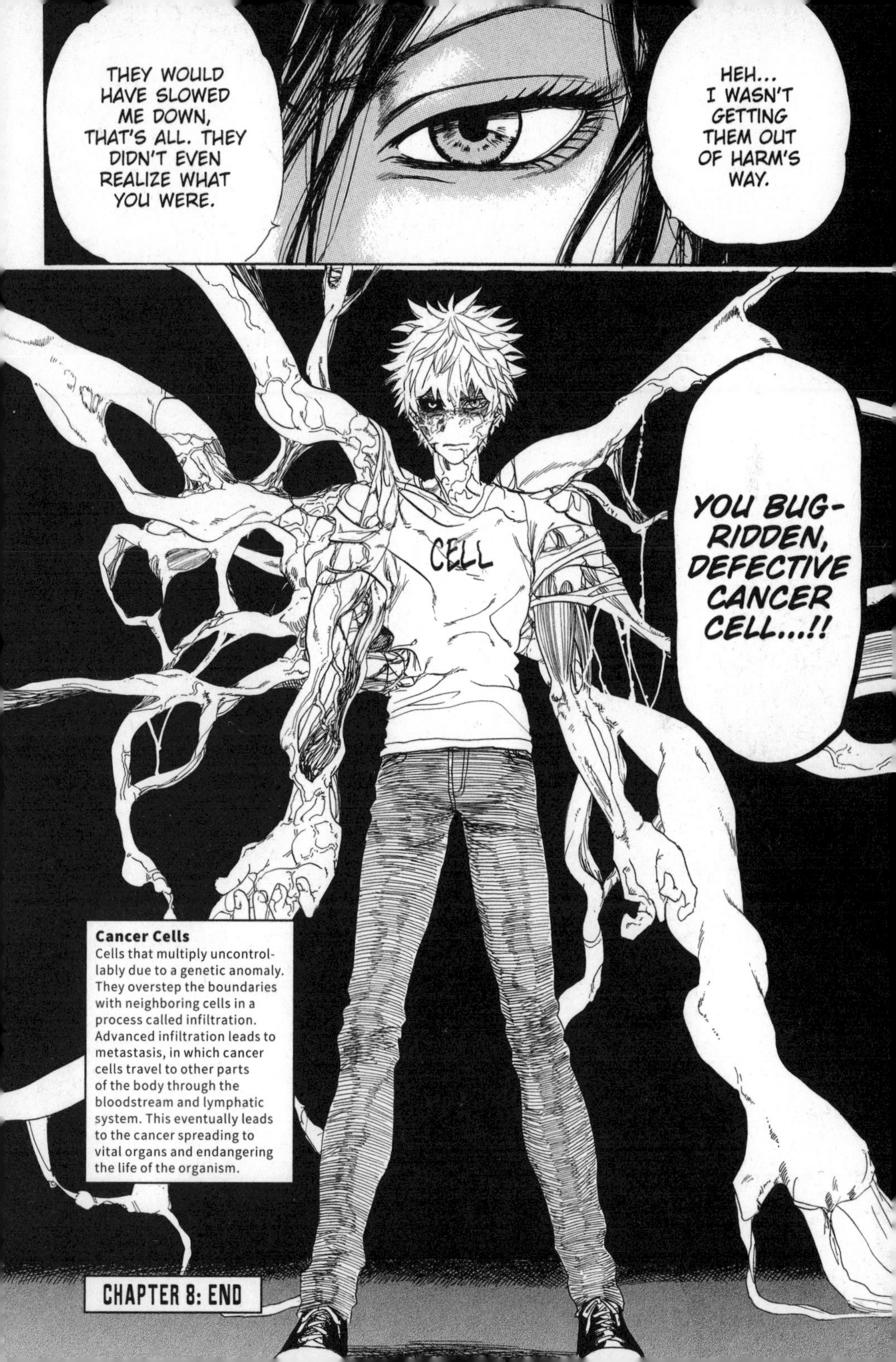
HEH... I WASN'T GETTING THEM OUT OF HARM'S WAY.
THEY WOULD HAVE SLOWED ME DOWN, THAT'S ALL. THEY DIDN'T EVEN REALIZE WHAT YOU WERE.
YOU BUG-RIDDEN, DEFECTIVE CANCER CELL...!!
CELL
Cancer Cells
Cells that multiply uncontrollably due to a genetic anomaly. They overstep the boundaries with neighboring cells in a process called infiltration. Advanced infiltration leads to metastasis, in which cancer cells travel to other parts of the body through the bloodstream and lymphatic system. This eventually leads to the cancer spreading to vital organs and endangering the life of the organism.
CHAPTER 8: END

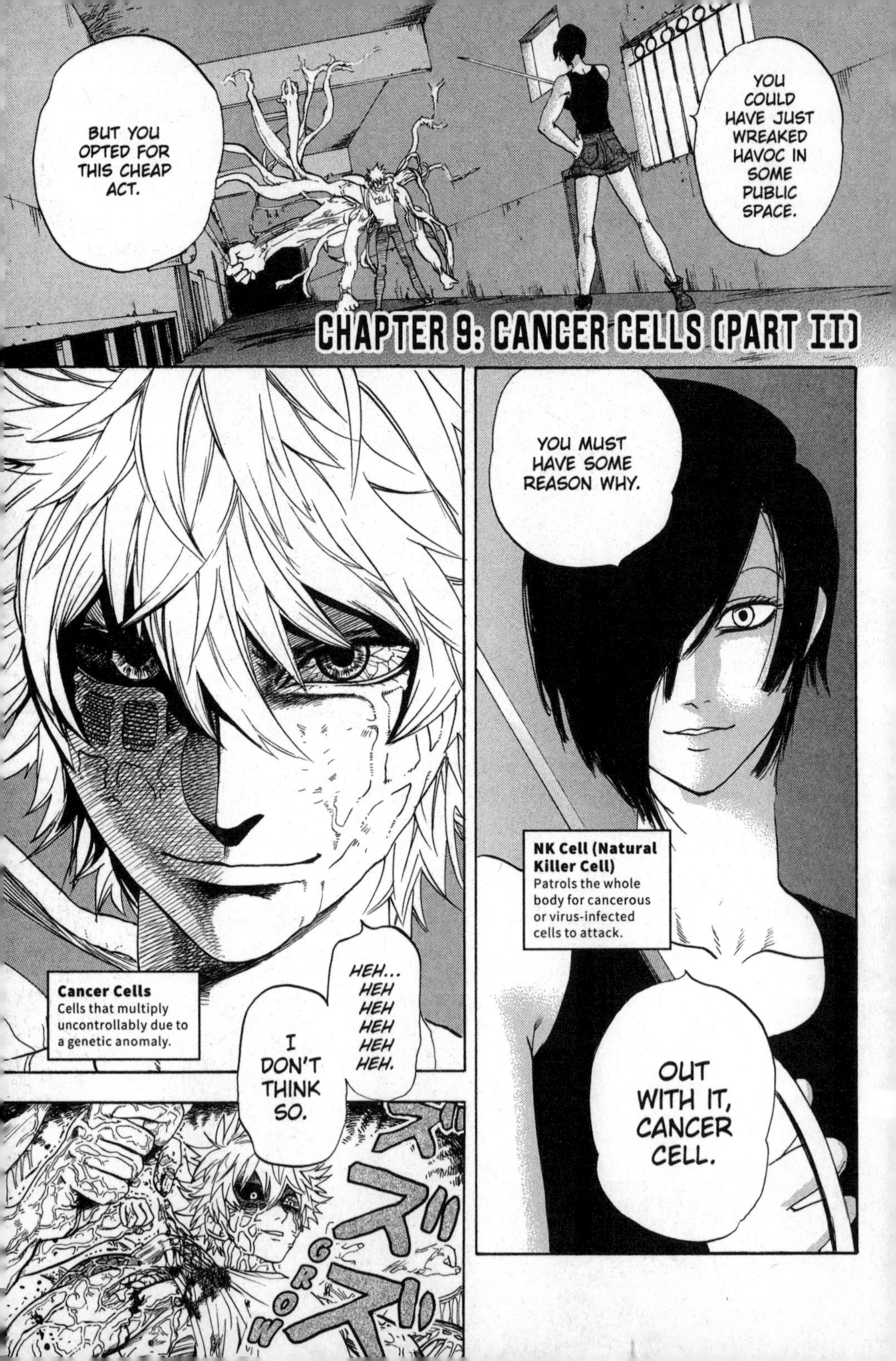
YOU COULD HAVE JUST WREAKED HAVOC IN SOME PUBLIC SPACE.
BUT YOU OPTED FOR THIS CHEAP ACT.
CHAPTER 9: CANCER CELLS (PART II)
YOU MUST HAVE SOME REASON WHY.
NK Cell (Natural Killer Cell)
Patrols the whole body for cancerous or virus-infected cells to attack.
OUT WITH IT, CANCER CELL.
Cancer Cells
Cells that multiply uncontrollably due to a genetic anomaly.
HEH... HEH HEH HEH HEH HEH.
I DON'T THINK SO.
GROW

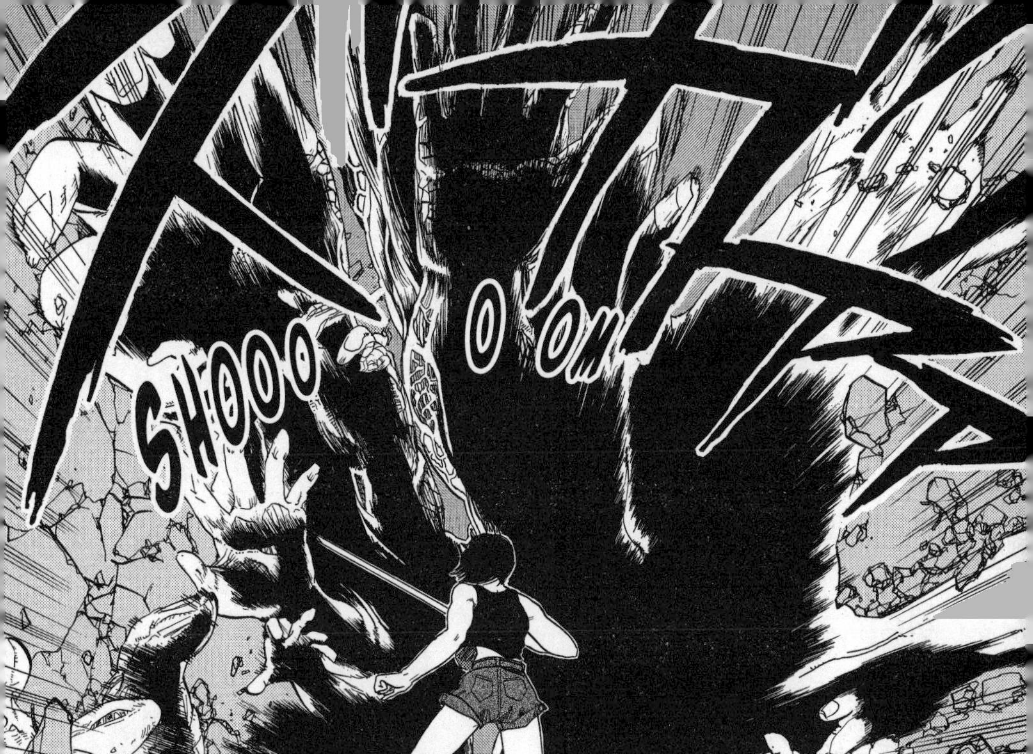
SHOOOOOOM

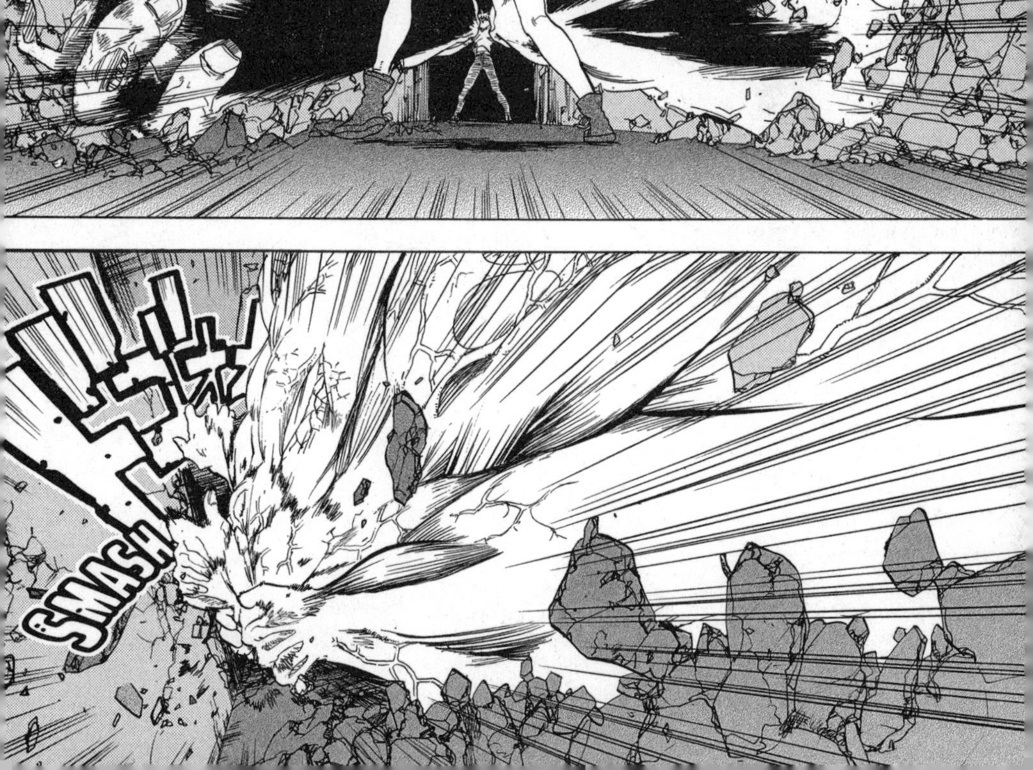
SMASH

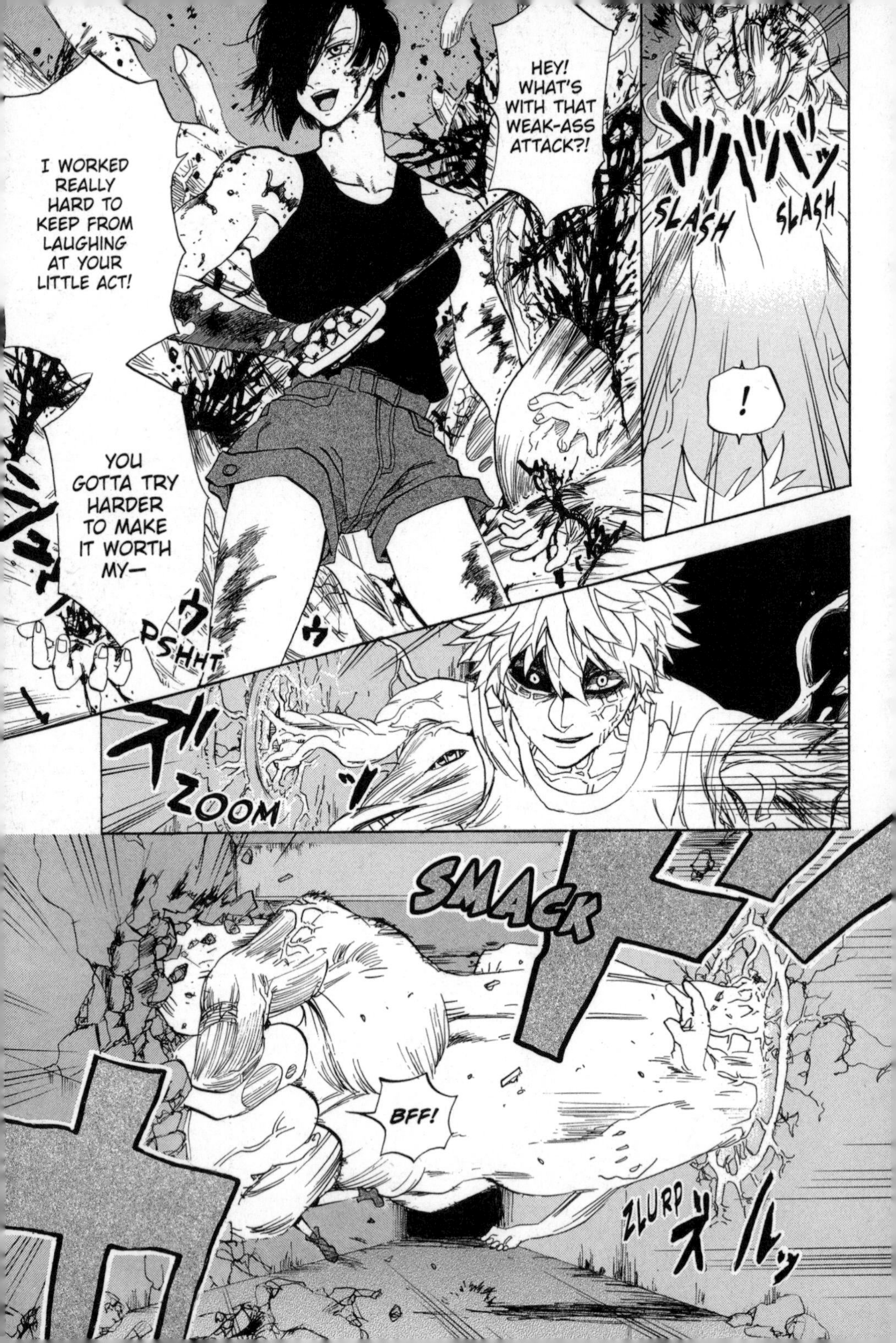
SLASH
SLASH
!
HEY! WHAT'S WITH THAT WEAK-ASS ATTACK?!
I WORKED REALLY HARD TO KEEP FROM LAUGHING AT YOUR LITTLE ACT!
YOU GOTTA TRY HARDER TO MAKE IT WORTH MY—
PSHHT
ZOOM
SMACK
BFF!
ZLURP

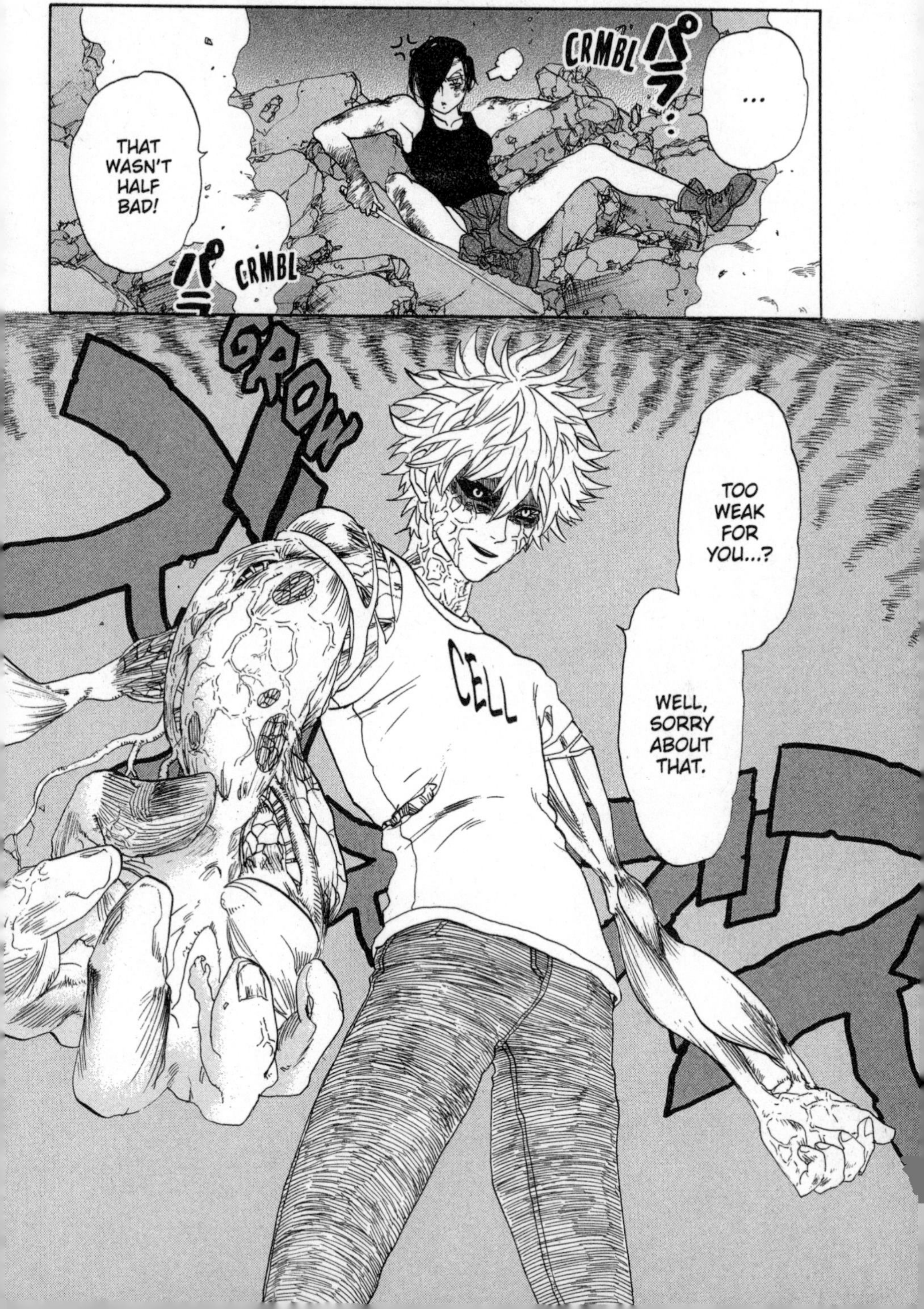

...
CRMBL
パラ
THAT WASN'T HALF BAD!
CRMBL
パラ
TOO WEAK FOR YOU...?
WELL, SORRY ABOUT THAT.
CELL

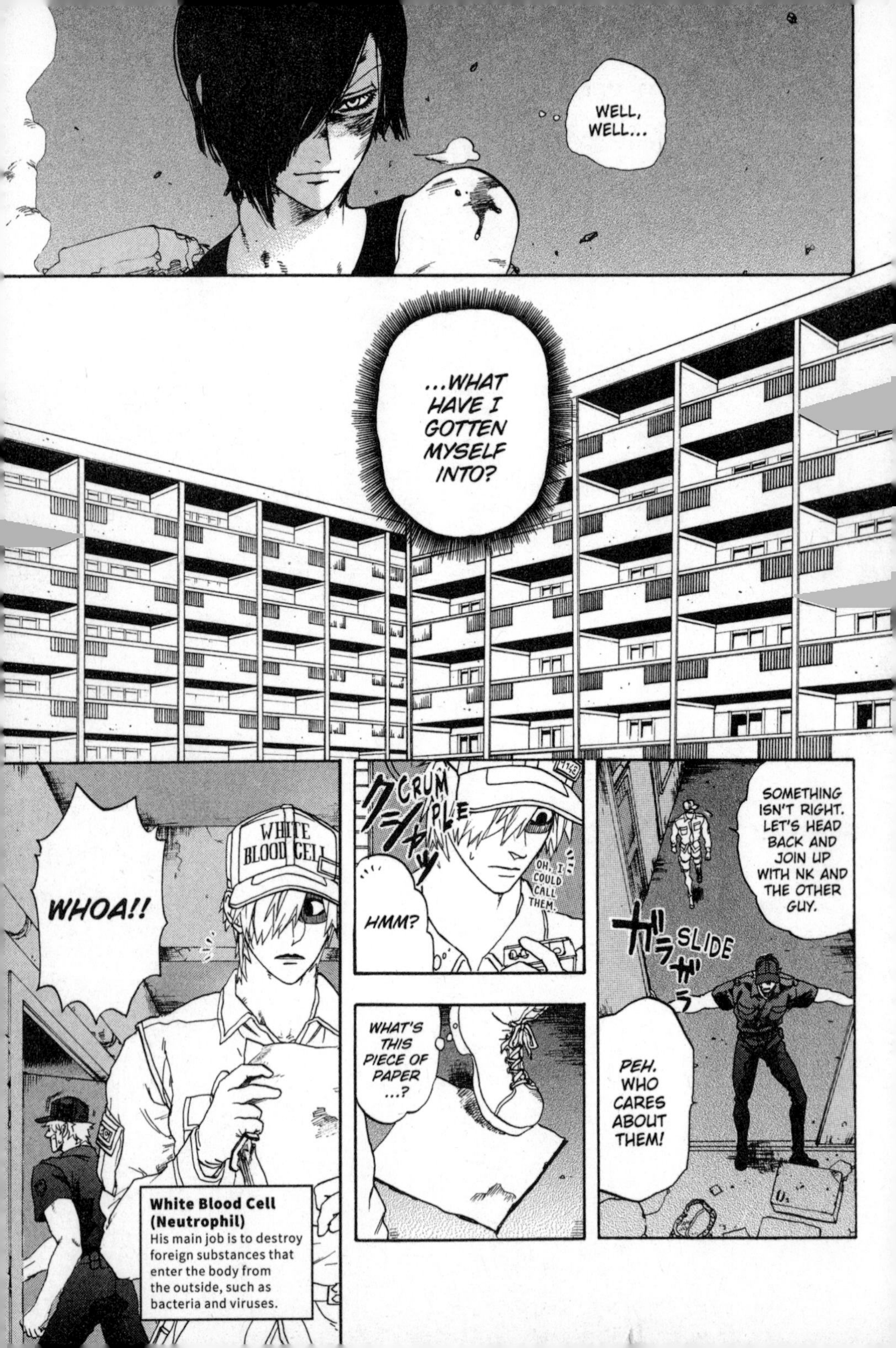

WELL, WELL...
...WHAT HAVE I GOTTEN MYSELF INTO?
SOMETHING ISN'T RIGHT. LET'S HEAD BACK AND JOIN UP WITH NK AND THE OTHER GUY.
SLIDE
PEH. WHO CARES ABOUT THEM!
CRUMPLE
OH, I COULD CALL THEM.
HMM?
WHAT'S THIS PIECE OF PAPER ...?
WHOA!!
White Blood Cell (Neutrophil)
His main job is to destroy foreign substances that enter the body from the outside, such as bacteria and viruses.

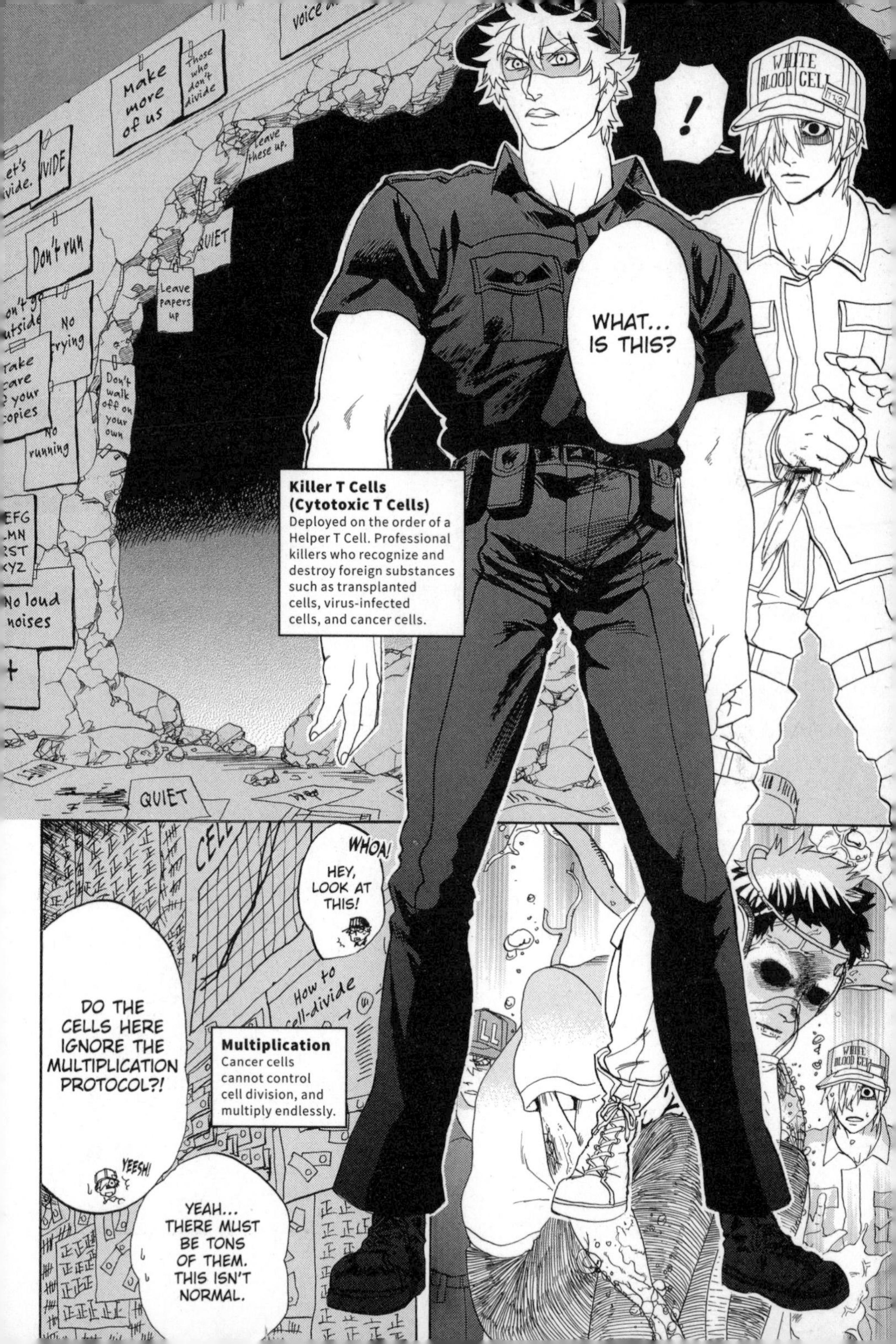

!
Make more of us
Those who don't divide
Leave these up.
Don't run
QUIET
Leave papers up
Don't walk off on your own
No running
No loud noises
QUIET
WHAT... IS THIS?
Killer T Cells (Cytotoxic T Cells)
Deployed on the order of a Helper T Cell. Professional killers who recognize and destroy foreign substances such as transplanted cells, virus-infected cells, and cancer cells.
WHITE BLOOD CELL
WHOA!
HEY, LOOK AT THIS!
How to cell-divide
DO THE CELLS HERE IGNORE THE MULTIPLICATION PROTOCOL?!
Multiplication
Cancer cells cannot control cell division, and multiply endlessly.
YEESH!
YEAH... THERE MUST BE TONS OF THEM. THIS ISN'T NORMAL.

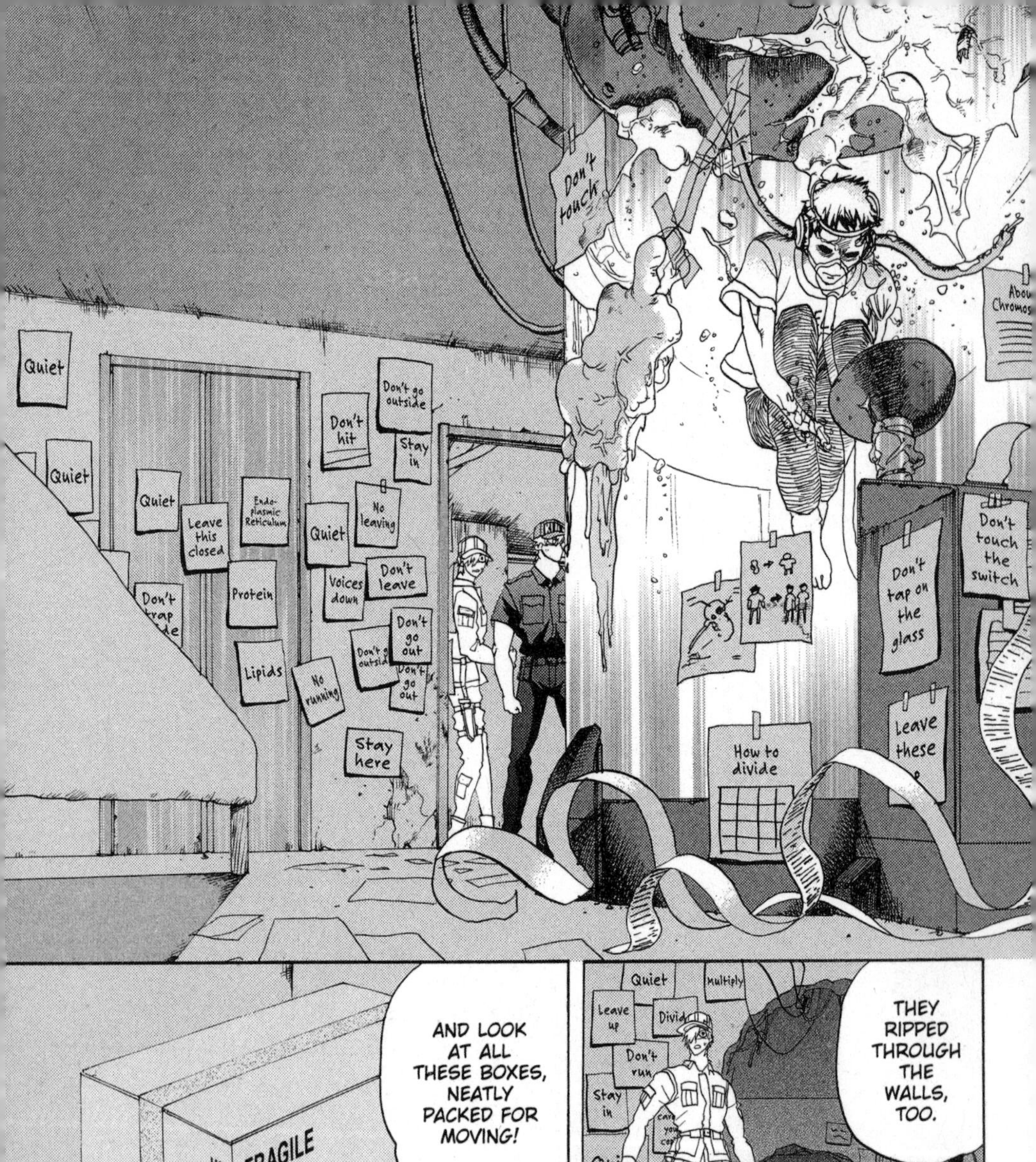
Don't touch
Quiet
Quiet
Don't go outside
Don't hit
Stay in
Quiet
Leave this closed
Endoplasmic Reticulum
Quiet
No leaving
Voices down
Don't leave
Protein
Don't go out
Lipids
No running
Don't go out
Stay here
How to divide
Don't tap on the glass
Don't touch the switch
Leave these

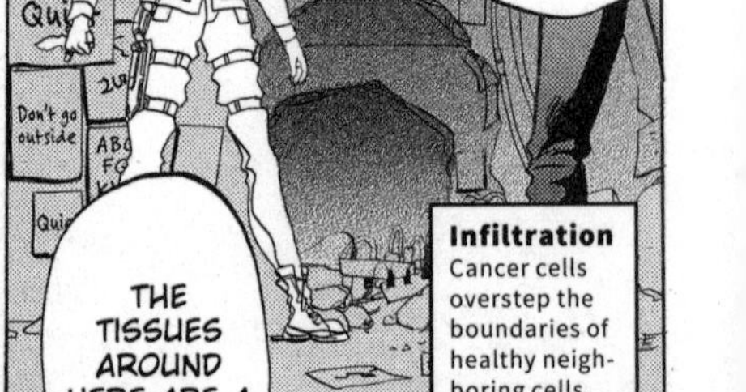
Quiet
Multiply
Leave up
Don't run
Stay in
Don't go outside
THEY RIPPED THROUGH THE WALLS, TOO.
THE TISSUES AROUND HERE ARE A MESS.
Infiltration
Cancer cells overstep the boundaries of healthy neighboring cells.

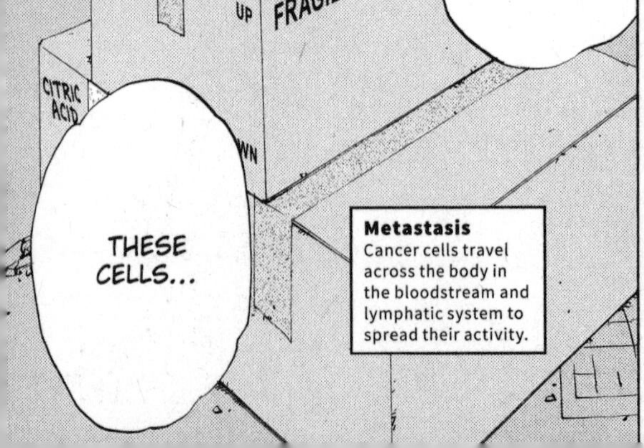
AND LOOK AT ALL THESE BOXES, NEATLY PACKED FOR MOVING!
UP
FRAGILE
CITRIC ACID
THESE CELLS...
Metastasis
Cancer cells travel across the body in the bloodstream and lymphatic system to spread their activity.

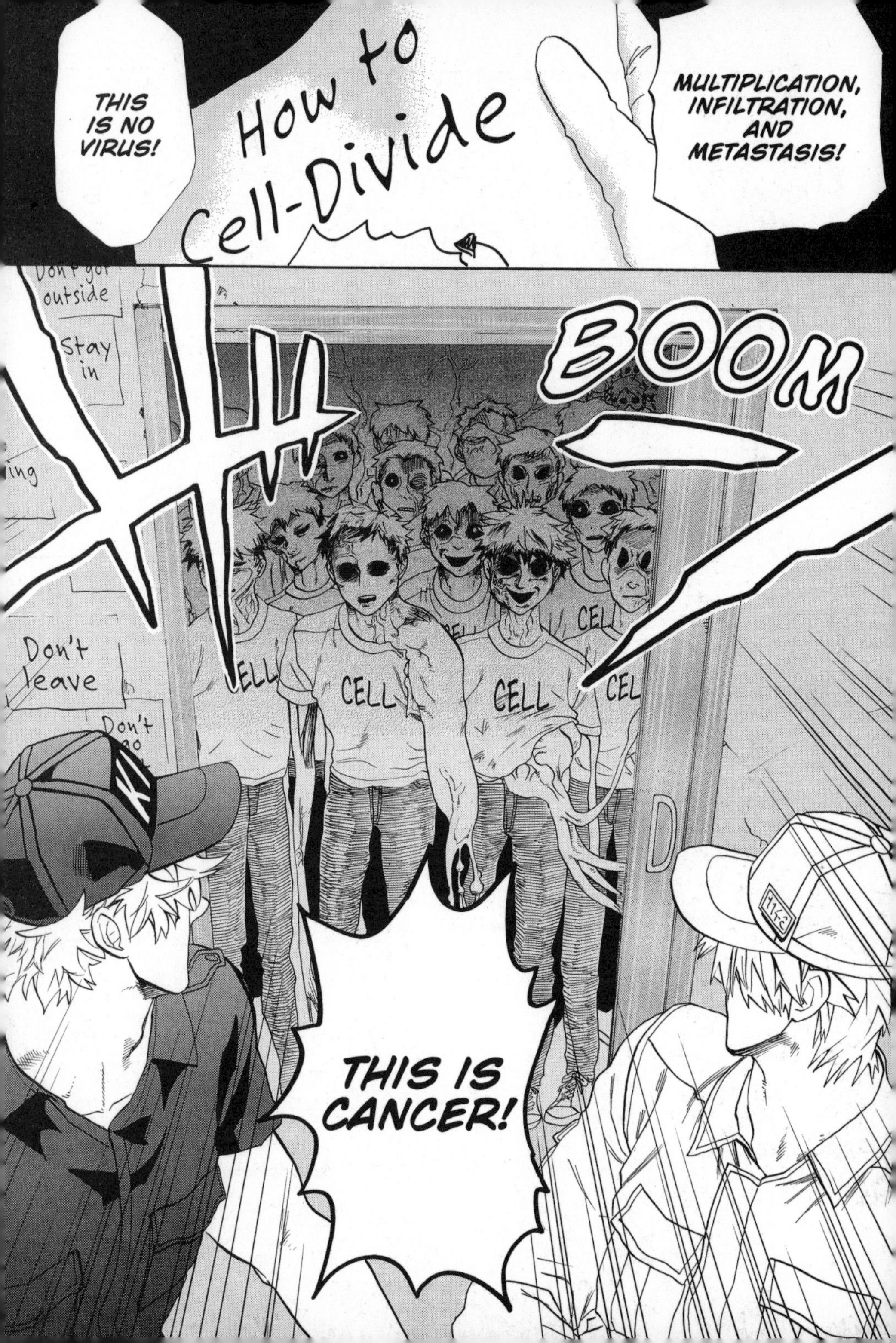
MULTIPLICATION, INFILTRATION, AND METASTASIS!
How to Cell-Divide
THIS IS NO VIRUS!
BOOM
outside
Stay in
Don't leave
CELL
CELL
CELL
THIS IS CANCER!

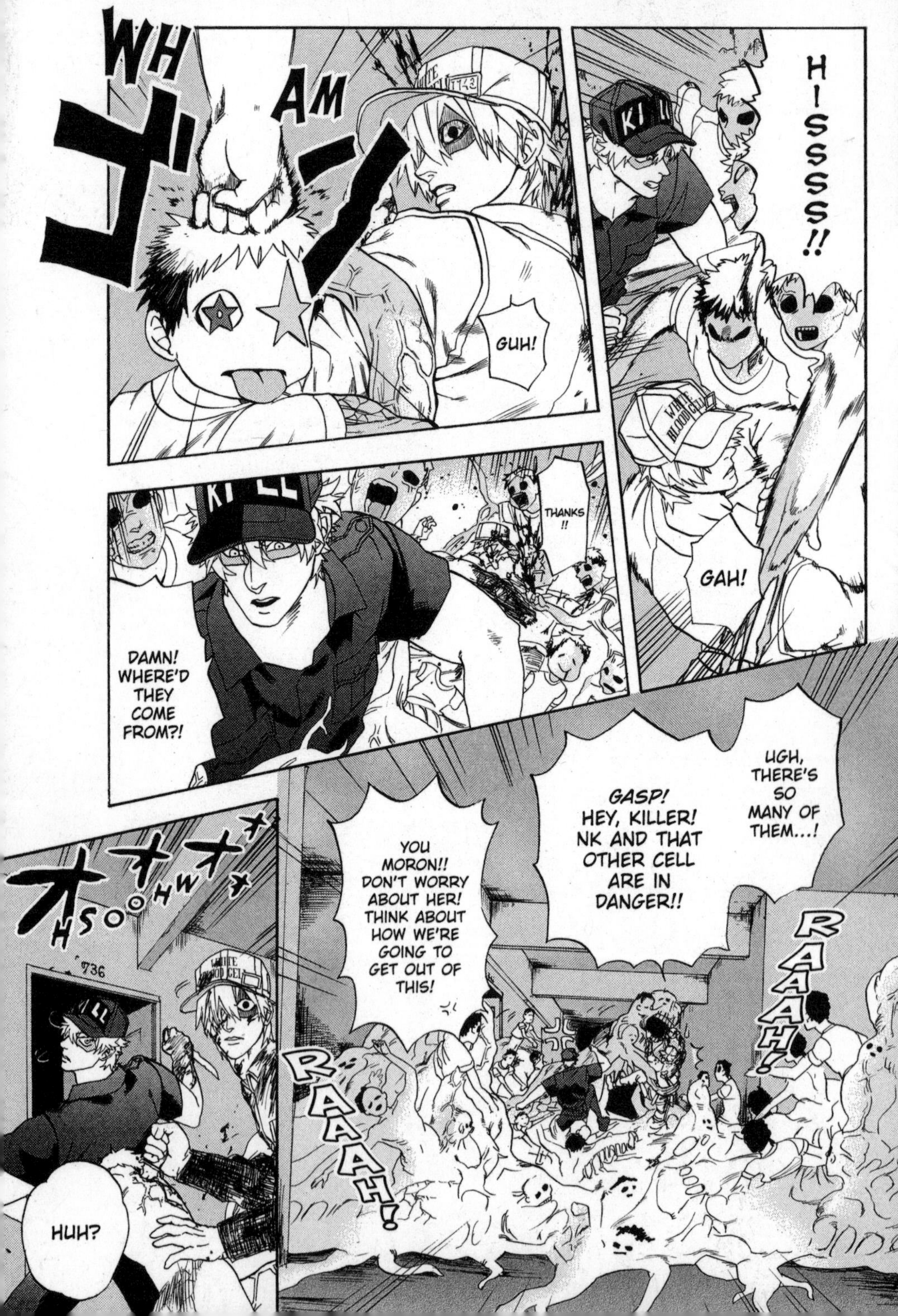
HISSSS!!
GAH!
WHAM
GUH!
THANKS!!
DAMN! WHERE'D THEY COME FROM?!
UGH, THERE'S SO MANY OF THEM...!
GASP! HEY, KILLER! NK AND THAT OTHER CELL ARE IN DANGER!!
YOU MORON!! DON'T WORRY ABOUT HER! THINK ABOUT HOW WE'RE GOING TO GET OUT OF THIS!
RAAAAH!
RAAAAH!
WHOOSH
736
HUH?

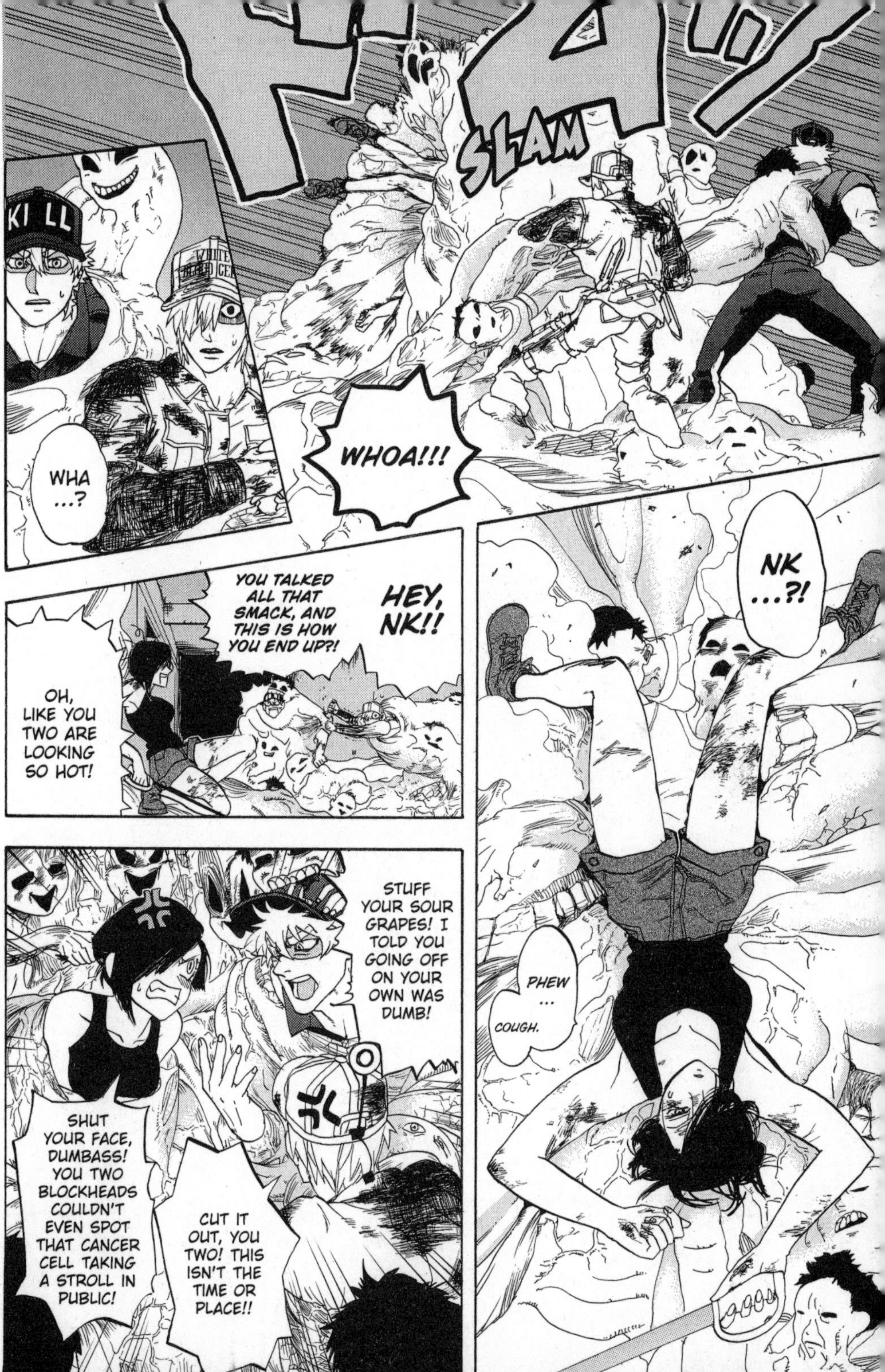
SLAM
WHOA!!!
WHA ...?
NK ...?!
PHEW ...
COUGH.
HEY, NK!!
YOU TALKED ALL THAT SMACK, AND THIS IS HOW YOU END UP?!
OH, LIKE YOU TWO ARE LOOKING SO HOT!
STUFF YOUR SOUR GRAPES! I TOLD YOU GOING OFF ON YOUR OWN WAS DUMB!
SHUT YOUR FACE, DUMBASS! YOU TWO BLOCKHEADS COULDN'T EVEN SPOT THAT CANCER CELL TAKING A STROLL IN PUBLIC!
CUT IT OUT, YOU TWO! THIS ISN'T THE TIME OR PLACE!!

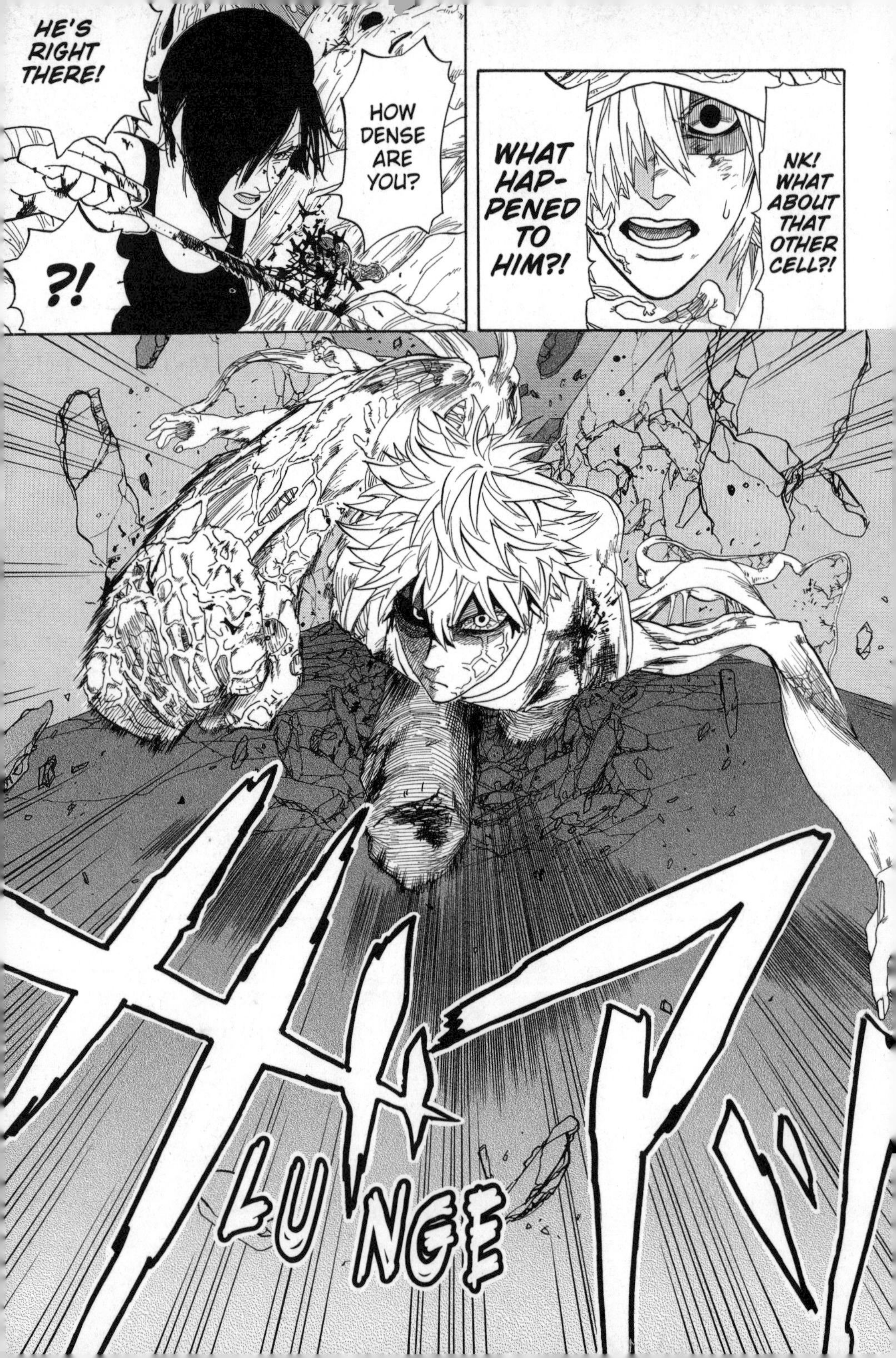
NK! WHAT ABOUT THAT OTHER CELL?!
WHAT HAPPENED TO HIM?!
HE'S RIGHT THERE!
HOW DENSE ARE YOU?
?!
LUNGE

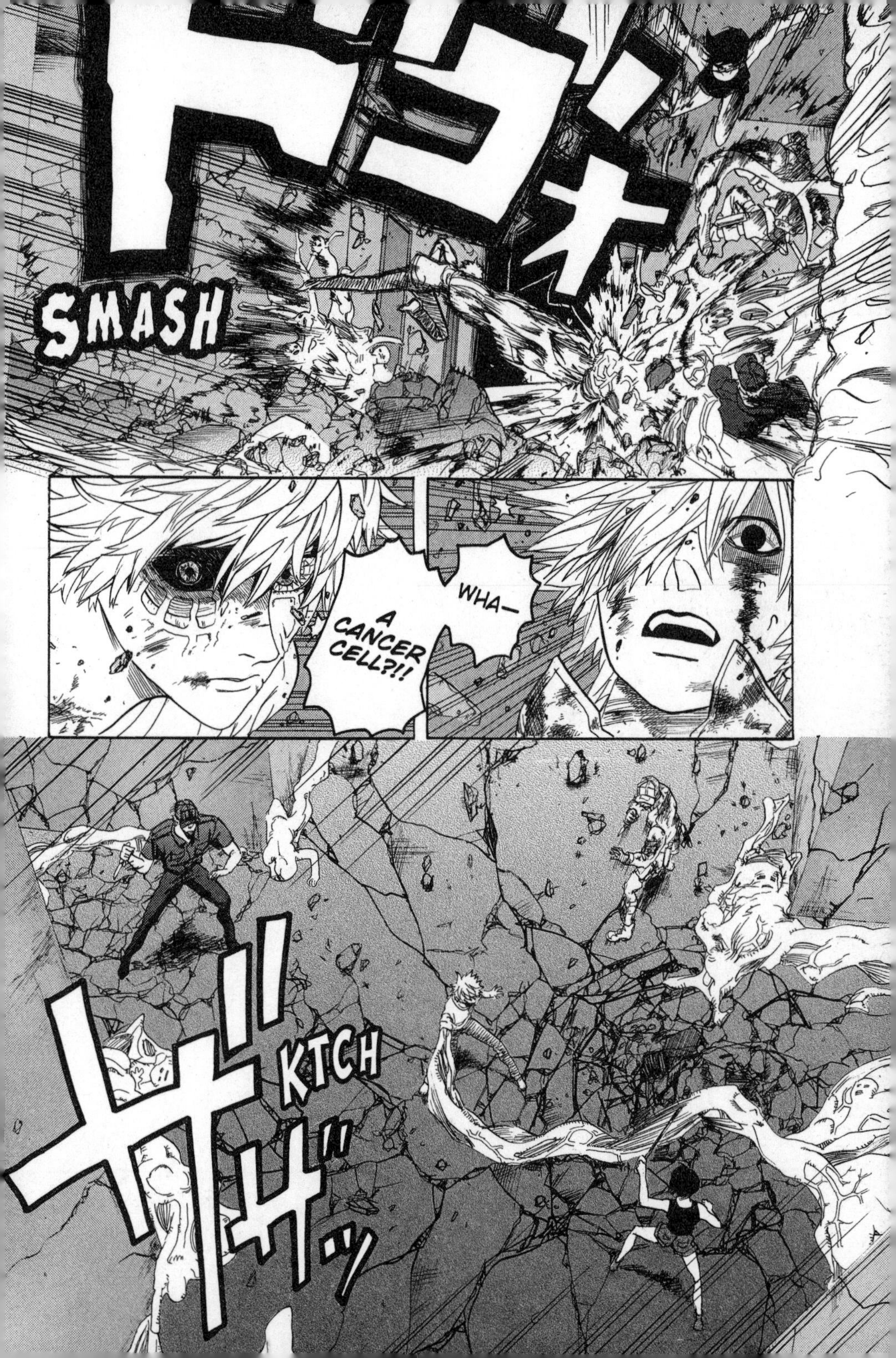
SMASH
WHA—
A CANCER CELL?!!
KTCH

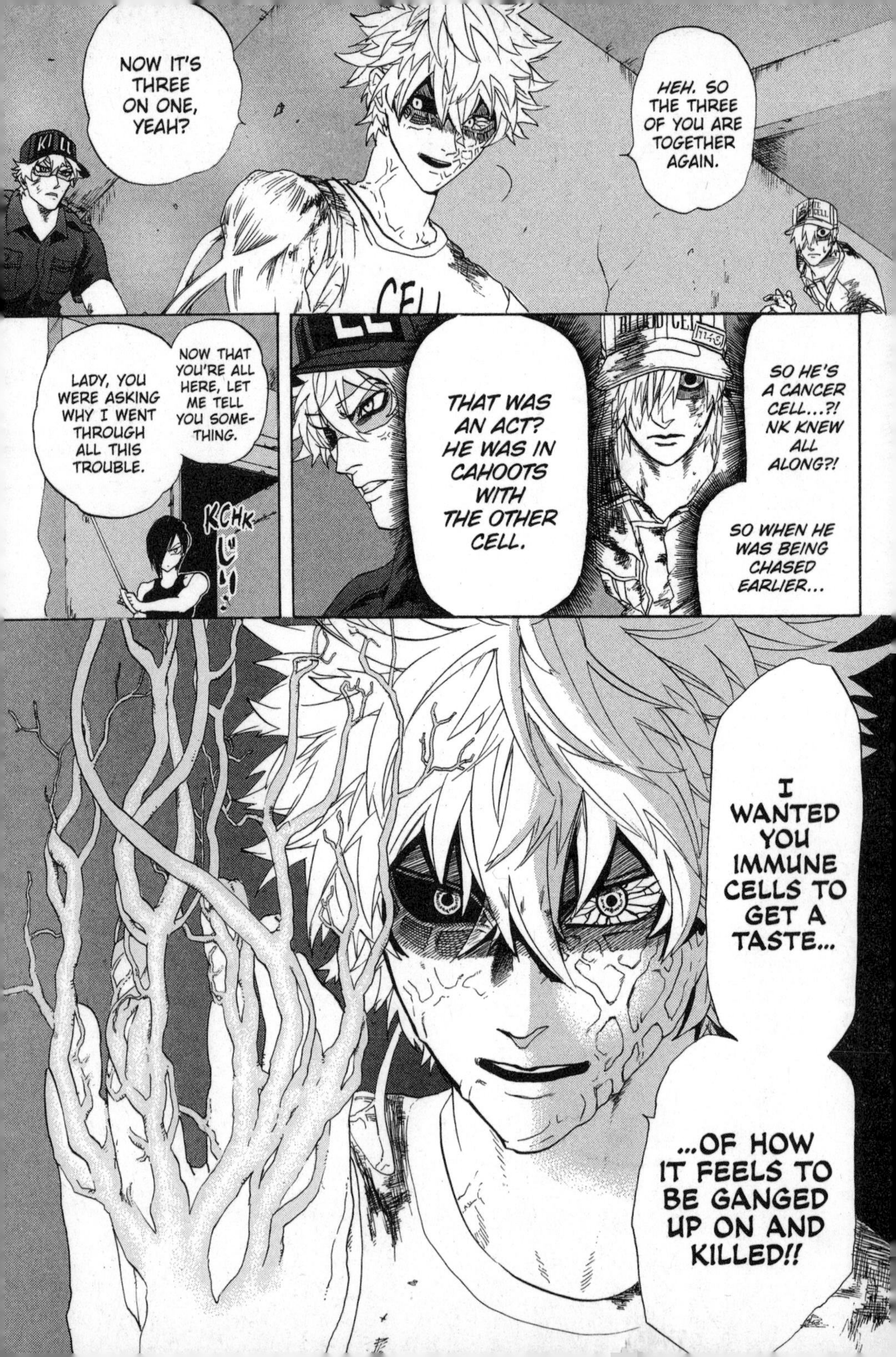
HEH. SO THE THREE OF YOU ARE TOGETHER AGAIN.
NOW IT'S THREE ON ONE, YEAH?
SO HE'S A CANCER CELL...?! NK KNEW ALL ALONG?!
SO WHEN HE WAS BEING CHASED EARLIER...
THAT WAS AN ACT? HE WAS IN CAHOOTS WITH THE OTHER CELL.
NOW THAT YOU'RE ALL HERE, LET ME TELL YOU SOME-THING.
LADY, YOU WERE ASKING WHY I WENT THROUGH ALL THIS TROUBLE.
KCHK
I WANTED YOU IMMUNE CELLS TO GET A TASTE...
...OF HOW IT FEELS TO BE GANGED UP ON AND KILLED!!

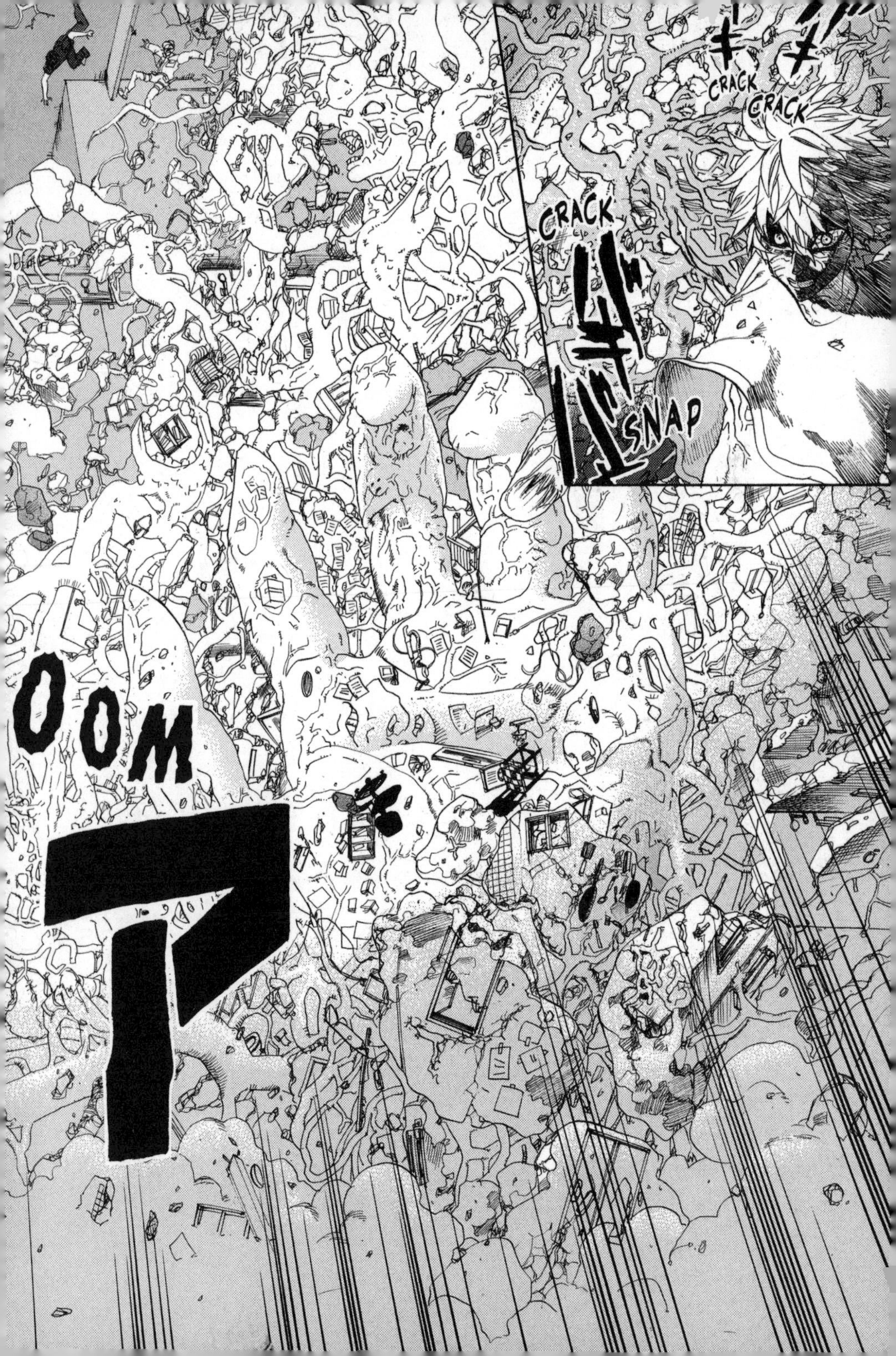
CRACK
CRACK
CRACK
SNAP
OOM

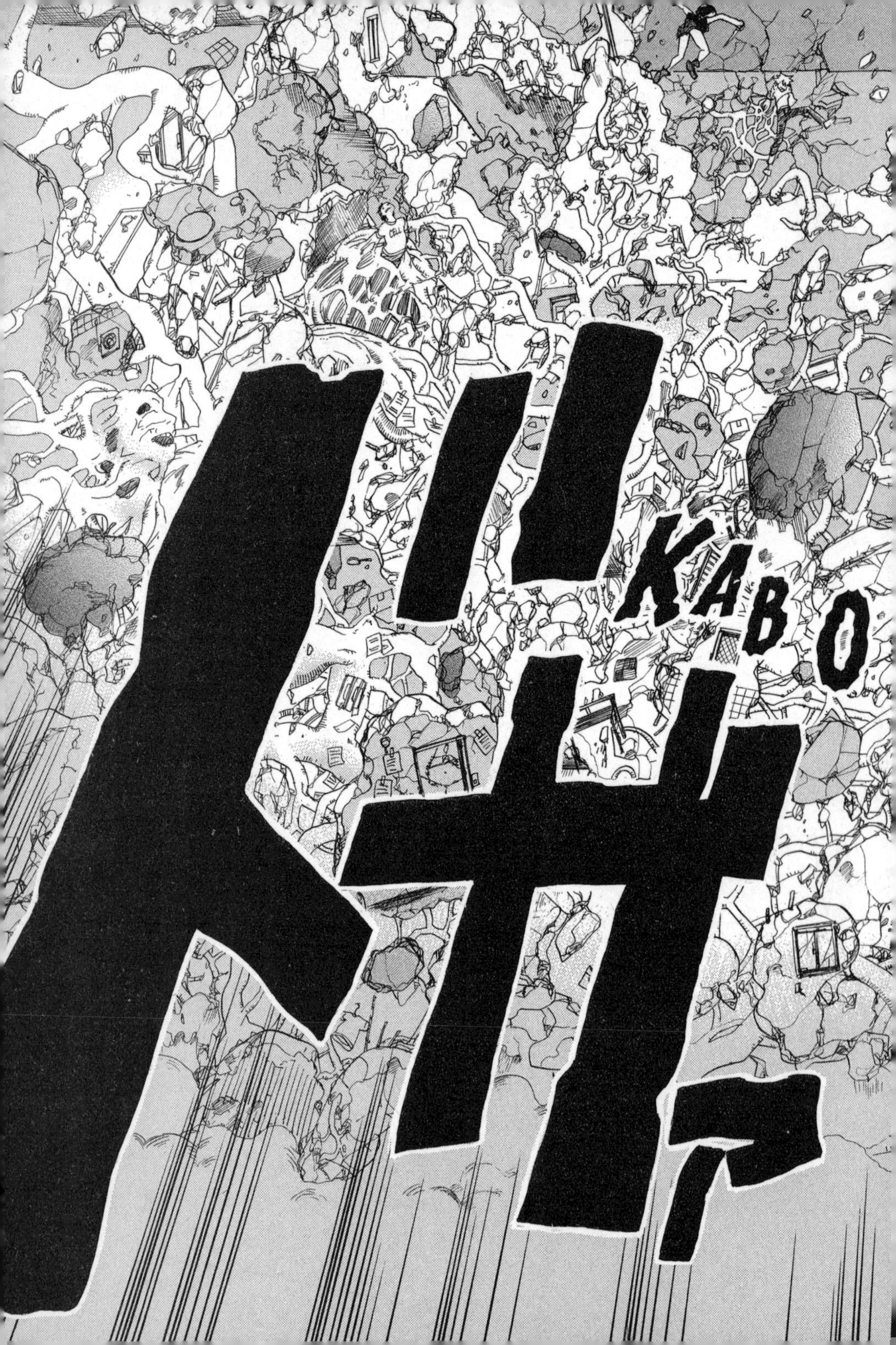
KABO

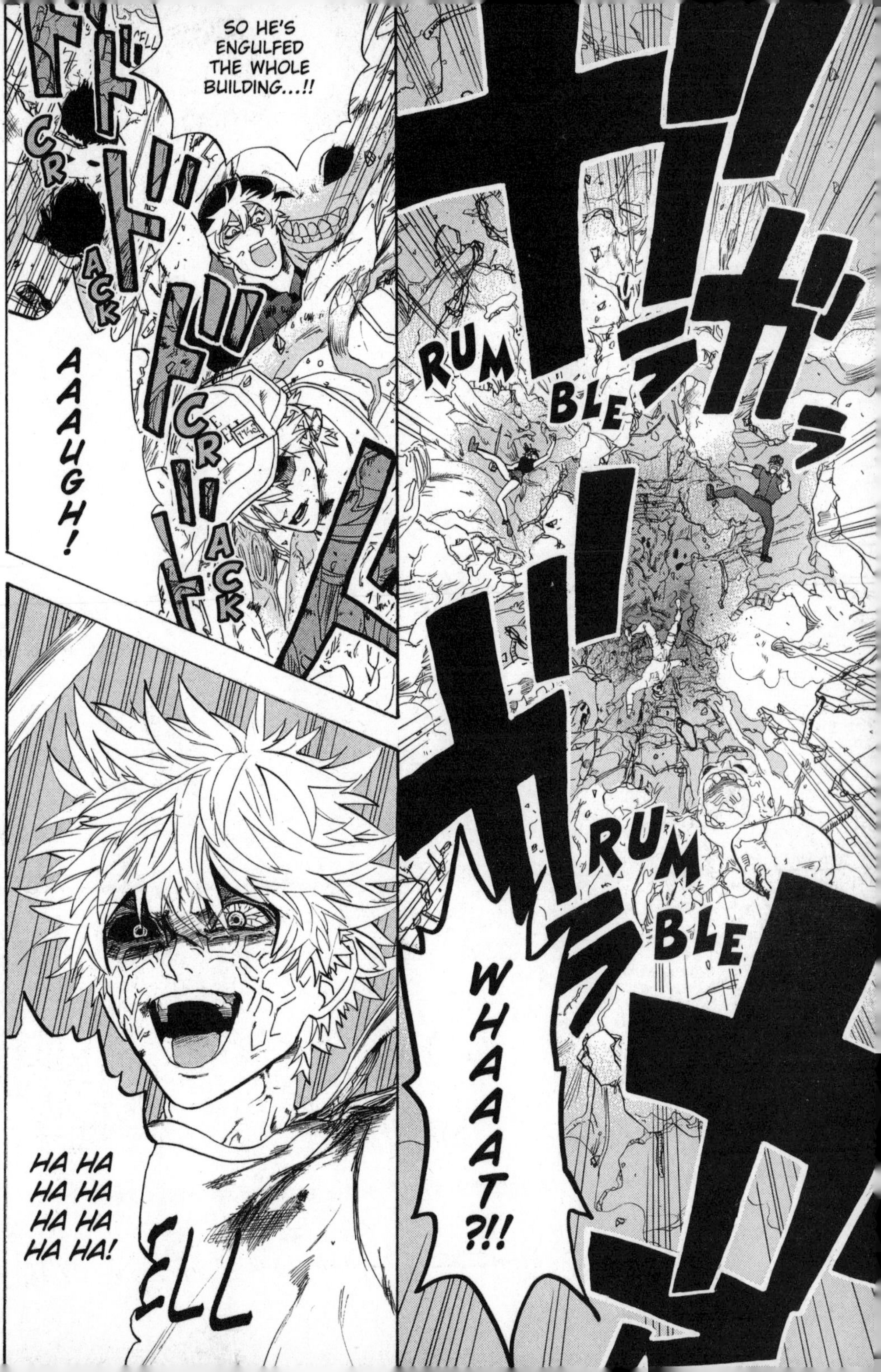
RUMBLE
RUMBLE
WHAAAAT?!!
SO HE'S ENGULFED THE WHOLE BUILDING...!!
CRACK
CRIIACK
AAAAUGH!
HA HA HA HA HA HA HA HA!
ELL

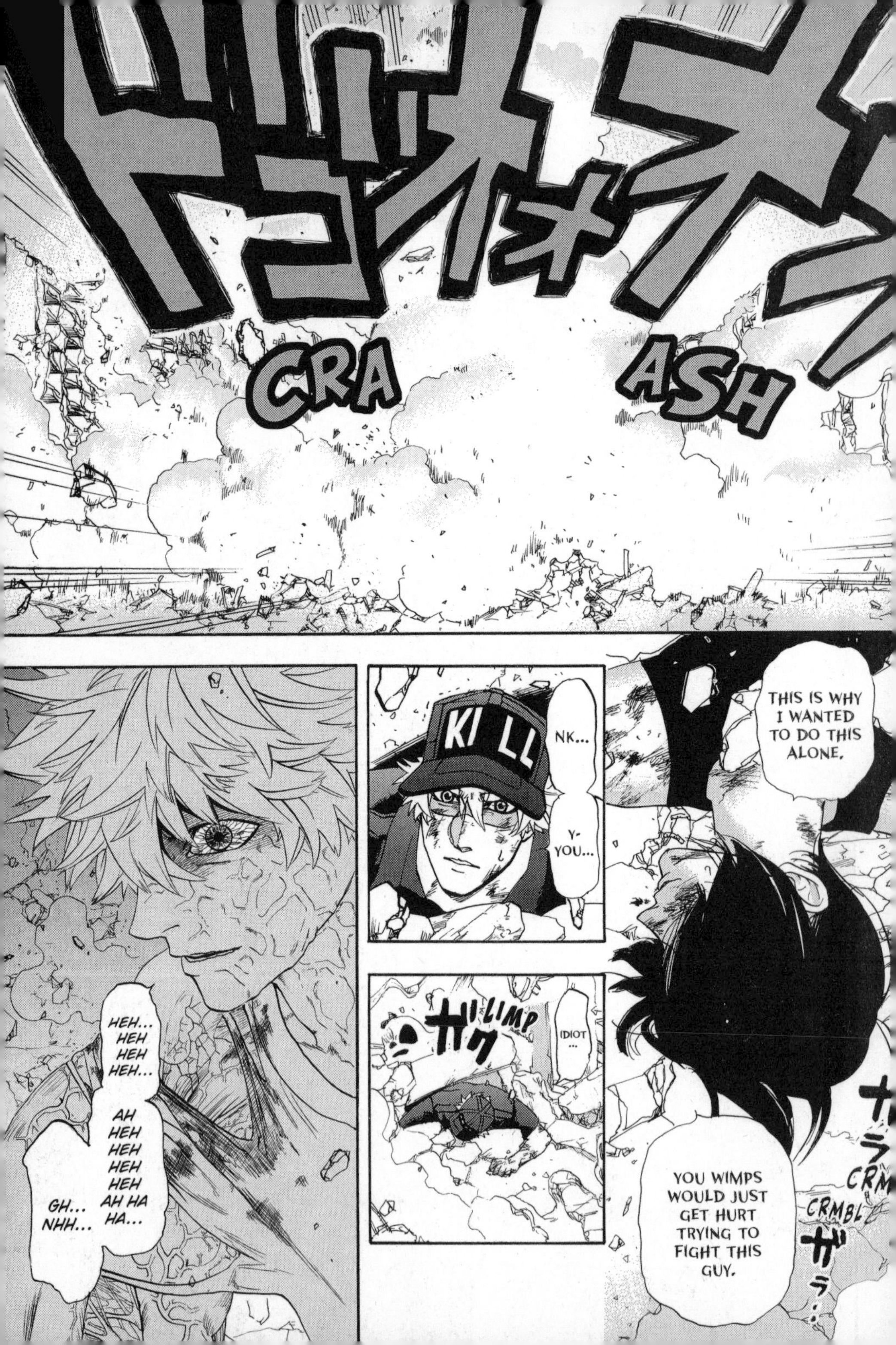
CRA
ASH
THIS IS WHY I WANTED TO DO THIS ALONE.
YOU WIMPS WOULD JUST GET HURT TRYING TO FIGHT THIS GUY.
CRMBL
CRMBL
ガラ
ガラ...
NK...
Y- YOU...
ガク
LIMP
IDIOT ...
HEH... HEH HEH HEH...
AH HEH HEH HEH HEH AH HA HA...
GH... NHH...

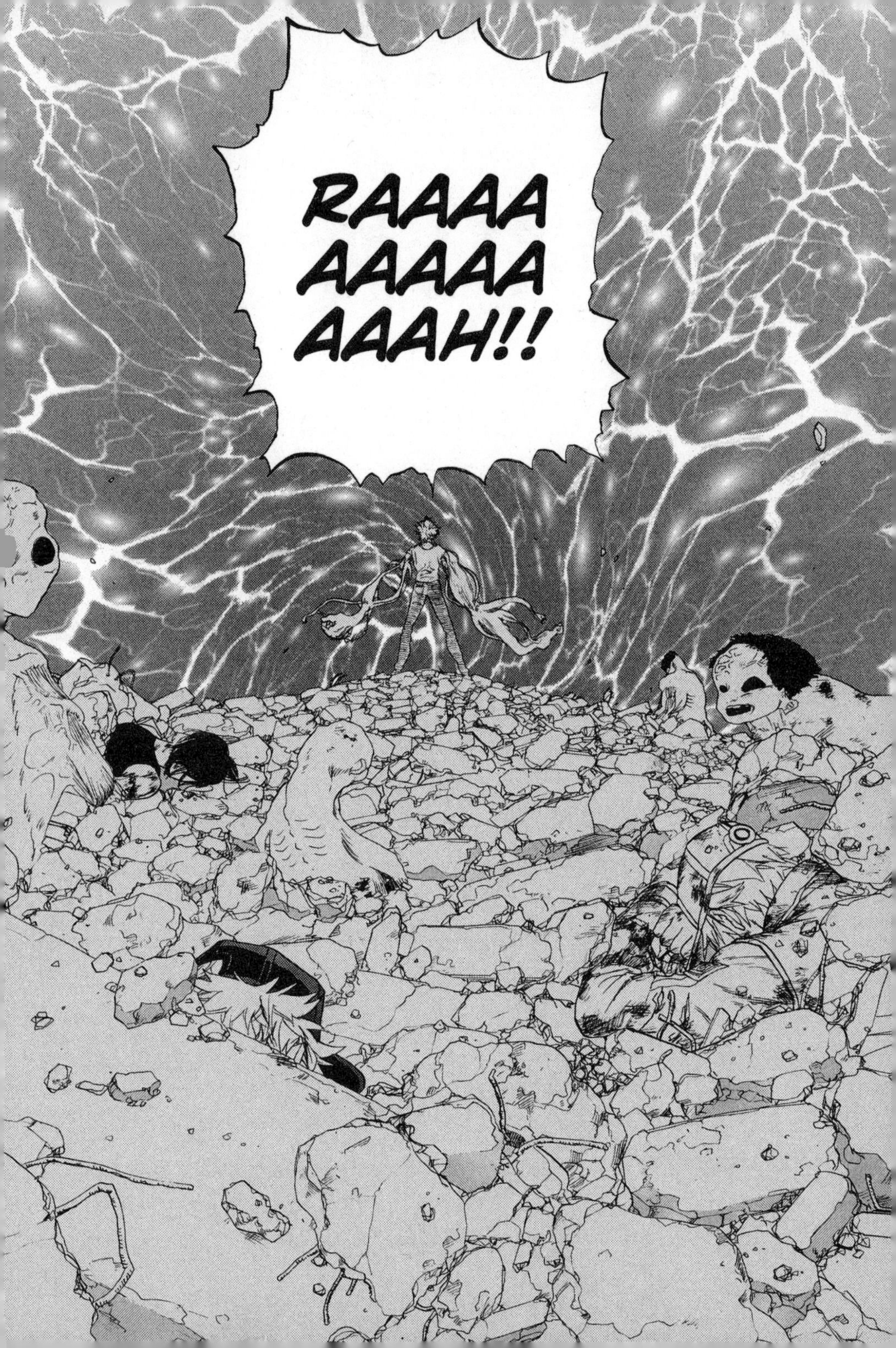
RAAAA AAAAA AAAH!!

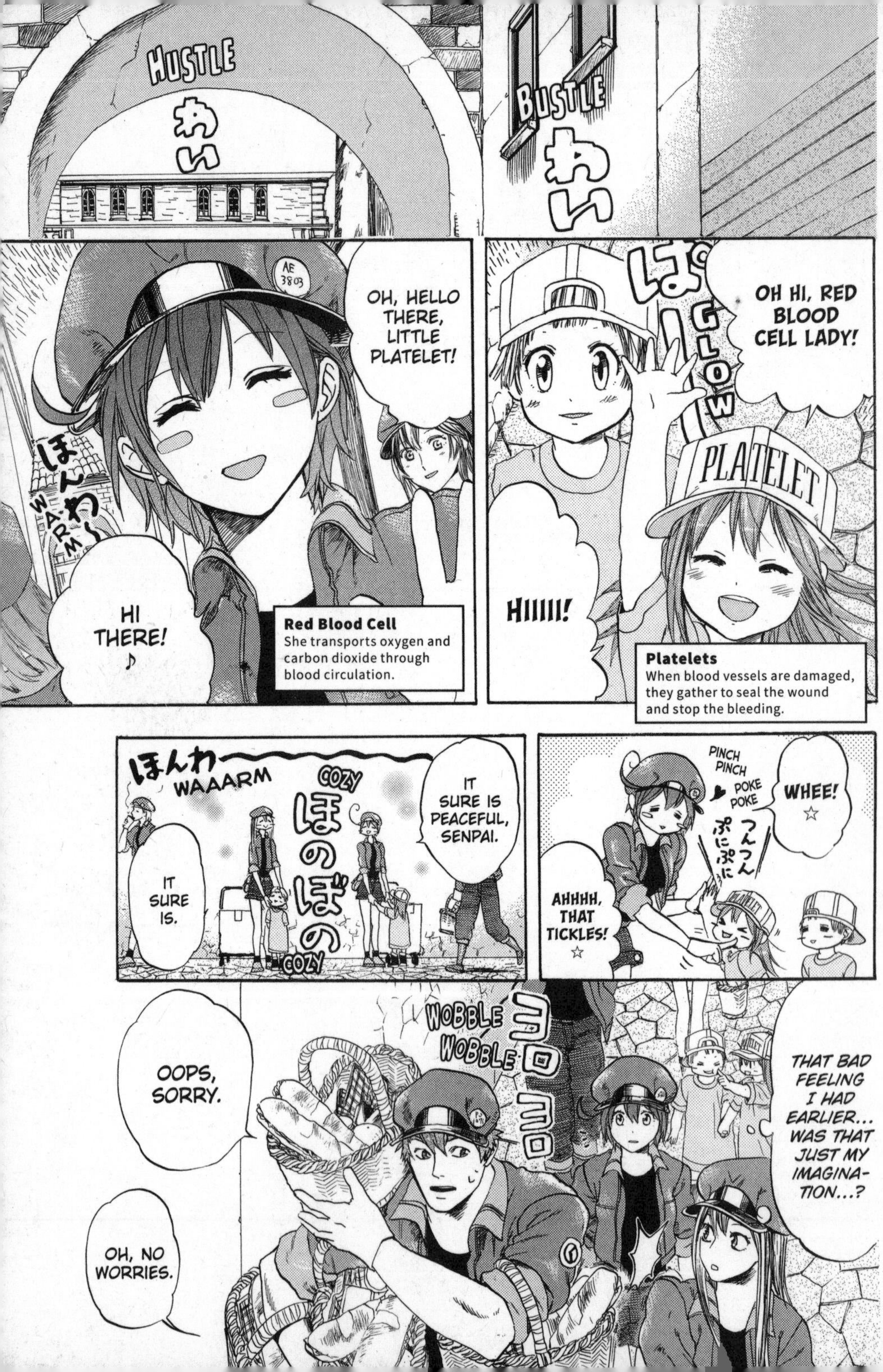
BUSTLE
わい
HUSTLE
わい
ぱ
GLOW
OH HI, RED BLOOD CELL LADY!
PLATELET
HIIIII!
Platelets
When blood vessels are damaged, they gather to seal the wound and stop the bleeding.
OH, HELLO THERE, LITTLE PLATELET!
AE 3803
ほんわ〜
WARM
HI THERE! ♪
Red Blood Cell
She transports oxygen and carbon dioxide through blood circulation.
WHEE! ☆
PINCH PINCH
POKE POKE
つんつん
ぷにぷに
AHHHH, THAT TICKLES! ☆
IT SURE IS PEACEFUL, SENPAI.
COZY
ほのぼの
COZY
ほんわ〜
WAAARM
IT SURE IS.
THAT BAD FEELING I HAD EARLIER... WAS THAT JUST MY IMAGINATION...?
ヨロヨロ
WOBBLE WOBBLE
OOPS, SORRY.
OH, NO WORRIES.

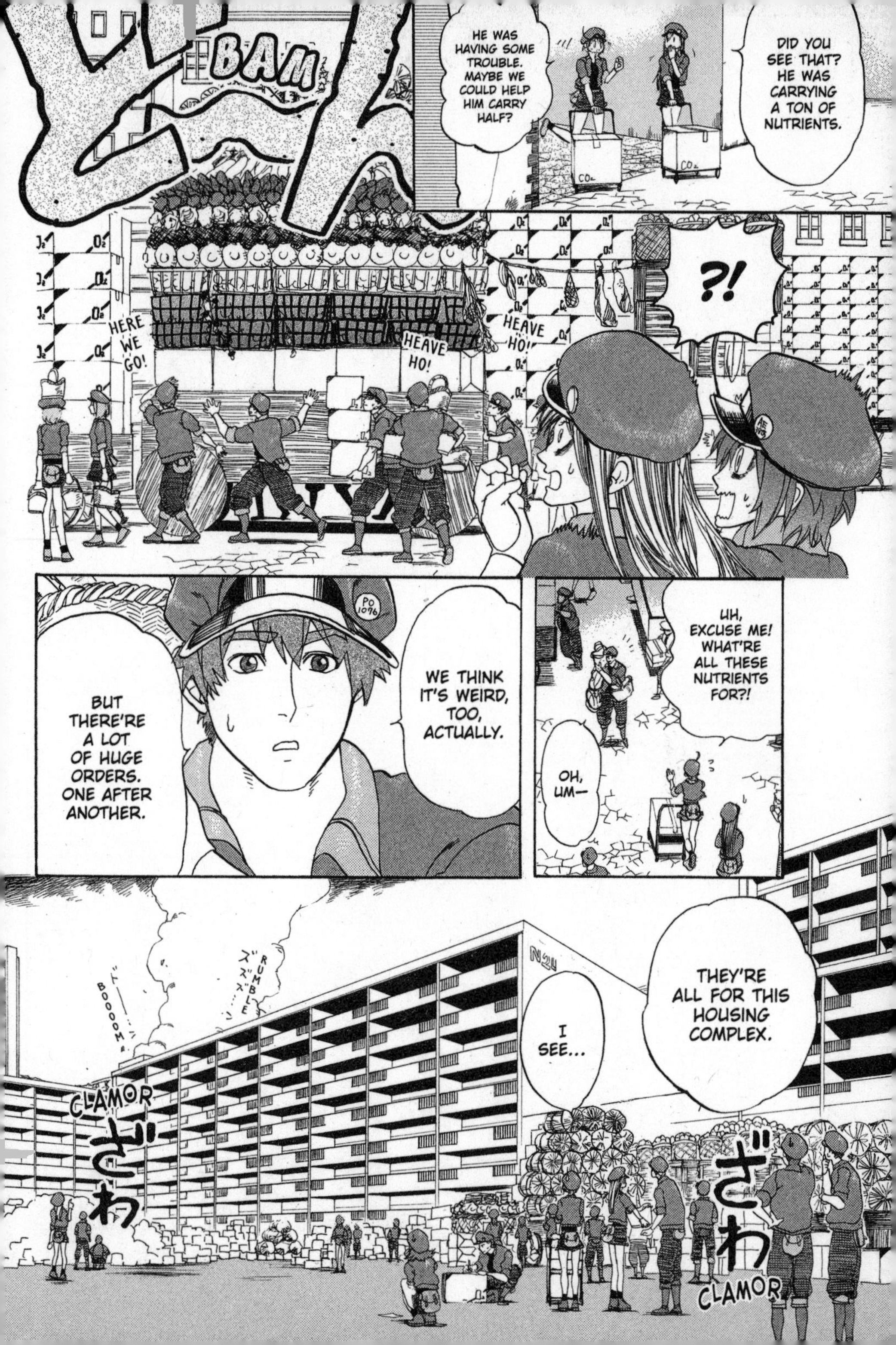
DID YOU SEE THAT? HE WAS CARRYING A TON OF NUTRIENTS.
HE WAS HAVING SOME TROUBLE. MAYBE WE COULD HELP HIM CARRY HALF?
BAM
?!
HEAVE HO!
HEAVE HO!
HERE WE GO!
UH, EXCUSE ME! WHAT'RE ALL THESE NUTRIENTS FOR?!
OH, UM—
WE THINK IT'S WEIRD, TOO, ACTUALLY.
BUT THERE'RE A LOT OF HUGE ORDERS. ONE AFTER ANOTHER.
THEY'RE ALL FOR THIS HOUSING COMPLEX.
I SEE...
RUMBLE
BOOOOOM
CLAMOR
ざわ
ざわ
CLAMOR

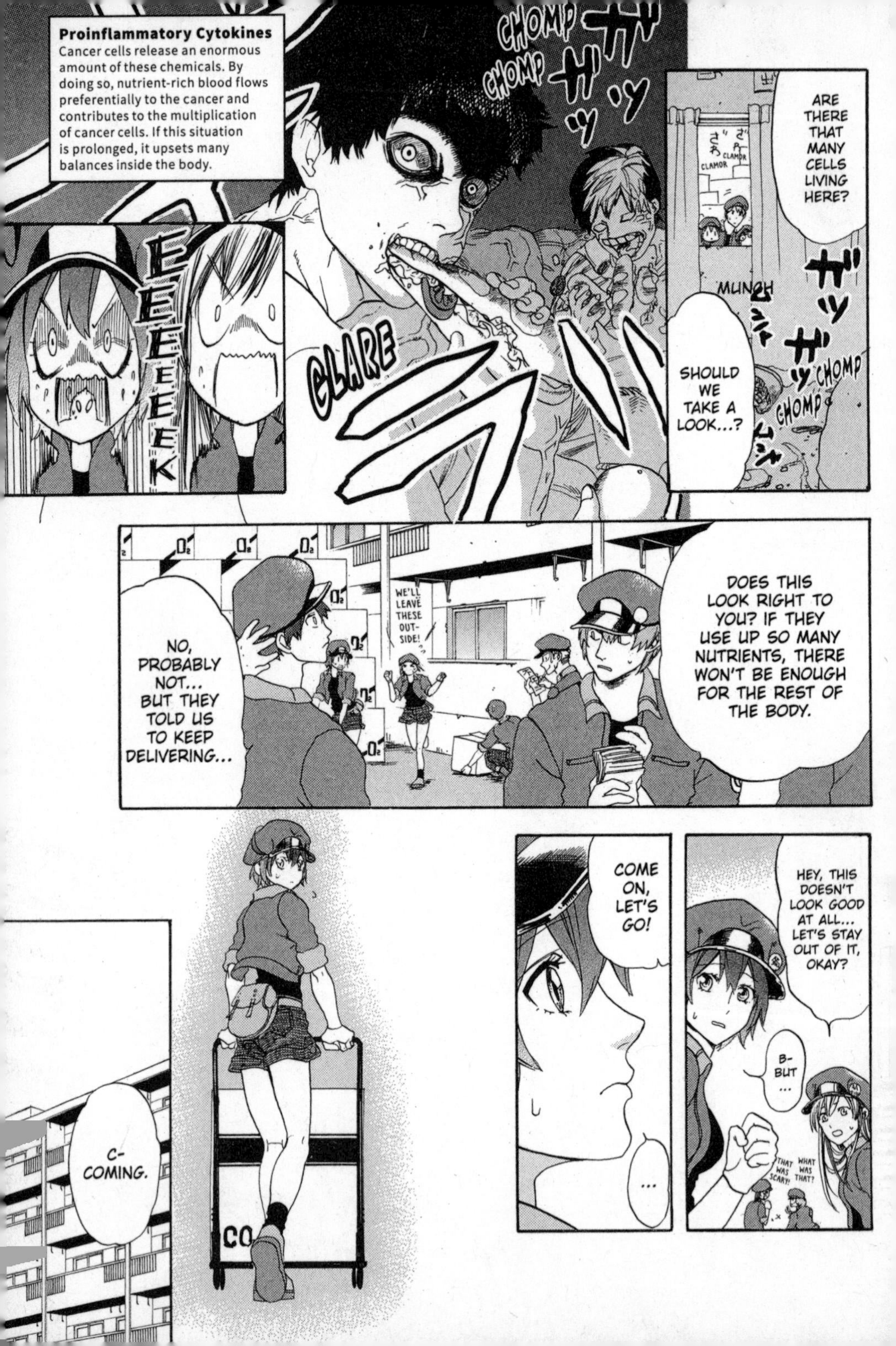
ARE THERE THAT MANY CELLS LIVING HERE?
CLAMOR CLAMOR
SHOULD WE TAKE A LOOK...?
MUNCH
CHOMP CHOMP
CHOMP CHOMP
Proinflammatory Cytokines
Cancer cells release an enormous amount of these chemicals. By doing so, nutrient-rich blood flows preferentially to the cancer and contributes to the multiplication of cancer cells. If this situation is prolonged, it upsets many balances inside the body.
GLARE
EEEEEEEEEK
DOES THIS LOOK RIGHT TO YOU? IF THEY USE UP SO MANY NUTRIENTS, THERE WON'T BE ENOUGH FOR THE REST OF THE BODY.
WE'LL LEAVE THESE OUT-SIDE!
NO, PROBABLY NOT... BUT THEY TOLD US TO KEEP DELIVERING...
HEY, THIS DOESN'T LOOK GOOD AT ALL... LET'S STAY OUT OF IT, OKAY?
B-BUT...
WHAT WAS THAT?
THAT WAS SCARY!
COME ON, LET'S GO!
...
C-COMING.

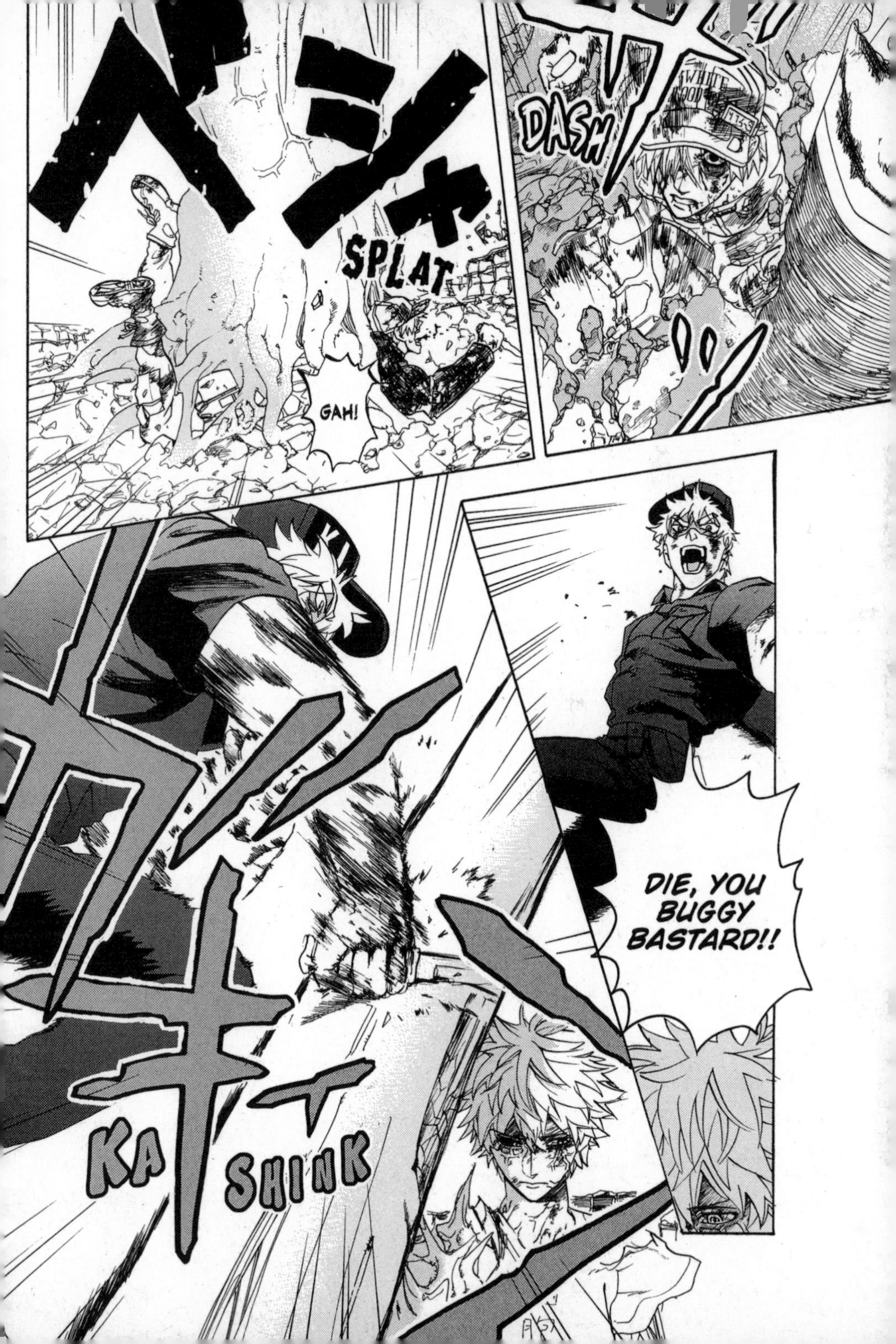
DASH
SPLAT
GAH!
DIE, YOU BUGGY BASTARD!!
KA SHINK

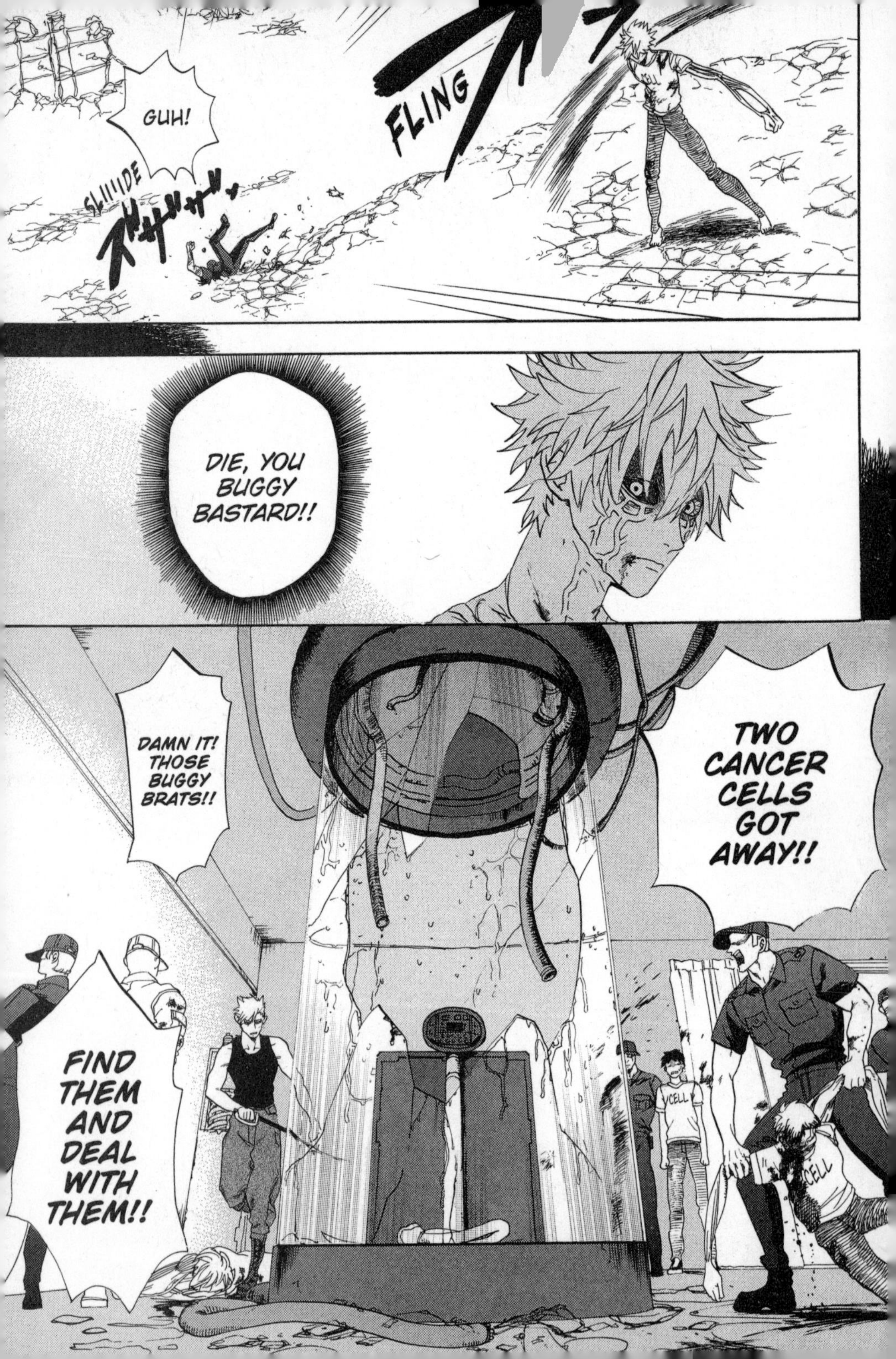
FLING
GUH!
SLIIIIDE
DIE, YOU BUGGY BASTARD!!
TWO CANCER CELLS GOT AWAY!!
CELL
CELL
DAMN IT! THOSE BUGGY BRATS!!
FIND THEM AND DEAL WITH THEM!!

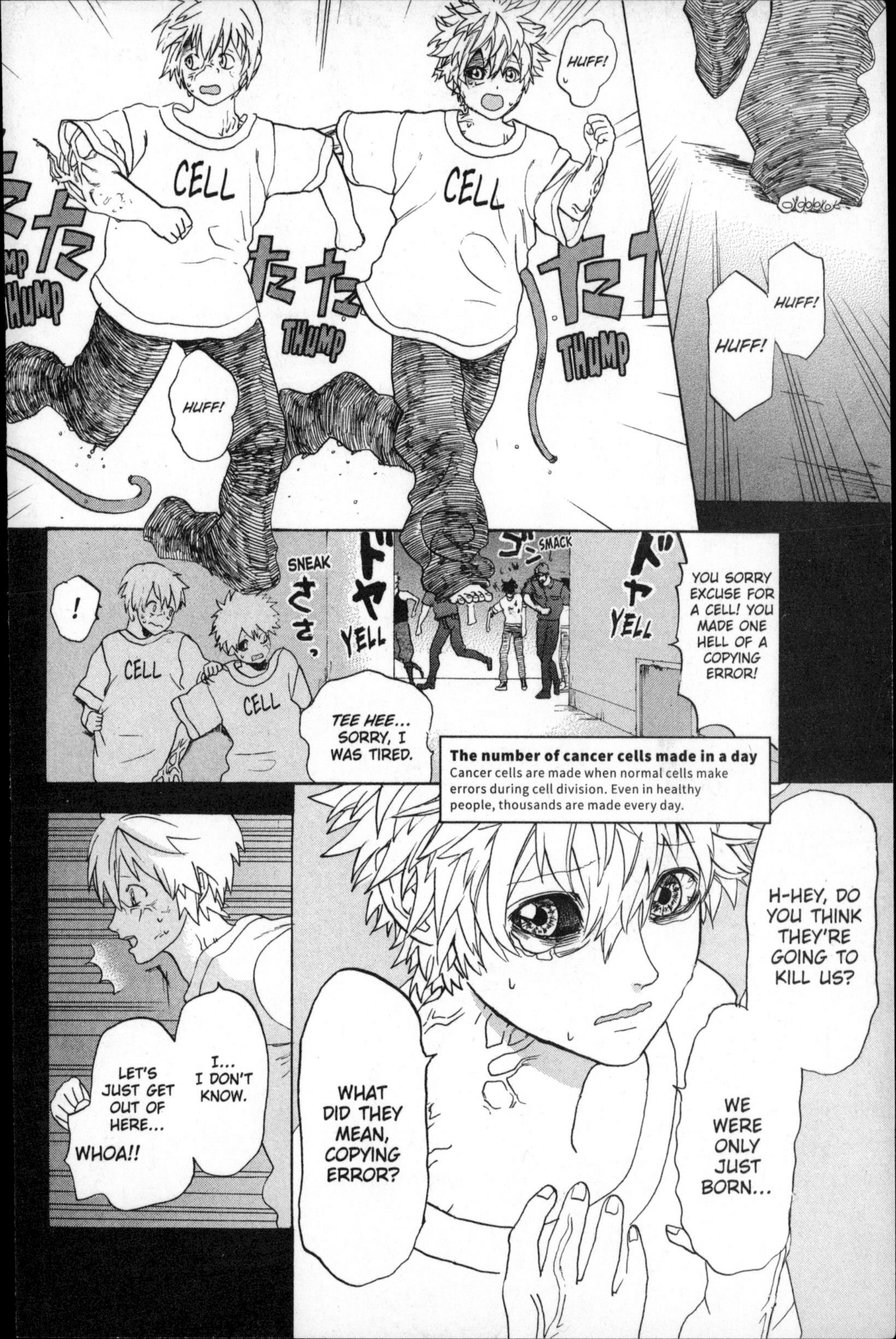
HUFF!
HUFF!
HUFF!
たた
THUMP THUMP
たた
THUMP
たた
THUMP
HUFF!
ドヤ
YELL
ゴン
SMACK
YOU SORRY EXCUSE FOR A CELL! YOU MADE ONE HELL OF A COPYING ERROR!
ドヤ
YELL
さっ
SNEAK
!
TEE HEE... SORRY, I WAS TIRED.
The number of cancer cells made in a day
Cancer cells are made when normal cells make errors during cell division. Even in healthy people, thousands are made every day.
H-HEY, DO YOU THINK THEY'RE GOING TO KILL US?
WE WERE ONLY JUST BORN...
WHAT DID THEY MEAN, COPYING ERROR?
I... I DON'T KNOW.
LET'S JUST GET OUT OF HERE...
WHOA!!

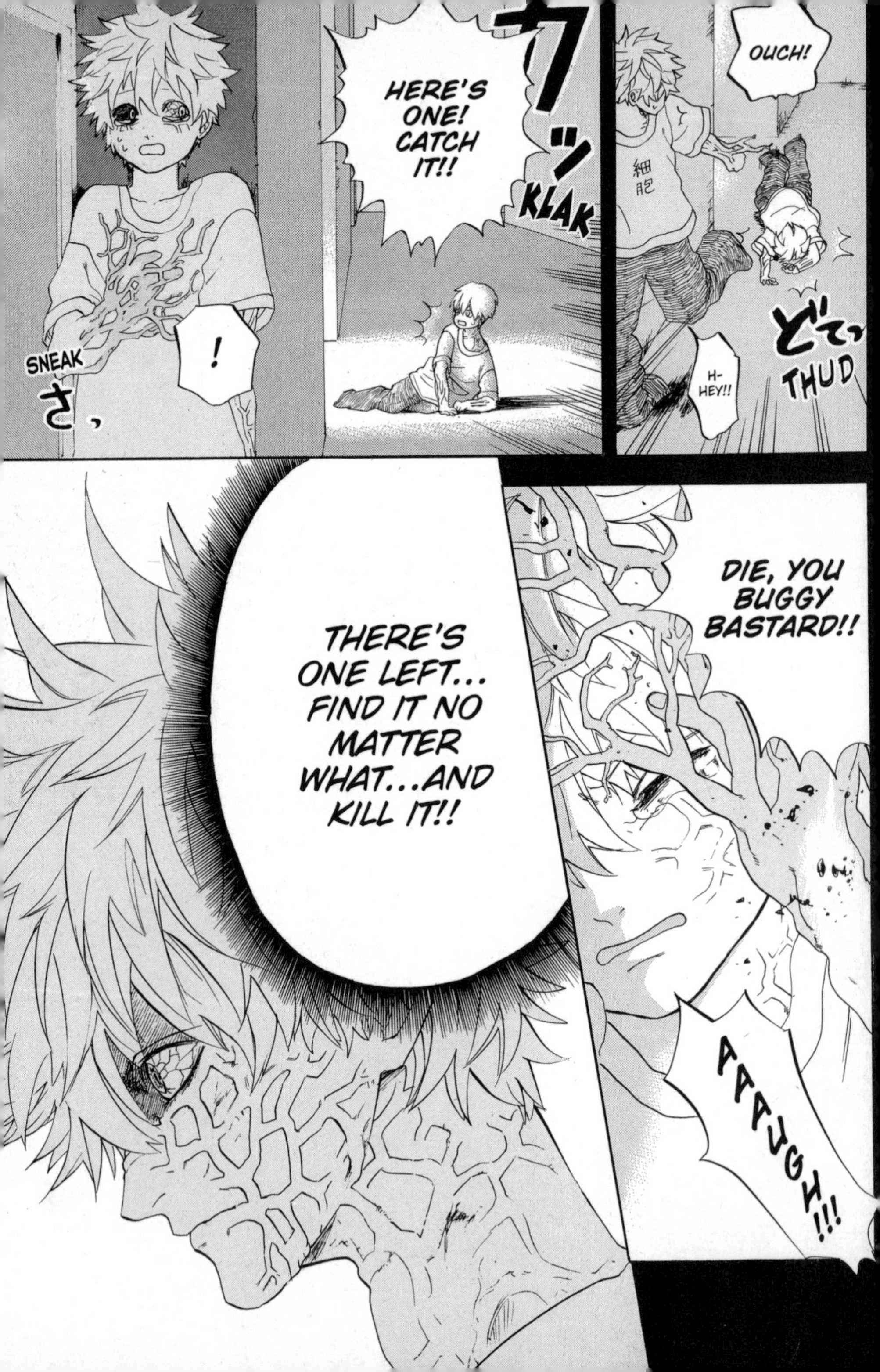
OUCH!
どでっ
THUD
H-HEY!!
カッ
KLAK
HERE'S ONE! CATCH IT!!
!
SNEAK
さ
DIE, YOU BUGGY BASTARD!!
AAAUGH!!!
THERE'S ONE LEFT... FIND IT NO MATTER WHAT...AND KILL IT!!

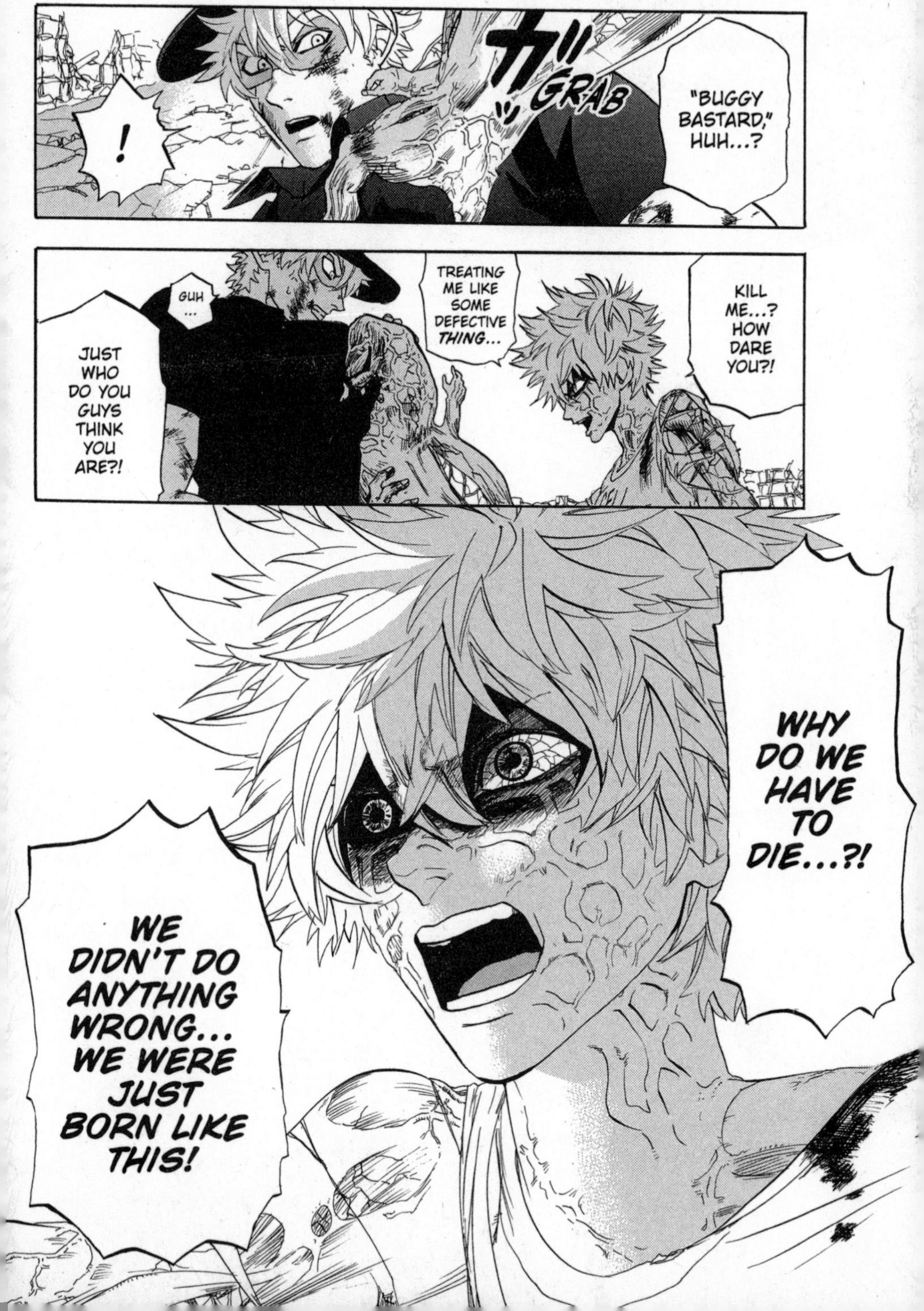
"BUGGY BASTARD," HUH...?
GRAB
!
KILL ME...? HOW DARE YOU?!
TREATING ME LIKE SOME DEFECTIVE *THING*...
GUH ...
JUST WHO DO YOU GUYS THINK YOU ARE?!
WHY DO WE HAVE TO DIE...?!
WE DIDN'T DO ANYTHING WRONG... WE WERE JUST BORN LIKE THIS!

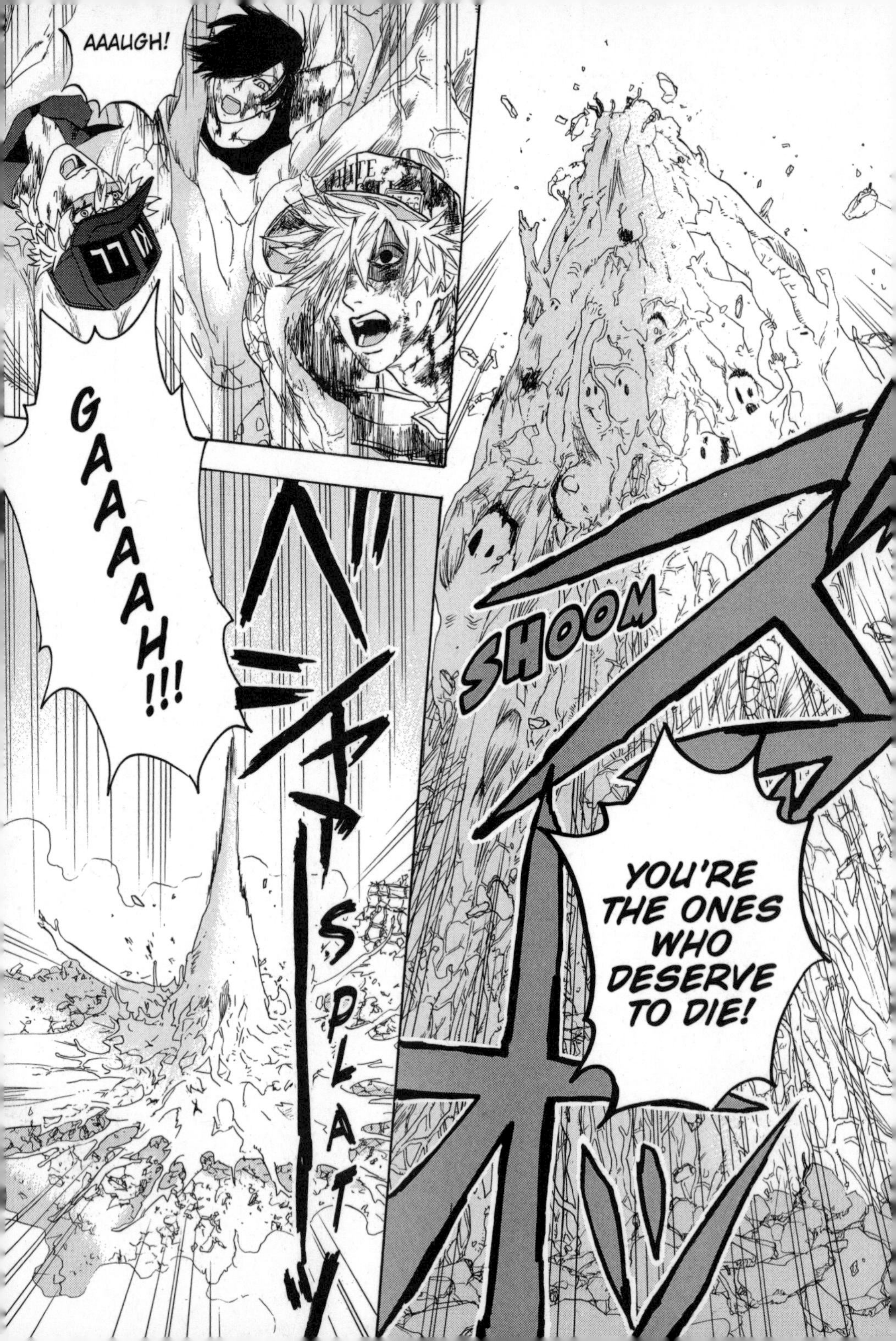
SHOOM
YOU'RE THE ONES WHO DESERVE TO DIE!
AAAUGH!
GAAAAAH!!!
SPLAT

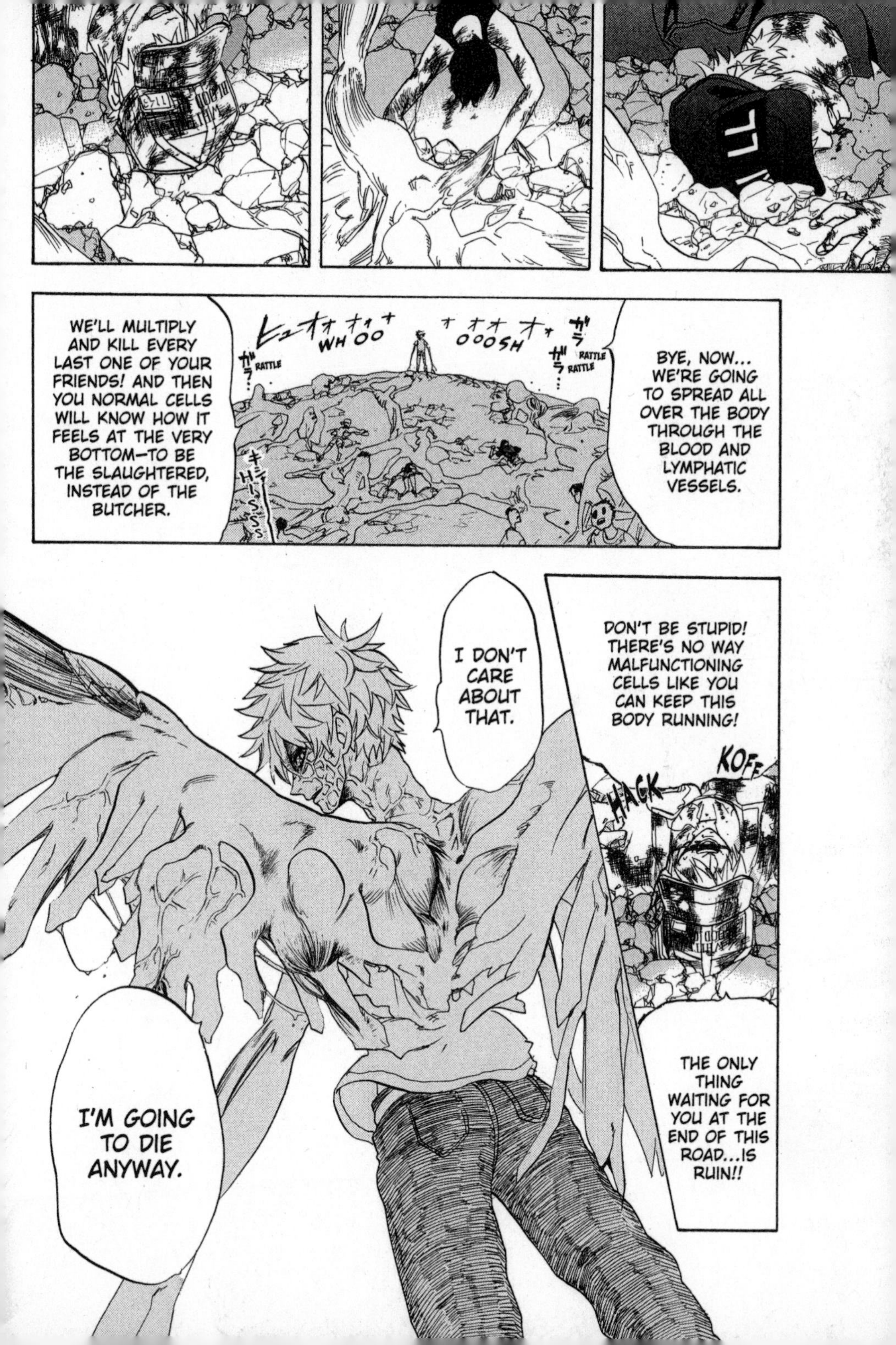
BYE, NOW... WE'RE GOING TO SPREAD ALL OVER THE BODY THROUGH THE BLOOD AND LYMPHATIC VESSELS.
RATTLE RATTLE
OOOSH
WHOO
RATTLE
HISSSS
WE'LL MULTIPLY AND KILL EVERY LAST ONE OF YOUR FRIENDS! AND THEN YOU NORMAL CELLS WILL KNOW HOW IT FEELS AT THE VERY BOTTOM—TO BE THE SLAUGHTERED, INSTEAD OF THE BUTCHER.
DON'T BE STUPID! THERE'S NO WAY MALFUNCTIONING CELLS LIKE YOU CAN KEEP THIS BODY RUNNING!
KOFF
HACK
THE ONLY THING WAITING FOR YOU AT THE END OF THIS ROAD...IS RUIN!!
I DON'T CARE ABOUT THAT.
I'M GOING TO DIE ANYWAY.

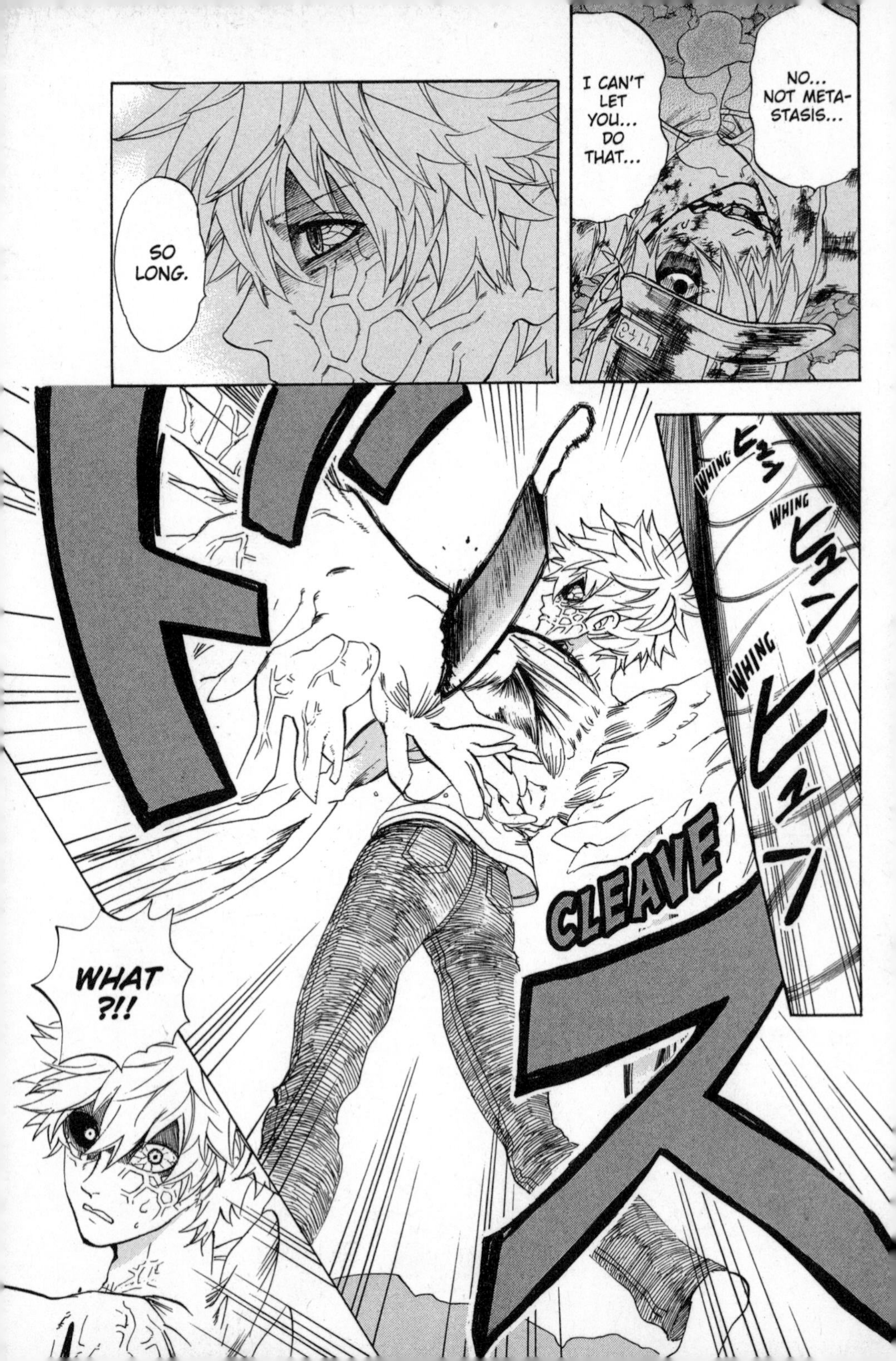
NO... NOT META-STASIS...
I CAN'T LET YOU... DO THAT...
SO LONG.
WHING
WHING
WHING
CLEAVE
WHAT ?!!

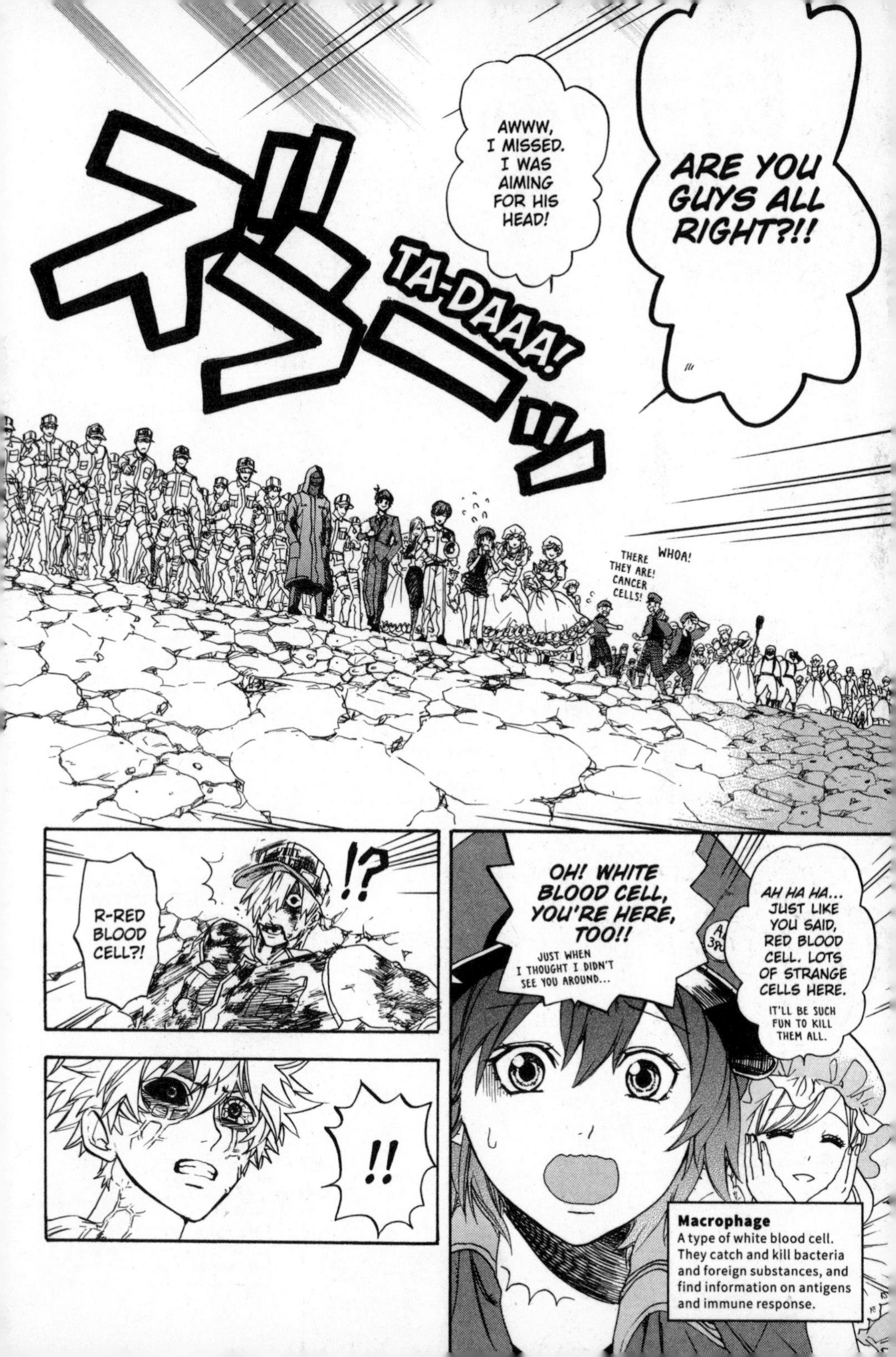
ARE YOU GUYS ALL RIGHT?!!
AWWW, I MISSED. I WAS AIMING FOR HIS HEAD!
TA-DAAA!
WHOA!
THERE THEY ARE! CANCER CELLS!
AH HA HA... JUST LIKE YOU SAID, RED BLOOD CELL. LOTS OF STRANGE CELLS HERE.
IT'LL BE SUCH FUN TO KILL THEM ALL.
OH! WHITE BLOOD CELL, YOU'RE HERE, TOO!!
JUST WHEN I THOUGHT I DIDN'T SEE YOU AROUND...
Macrophage
A type of white blood cell. They catch and kill bacteria and foreign substances, and find information on antigens and immune response.
!?
R-RED BLOOD CELL?!
!!

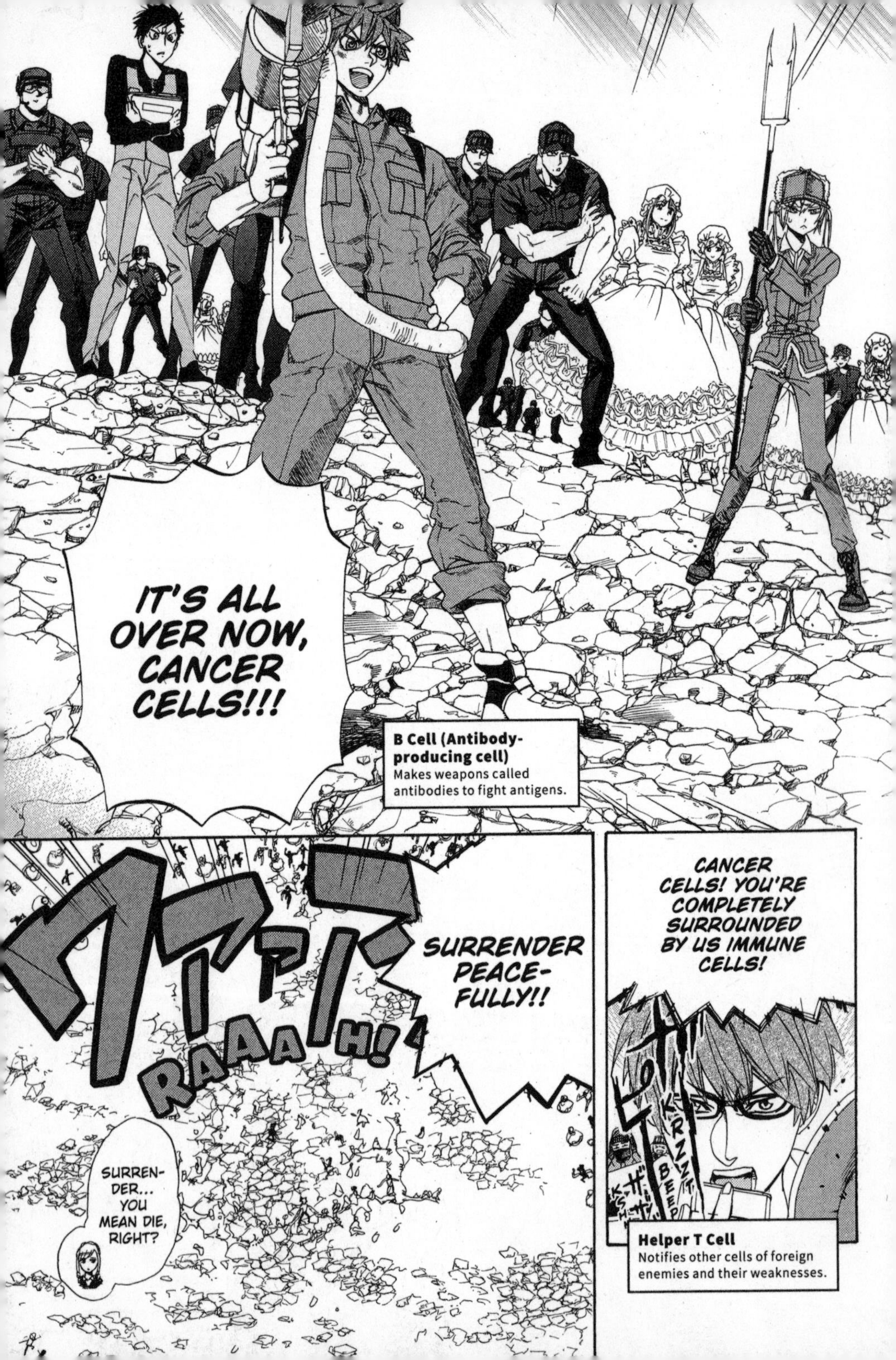
IT'S ALL OVER NOW, CANCER CELLS!!!
B Cell (Antibody-producing cell)
Makes weapons called antibodies to fight antigens.
CANCER CELLS! YOU'RE COMPLETELY SURROUNDED BY US IMMUNE CELLS!
KRZZT
BEEP
Helper T Cell
Notifies other cells of foreign enemies and their weaknesses.
SURRENDER PEACE-FULLY!!
RAAAAH!
SURREN-DER... YOU MEAN DIE, RIGHT?

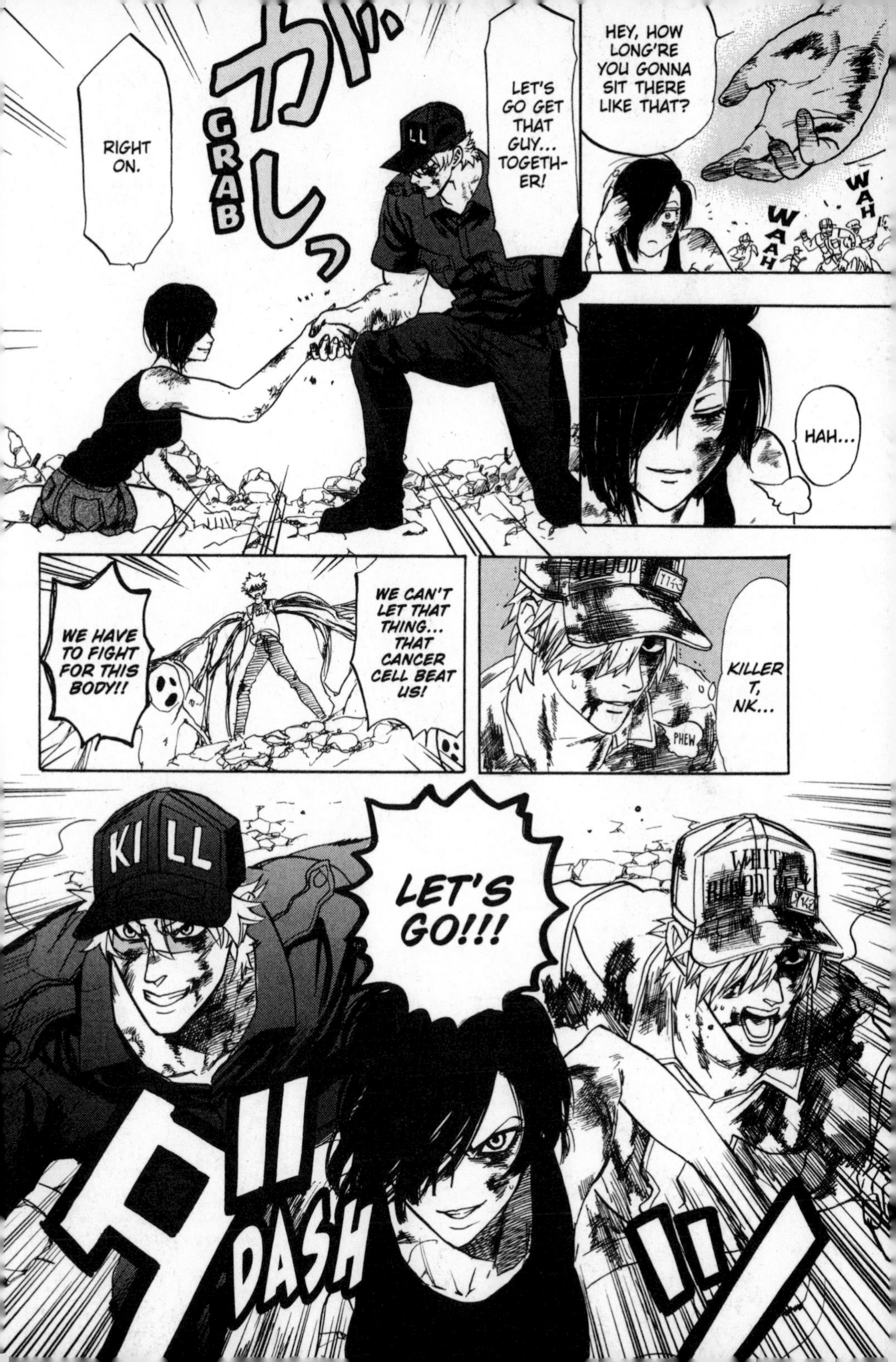
HEY, HOW LONG'RE YOU GONNA SIT THERE LIKE THAT?
WAH
WAH
WAH
HAH...
LET'S GO GET THAT GUY... TOGETH-ER!
GRAB
RIGHT ON.
KILLER T, NK...
PHEW
WE CAN'T LET THAT THING... THAT CANCER CELL BEAT US!
WE HAVE TO FIGHT FOR THIS BODY!!
LET'S GO!!!
DASH

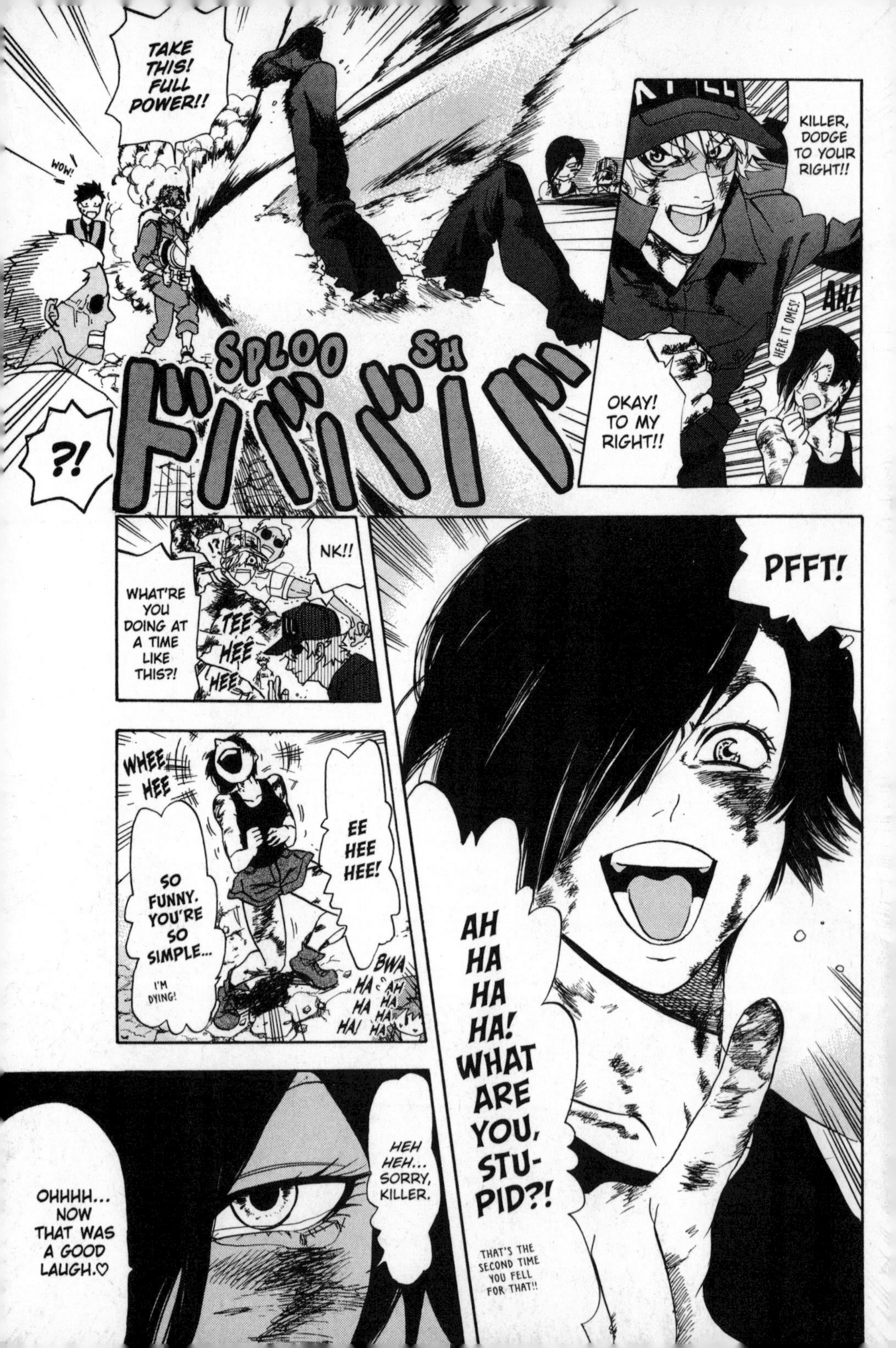
KILLER, DODGE TO YOUR RIGHT!!
AH!
HERE IT OMES!
OKAY! TO MY RIGHT!!
TAKE THIS! FULL POWER!!
WOW!
SPLOO SH
ドバババ
?!
PFFT!
AH HA HA HA! WHAT ARE YOU, STU-PID?!
THAT'S THE SECOND TIME YOU FELL FOR THAT!!
NK!!
WHAT'RE YOU DOING AT A TIME LIKE THIS?!
TEE HEE HEE
EE HEE HEE!
WHEE HEE
SO FUNNY. YOU'RE SO SIMPLE...
I'M DYING!
BWA HA HA HA!
AH HA HA HA
HEH HEH... SORRY, KILLER.
OHHHH... NOW THAT WAS A GOOD LAUGH.♡

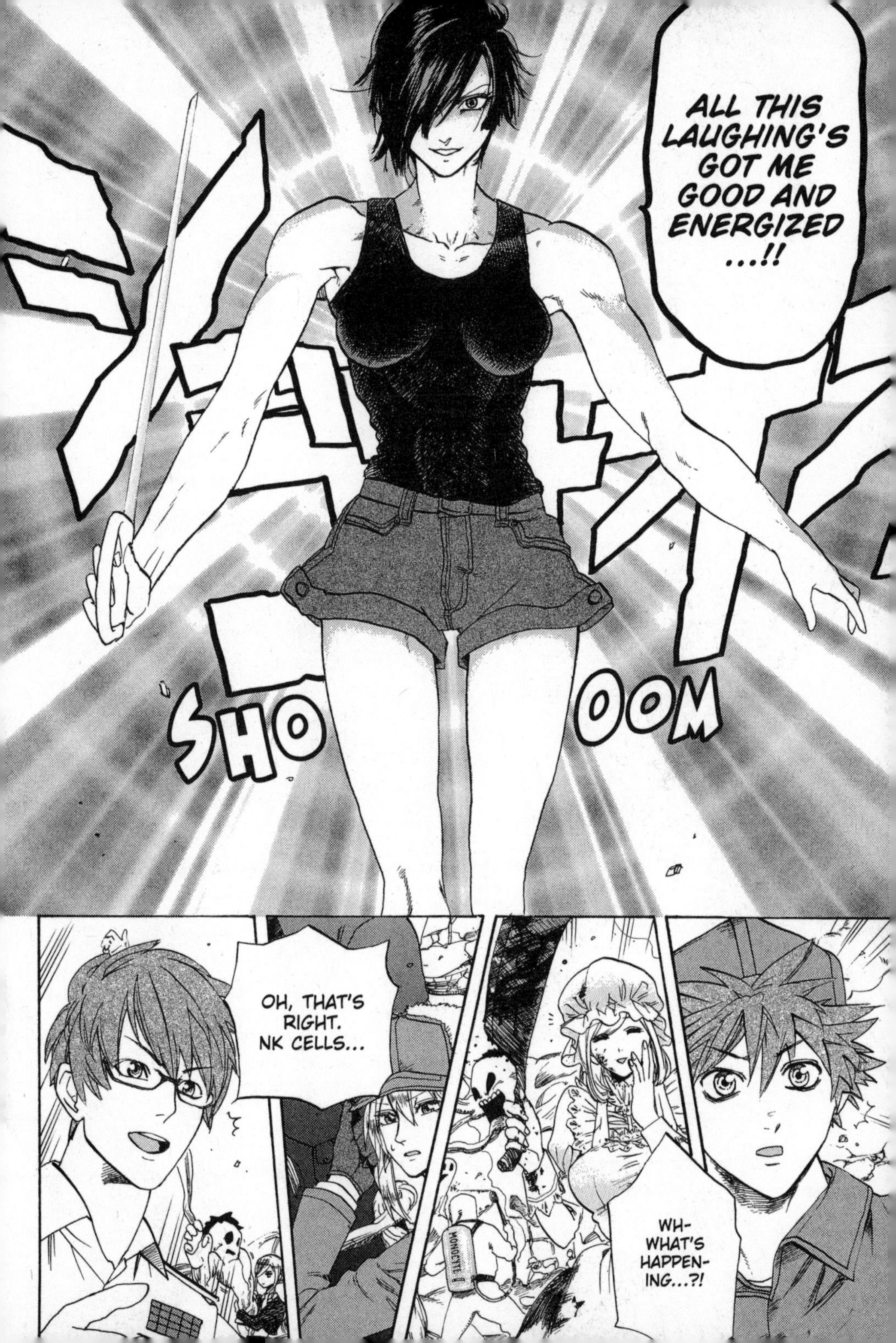
ALL THIS LAUGHING'S GOT ME GOOD AND ENERGIZED ...!!
SHO OOM
WH- WHAT'S HAPPEN- ING...?!
OH, THAT'S RIGHT. NK CELLS...

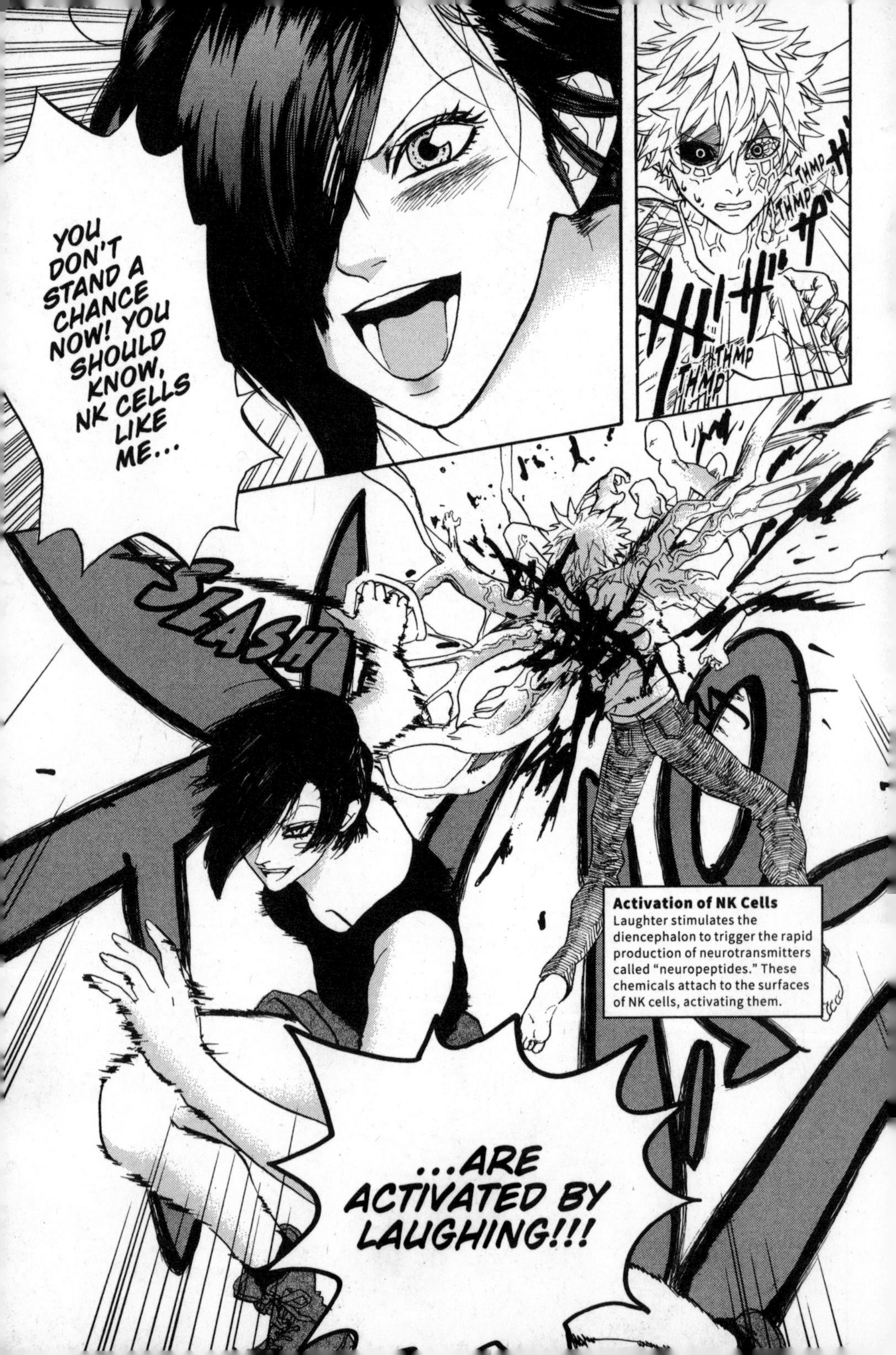
THMP
THMP
THMP
THMP
YOU DON'T STAND A CHANCE NOW! YOU SHOULD KNOW, NK CELLS LIKE ME...
SLASH
Activation of NK Cells
Laughter stimulates the diencephalon to trigger the rapid production of neurotransmitters called "neuropeptides." These chemicals attach to the surfaces of NK cells, activating them.
...ARE ACTIVATED BY LAUGHING!!!

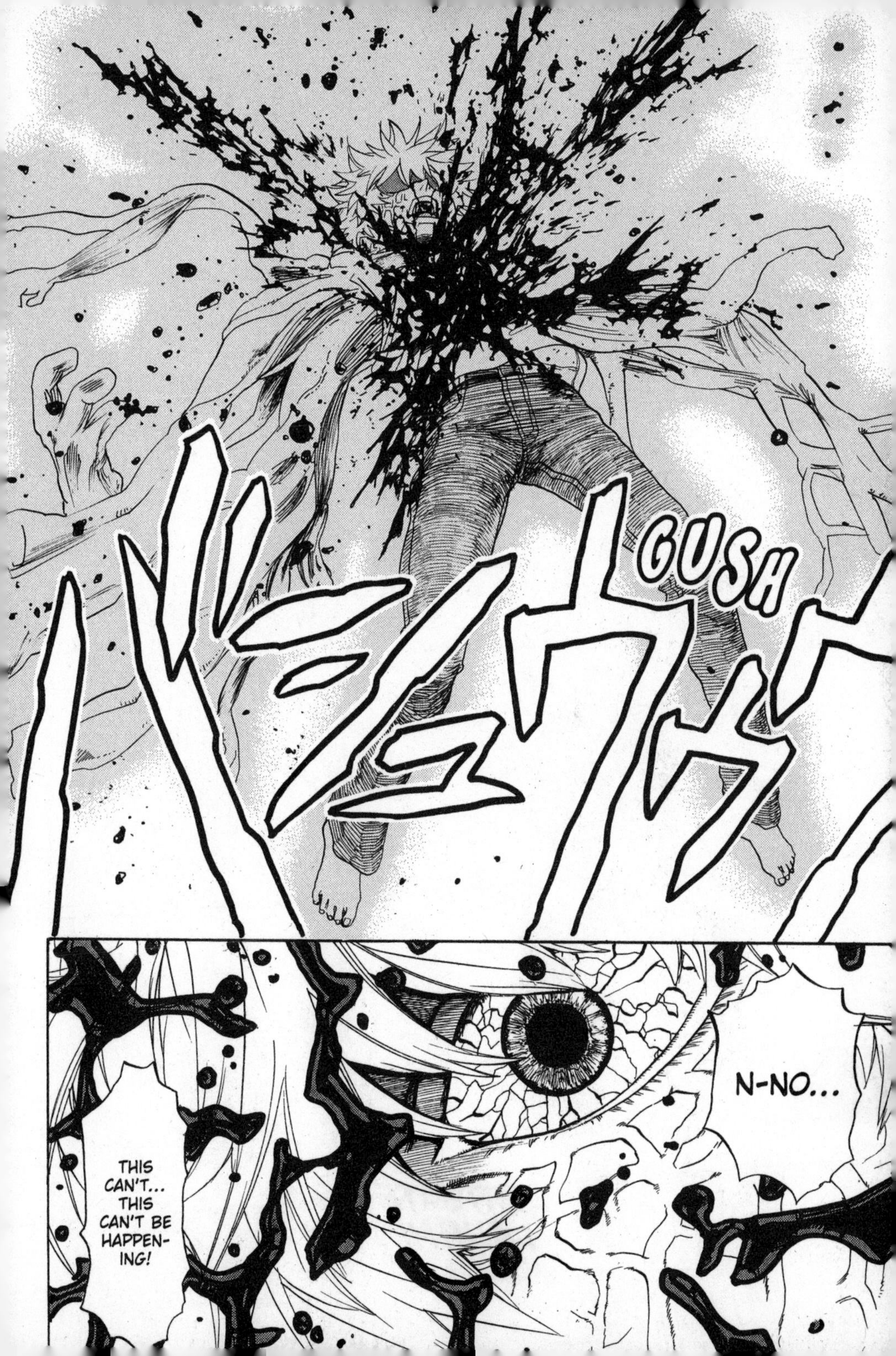
GUSH
N-NO...
THIS CAN'T... THIS CAN'T BE HAPPEN-ING!

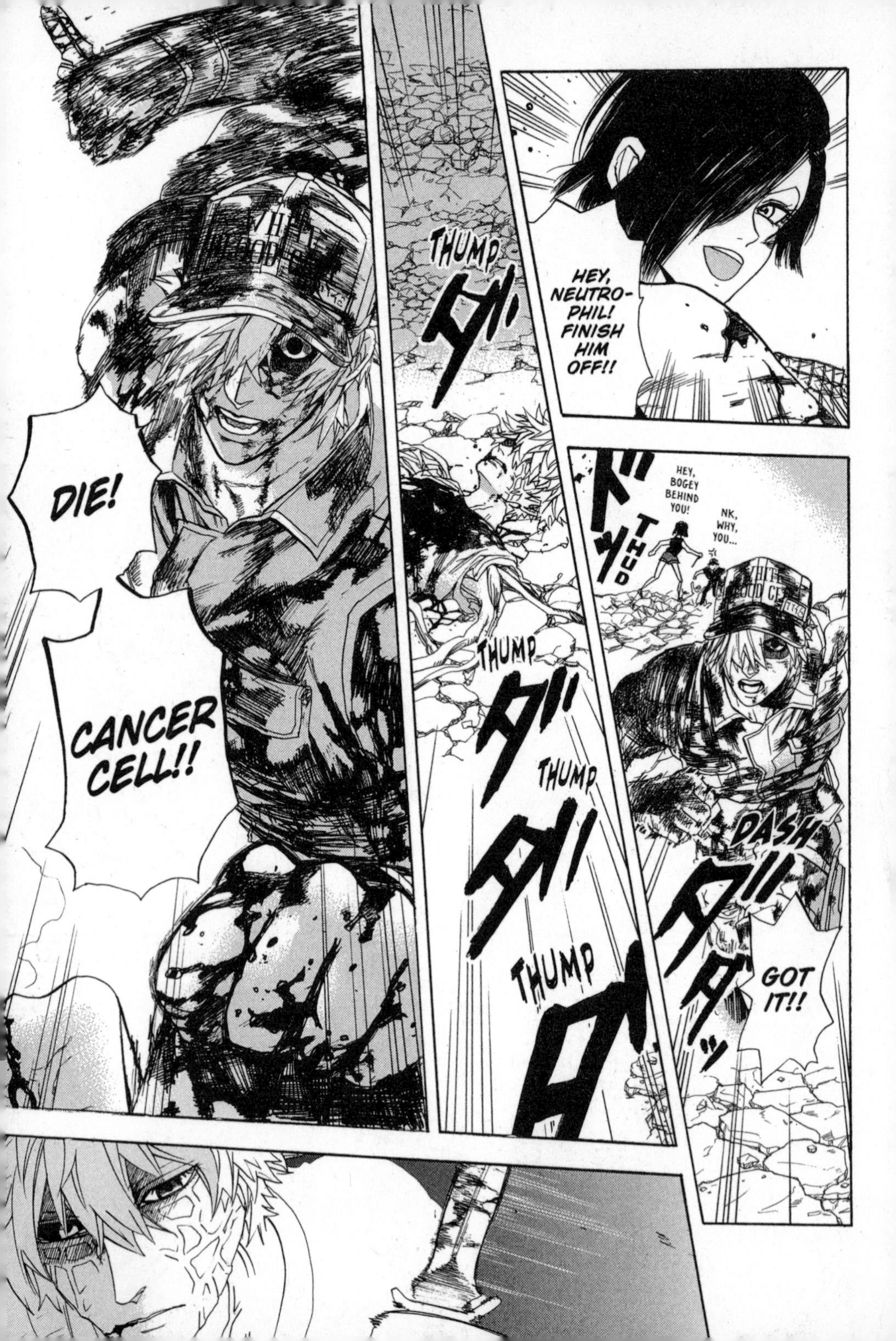
HEY, NEUTRO-PHIL! FINISH HIM OFF!!
THUD
HEY, BOGEY BEHIND YOU!
NK, WHY, YOU...
DASH
GOT IT!!
THUMP
THUMP
THUMP
THUMP
DIE!
CANCER CELL!!

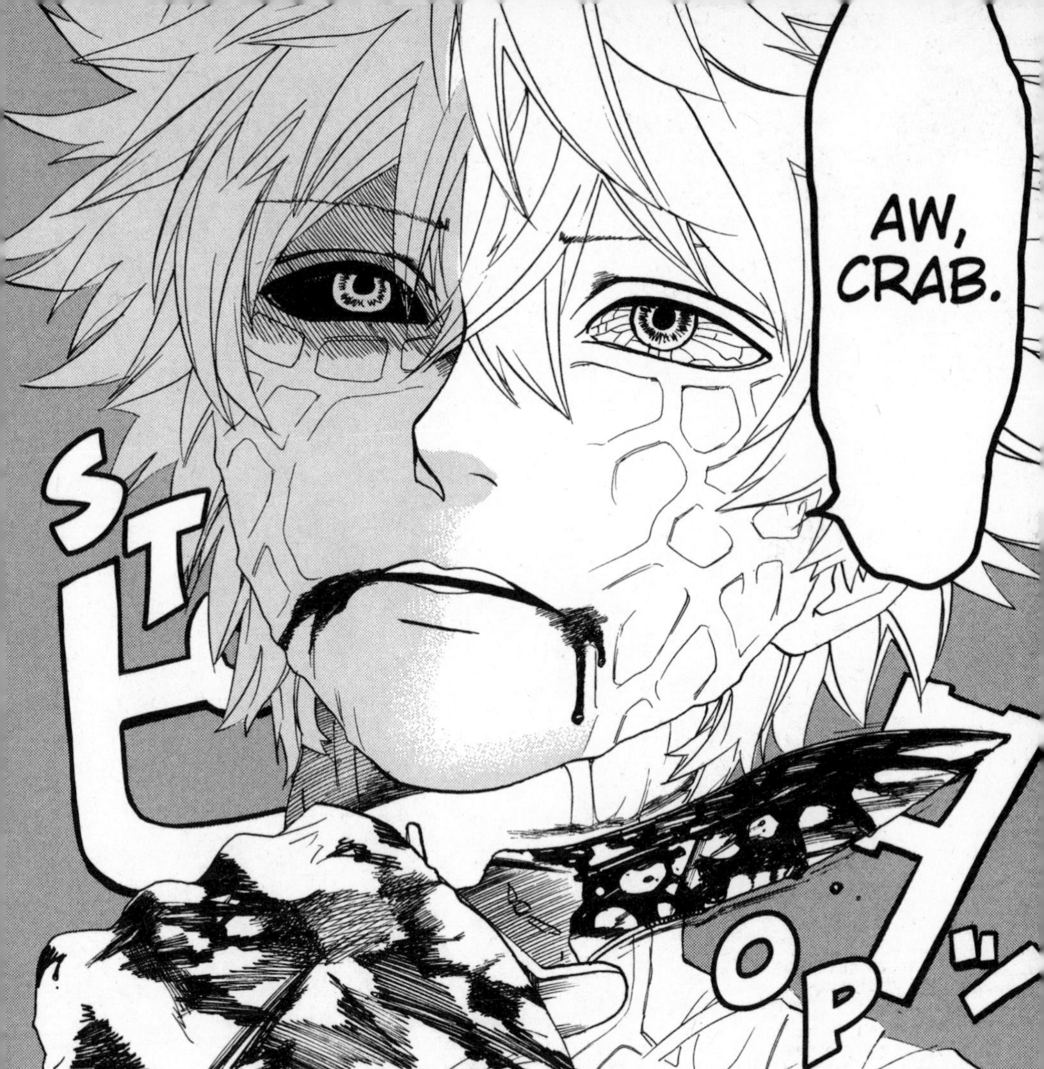
AW, CRAB.
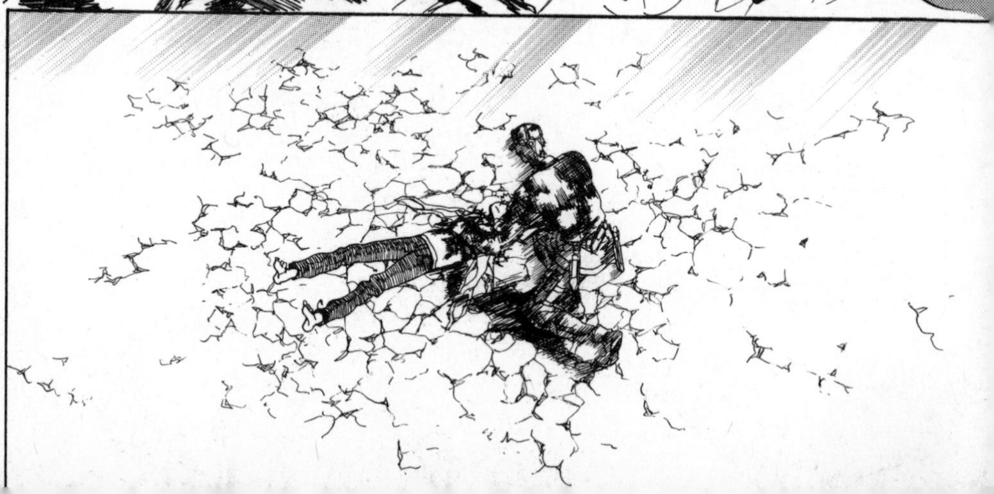

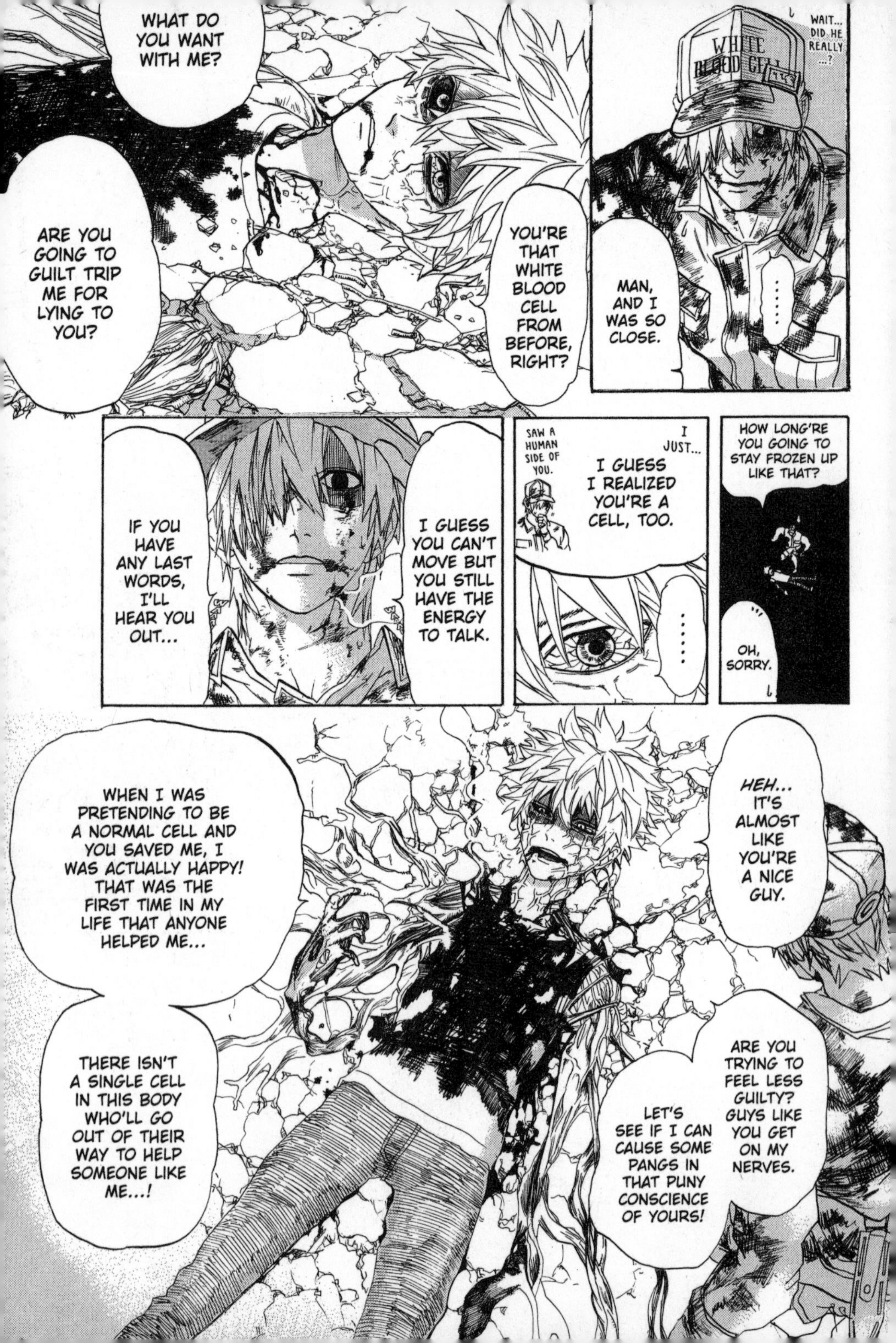
WAIT... DID HE REALLY ...?
MAN, AND I WAS SO CLOSE.
......
YOU'RE THAT WHITE BLOOD CELL FROM BEFORE, RIGHT?
WHAT DO YOU WANT WITH ME?
ARE YOU GOING TO GUILT TRIP ME FOR LYING TO YOU?
HOW LONG'RE YOU GOING TO STAY FROZEN UP LIKE THAT?
OH, SORRY.
I JUST...
SAW A HUMAN SIDE OF YOU.
I GUESS I REALIZED YOU'RE A CELL, TOO.
......
I GUESS YOU CAN'T MOVE BUT YOU STILL HAVE THE ENERGY TO TALK.
IF YOU HAVE ANY LAST WORDS, I'LL HEAR YOU OUT...
HEH... IT'S ALMOST LIKE YOU'RE A NICE GUY.
WHEN I WAS PRETENDING TO BE A NORMAL CELL AND YOU SAVED ME, I WAS ACTUALLY HAPPY! THAT WAS THE FIRST TIME IN MY LIFE THAT ANYONE HELPED ME...
ARE YOU TRYING TO FEEL LESS GUILTY? GUYS LIKE YOU GET ON MY NERVES.
LET'S SEE IF I CAN CAUSE SOME PANGS IN THAT PUNY CONSCIENCE OF YOURS!
THERE ISN'T A SINGLE CELL IN THIS BODY WHO'LL GO OUT OF THEIR WAY TO HELP SOMEONE LIKE ME...!

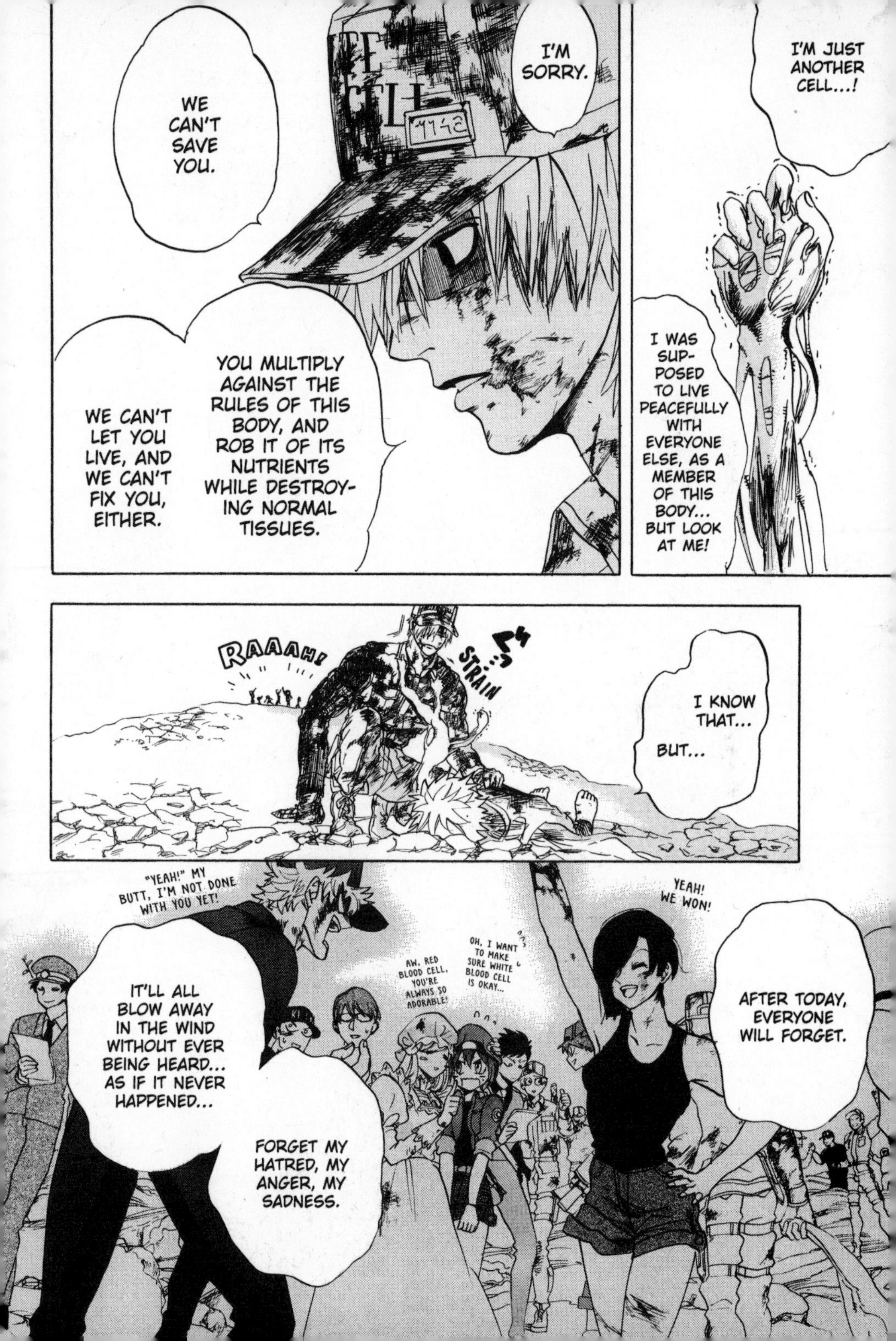
I'M JUST ANOTHER CELL...!
I WAS SUP-POSED TO LIVE PEACEFULLY WITH EVERYONE ELSE, AS A MEMBER OF THIS BODY... BUT LOOK AT ME!
I'M SORRY.
WE CAN'T SAVE YOU.
YOU MULTIPLY AGAINST THE RULES OF THIS BODY, AND ROB IT OF ITS NUTRIENTS WHILE DESTROY-ING NORMAL TISSUES.
WE CAN'T LET YOU LIVE, AND WE CAN'T FIX YOU, EITHER.
I KNOW THAT...
BUT...
STRAIN
RAAAH!
YEAH! WE WON!
AFTER TODAY, EVERYONE WILL FORGET.
OH, I WANT TO MAKE SURE WHITE BLOOD CELL IS OKAY...
AW, RED BLOOD CELL, YOU'RE ALWAYS SO ADORABLE!
FORGET MY HATRED, MY ANGER, MY SADNESS.
"YEAH!" MY BUTT, I'M NOT DONE WITH YOU YET!
IT'LL ALL BLOW AWAY IN THE WIND WITHOUT EVER BEING HEARD... AS IF IT NEVER HAPPENED...

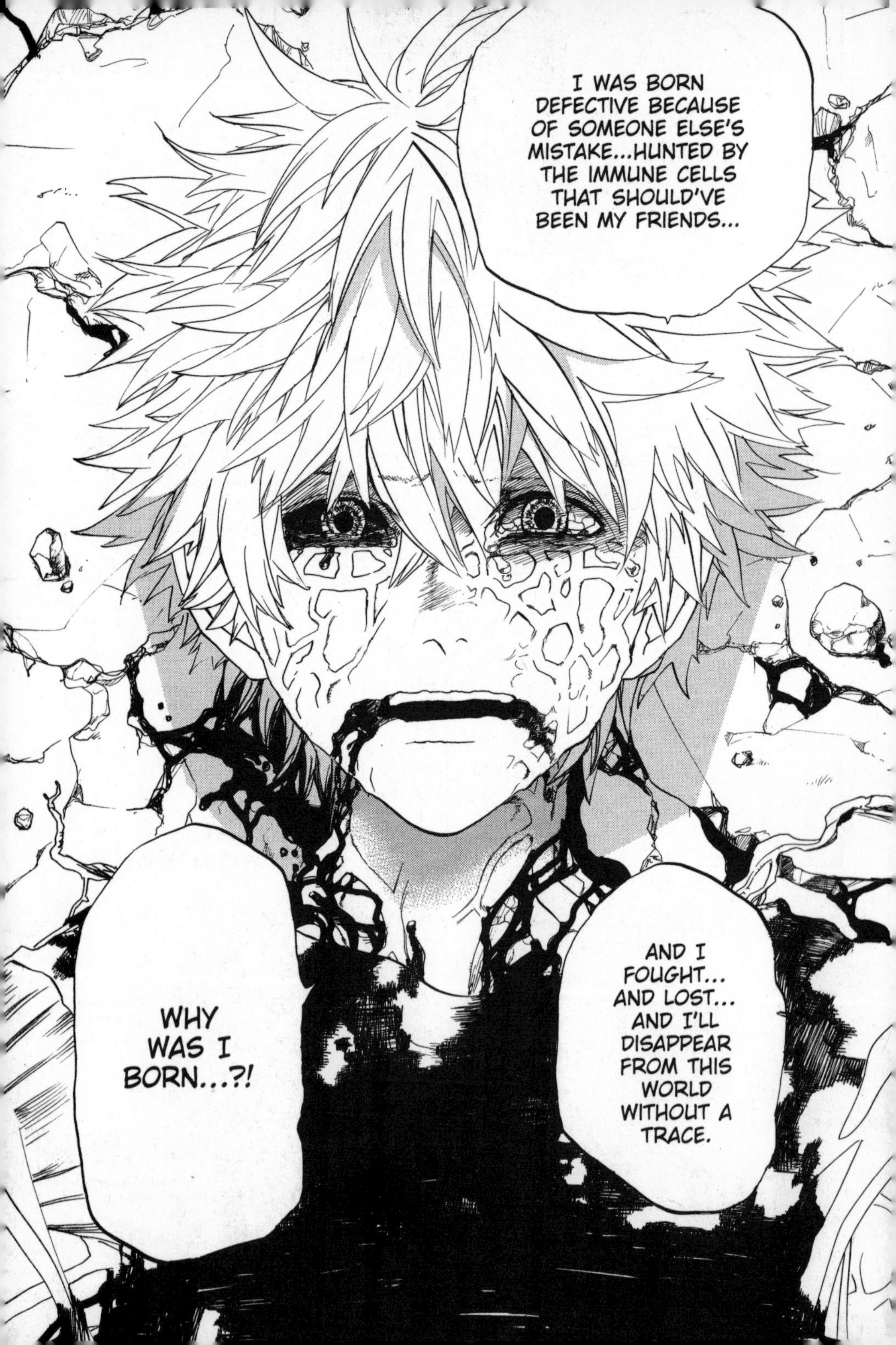
I WAS BORN DEFECTIVE BECAUSE OF SOMEONE ELSE'S MISTAKE...HUNTED BY THE IMMUNE CELLS THAT SHOULD'VE BEEN MY FRIENDS...
AND I FOUGHT... AND LOST... AND I'LL DISAPPEAR FROM THIS WORLD WITHOUT A TRACE.
WHY WAS I BORN...?!

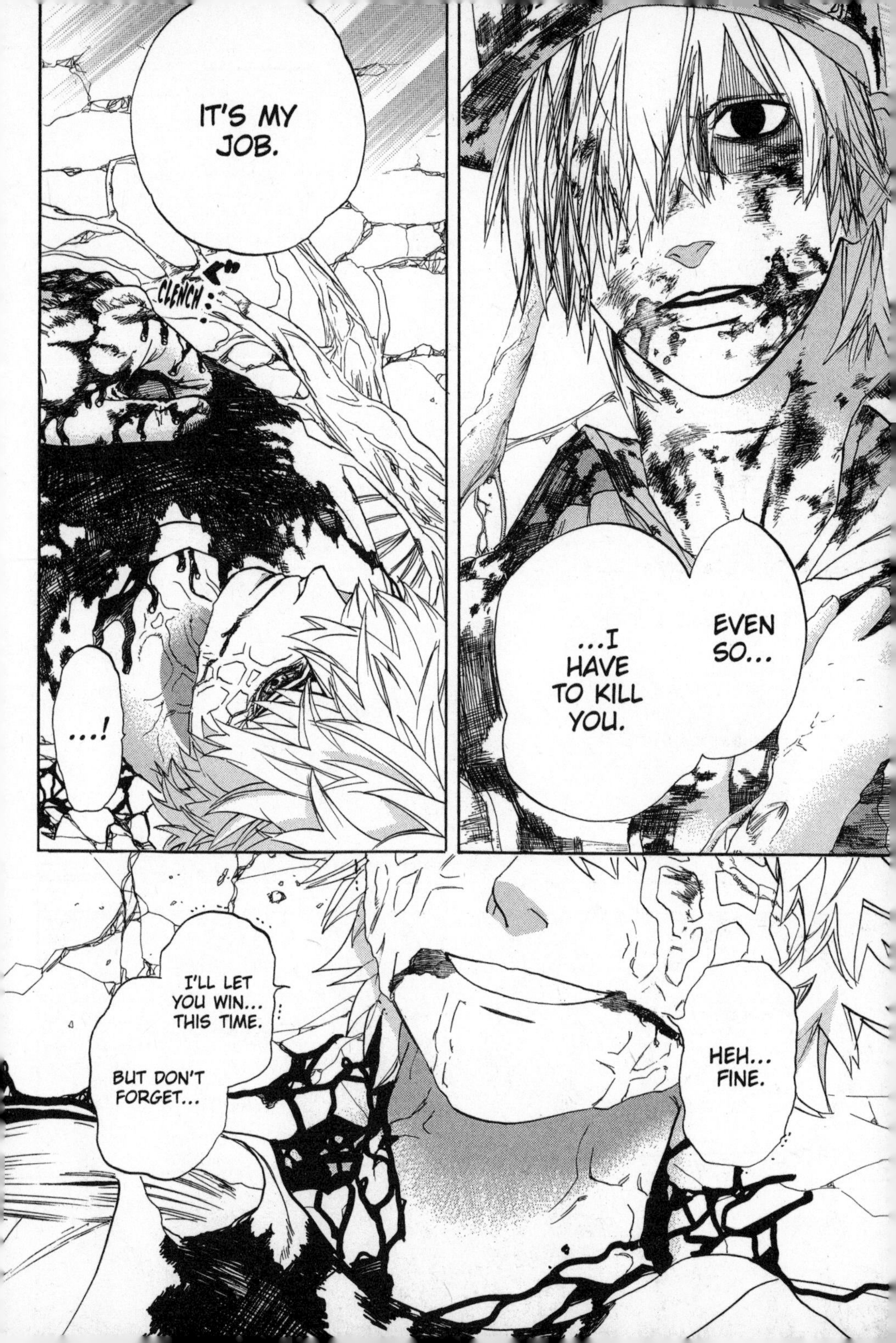
EVEN SO...
...I HAVE TO KILL YOU.
IT'S MY JOB.
CLENCH
...!
HEH... FINE.
I'LL LET YOU WIN... THIS TIME.
BUT DON'T FORGET...

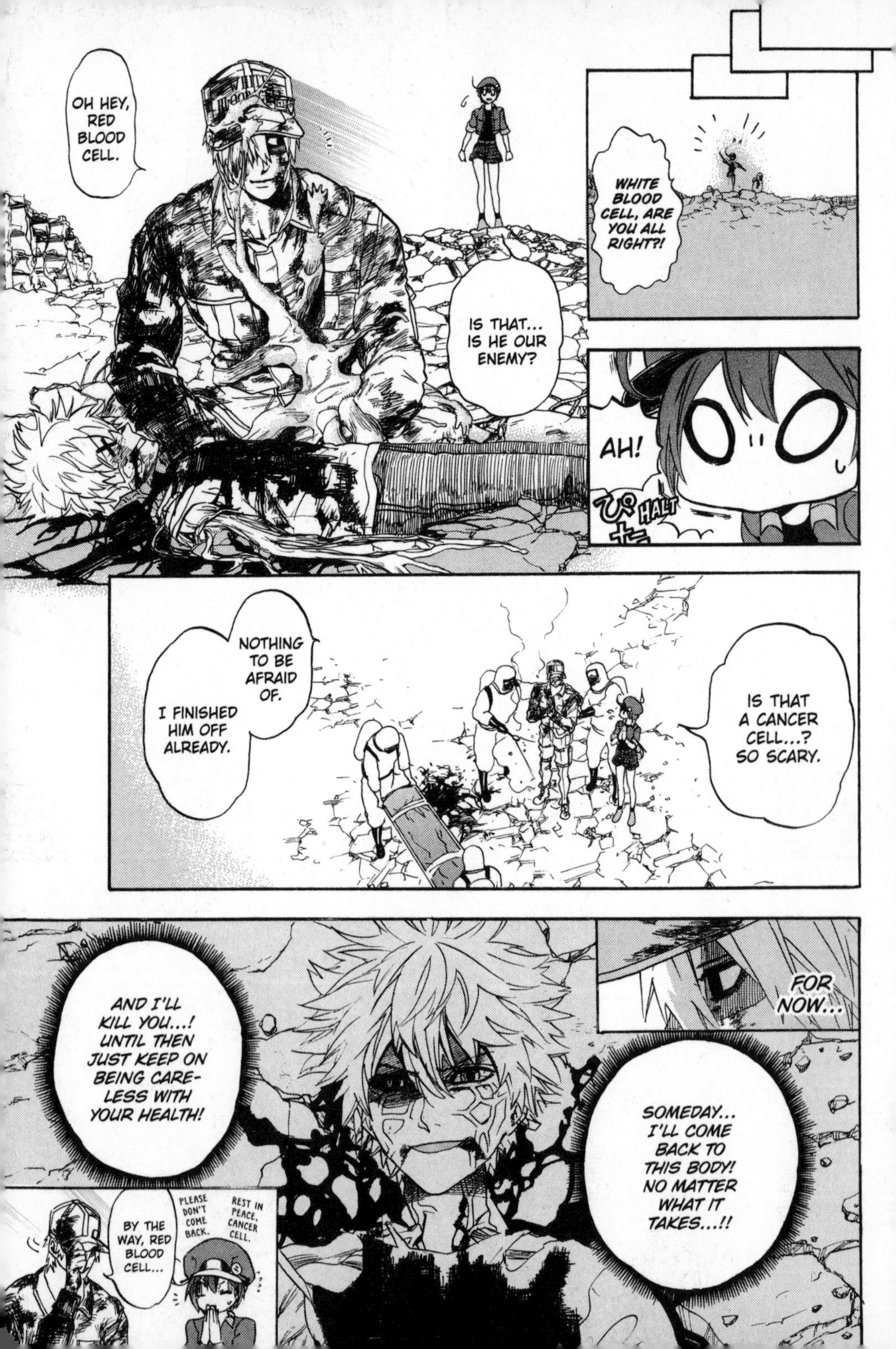
WHITE BLOOD CELL, ARE YOU ALL RIGHT?!
AH!
HALT
OH HEY, RED BLOOD CELL.
IS THAT... IS HE OUR ENEMY?
IS THAT A CANCER CELL...? SO SCARY.
NOTHING TO BE AFRAID OF.
I FINISHED HIM OFF ALREADY.
FOR NOW...
SOMEDAY... I'LL COME BACK TO THIS BODY! NO MATTER WHAT IT TAKES...!!
AND I'LL KILL YOU...! UNTIL THEN JUST KEEP ON BEING CARE-LESS WITH YOUR HEALTH!
REST IN PEACE, CANCER CELL.
PLEASE DON'T COME BACK.
BY THE WAY, RED BLOOD CELL...

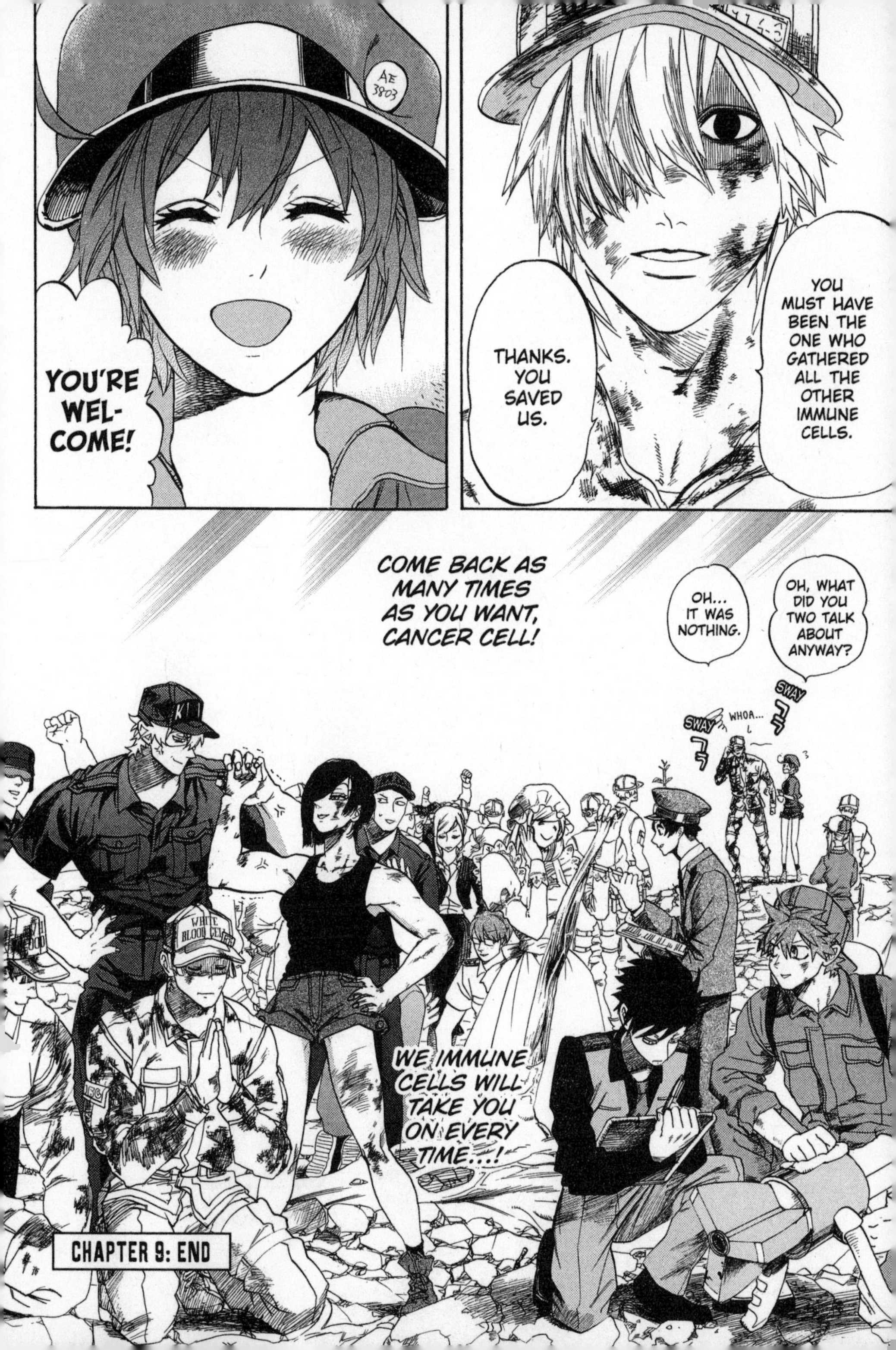
YOU MUST HAVE BEEN THE ONE WHO GATHERED ALL THE OTHER IMMUNE CELLS.
THANKS. YOU SAVED US.
YOU'RE WEL-COME!
OH, WHAT DID YOU TWO TALK ABOUT ANYWAY?
OH... IT WAS NOTHING.
SWAY
WHOA...
SWAY
COME BACK AS MANY TIMES AS YOU WANT, CANCER CELL!
WE IMMUNE CELLS WILL TAKE YOU ON EVERY TIME...!
CHAPTER 9: END

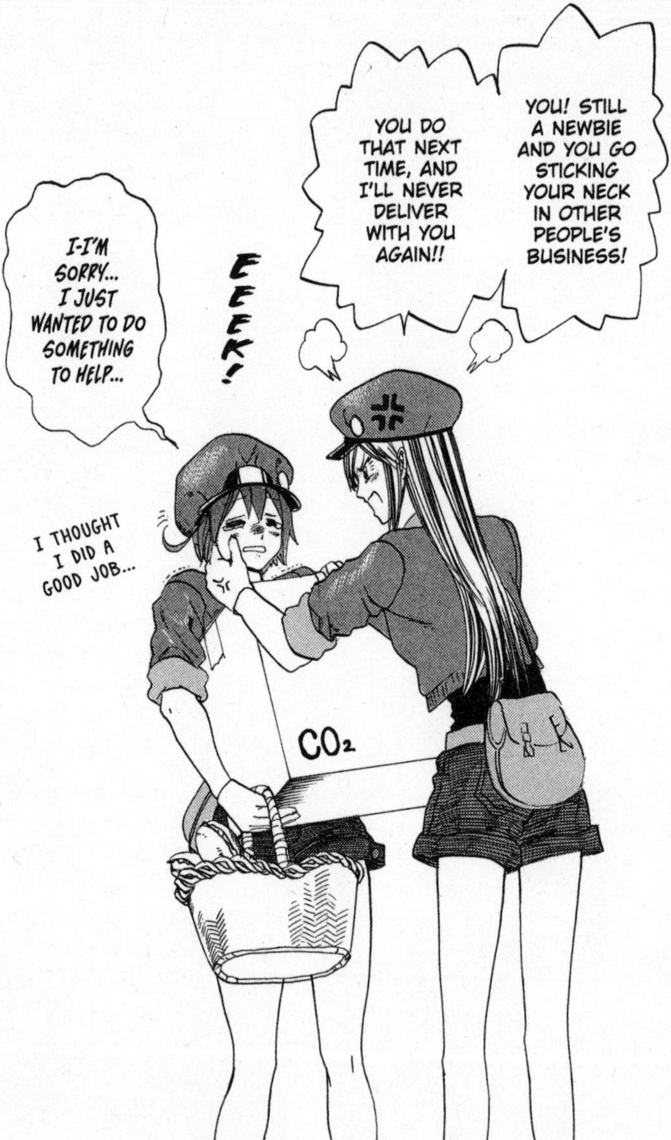
YOU! STILL A NEWBIE AND YOU GO STICKING YOUR NECK IN OTHER PEOPLE'S BUSINESS!
YOU DO THAT NEXT TIME, AND I'LL NEVER DELIVER WITH YOU AGAIN!!
EEEK!
I-I'M SORRY... I JUST WANTED TO DO SOMETHING TO HELP...
I THOUGHT I DID A GOOD JOB...
CO2

CELLS AT WORK! VOLUME 2: END

Medical Editor: Tomoyuki Harada

TRANSLATION NOTES

Tally marks

Page 124

The Japanese character 正 (meaning "right," "true," or "correct") is commonly used to count to five, just like tally counts using four vertical lines and one slash through them for "five" (卌).

cannot control cell division, and multiply endlessly.
PROTOCOL?!
YEESH!
YEAH... THERE MUST BE TONS OF THEM. THIS ISN'T NORMAL.

DIE, YOU BUGGY BASTARD!!

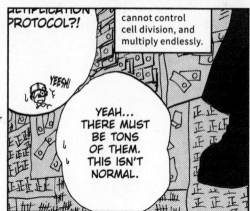

Buggy bastard

Page 140

In the Japanese edition, the immune cells insult the cancer cell by calling him *baguri-yaro*. The term "baguri" comes from the verb "baguru," which a slang term describing what software does when it has bugs—an apt insult for a renegade cancer cell. Baguri also may echo the term *pakuri*, meaning plagiarism, which would make sense given that cancerous cells are poor copies of the original.

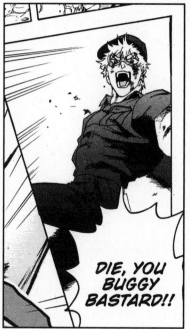

Aw, crab

Page 156

In his final moments, the cancer cell makes a terrible pun. He says "Gaan," which is an exclamation expressing shock or dismay. "Gan" is also the Japanese word for cancer. In this version, he murmurs "crab," the Latin term for which gives us the word "cancer" (and is the namesake for the constellation).

AW, CRAB.

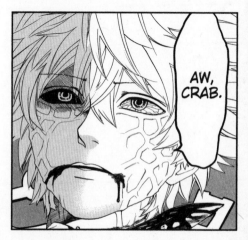

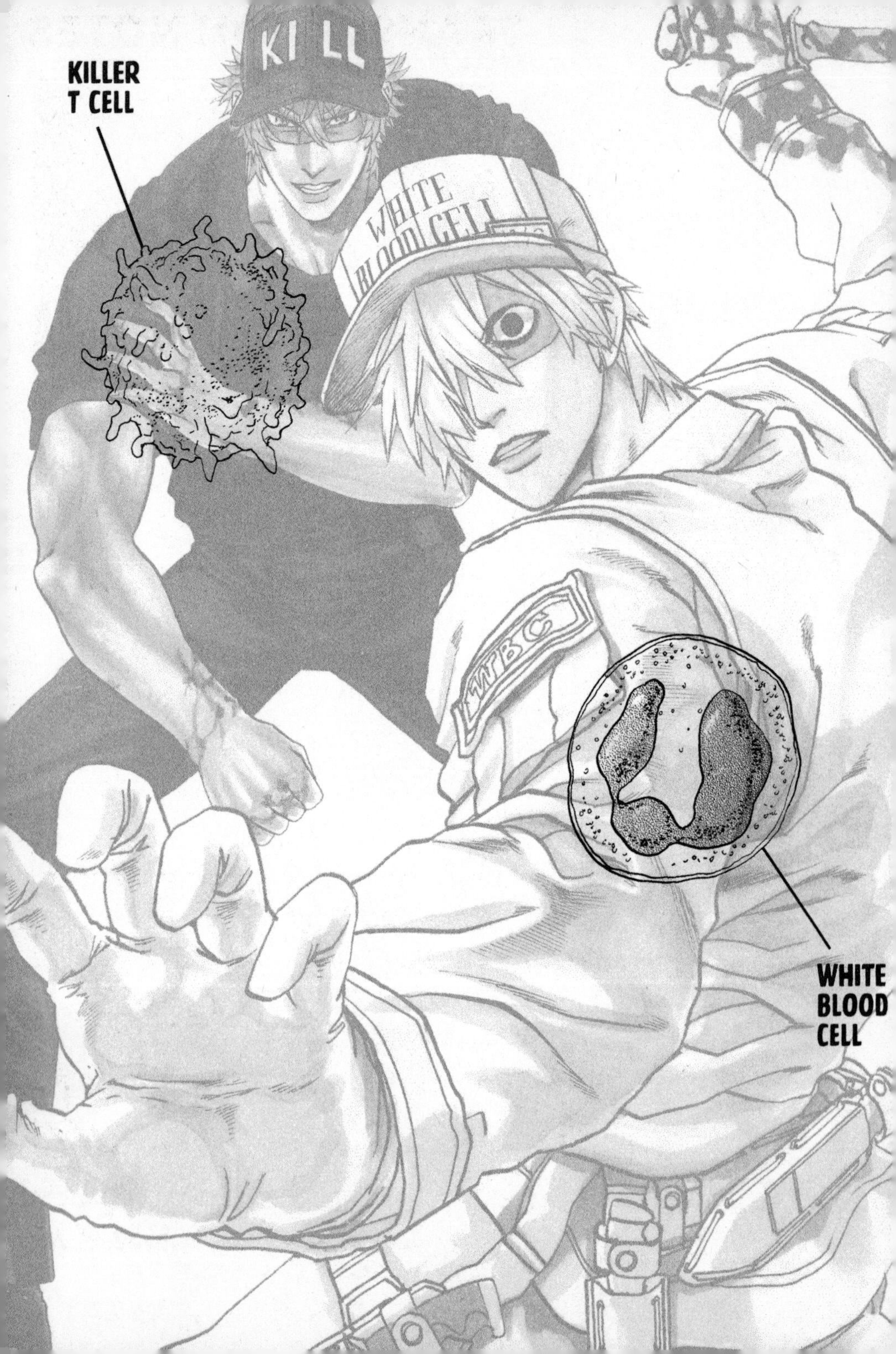
KILLER T CELL
KILL
WHITE BLOOD CELL
WBC
WHITE BLOOD CELL

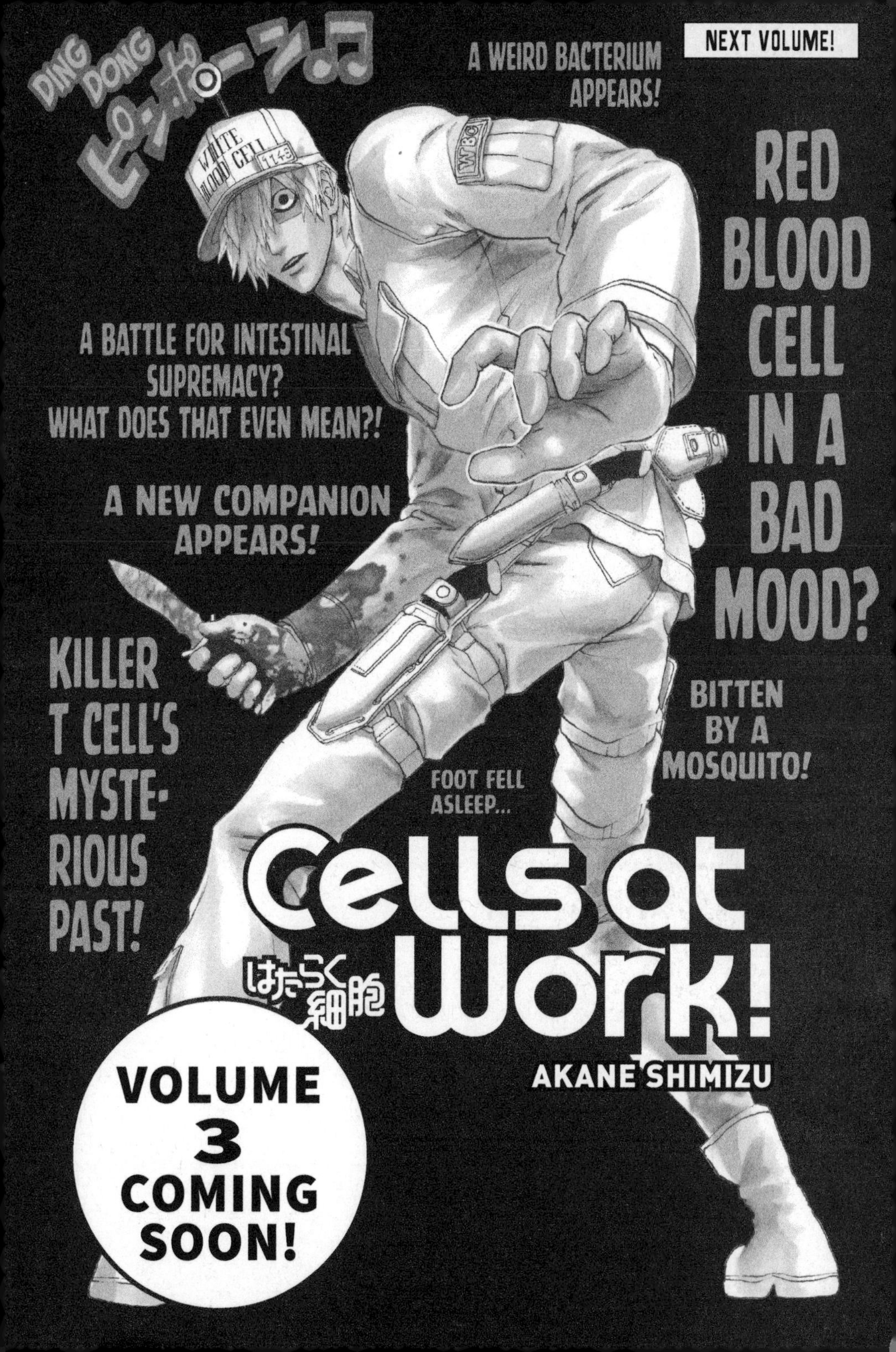
NEXT VOLUME!
DING DONG
ピンポーン♪♫
A WEIRD BACTERIUM APPEARS!
WHITE BLOOD CELL
1143
WBC
RED BLOOD CELL IN A BAD MOOD?
A BATTLE FOR INTESTINAL SUPREMACY? WHAT DOES THAT EVEN MEAN?!
A NEW COMPANION APPEARS!
KILLER T CELL'S MYSTE-RIOUS PAST!
BITTEN BY A MOSQUITO!
FOOT FELL ASLEEP...
Cells at Work!
はたらく細胞
AKANE SHIMIZU
VOLUME 3 COMING SOON!

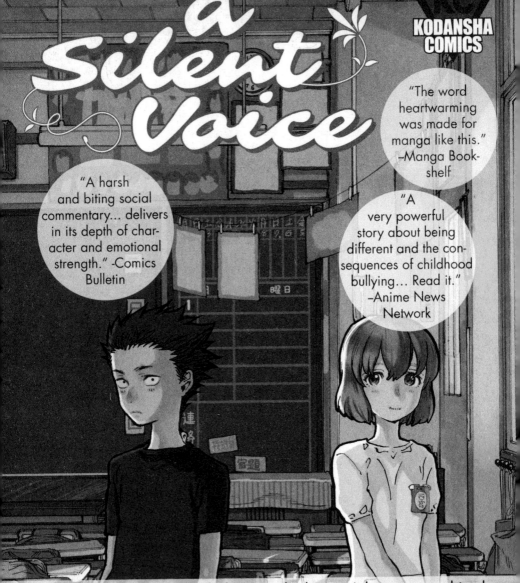

a Silent Voice

KODANSHA COMICS

"The word heartwarming was made for manga like this." –Manga Book-shelf

"A harsh and biting social commentary... delivers in its depth of char-acter and emotional strength." -Comics Bulletin

"A very powerful story about being different and the con-sequences of childhood bullying... Read it." –Anime News Network

Shoya is a bully. When Shoko, a girl who can't hear, enters his ele-mentary school class, she becomes their favorite target, and Shoya and his friends goad each other into devising new tortures for her. But the children's cruelty goes too far. Shoko is forced to leave the school, and Shoya ends up shouldering all the blame. Six years lat-er, the two meet again. Can Shoya make up for his past mistakes, or is it too late?

Available now in print and digitally!

Say I Love You.

KC KODANSHA COMICS

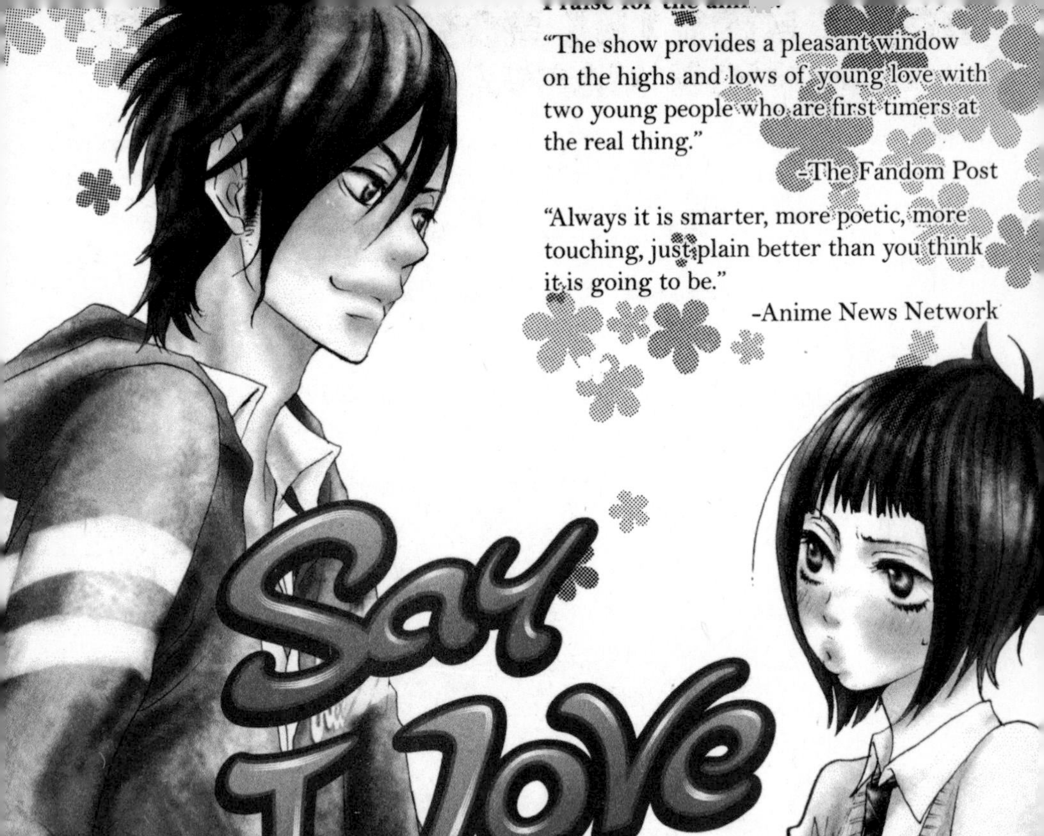

Mei Tachibana has no friends — and says she doesn't need them!

But everything changes when she accidentally roundhouse kicks the most popular boy in school! However, Yamato Kurosawa isn't angry in the slightest— in fact, he thinks his ordinary life could use an unusual girl like Mei. But winning Mei's trust will be a tough task. How long will she refuse to say "I love you"?

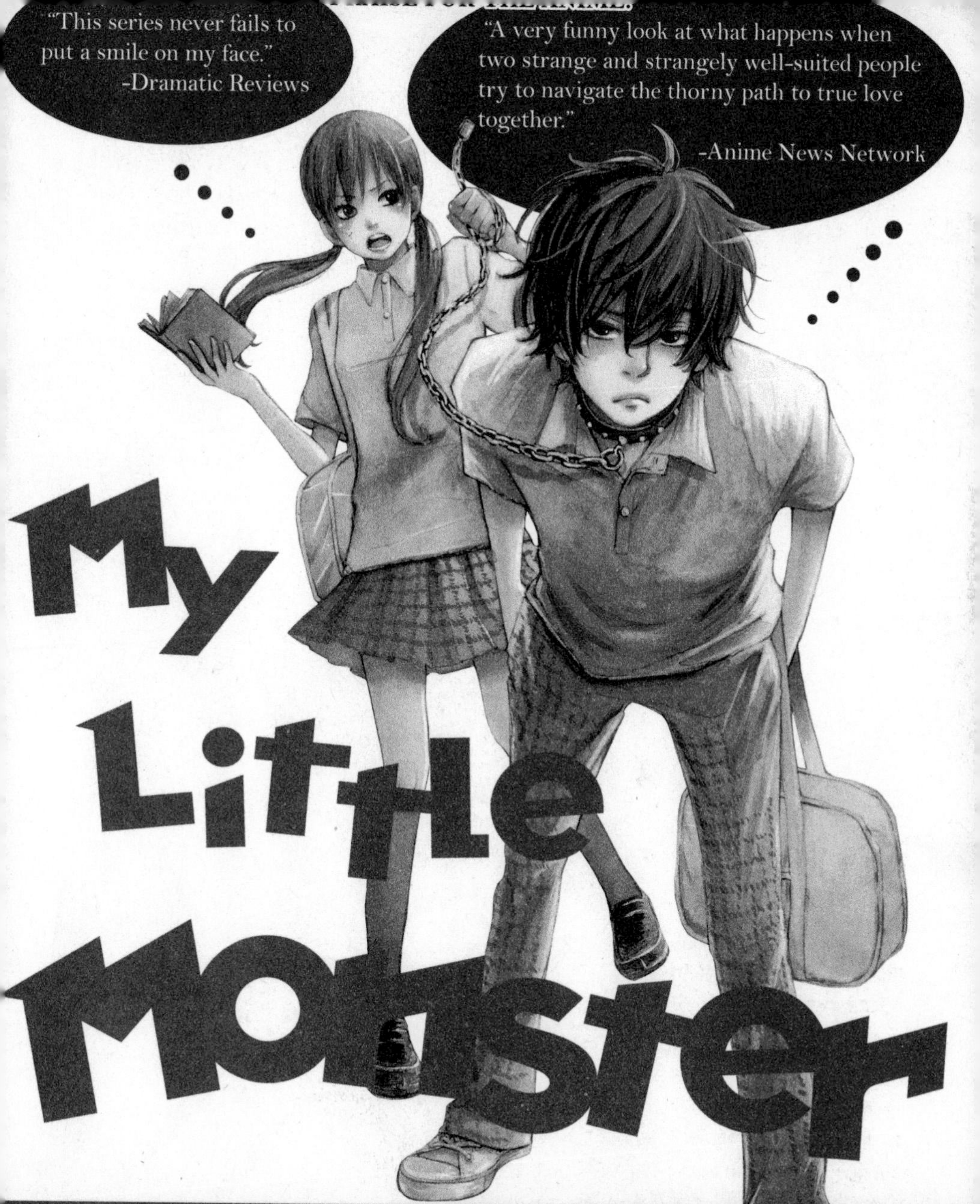

My Little Monster

OPPOSITES ATTRACT...MAYBE?

Haru Yoshida is feared as an unstable and violent "monster." Mizutani Shizuku is a grade-obsessed student with no friends. Fate brings these two together to form the most unlikely pair. Haru firmly believes he's in love with Mizutani and she firmly believes he's insane.

KC
KODANSHA
COMICS

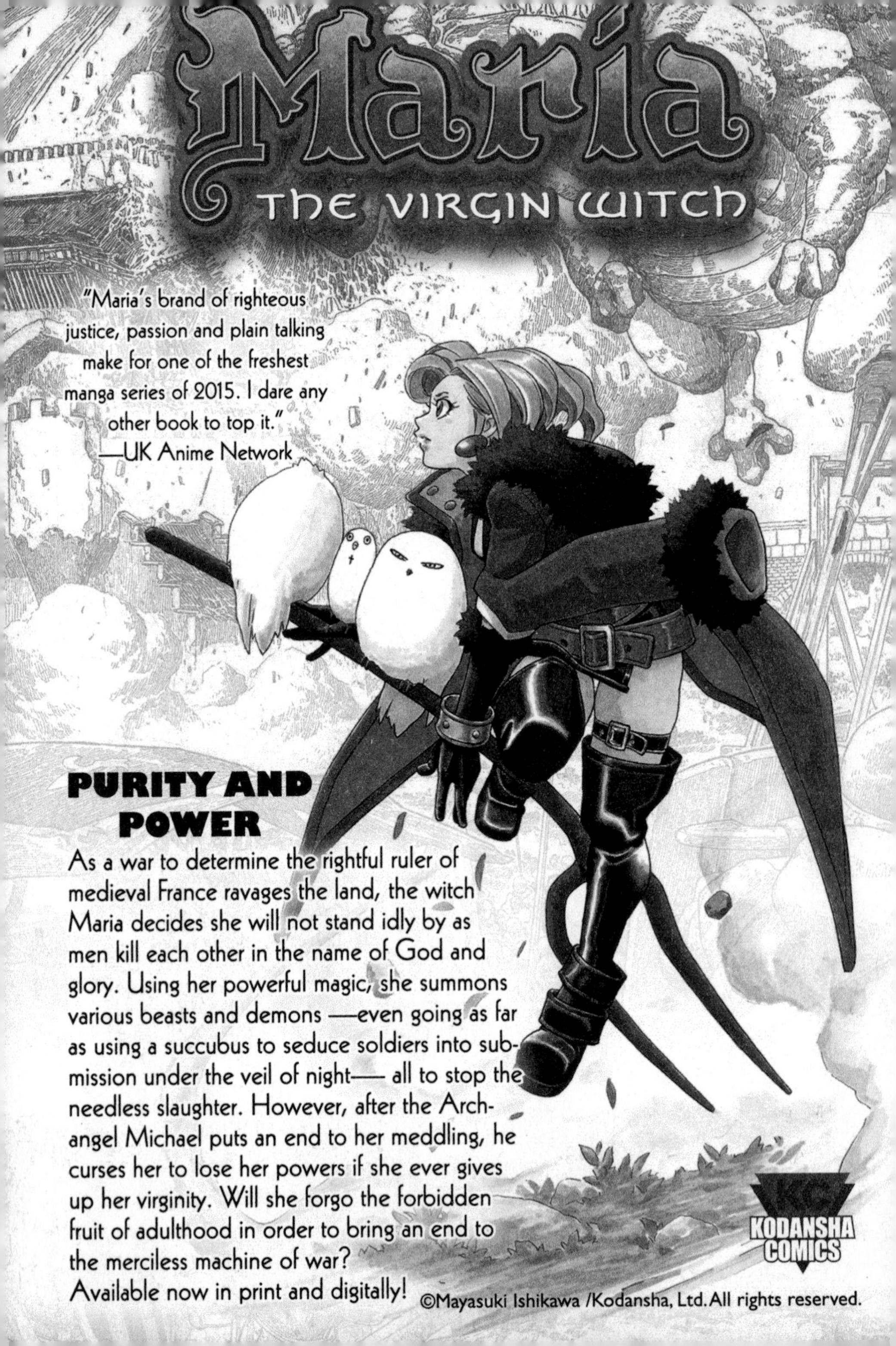

Maria
THE VIRGIN WITCH

"Maria's brand of righteous justice, passion and plain talking make for one of the freshest manga series of 2015. I dare any other book to top it."
—UK Anime Network

PURITY AND POWER

As a war to determine the rightful ruler of medieval France ravages the land, the witch Maria decides she will not stand idly by as men kill each other in the name of God and glory. Using her powerful magic, she summons various beasts and demons —even going as far as using a succubus to seduce soldiers into submission under the veil of night— all to stop the needless slaughter. However, after the Archangel Michael puts an end to her meddling, he curses her to lose her powers if she ever gives up her virginity. Will she forgo the forbidden fruit of adulthood in order to bring an end to the merciless machine of war?
Available now in print and digitally!

KC
KODANSHA COMICS

INUYASHIKI

A superhero like none you've ever seen, from the creator of "Gantz"!

Ichiro Inuyashiki is down on his luck. He looks much older than his 58 years, his children despise him, and his wife thinks he's a useless coward. So when he's diagnosed with stomach cancer and given three months to live, it seems the only one who'll miss him is his dog.

Then a blinding light fills the sky, and the old man is killed... only to wake up later in a body he almost recognizes as his own. Can it be that Ichiro Inuyashiki is no longer human?

Comes in extra-large editions with color pages!

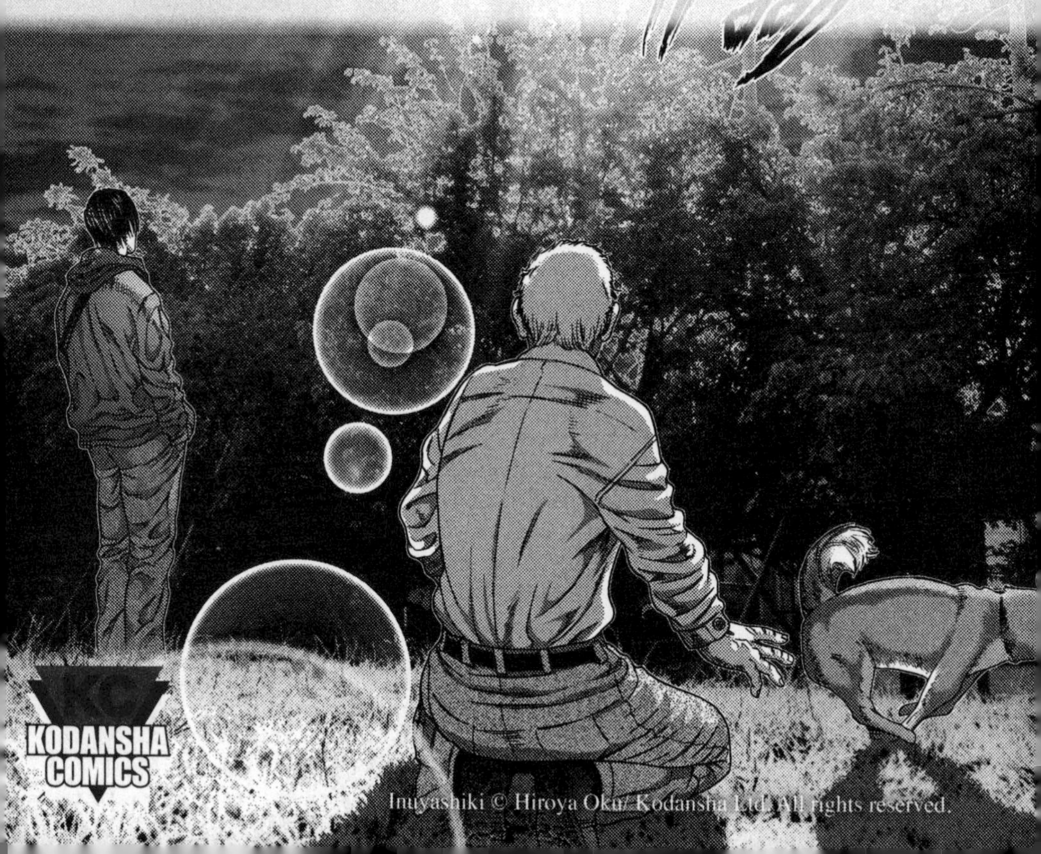

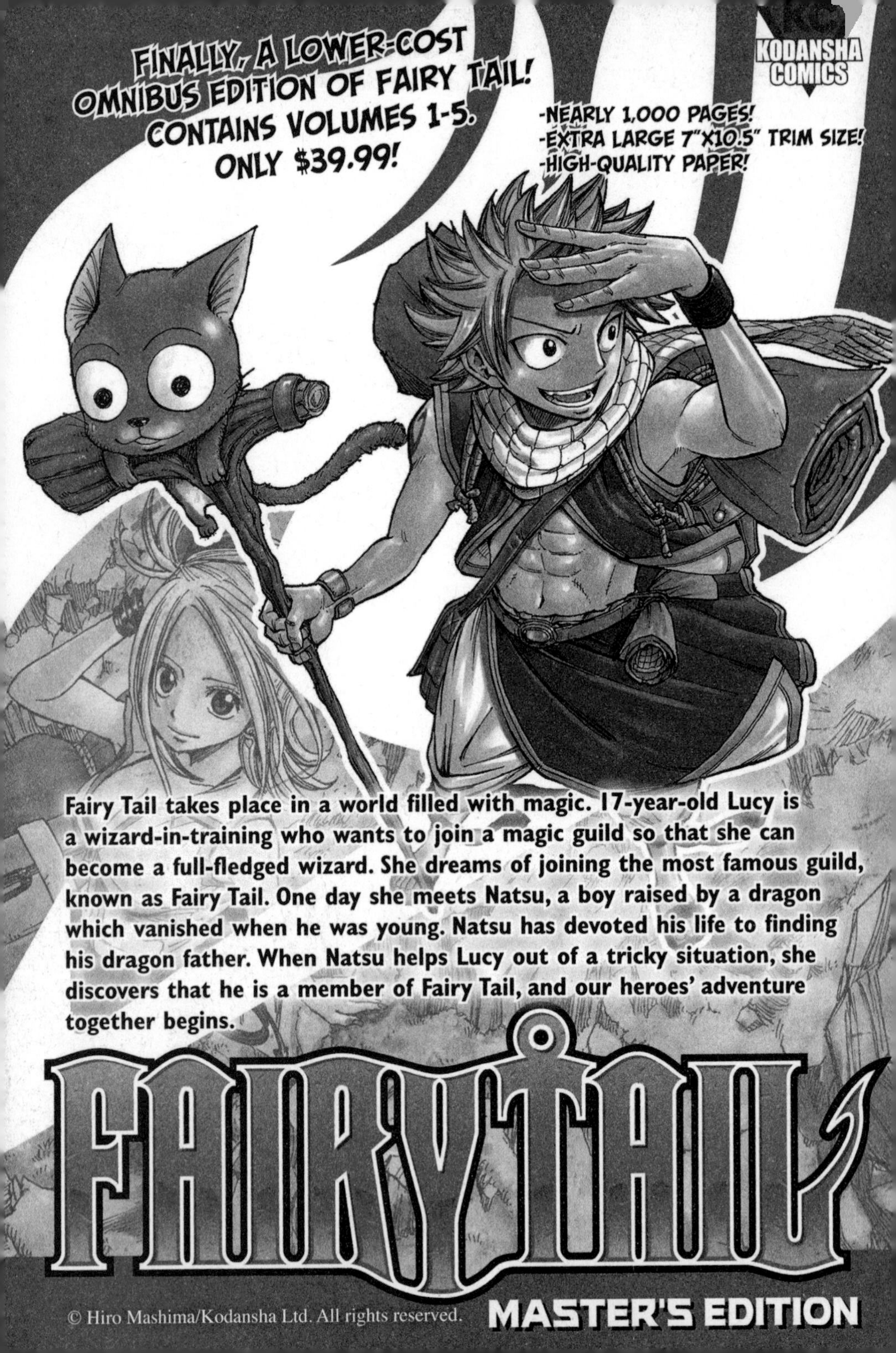
KODANSHA COMICS
FINALLY, A LOWER-COST OMNIBUS EDITION OF FAIRY TAIL! CONTAINS VOLUMES 1-5. ONLY $39.99!
-NEARLY 1,000 PAGES!
-EXTRA LARGE 7"X10.5" TRIM SIZE!
-HIGH-QUALITY PAPER!
Fairy Tail takes place in a world filled with magic. 17-year-old Lucy is a wizard-in-training who wants to join a magic guild so that she can become a full-fledged wizard. She dreams of joining the most famous guild, known as Fairy Tail. One day she meets Natsu, a boy raised by a dragon which vanished when he was young. Natsu has devoted his life to finding his dragon father. When Natsu helps Lucy out of a tricky situation, she discovers that he is a member of Fairy Tail, and our heroes' adventure together begins.
FAIRY TAIL
MASTER'S EDITION
© Hiro Mashima/Kodansha Ltd. All rights reserved.

Cells at Work! volume 2 is a work of fiction. Names, characters, places, and incidents are the products of the author's imagination or are used fictitiously. Any resemblance to actual events, locales, or persons, living or dead, is entirely coincidental.

A Kodansha Comics Trade Paperback Original.

Published in the United States by Kodansha Comics,
an imprint of Kodansha USA Publishing, LLC, New York.

Publication rights for this English edition arranged through Kodansha Ltd., Tokyo.

First published in Japan in 2015 by Kodansha Ltd., Tokyo, as *Hataraku Saibou* volume 2.

ISBN 978-1-63236-357-2

Printed in the United States of America.

www.kodanshacomics.com

9 8 7 6 5 4 3 2 1

Translation: Yamato Tanaka
Lettering: Abigail Blackman
Editing: Paul Starr
Kodansha Comics edition cover design: Phil Balsman

HOW TO READ MANGA

Japanese is written right to left and top to bottom. This means that for a reader accustomed to Western languages, Japanese books read "backwards." Since most manga published in English now keeps the Japanese page order, it can take a little getting used to—but once you learn how, it's a snap. Here's a handy guide!

Here you can see pages 10-11 from Volume 1 of *Cells at Work*. The speech balloons have been numbered in the order you should read them in.

Page 10*—read this one first!*

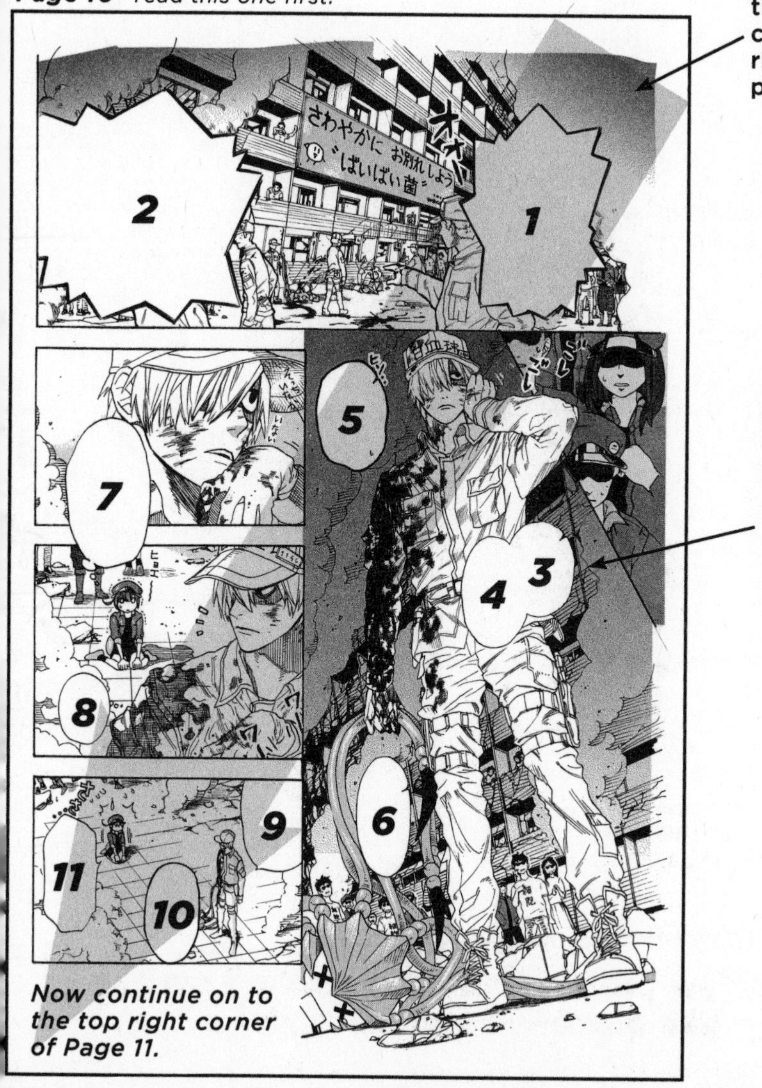
さわやかに お別れしよう
ばいばい菌
1
2
3
4
5
6
7
8
9
10
11

Start here, at the top right corner of the right hand page.

Read right to left, then top to bottom. In this panel, the leftmost speech balloon comes before the one in the top left corner.

Now continue on to the top right corner of Page 11.

Page 11

On this page, the top two panels are read first.

This panel is the top right-most after the first two, so it's next.

If you go to this panel next, you would have to move backwards (right) to read balloons 6 and 7.

Instead, after reading balloon 5, you move down to 6 and 7, then left...

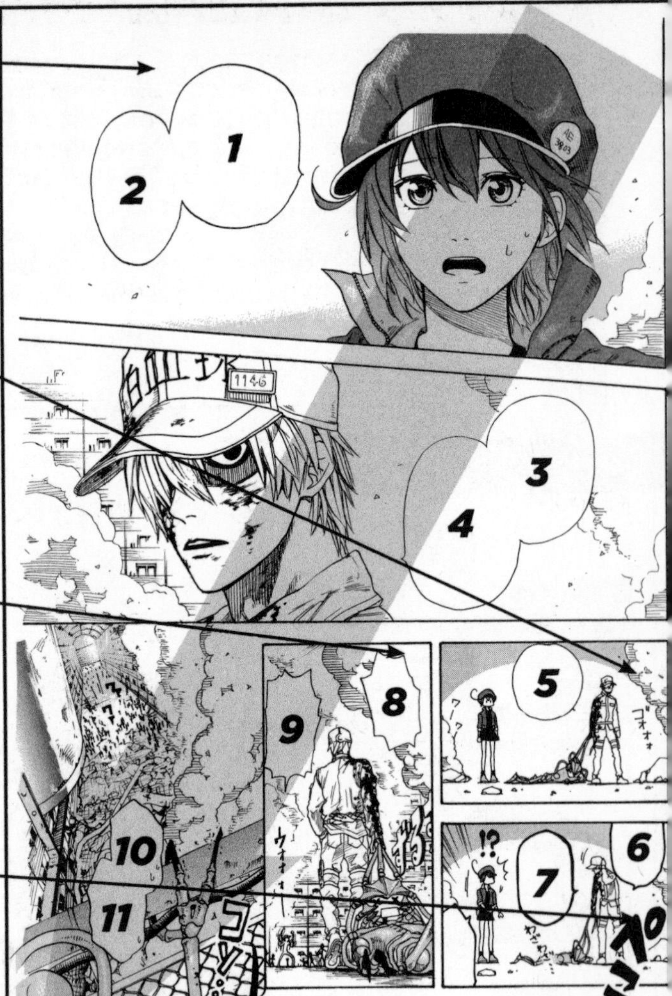
1
2
3
4
5
6
7
8
9
10
11

...and then you arrive at the end of the page!

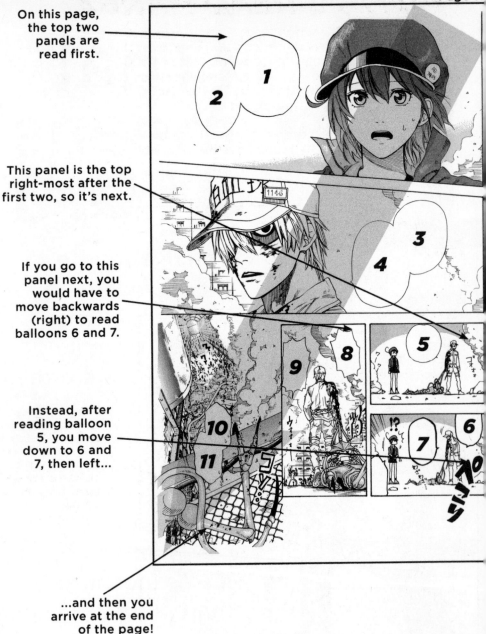

After a few pages, you'll be reading manga like a pro—*Japanese-style!*

止まれ

(That means STOP)

You're about to read a *manga*—a Japanese comic—presented in its original page order, which means you start at the other end of the book. If you need a quick guide on how to read manga the way it was meant to be read, flip to the next pag⎯ ⎯⎯⎯⎯ turr⎯ an⎯